The Templars

The Templars

The Rise and Spectacular Fall
of God's Holy Warriors

DAN JONES

VIKING

VIKING
An imprint of Penguin Random House LLC
375 Hudson Street
New York, New York 10014
penguin.com

Illustration credits: **Page 1:** Map of Jerusalem, ca. 1200; Alamy. **Page 2:** *(top)* Christ's tomb,
Church of the Holy Sepulchre; Getty Images. *(Bottom)*: Al-Aqsa Mosque; Andrew Shiva/
Wikipedia. **Page 3:** *(top)* Saint Bernard of Clairvaux; Jastrow/Wikimedia commons.
(Bottom): Templars playing chess, from the Libro de los Juegos ("Book of games"),
commissioned by Alfonso X of Castile; Wikimedia commons. **Page 4:** *(top)* Templar fresco
from Cressac-Saint-Genis, Charente; Getty Images. *(Bottom)*: Templar banners; Corpus
Christi College, Cambridge. **Page 5:** *(top)* Monzón Castle, Aragon; ecelan/Wikimedia
commons. *(Bottom)*: Syrian horseman in battle, fresco at Pernes-les-Fontaines, Vaucluse;
Véronique Pagnier/Wikimedia commons. **Page 6:** *(top)* Louis VII and Eleanor of Aquitaine;
Getty Images. *(Bottom)*: Saladin, as portrayed by the sixteenth-century Italian painter
Cristofano dell'Altissimo; Wikimedia commons. **Page 7:** Battle of Hattin, British Library.
Page 8: *(top)* Richard the Lionheart, Getty Images. *(Bottom)*: Richard the Lionheart and
Philip Augustus at Acre, 1191; Getty Images. **Page 9:** *(top)* Giotto di Bondone, Saint Francis
before the Sultan, Upper Church, San Francesco, Assisi; Wikimedia commons. *(Bottom)*:
Frederick II Hohenstaufen: Art Collection 3/Alamy Stock photo **Page 10:** *(top)* Templar
tunnels beneath Acre; Shutterstock. *(Bottom)*: Louis IX sets off for Damietta, illumination
from the Vie et miracles de Saint Louis; Wikimedia commons. **Page 11:** Hülagü Khan:
DeAgostini/Getty Images. **Page 12:** Crusaders vs. Khwarizmians; Library of Corpus
Christi College, Cambridge. **Page 13:** *(top)* Detail of a fourteenth-century brass basin
known as the Baptistère de Saint Louis, made by Mohammed ibn al-Zain; Wikimedia
commons. *(Bottom)*: Philip IV of France photo 12/UIG via Getty Images. **Page 14:** *(top)*
The Paris Temple, ca. 1795; Wikimedia commons. *(Bottom)* Pope Clement V; Getty
Images. **Page 15:** *(top)* Arrest of the Templars, depicted in a fourteenth-century miniature,
in *Les Grandes Chroniques de France*; British Library. *(Bottom)*: Vatican transcript, Getty
Images. **Page 16:** The burning of the Templars and the death of Philip IV; British Library.

LIBRARY OF CONGRESS CATALOGING-IN-PUBLICATION DATA AVAILABLE
ISBN: 978-0-525-42830-5 (HC)
978-0-698-18643-9 (EL)

Printed in the United States of America
1 3 5 7 9 10 8 6 4 2

Set in Adobe Jenson Pro
Designed by Francesca Belanger
Maps by Jeffrey L. Ward

For Georgina

Think not that I am come to send peace on earth:
I came not to send peace, but a sword.

—Matthew 10:34

CONTENTS

PART III

Bankers

1189–1260

PART IV

Heretics

1260–1314

An illustration insert falls between pages 268 and 269

LIST OF MAPS

AUTHOR'S NOTE

The story of the Templars takes us across a broad sweep of times, territories and cultures. Some of these are familiar to Western readers, others less so. Naming conventions for people and places vary significantly between English, French, German, Spanish, Italian, Latin, Greek, Arabic, Turkish and every tongue that was in use during the period this book covers, and spelling very often lacks consistency in the original sources.

Rendering Arabic and Turkish names into English is challenging. There is no single accepted formula for doing so, and no unchallenged agreement on the best way to spell in English even as important a name as Muhammad, let alone the names of less famous individuals. In writing this book I found myself constantly making choices, frequently arbitrarily.

For example, Salah al-Din Yusuf ibn Ayyub, the great Kurdish sultan of Egypt and Syria and scourge of the Templars, is best known to most English and American readers by his crudely reduced crusader nickname of Saladin. Salah al-Din is sometimes considered more sensitive shorthand today, but it would not have been quite so clear who I meant. So Saladin is what I have called him. However, I have called his less well-known brother and successor al-Adil rather than Saphadin, following the conventions of modern scholarship rather than those of medieval Christian chroniclers.

Not every case is this straightforward. How do we render the name of the empire established by the Turkic people of the steppe, who rode into Baghdad in 1055 and were holding much of the Holy Land when the crusaders arrived a few decades later? We could transliterate the Arabic and get Saljuq, or render the Turkish into Selcük. There are other popular variations, including "Seljuk" and "Seljuq." In cases such as this, where there are many plausible options but no obvious best, I have turned to *The New Encyclopedia of Islam* for guidance. (It says Seljuq.) Early on I also asked Paul M. Cobb, professor of Islamic History at the University of Pennsylvania, for his guidance on the matter. As always, he gave me sensible advice, for which I am grateful. Those illiteracies that remain are my fault alone.

Other choices: I have decided not to include the marks sometimes used for transliterating Arabic into Roman script, on the basis that these are often more distracting than helpful to readers in a text that is not solely produced for academic reference. I have consistently translated the names of most characters in this book into their standard English form, so that we have James of Molay and not Jacques de Molay, as is standard practice in most modern English works about this historical period.

In many cases I have modernized or at least updated place-names for the sake of clarity; thus, in chapter 1, Joppa becomes Jaffa (although the settlement I describe is today to be found in Tel Aviv-Yafo). Cairo has been substituted for the archaic crusader term Babylon. Yet on occasion modernization would be inappropriate, which is why I refer to Constantinople rather than Istanbul.

In the case of crusader settlements in the Holy Land, there are sometimes three or more different renderings possible for the same place. The great Templar fortress south of Acre (modern-day Akka) was known by the men who built it as Castel Pèlerin. Today scholars call it 'Atlit or Athlit. But I have chosen to modernize the French and call it Château Pèlerin, giving 'Atlit in parentheses at the first instance of use. I have chosen *not* to translate it fully into English, which would have been Castle Pilgrim.

None of this amounts to a system, except to say that I have sought readability rather than consistency. From time to time I may have achieved neither: I can ask only for your patience and understanding.

The Templars

NORWAY

SWEDEN

SCOTLAND

North Sea

DANES

POMERANIA

Dublin

York

Lincoln

IRELAND

WALES ENGLAND

Hamburg

London *Thames R.*

Winchester

Canterbury

FRISIANS

GERMANY

Cologne

Elbe R.

HOLY

Prague

Atlantic Ocean

Rouen

Paris

Worms

Rhine R.

Danube R.

Vienna

Normandy

Seine R.

Troyes

ROMAN

Citeaux

Loire R.

Clairvaux

Vézelay Dijon

Nantes

Cluny

Geneva

EMPIRE

FRANCE

Garonne R.

Lyon

Milan

Venice

Compostela

Oviedo

Leon

NAVARRE

ARLES

Genoa

CROATIA

DALMATIA

Burgos

Rhône R.

Avignon

Adriatic Sea

LEON & CASTILE

Pamplona

Toulouse

Florence

ITALY

PORTUGAL

ARAGON

COUNTY OF
BARCELONA

CORSICA

Rome

Salamanca

Ebro R.

Madrid

Zaragoza

Lerida

APULIA Bari

Lisbon *Tagus R.*

Toledo

Tortosa

Naples Salerno

AL-ANDALUS

SARDINIA

Cordoba

BALEARIC
ISLANDS

Seville

Mediterranean Sea

Palermo Messina

SICILY

Fez

ALMORAVID EMPIRE

MALTA

Marrakesh

© 2017 Jeffrey L. Ward

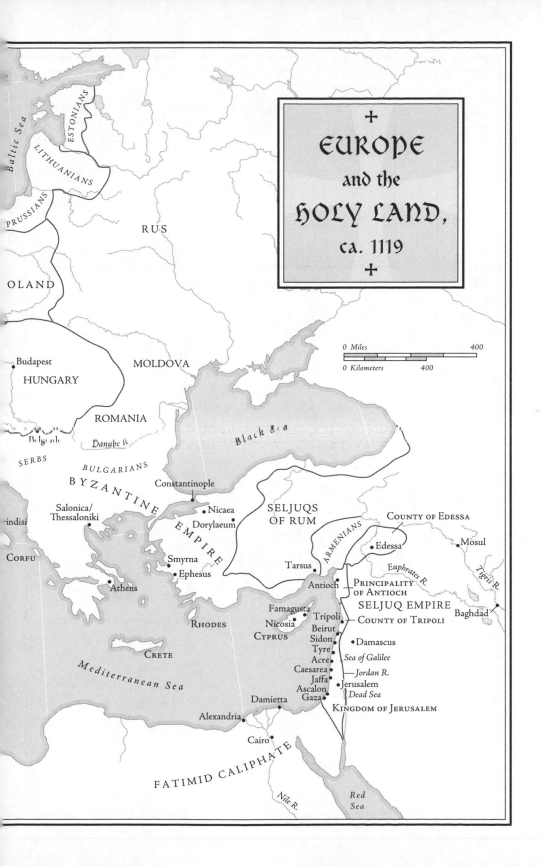

EUROPE
and the
HOLY LAND,
ca. 1119

Baltic Sea

ESTONIANS

LITHUANIANS

PRUSSIANS

RUS

OLAND

Budapest

HUNGARY

MOLDOVA

ROMANIA

Belgrade

Danube R.

SERBS

BULGARIANS

BYZANTINE

Black Sea

0 Miles 400
0 Kilometers 400

Constantinople

Salonica/
Thessaloniki

Nicaea

Dorylaeum

SELJUQS
OF RUM

COUNTY OF EDESSA

ARMENIANS

Edessa

Mosul

rindisi

EMPIRE

Smyrna

Euphrates R.

Tigris R.

CORFU

Ephesus

Tarsus

Antioch

PRINCIPALITY
OF ANTIOCH

Athens

SELJUQ EMPIRE

Baghdad

Famagusta

RHODES

Nicosia

CYPRUS

Tripoli

COUNTY OF TRIPOLI

Beirut

Sidon

Damascus

Tyre

Acre

Sea of Galilee

CRETE

Caesarea

Jordan R.

Mediterranean Sea

Jaffa

Ascalon

Jerusalem

Gaza

Dead Sea

Damietta

KINGDOM OF JERUSALEM

Alexandria

Cairo

FATIMID CALIPHATE

Nile R.

Red
Sea

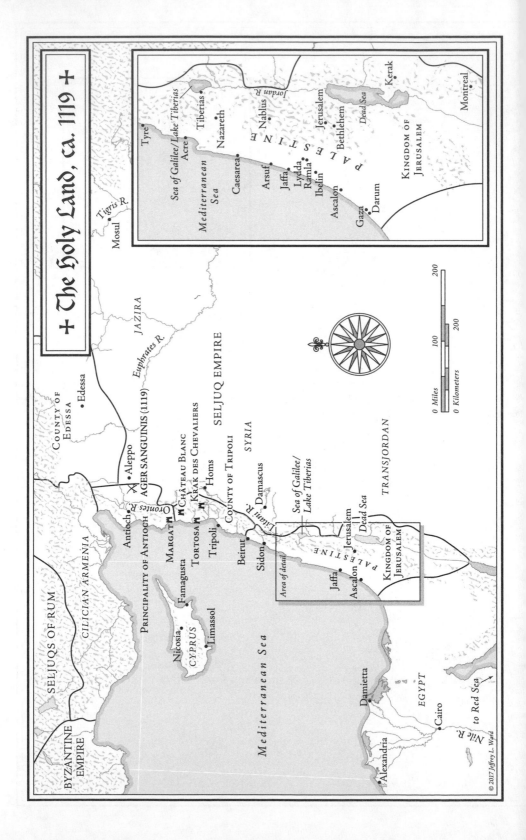

✠ The Holy Land, ca. 1119 ✠

Kerak
Montreal
Jordan R.
Tiberias
Nazareth
Nablus
Jerusalem
Dead Sea
Bethlehem
Tyre
Sea of Galilee/Lake Tiberias
Acre
PALESTINE
Caesarea
Mediterranean Sea
Arsuf
Jaffa
Lydda
Ramla
Ibelin
Ascalon
Darum
Gaza
KINGDOM OF JERUSALEM

Tigris R.
Mosul
JAZIRA
Euphrates R.
COUNTY OF EDESSA
Edessa
Aleppo
AGER SANGUINIS (1119)
CHÂTEAU BLANC
KRAK DES CHEVALIERS
Homs
SELJUQ EMPIRE
SYRIA
Damascus
Sea of Galilee/Lake Tiberias
Dead Sea
Jerusalem
PALESTINE
TRANSJORDAN
KINGDOM OF JERUSALEM
Area of detail
Jaffa
Ascalon

SELJUQS OF RUM
CILICIAN ARMENIA
BYZANTINE EMPIRE
Antioch
Orontes R.
PRINCIPALITY OF ANTIOCH
MARGAT
TORTOSA
Tripoli
COUNTY OF TRIPOLI
Litani R.
Beirut
Sidon
Famagusta
Nicosia
CYPRUS
Limassol
Mediterranean Sea
Damietta
EGYPT
Cairo
Alexandria
Nile R.
to Red Sea

0 Miles 100 200
0 Kilometers 200

© 2017 Jeffrey L. Ward

Introduction

THE TEMPLARS were holy soldiers. Men of religion and men of the sword, pilgrims and warriors, paupers and bankers. Their uniforms were emblazoned with a red cross, symbolizing the blood Christ had shed for mankind and that they themselves were prepared to spill in the Lord's service. Although the Templars were only one among a host of religious orders that sprang up in medieval Europe and the Holy Land between the eleventh and fourteenth centuries, they were by far the best known and the most controversial.

Their order was a product of the crusades, the wars instigated by the medieval Church, which took aim primarily, although not exclusively, at the Islamic rulers of Palestine, Syria, Asia Minor, Egypt, northwest Africa and southern Spain. As such, Templars could be found across a vast swath of the Mediterranean world and beyond: on the battlefields of the Near East and in towns and villages throughout Europe, where they managed extensive estates that funded their military adventures. The word "Templars"—shorthand for "the Poor Knighthood of the Temple" or, less frequently, "the Poor Fellow-Soldiers of Christ and the Temple of Jerusalem"—advertised their origins on the Temple Mount in Christianity's holiest city. But their presence was felt almost everywhere. Even in their own lifetimes the Templars were semilegendary figures, featuring in popular stories, artworks, ballads and histories. They were part of the mental landscape of the crusades—a position they still occupy today.

The Templars were founded in 1119 on the principles of chastity, obedience and poverty—the last of which was memorialized in the master's official seal, showing two armed brothers sharing a single horse. But the order soon grew rich and influential. Senior Templar officials in the Holy Land and the West counted among their friends (and enemies) kings and princes, queens and countesses, patriarchs and popes. The order helped finance wars, loaned money to pay kings' ransoms, subcontracted the financial management of royal governments, collected taxes, built castles, ran cities, raised armies, interfered in trade disputes, engaged in private wars against other military orders, carried out political assassinations and even helped make men kings. From meager beginnings they became as mighty an outfit as existed during the later Middle Ages.

Yet—perhaps strangely—the Templars also had broad popular appeal. For many people they were not distant elites but local heroes. The prayers that the order's many nonfighting brothers said in their religious houses across Europe were just as important as the sacrifices Templar knights and sergeants made on the battlefield, and both were of the utmost importance in seeking heavenly salvation for all Christians. Some of the order's wealth came from the patronage of the pious nobility, but just as much grew from the small donations of ordinary men and women, who gave what little they had—a jacket here, a vegetable patch there—to their local branch to help fund the order's militant mission in the East.

Of course, there were dissenters. To some observers the order was dangerously unaccountable and a corruption of the supposedly peaceful principles of Christianity. At times the Templars were the subject of fierce attacks, particularly from scholars and monks suspicious of their privileged status: protected by the authority of the pope and exempted from the rules and taxes that were imposed on other religious groups. Bernard of Clairvaux—a sort of godfather to the order—hailed the Templars as "a new knighthood," but a century later another learned French monk dismissed them as "a new monstrosity."

Nevertheless, the sudden dissolution of the order in the early fourteenth century, which involved mass arrests, persecution, torture, show trials, group burnings and the seizure of all the Templars' assets, shocked the whole of Christendom. Within a few years the order was shut down, wound up and dissolved, its members accused of a list of crimes designed specifically to cause outrage and disgust. The end came so suddenly and so violently that it only added to the Templar legend. Today, more than seven hundred years after their demise, the Templars remain the object of fascination, imitation and obsession.

So who were the Templars? It is sometimes hard to tell. Featured in numerous works of fiction, television shows and films, the Templars have been presented variously as heroes, martyrs, thugs, bullies, victims, criminals, perverts, heretics, depraved subversives, guardians of the Holy Grail, protectors of Christ's secret bloodline and time-traveling agents of global conspiracy. Within the field of "popular" history, a cottage industry exists in exposing "the mysteries of the Templars"—suggesting their role in some timeless plot to conceal Christianity's dirty secrets and hinting that the medieval order is still out there, manipulating the world from the shadows. Occasionally this is very entertaining. None of it has very much to do with the Templars themselves.

This book seeks to tell the story of the Templars as they were, not as legend has embellished them. My goal is not so much to debunk or even engage with the more outlandish themes of Templar mythology, but rather to show that their real deeds were even more extraordinary than the romances, half-truths and voodoo histories that have swirled around them since they fell. I also believe that the themes of the Templar story resonate powerfully today. This is a book about a seemingly endless war in Palestine, Syria and Egypt, where factions of Sunni and Shi'a Muslims clashed with militant Christian invaders from the West; about a "globalized," tax-exempt organization that grew so rich that it became more powerful than some governments; about the relationship between international finance and geopolitics; about the power of propaganda and mythmaking; about violence, treachery, betrayal and greed.

Readers of my books about Plantagenet England will not be surprised to learn that this is a narrative history. It tells the story of the Templars from their creation to their dissolution, exploring the order's changing nature, its spread across the Near East and Europe and the part it played in the medieval wars between Christian armies and the forces of Islam. I have presented the text with detailed endnotes and a bibliography pointing readers to a wide range of original sources and academic studies, but I have not strayed from my usual ambition, which is to write a book that will entertain as well as inform.

To guide readers through the two centuries from the order's unremarkable birth to its spectacular annihilation, I have divided the book into four sections. Part I, "Pilgrims," describes the Templars' origins in the early twelfth century, when they were founded as an order of Christian religious warriors by a French knight, Hugh of Payns, and (so it was later

said) eight of his companions, who were looking for a purpose in Jerusalem in the turbulent aftermath of the First Crusade. The initial intention
of this little band was to form a permanent bodyguard for Western pilgrims following in Christ's footsteps on the dangerous roads of the Holy
Land. They took their lead in part from a group of volunteer medics who
had established a hospital in Jerusalem around 1080, known as the Hospital of Saint John or the Hospitallers. Having received royal approval
from the Christian king of Jerusalem, and papal blessing from Rome, the
Templars quickly institutionalized and expanded. They set up headquarters in the Holy City in the al-Aqsa Mosque on the Temple Mount
(known to Muslims as the Haram al-Sharif), sent emissaries to Europe
to round up men and financial support and sought out famous patrons.
Their spiritual guide was Bernard of Clairvaux, who helped write their
rule, and early supporters included the leading crusaders of the day, such
as the Plantagenet forefather Fulk, Count of Anjou, who with a little
help from the Templars became king of Jerusalem. Within a couple of
decades the Templars were no longer nine penniless warriors in search of
a cause: they were an ambitious organization with a clear purpose and
the means to achieve it.

The second part, "Soldiers," shows how the Templars transformed themselves from a roadside rescue team into an elite military unit at the forefront of the crusader wars. It describes the Templars' crucial role in the
Second Crusade, when they helped guide not a handful of pilgrims but
an entire army under the king of France through the mountains of Asia
Minor, delivering them safely to the Holy Land, bailing out their bankrupt commander, then fighting in the front line as the crusaders attempted
to conquer Damascus, one of the greatest cities in the Islamic world. From
this point on the Templars were prominent agents in the political and
military history of the Christian crusader states (the kingdom of Jerusalem, county of Tripoli and principality of Antioch). Part II follows them
as they developed a network of castles, a set of military protocols and the
institutional expertise necessary to carry out their task. It also features
some of the most extraordinary characters in the whole history of crusading: the pious but unlucky Louis VII of France, the suicidally proud
Templar Master Gerard of Ridefort who helped lead the armies of God
into an apocalyptic battle at Hattin in 1187, the miserably afflicted leper

king of Jerusalem Baldwin IV and the most famous Muslim sultan who ever lived, Saladin, who made it his personal mission to wipe the crusaders off the map, and personally oversaw the execution of hundreds of Templar knights in a single day.

Part III, "Bankers," examines how the Order of the Temple matured from a crusading auxillary force supported by donations from the West into an institution that combined military capability with a sophisticated network of properties and personnel across Christendom, binding together the Christian West with the Eastern war zone at a time when crusading fervor was beginning to ebb.

Having been nearly wiped out as a fighting force by Saladin, the Templars were rebuilt in the 1190s with the help of a brilliant and brutal king of England, Richard the Lionheart, whose trust in and reliance on the Templars' leading officials suggested the direction the order would take during the thirteenth century. Protected by royal patronage, which was soon mimicked by nobles and urban authorities, the Templars grew their landholdings, expanded their property portfolio and were granted lucrative tax breaks. They became dazzlingly wealthy and financially sophisticated, and in due course popes and kings turned to them to manage bookkeeping, guard treasure, organize wars and raise bailouts in times of crisis.

There were certainly many of those times, and Part III shows the Templars still deeply embedded in the wars against Islam. Two massive assaults on the Egyptian Delta city of Damietta were facilitated by the Templars' financial know-how. Both ended in chaos, with the order's knights and sergeants fighting desperate rearguard actions in the diseased swamps of a flooded Nile. As the Templars discovered, raising and organizing war funds was one thing; fighting long campaigns on unfamiliar foreign terrain against an enemy far better schooled in the conditions was quite another.

Part III also shows the Templars assuming ever more responsibility for the security of the crusader states, which brought them into contact with some of the thirteenth century's most memorable characters, including the sainted French king Louis IX, with whom they got on famously, and Frederick II Hohenstaufen, the bombastic and freethinking Holy Roman Emperor who claimed to be the king of Jerusalem and promptly started a war against the men who were tasked with defending it. At this point the Templars had to contend with the appearance of Frederick's protégés, the Teutonic Order: one of a number of military orders set up in parallel with (and sometimes in imitation of) the Templars. These included the Order of Saint Lazarus, which attended to pilgrims suffering from leprosy; the orders of Calatrava, Santiago and Alcántara, set up in the kingdoms of Spain; the Sword Brothers of Livonia, who made war on pagans in the Baltic; and the Hospitallers, alongside whom the Templars had lived from the very beginning and alongside whom they would fight some of their greatest battles. In the Holy Land the increasing importance of the military orders combined with their growing diversity exacerbated factional conflict, and the Templars were dragged into wars between rival groups of Italian merchants and self-interested barons. Ultimately this damaged the political foundation of the crusader states so badly that when a new threat arose in the 1260s the Templars were as helpless as the rest of their Christian counterparts to resist.

Part IV, "Heretics," traces the roots of the Templars' destruction to events in the 1260s, when the brothers in the East were on the front line of a war against the two most dangerous enemies the crusaders ever faced: Mongol armies under the descendants of Genghis Khan and a caste of Muslim slave soldiers known as the Mamluks. Defeat at the hands of the Mamluks gave license for more widespread criticism of the Templars than ever before, as their plentiful resources and close association with the fortunes of the wars against Islam now became sticks with which to beat them.

As pressure on the order mounted, they grew open to political attack. This came suddenly and violently in 1307 in an assault by the pious but unscrupulous French king Philip IV. His arrest of every Templar in France on Friday, October 13, was the start of an entirely self-interested move to wind up the order and seize its assets. Alternately abetted and resisted by a compromised Pope Clement V, Philip IV and his ministers turned a raid on Templar property into an all-out war on the order across the Christian world, using methods that had already been practiced on other vulnerable targets, including France's Jewish population. Although France had traditionally been the realm from which the Templars derived their greatest support, Philip made it his unwavering mission to try, torture and kill the order's members, starting at the top with the last Templar grand master,[1] James of Molay, who was burned to death in Paris in 1314, his final words a promise that God would have revenge on the order's behalf.

Philip's motives in breaking the Templars with the dual rods of judicial inquiry and personal barbarity had very little to do with the real character or conduct of the members either on the front line of the war against Islam or in France, where their lives for the most part resembled those of monks. Philip's actions derived from his political preoccupations and his extreme, cruel and callous personal pathology, but he hit the order at a moment when it was more susceptible than usual to attack and slander, and when public interest in crusading was, if not dead, then certainly vastly diminished. James of Molay's demise signaled the end of the Templars as an organization, nearly two hundred years after their humble origins in Jerusalem. Their legend, however, was only just beginning. This book's epilogue summarizes the Templars' journey into the popular imagination and considers the process by which the order has been romanticized and even resurrected ever since.

One distinguished scholar has suggested that a narrative history of the Templars is "misleading, because it implies that the order rose and declined, that criticism increased steadily and that certain events caused later events."[2] This is right and it is wrong. Certainly it would be a fool's task to attempt to write within a chronological framework a comprehensive account of the two centuries during which the order was active in the kingdom of Jerusalem, the Iberian Peninsula, France, England, Italy, Poland, Germany, Hungary, Cyprus and elsewhere. The experiences of the thousands of men and women who lived as fully professed Templars or associate members cannot all be contained in a coherent account of their most notable activities. Nevertheless, the order undeniably began, existed and ended, and this process occurred over a fixed period in which time advanced in the usual fashion. Following this takes us through the broader sweep of the crusades, linking up several theaters of war and a dozen generations of men and women. It is also a story that is more usually told thematically, a treatment that all too often becomes digressive and even dull. My choosing to tell this story as a *story* in the traditional way does not imply an inevitable moral journey from honor to corruption to hubris to destruction, for such thinking has bedeviled the long tradition of writing about the Templars, dating back at least to the seventeeth century.[3] I simply believe that an account of the Templars can be told chronologically to satisfy readers who like their history told in sequence. I hope that in doing so I have not slipped too deep into teleology or misrepresented the lives and experiences of the people who lived, fought and died with a red cross on their breast. I also hope that this book will encourage readers to explore the voluminous scholarly literature that exists on the military orders and on the Templars in particular, by distinguished and brilliant academics including Malcolm Barber, Helen Nicholson, Alan Forey, Jochen Burgtorf, Alain Demurger, Jonathan Riley-Smith, Judi Upton-Ward, Anthony Luttrell, Jonathan Phillips, Norman Housley, Jochen Schenk, Paul Crawford, Peter Edbury, Anne Gilmour-Bryson and many others, on which I have drawn here with the greatest respect and gratitude.

The Templars charged into battle under a black-and-white flag, and as they rode they would sometimes sing a psalm to give them strength. It feels appropriate to quote those lines as we begin our story:

Not to us, O lord, not to us, but to your name give glory, for the sake of your steadfast love and your faithfulness!

Enjoy the ride.

PART I

Pilgrims

1102–1144

Fight, I beseech you, for the salvation of your souls!

—Baldwin I, king of Jerusalem

"A Golden Basin Filled with Scorpions"

IT WAS a foul autumn morning in Jaffa when the pilgrims came out of the church. They were immediately swept up in the stampede of a crowd heading toward the sea, drawn by a dreadful cacophony: the scream of timber being wrenched apart and, scarcely audible below the roar of the wind and explosions of waves, the shrieks of terrified men and women fighting for their lives. A violent storm, building over the previous day, had burst during the night and thirty or so ships anchored off Jaffa's steeply shelving beach were being hurled about upon great mountains of water. The largest and most robust among them were ripped from their anchors, driven into sharp rocks and hammered into sandbanks until, in the words of one onlooker, all had been "torn to pieces by the tempest."[1]

The crowd on the shore watched helplessly as sailors and passengers were washed from the decks. Some tried to stay afloat by hanging on to splintered masts and spars, but most were doomed. "Some, as they were clinging, were cut apart by the timbers of their own ships," wrote the observer. "Some, who knew how to swim, voluntarily committed themselves to the waves, and thus many of them perished."[2] On the shore, corpses had begun to wash up with the surf. The dead would eventually number one thousand, and only seven ships would survive the storm unwrecked. "A greater misery on one day no eye ever saw," the pilgrim wrote. It was Monday, October 13, 1102.

The pilgrim to whom we owe this account was an Englishman known as Saewulf.* He had been traveling for several months, having left Monopoli, on the coast of Apulia (the heel of the boot in modern Italy) on

---

* Saewulf makes no mention of his birthplace in his Latin account of the Holy Land, and we have almost no knowledge of his biography save what is contained in his pilgrimage diary. But it is reasonable to assume that he was from England: he drew on materials compiled by the Northumbrian saint Bede, and the one medieval copy of his account

July 13, a day he described as *hora egyptiaca*, as it had been thought since the age of the Pharaohs that this was an astrologically accursed date on which to begin an important task.[3] And so it had proved to be. Saewulf had already suffered one shipwreck on his passage from England to the eastern Mediterranean. Mercifully he had survived. His subsequent route had taken him to Corfu, Cephalonia and Corinth, overland via Thebes to the Aegean Sea, then southeastward through the Cyclades and Dodecanese islands to Rhodes. Several more days at sea had brought him to the Cypriot port of Paphos from where, after exactly thirteen weeks during which he had traveled some two thousand miles, he finally arrived in Jaffa, the main port of the Christian kingdom of Jerusalem. He was rowed to shore just hours before the fatal storm struck.

Despite the many privations and terrible risks of seafaring, Saewulf had seen great things on his journey east as he and his fellow travelers had alighted their boat every few days to beg accommodation from islanders whom he called, generically, the Greeks. He had gazed on the silk workshops of Andros and had been to the site of the long-vanished Colossus of Rhodes. He had visited the ancient city of Myra, with its beautiful semicircular theater, and had been to Finike, a windswept trading port founded by the Phoenicians in an area known by the local people as "sixty oars," due to the roughness of the seas. He had prayed at the tomb of Saint Nicholas and had walked, in Cyprus, in the footsteps of Saint Peter. Yet his real prize lay one step farther. Once the storm had abated, he would be heading to the most important city on earth: he would set out on the road southeast to Jerusalem, where he intended to pray at the tomb of Jesus Christ, the Son of God and savior of mankind.

For a Christian like Saewulf, who piously described himself as "unworthy and sinful," a visit to Jerusalem was a redemptive journey to the center of the world.[4] God had told the Old Testament prophet Ezekiel that he had set Jerusalem "in the midst of the nations," and this was regarded as more than a mere figure of speech.[5] Maps produced in Europe at the time represented the Holy City as the kernel around which all

---

found its way to the library of Matthew Parker, the sixteenth-century archbishop of Canterbury.

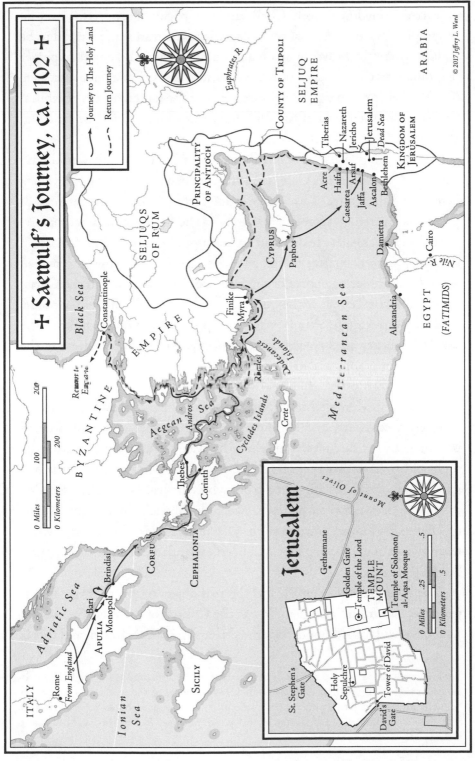

✝ Saewulf's Journey, ca. 1102 ✝

→ Journey to The Holy Land
⇢ Return Journey

ITALY
Rome
From England
Adriatic Sea
Bari
APULIA
Monopoli
Brindisi
Ionian Sea
SICILY
CORFU
CEPHALONIA
Thebes
Corinth
Aegean Sea
Andros
BYZANTINE EMPIRE
Black Sea
Constantinople
Return to Empire
SELJUQS OF RUM
Euphrates R.
PRINCIPALITY OF ANTIOCH
COUNTY OF TRIPOLI
SELJUQ EMPIRE
Cyclades Islands
Crete
Rhodes
Dodecanese Islands
Finike
Myra
CYPRUS
Paphos
Mediterranean Sea
Acre
Haifa
Caesarea
Arsuf
Jaffa
Ascalon
Bethlehem
Tiberias
Nazareth
Jericho
Jerusalem
Dead Sea
KINGDOM OF JERUSALEM
Damietta
Alexandria
Nile R.
Cairo
EGYPT (FATIMIDS)
ARABIA

© 2017 Jeffrey L. Ward

0 Miles   100   200
0 Kilometers   200

Jerusalem

Mount of Olives
Gethsemane
Golden Gate
Temple of the Lord
TEMPLE MOUNT
Temple of Solomon/ al-Aqsa Mosque
St. Stephen's Gate
Holy Sepulchre
Tower of David
David's Gate

0 Miles   .25   .5
0 Kilometers   .5

of earth's kingdoms, both Christian and pagan, grew.* This fact of geography was also a fact of cosmology. Jerusalem was understood to be a place where the heavenly was made manifest, and the power of prayer magnified by the presence of relics and holy sites. It was not just seen, but felt: a visitor could personally experience the sacred details of biblical stories, from the deeds of the Old Testament kings to Christ's life and Passion.

Approaching Jerusalem on the road from Jaffa, Saewulf would have entered through David's Gate, a heavily fortified portal in the city's thick defensive walls, guarded by a large stone citadel built on the remains of a fortress erected by Herod: the king who the Bible claimed had put every baby in Bethlehem to death in an attempt to kill the infant Christ. In the southeastern quarter of the city was the Temple Mount, crowned with the shimmering cupola of the Dome of the Rock, which the Christians called the Temple of the Lord. Beside this was the al-Aqsa Mosque, a wide, low, rectangular building also topped with a dome, built in the seventh century and converted to Christian use as a palace for the Christian king of Jerusalem, a wealthy soldier from Boulogne known as Baldwin I.

Beyond the Temple Mount, on the other side of Jerusalem's eastern wall, lay a cemetery, and beyond that Gethsemane, where Christ had prayed with his disciples, and where he was betrayed by Judas on the night of his arrest. Farther on lay the Mount of Olives, where Jesus had spent many weeks teaching, and from where he had eventually ascended to heaven. Saewulf wrote in his diary that he himself climbed the Mount of Olives and looked down over the city of Jerusalem, examining where the city's walls and boundaries had been expanded during its occupation by the Romans.

The most holy place of all, and the real object of every Christian pilgrimage, lay within Jerusalem. It was the Church of the Holy Sepulchre, which Saewulf called "more celebrated than any other church, and this is

---

* A fine example is the Mappa Mundi held at Hereford Cathedral in England. This was created ca. 1300, but it illustrates the medieval conception of the world as it existed in Saewulf's time, and Jerusalem's central place in it. Pilgrim guidebooks advised visitors that they could find the exact center of the world "thirteen feet to the west of Mount Calvary."

meet and right, since all the prophecies and foretellings in the whole world about our Saviour Jesus Christ were all truly fulfilled there."[6]

It was a double-storied complex of interlinked chapels and courtyards, many of which commemorated, and were thought literally to mark the sites of, the central events in the Passion. Saewulf listed them: the prison cell where Jesus was kept after his betrayal; the spot where a fragment of the Cross had been found; a pillar against which the Lord had been bound when he was flogged by Roman soldiers and "the place where he was made to put on the purple robe and crowned with the crown of thorns" and Calvary, where Christ was crucified—here Saewulf examined the hole in which the Cross had been held, and a rock split in two, as had been described in the Gospel of Matthew.[7] There were chapels dedicated to Mary Magdalen and Saint John the Apostle, to the Virgin Mary and Saint James. Most important and impressive of all, though, was the great rotunda at the western end of the church, for here lay the Sepulchre itself: the tomb of Christ. This was the cave in which Jesus had been buried following his Crucifixion, before the Resurrection. The shrine was surrounded by continuously burning oil lamps and paved with slabs of marble: a still, fragrant place for prayer and devotion.[8] Nowhere on earth or in history was more sacred to Christians. Saewulf acknowledged as much in the very first line of his memoir: "I was on my way to Jerusalem to pray at the Lord's tomb." To stand before the Sepulchre was to venture to the cradle of Christianity, which was why pilgrims like Saewulf were willing to risk their lives to go there.

Pilgrimage was a centrally important part of Christian life in the early twelfth century, and had been for nearly one thousand years. People traveled incredible distances to visit saints' shrines and the sites of famous Christian deeds. They did it for the good of their souls: sometimes to seek divine relief from illness, sometimes as penance to atone for their sins. Some thought that praying at a certain shrine would ensure the protection of that saint in their passage through the afterlife. All believed that God looked kindly on pilgrims and that a man or woman who ventured humbly and faithfully to the center of the world would improve his or her standing in the eyes of God.

Yet Saewulf's perilous journey was not just devout. It was also timely. Although Christians had been visiting Jerusalem on pilgrimage since at least the fourth century, it had never been entirely friendly territory. For most of the previous seven hundred years the city and surrounding area had been under the control of Roman emperors, Persian kings, Umayyad caliphs and Seljuq rulers called beys (or emirs). From the seventh century until the end of the eleventh century, Jerusalem had been in Muslim hands. To the followers of Islam, it was the third-holiest city in the world, after Mecca and Medina. Muslims recognized it as the location of al-Masjid al-Aqsa (the Furthest Mosque), the place where, according to the Qur'an, the Prophet Muhammad was brought on his "Night Journey," when the angel Gabriel transported him from Mecca to the Temple Mount, from which they ascended together into the heavens.[9]

Recently, however, conditions had changed profoundly. Three years before Saewulf's journey, a dramatic upheaval had torn through the city and the wider coastal region of Palestine and Syria, which had fundamentally changed the appeal and nature of pilgrimage for men and women of the Latin West. Following a bitter and sustained war that raged between 1096 and 1099, major parts of the Holy Land had been conquered by the armies of what would come to be known as the First Crusade.

Several large expeditions of warrior pilgrims had traveled from Western Europe to the Holy Land (sometimes they called this "Outremer," which translates simply as "overseas"). These pilgrims were known collectively by Christian writers as the "Latins" or the "Franks," a term mirrored in Muslim texts, which referred to them as *Ifranj*.[10] Reacting to a cry for military assistance from the Byzantine emperor Alexius I Comnenus, backed by the enthusiastic preaching of Pope Urban II, these men and women had marched first to Constantinople and then on to the Levantine coast to fight the Muslims who held sway there. Urban promised, alluringly, that going on crusade could be substituted for all penances the Church had imposed on individuals for their sins—an entire lifetime's wrongdoing could theoretically be wiped out in a single journey. Initially these armed pilgrims had been little more than an undisciplined, violent mob led by rabble-rousers such as the French priest Peter the Hermit, who whipped his followers into a frenzy of devotion, but was unable either to provision them properly or to control their violent urges. Subsequent waves of crusaders were led by noblemen from France, Normandy,

England, Flanders, Bavaria, Lombardy and Sicily, driven by a genuinely righteous sense that it was their Christian duty to liberate the holy places from their Muslim occupiers, and encouraged by the fact that Jerusalem and the surrounding area were politically and militarily divided between numerous mutually hostile factions of the Islamic world.

The fissures were political, dynastic and sectarian. On one side were the Seljuqs, originally from central Asia, who had built an empire stretching from Asia Minor to the Hindu Kush, blending Turkic and Persian culture and observing religious loyalty to the Abbasid caliph in Baghdad, the spiritual leader of Sunni Islam. For twenty years before 1092 the Seljuq empire was ruled by Sultan Malikshah I, but on his death the empire split between his four sons, who fell into fractious dispute.

Pitted against the Seljuqs was the rump of the Fatimid caliphate, with its heartlands in Egypt, whose leaders claimed descent from Muhammad's daughter Fatima. From the mid-tenth century the Fatimids ruled most of North Africa, Syria, Palestine, the Hijaz and even Sicily, loyal to their own Shi'a caliph in Cairo. In the late eleventh century the Fatimid empire was also breaking up, losing territory and influence and contracting back toward its Egyptian heartlands. Sectarian and political rivalry between the Seljuqs and the Fatimids, as well as within the Seljuq empire itself, had caused a period of exceptional disunity within the Islamic world. As one of their own chroniclers put it, the various rulers were "all at odds with one another."[11]

So it was that the Christians of the First Crusade had enjoyed a staggering series of victories. Jerusalem had fallen on July 15, 1099, an astonishing military coup that was accompanied by disgraceful plundering and massacres of the city's Jewish and Muslim inhabitants, whose beheaded bodies were left lying in piles in the streets, many with their bellies slit open so that the Christian conquerors could retrieve gold coins their victims had swallowed in a bid to hide them from the marauding invaders.[12] Greek Orthodox priests in Jerusalem were tortured until they revealed the location of some of their finest relics, including a fragment of wood from the True Cross on which Christ had died, embedded in a beautiful gold, crucifix-shaped reliquary.

The crusaders took the major northern cities of Edessa and Antioch, as well as smaller towns including Alexandretta, Bethlehem, Haifa, Tiberias and Jaffa. Other coastal settlements including Arsuf, Acre, Caesarea and Ascalon remained in Muslim hands but agreed to pay tributes to be left alone and were in time conquered. A series of new Christian states was established along the Mediterranean coast: the county of Edessa and the principality of Antioch in the north were bordered to the south by the county of Tripoli and the kingdom of Jerusalem, which claimed theoretical feudal lordship over the whole region—although this was only ever very loosely enforced.

Given the unprecedented conditions of their arrival, the sheer distance from home and the sapping nature of waging war in such an unforgiving climate, the Christians' hold on these lands was still incomplete. By the time of Saewulf's pilgrimage to Jerusalem, troops, boats and holy men arriving from the West had helped expand the territories subject to the rule of Jerusalem's first crusader king, Baldwin I. But there were not very many of them and they were threatened by multiple enemies from outside, and internal divisions among the crusaders, drawn as they were from parts of the West not renowned for easy cooperation.

In the summer of 1102, Saewulf thus found himself in a new, small, occasionally beleaguered but aggressive Christian kingdom of the East, whose very existence was thought by the zealots who had established it to be evidence that God had "opened to us the abundance of His blessing and mercy." The Muslims who had been displaced not surprisingly saw things otherwise. They referred to their new neighbors as the product of "a time of disasters" brought about by the "enemies of God."[13]

✛

For the next six months Saewulf explored every inch of the Holy City and its surrounding area, comparing the things he saw with his knowledge of Scripture and previous accounts of Jerusalem, including one written by the eighth-century English monk and theologian known as the Venerable Bede. Saewulf marveled at the Temple of the Lord and the Church of the Holy Sepulchre, the Mount of Olives and the Garden of Gethsemane. He went to the Monastery of the Holy Cross, where visitors could peer beneath the great altar and see the stump of the tree from which Jesus' crucifix had been made, encased in a box of white marble with a little viewing window. He was stunned by the magnificence of what he saw. Of the Temple of the Lord he remarked that "its height was more than the hills around it and in its beauty and its glory it excelled all other houses and buildings."[14] He admired glorious sculpture and the city's formidable defenses. In everything he saw Scripture coming to life: the place where Peter cured the lame man and where Jesus rode into Jerusalem "sitting on an ass, when the boys were singing *Hosanna to the Son of David!*"[15]

Nevertheless, Saewulf often found the pilgrim roads around Jerusalem eerie and unsafe. The trail inland from Jaffa had been particularly grueling: a long, tough journey along a "very hard mountain road."[16] The general instability of the crusader kingdom was evident all around. Muslim brigands—Saewulf called them "Saracens"—fanned out across the countryside, living in rocky caves, spooking pilgrims who believed that "they were awake day and night, always keeping a look-out for someone to attack." From time to time Saewulf and his party would glimpse frightening figures ahead or behind them, menacing them from a distance before disappearing out of view. They traveled in fear, knowing that anyone who tired and dropped behind was liable to suffer a grisly fate.

Everywhere corpses lay rotting in the heat. Some were on the path itself, others just off it, a number of them "torn up by wild beasts." (Cliff foxes, jackals and leopards were all native to the mountains of Palestine.) These Christians had been abandoned by their fellow travelers without any attempt to give them a decent burial, for in the sunbaked earth the task would have been impossible. "There is little soil there and the rocks are not easy to move," wrote Saewulf. "Even if the soil were there, who would be stupid enough to leave his brethren and be alone digging a grave? Anybody who did this would dig a grave not for his fellow Christian but for himself."[17]

Six miles to the south of Jerusalem he found Bethlehem "all ruined," except for the large monastery of the Blessed Virgin Mary, which contained "the manger where the ox and ass stood" at the time of Christ's birth, as well as a marble table where the Virgin supposedly had supper with the Magi.[18] Farther south still was Hebron, also "ruined by the

Saracens," notable for being the burial place of "the Holy Patriarchs Abraham, Isaac and Jacob" as well as "Adam, the first-created man."[19] In the east he saw the Dead Sea, "where the water of the Jordan is whiter and more like milk than the other waters."[20] In the north, three days' ride away, he visited Nazareth, the Sea of Galilee and the city of Tiberias, where Jesus had performed miracles, including the feeding of the five thousand.

The sheer concentration of holy places was deeply affecting, and he kept a detailed record of it all, recording even the "smell of balsam and very precious spices" that stayed in his nostrils when he visited particularly popular shrines.[21] Yet he was constantly aware that his pious travels were made through treacherous lands. Churches and towns lay collapsed into jagged stone ruins. Monasteries mourned dozens of brethren massacred for their faith. Horrors old and new commingled. Here was a place where in ancient times Saint Peter had wet the earth with his tears after betraying the Lord; there a church deserted more recently for fear of "the pagans" who had amassed on the far banks of the river Jordan, "in Arabia, which is very hostile to Christians and hates all worshippers of God."[22]

By the late spring of 1103 Saewulf had traveled as far as he could and amply fulfilled his purpose as a pilgrim. "I had explored as far as I was able each one of the Holy Places of the city of Jerusalem and the cities near it, and venerated them," he wrote. He returned to Jaffa and sought out a berth on a merchant ship heading west. Still his safety was not guaranteed. The open waters toward Cyprus were patrolled by enemy ships from Fatimid Egypt, which commanded enough coastal cities to keep their fleet active at sea, readily replenished with food and water. No Christian ships dared to make a long journey out of sight of land, for fear of attack. On May 17 Saewulf boarded one of three large ships known as dromonds, which were traveling north together, hugging the coast, stopping at friendly ports and hurrying past unfriendly ones as fast as the prevailing wind and their oarsmen would carry them.

Some seventy-five miles into the journey, as the dromonds were approaching Acre, twenty-six Arab warships came into view. They were Fatimid vessels, which prompted panic on the decks. Saewulf watched, presumably in some disquiet, as the two dromonds accompanying his own dipped their oars frantically and fled for the safety of the Christian-held town of Caesarea. Saewulf's ship was left stranded. The enemy formed a ring around her, staying just out of range of crossbow fire, whooping with delight at the promise of such a prize. The pilgrims armed themselves for a fight and fell into defensive ranks on the decks. "Our men," wrote Saewulf, "were prepared to die for Christ."[23]

Mercifully, this show of defiance was enough to make the Fatimid commander think twice before making his attack. After a tense hour of consideration, he decided there were easier targets to be found, abandoned the assault and made for deeper waters and less determined opposition. Saewulf and his fellow travelers praised the Lord and went on their way, crossing to Cyprus eight days later, then hopping back to the coast of Asia Minor and continuing along much the same route he had traveled on his outbound journey. Finally they swung north through the Dardanelles toward the great city of Constantinople, itself packed with holy relics to inspect and adore. Throughout their journey they were harassed by pirates and tossed by storms. As Saewulf contemplated the journey of a lifetime from the safety of his home, he mused that the only thing that had protected him was the grace of God.

✝

Saewulf was just one among thousands of pilgrims to make this similar journey to the Holy Land in the aftermath of the First Crusade. They came from all over the Christian world: accounts of the Christian kingdom of Jerusalem, new and fragile in its first decades, survive from men who traveled from Portugal, Flanders, Germany, Russia and even Iceland. As the Holy Land was in effect a war zone, many found it a hair-raising place. The chronicler Fulcher of Chartres noted in 1101 that when pilgrims visited Jersualem they came "very timidly . . . through the midst of hostile pirates and past the ports of the Saracens, with the Lord showing the way."[24] A Russian writer known as Daniel the Abbot traveled on pilgrimage from Kiev between about 1106 and 1108. He, too, wrote of the terrifying road between Jaffa and Jerusalem, where "Saracens sally forth and kill travelers," and complained of the number of venerable sites "destroyed by the pagans." On the road to Lake Tiberias he dodged "fierce pagans who attack travelers at the river-fords" and lions that roamed the countryside in "great numbers." Walking unescorted on the high, narrow pass between Mount Tabor and Nazareth, Daniel prayed for his life, having been warned that the local villagers "kill travelers in those terrible mountains."[25] Fortunately, he survived, returning home to Kiev with a small piece of the rock of Christ's tomb, broken off surreptitiously by the key keeper and given to him as a relic.

Pilgrims in any age expect a certain degree of danger from brigands and robbers. But the hostility of the Muslims who lived in and around the new crusader states was more than merely opportunistic. The losses their people had suffered from the first appearance of the Franks in 1096 were considered shameful and perplexing—a sign of God's displeasure at divisions in the Muslim world and a call to all the faithful to rise in arms to fight back against the invaders. "Armies like mountains, coming again and again, have ranged forth from the lands of the Franks," wrote the Syrian poet Ibn al-Khayyat, before 1109. "The heads of the polytheists have already ripened, so do not neglect them as a vintage and a harvest!"[26] Other writers, such as the farsighted and wise Ali ibn Tahir al-Sulami, called for a united effort from across the Islamic world—Turks and Arabs, Sunni and Shi'a—to pull together and wage jihad, or holy war, to achieve "the taking back of what [the Franks] took from the country of the Muslims [and] the displaying of the religion of Islam in them."[27]

The jihadist counterattack al-Sulami had hoped for did not occur— at least, not in the years immediately following the establishment of the Christian kingdom. Bitter divisions continued, making a serious, sustained and effective response to occupation impossible. At the level of high politics and warring princes, the Franks were in Jerusalem to stay. Yet at the same time, for those Christians who risked everything they owned, even their lives, traveling for thousands of miles to visit the holy sites in the East, the kingdom of Jerusalem was a place where rapture and terror were to be experienced side by side, often over the course of the same day. Jerusalem was, as one writer noted, quoting the Torah, "a golden basin filled with scorpions."[28] The desire to brave these dangers added to the allure of a pilgrimage, as discomfort and suffering were thought to be necessary for the redemption of the soul and remission of sins sought by every pilgrim. Yet there were only so many bodies that could reasonably be allowed to stack up by the side of the road, their throats slit and flesh torn to pieces. As the crusading Christians put down roots in this new kingdom at the center of the world, it became clear that they would need protection.

That is where the story of the Templars begins.

2

"The Defense of Jerusalem"

THE KNIGHTS OF THE TEMPLE were founded in Jerusalem in 1119 and officially recognized at some point between January 14 and September 13 of the year 1120.[1] Barely anyone noticed. The Templars did not arrive on a wave of popular demand, nor was their creation the product of some farsighted planning between the nascent crusader states and religious authorities in Western Christendom. No surviving chronicles of the immediate time, either Christian or Muslim, paid any attention to the first stirrings of the order—indeed, it was only several generations later that the story of the Templars' earliest origins was written down, by which time it was colored by what the order had become.[2] But this was hardly surprising. Much like Jerusalem's rulers and inhabitants, the historians and gossip collectors of the Holy Land in the year 1120 had other, bigger things to worry about.

The crusaders who stayed to rule in the Holy Land were foreign invaders, trying to establish their command over a mixed population of Sunni and Shi'a Muslims, Jews, Greek and Syrian Orthodox Christians, Samaritans and poor settlers from all over Europe. This was a society naturally divided by language, religion, culture and loyalty, contending with an environment that sometimes seemed naturally hostile to settlement. In 1113 and 1114, Syria and Palestine were shaken by severe earthquakes, which razed whole towns and left people suffocating to death beneath collapsed buildings. Virtually every springtime brought plagues of mice and locusts, which swarmed over vines and fields, ruining crops and stripping the bark from the trees. From time to time strange eclipses stained the moon and the sky bloodred. All of these things played on the settlers' superstitious minds. It was as if the land wished to cast out the crusaders and the heavens to punish them for their conquest.[3]

Just as serious as the plagues and omens was the matter of safety and security. Over the twenty years since the Franks had conquered Jerusalem and established their four crusader states, they had been forced to fight hard for a foothold on the coast. There were some major gains: the cities of Acre, Beirut and Tripoli were taken, thanks in part to regular influxes of troops from the Christian West (including a major expedition from Scandinavia commanded by Sigurd, king of Norway, who helped King Baldwin capture Sidon in 1110). Yet these impressive territorial advances could not change the reality of life beneath the scorching sun of the Levantine coast: unpredictable and violent.

In 1118, Baldwin I died. He was followed to the grave three weeks later by the leading Latin churchman in the kingdom: Arnulf, patriarch of Jerusalem. These two men were succeeded by the Count of Edessa, an experienced crusader who became King Baldwin II, and Warmund of Picquigny, a spirited cleric from a prominent family in northern France. Both were formidable characters, but the transition nevertheless prompted simultaneous invasions from the Seljuqs in eastern Syria and the Fatimids in Egypt, bringing a new round of skirmishes and warfare. Defending the kingdom was costly in manpower and morale, and the Frankish forces were constantly overstretched. The chronicler Fulcher of Chartres considered it "a wonderful miracle that we lived among so many thousands of thousands [of enemies]."[4]

In the year 1119 things were as bad as they had ever been, thanks to two particularly grave events. The first took place on Holy Saturday, March 29, following the miracle of the Holy Fire at the Church of the Holy Sepulchre. In this yearly ritual an oil lamp kept beside the rock of Christ's tomb would spontaneously burst alight on the eve of Easter; the sacred flame was then used to light the individual candles and lamps of faithful men and women who gathered to witness it. Unfortunately in 1119, once the miracle had taken place, seven hundred ecstatic pilgrims ran out of the church and streamed into the desert in the direction of the river Jordan, intending to bathe in its waters and thank God. The river was about twenty miles from the eastern walls of Jerusalem and the pilgrims never made it to their destination. The chronicler Albert of Aachen recorded that once they had descended from the mountains to "a place of solitude" near the river, all of a sudden "there appeared Saracens from Tyre and Ascalon [two cities still in Muslim hands], armed and very fierce." They fell upon the pilgrims, who were "virtually unarmed" and "weary after a journey of many days, weakened by fasting for Jesus' name."

It was no fight at all. "The wicked butchers pursued them, putting three hundred to the sword and holding sixty captive," wrote Albert.[5]

As soon as Baldwin II heard of the outrage, he scrambled troops out of Jerusalem to take revenge. But he was too late. The attackers were already safely back in their redoubts, counting their prisoners and delighting in the spoils of their raid.

Scarcely two months later, more dreadful news arrived from the north. On June 28, 1119, at Sarmada in northwest Syria, a very large force of Christians who were occupying Antioch went into battle against an army led by an Artuqid ruler known as Il-ghazi,* a drunkard but a dangerous general who occupied nearby Aleppo. According to an eyewitness, the battle was fought in a fierce dust storm: a "whirlwind . . . twisting itself upward like an enormous jar on the potter's wheel, burnt up by sulphurous fires."

The Christians were slaughtered by the hundreds. Their leader, Roger of Salerno, was "struck by a knight's sword through the middle of his nose right into his brain" and died instantly. All around him the countryside was littered with human corpses and dying horses so thickly pierced with arrows they looked like hedgehogs.[6] "The cavalry was destroyed, the infantry cut to pieces, the followers and servants were all taken prisoner," wrote the Arab historian Ibn al-Adim approvingly.[7] This was not all. After the battle, several hundred Christian captives were bound together by their necks and marched through the blistering heat of the day, tortured by the sight of a water barrel from which they were not allowed to drink. Some were beaten. Some were flayed. Some were stoned to death. Others were beheaded.[8] Fulcher of Chartres estimated that, in all, seven thousand Christians were killed, taking with them just twenty of Il-ghazi's men.[9] Fulcher may have exaggerated the numbers, but this demoralizing defeat was known thereafter among the Franks as *ager sanguinis*: the Field of Blood.[†] The defeat at Sarmada was a ghastly moment not only

---

* The Artuqids were a tribal Sunni Turkish dynasty begun by a soldier called Artuq Bey, who had worked as a general for the Seljuq sultan Malikshah I. Artuq's descendants carved out an independent territory in northern Mesopotamia, northern Syria and eastern Anatolia.

† There was an echo here, perhaps deliberate, of the biblical name given to a certain field used for burying strangers, which had been bought by the elders of Jerusalem using the

for the Christians of Antioch, but for the Franks in general. Yet out of it came the germ of an idea that would lie at the heart of Templar ideology.

Following the battle, desperate measures were required to resist any further losses in Antioch. Il-ghazi was preparing a direct assault on the city. According to the writer Walter the Chancellor, a senior bureaucrat from Antioch who was almost certainly present and very likely taken prisoner at the Field of Blood, "almost the entire military force of Frankish citizens was lost." Armed assistance had been urgently requested from the kingdom of Jerusalem, but plainly it would take some time for this to arrive.

Into the vacuum stepped a man named Bernard of Valence, Latin patriarch of Antioch.[10] Bernard was one of the highest-ranking churchmen in all the crusader states. He had been patriarch since 1100, when the Western invaders who conquered Antioch chased out the Greek Orthodox patriarch and installed their own man, who followed the traditions of the Roman Church. During that time he had frequently helped Christian armies to prepare themselves spiritually for battle: preaching to soldiers and hearing the confession of those who had shed blood in the course of the wars. Now it was not only souls that he would have to save. It was his city.

"Of necessity, all came down to the clergy," wrote Walter the Chancellor, and this was no mere rhetoric.[11] As Il-ghazi mustered his troops, inside Antioch the patriarch took supreme military command. He ordered a nightly curfew and decreed that no one was to carry arms within the city except for the Franks. Then he ensured that every tower along Antioch's defenses was "garrisoned at once with monks and clerics," supported by what suitable Christian laymen they could find to assist them. Bernard arranged for constant prayers to be said "for the safety and defense of the Christian people," and while these took place he "did not cease . . . to visit in turn, night and day, with his armed clergy and knights, in the manner of warriors, the gates, ramparts and towers and walls."[12]

These were the actions of a soldier prince, rather than the defensive measures of a man of the Church. And they were stunningly successful.

---

thirty pieces of silver returned to them by Judas Iscariot shortly before his suicide (Matthew 27:6–8).

Seeing that the city was well defended, Il-ghazi declined to attack. The lull in hostilities allowed Baldwin II to muster troops and take over the campaign. Antioch had been saved. In the words of Walter the Chancellor, "the clergy . . . acted the part of military service wisely and vigorously, inside and outside, and with God's strength kept the city intact from the enemy."[13] It was a taste of what lay ahead.

+

The notion that churchmen might go into battle armed not only with prayer but with deadly weapons was hardly new. It spoke to a tension at the heart of Christian thought for a thousand years, as the pacifism suggested by the example of Christ's life rubbed against a martial mentality embedded in the language of Christian rhetoric and Scripture.[14] It also followed naturally from the ideas underpinning the whole crusading movement.

On the face of it, Christianity was a faith rooted in peace. Jesus had admonished his disciples for resorting to violence even under the most extreme provocation—urging them to sheathe their weapons during his arrest in the Garden of Gethsemane, and saying "they that take the sword will perish by the sword."[15] But during the decades immediately following his death, Saint Paul had exhorted the Ephesians to arm themselves with "the breastplate of righteousness," "the helmet of salvation" and "the sword of the Spirit, which is the word of God."[16] The warfare Paul advocated was spiritual rather than physical, but the terms of Christian ideology drew directly from the language of war. The idea of Christian existence as an act of cosmic, spiritual battle—a fight against the devil—dominated the worldview of many of the great Christian thinkers of the classical world, such as Saint Ambrose and Saint Augustine of Hippo. This was perhaps no surprise, given how frequently during the first centuries of Christianity's emergence the faithful had found themselves compelled to commit or endure bodily violence, whether in the amphitheaters of the Romans or in suffering the death throes of martyrdom. Indeed, martyrdom had become an admirable thing in itself, and a staple part of the notion of sainthood.

By the time of the First Crusade, the notion of Christian war was not just metaphorical. Christian societies in Europe were structured around the existence of a warrior caste—knights—and churchmen had occasionally begun to engage more directly in warfare, no longer contenting themselves with the struggles of the soul. Rudolf I, bishop of Würzburg, died fighting the Magyars in 908. An English record known as the Abingdon Chronicle, compiled shortly before the First Crusade, describes how the abbot of Abingdon commanded a retinue of knights.[17] This is not to say that the practice of holy warfare was universally accepted: in the ninth century Pope Nicholas I had specifically stated that for churchmen, self-defense must mean following Christ's example and turning the other cheek, while the Byzantine princess and biographer Anna Comnena frequently expressed in her writings a marked distaste for the idea of Christian clerics having any involvement in maiming or killing people.[18]

But in the white heat of war in Syria and Palestine a restriction on Christians of any sort bearing arms was increasingly impractical. For a start, a significant factor behind the existence of the crusade movement was a widespread acceptance of the concept of Christian holy war, waged by secular men for spiritual reward. Successive popes had worked this up into a practical philosophy of Christian violence, manifested in the First Crusade. Laymen who went to fight Muslims in the East were described as having joined the "knighthood of Christ" (*militiae Christi*), and having taken up the "gospel knighthood" (*evangelicam militiam*).[19]

From here it was a relatively small step to argue that if fighting men could become holy, then it was possible to imagine that holy men could fight. Indeed, given the strain on resources in the crusader states in the 1120s, it was a matter of necessity to concede that a cleric could from time to time wield weapons without reproach—as Patriarch Bernard had done at Antioch. Several months later, at a grand gathering of clerical and secular leaders from the kingdom of Jerusalem, the idea of religious men bearing arms was institutionalized for the first time.

The Council of Nablus convened on January 16, 1120, under the auspices of King Baldwin II and Warmund, the Latin patriarch of Jersualem. It was attended by many of the highest-ranking churchmen in the Holy Land, including the archbishop of Caesarea, the bishops of Nazareth, Bethlehem and Ramla, and—significantly, as it would later turn out—the priors of the Holy Sepulchre and the Temple of the Lord in Jerusalem. The purpose of this gathering at Nablus—a town nestled in a valley between two mountains in central Palestine, notable for its plentiful olive trees—was to provide a set of written laws, or "canons," by which the kingdom could be properly governed in a manner pleasing to God.[20]

The Council of Nablus produced twenty-five decrees, which touched initially on matters of jurisdiction between the secular and clerical authorities, and for the most part focused on sex.[21] Declarations were made against sins including adultery, sodomy, bigamy, pimping, prostitution, theft and sexual relations with Muslims, for which the prescribed punishments ranged from penance and exile to castration and nose slicing. Tucked among these was a dictum that would be of fundamental importance to the origins and history of the Knights Templar. It was canon 20, and its first line stated simply that "if a cleric takes up arms in the cause of self-defense, he shall not bear any guilt." The second line suggested that this was envisaged as a temporary measure, and that the abandonment of the holy duty for a martial one was to be carried out only under duress. (Clerics who permanently abandoned their tonsures to become knights or join secular society could be disciplined by the patriarch and the king.) Nevertheless, in the context of the early months of 1120, this was significant indeed. The men who met in Nablus were not just working out a code of law and morality for the Holy Land. They were seeding in law a revolutionary idea, which would evolve before long into the notion—and fact—that religious men under arms might serve as a central plank in the defense of the crusader states.

+

"At the beginning of the reign of Baldwin II," wrote a late-twelfth-century churchman called Michael the Syrian, "a Frenchman came from Rome to Jerusalem to pray."[22] This Frenchman's name was Hugh of Payns. He was born some time before the year 1070, probably in the village of Payns, near the town of Troyes, some ninety miles southeast of Paris in the county of Champagne. We know little else about Hugh of Payns's early life, other than that he was of sufficiently high rank to witness charters for local noblemen in France. If Michael the Syrian was correct, by the time the Council of Nablus assembled in January 1120, Hugh of Payns had been in the Holy Land for roughly as long as Baldwin had been king—a matter of some twenty months. This was long enough for him to see the sights, assess the dangers of the region and, evidently, to determine that rather than fleeing home by way of the pirate-infested waters of the eastern Mediterranean, he would see out a substantial number of his remaining years as part of the community of occupying Franks in Jerusalem. He planned first to serve in the royal army, and then to retire from the hard-bitten life on the front line to become a monk.[23]

Hugh was not alone in making this decision. There were other men of the knightly sort in the city of Jerusalem at the time, and they began to cluster together at the most obvious spot for tourists and newcomers of all backgrounds and nationalities to meet: the Church of the Holy Sepulchre.

Indeed, they did more than cluster. It would seem that in the months preceding the Council of Nablus a handful of Jerusalem's expatriate knights (later sources suggested it was initially between nine and thirty men) had formed a sort of loose brotherhood, or confraternity, of the sort that had cropped up in the West during the previous century for the purpose of defending churches and shrines from bandits.[24] They had sworn oaths of obedience to Gerard, prior of the Holy Sepulchre, on whose patronage and hospitality they depended for their day-to-day livelihood.[25] They were not, strictly speaking, clergymen, but rather able-bodied warrior pilgrims who could fight and who had made a significant decision to live a quasi-monastic life of penitence, poverty, obedience and duty beyond the normal vows of a crusader.

By the beginning of January 1120 there was a feeling that these religiously minded soldiers were being underused. One later writer characterized the lives of Hugh of Payns and his companions at that time as squandered in underemployed frustration: "drinking, eating, wasting . . . time and doing nothing" at the Holy Sepulchre.[26] If true, this was clearly a shameful misuse of talent. Already there existed an order of religious volunteers who dedicated themselves to tending the sick and wounded pilgrims at the infirmary known as the Hospital of Saint John of Jerusalem. That order—the Hospitallers—had been granted official papal recognition in 1113, and operated from premises that were not far from the

Holy Sepulchre. They were not soldiers (although they would later become so), and their contribution to life in Jerusalem was generations old and highly valued. It must have seemed that a complementary order of armed escorts could lighten the load on the Hospitallers and further improve conditions for the thousands of pilgrims who passed through the region.

Around the time of the Council of Nablus it was decided that instead of being attached to the Holy Sepulchre, this pious band of knights should be given independence, some means of feeding and clothing themselves, access to priests who could lead prayers for them at the appropriate hours of the day and a place to live in one of the prominent areas of Jerusalem. The Crown would assist with the means of their upkeep, but their main task would be one of equal interest to king, patriarch and every other Christian visitor to the Holy Lands. They would be responsible, in the words of a charter produced in 1137, for "the defense of Jerusalem and the protection of pilgrims."[27] Part bodyguards, part paupers, a tiny brotherhood devoted only to arms and prayer: these were the men who became the first Knights of the Temple.

✝

Temples had stood on the eastern side of Jerusalem for thousands of years. The first was a huge complex erected by King Solomon, the fabulously rich, wise and worldly Old Testament monarch who had ruled over the tribes of Israel after the death of his father, King David. The construction of Solomon's Temple was described at length in the book of Kings. It was made of "costly stones," paneled with delicately carved olive wood, cedarwood and gold and held up by countless pillars, concealing at its heart the Holy of Holies, a sacred room where God's name "lived" and where the Ark of the Covenant—the repository of the original tablets inscribed with the Ten Commandments—was stored.[28]

The Babylonian king Nebuchadnezzar II destroyed Solomon's Temple in 586 B.C. and at that point the Ark of the Covenant disappeared. But a few decades later the Temple rose again. The Second Temple was built by Jewish exiles returning to Jerusalem in 520 B.C. and massively enlarged half a millennium later during the reign of Herod the Great. It stood on a vast stone platform covering a natural hill—the Temple Mount—and served as a place for sacrifice, prayer, worship, trade, medical care and entertainment. It was completed around 10 B.C. and was the center of Jewish life in Jerusalem at the time of Jesus' ministry. Like Solomon's original Temple, the Second Temple was destroyed by the wrath of an outside empire: wrecked by fire in A.D. 70 during the suppression of a Jewish revolt against the Roman emperor Titus. Sixty-five years later its ruins were demolished for good and pagan statues were erected on the site.

By the time Hugh of Payns set up his order in Jerusalem, the Temple Mount had been refashioned once again: not by Jews or Christians, but by the Umayyads—the all-powerful Sunni caliphate whose armies had conquered the city a few decades after Muhammad's death in the late seventh century A.D. Two extraordinary buildings now dominated Jerusalem's skyline. The Dome of the Rock's huge golden roof shimmered like a fireball, visible for miles around. ("As soon as the beams of the sun strike the cupola and the drum radiates the light, then indeed is this marvelous to behold," recorded one Muslim traveler and geographer of the tenth century.)[29] At the other end of the Temple Mount complex was another imposing building: al-Aqsa Mosque, most recently refashioned in the 1030s. This was regarded as the most important and most beautiful mosque outside Arabia, more magnificent even than the Great Mosque of Damascus. When a Persian traveler visited al-Aqsa in its heyday, he described seeing "two hundred and eighty marble columns, supporting arches that are fashioned of stone, and both the shafts and the capitals of the columns are sculptured . . . the mosque is everywhere flagged with colored marble, with the joints riveted in lead. . . . Above rises a mighty dome that is ornamented with enamel work."[30] Around this lived devout men who had retired from the world and given themselves over to the religious life: the chronicler Ibn al-Athir wrote that at the time of the First Crusade the mosque was frequented by "imams, ulema, righteous men and ascetics, Muslims who had left their native lands and come to live a holy life in this august spot."[31]

Under crusader rule, both the Dome of the Rock and al-Aqsa Mosque were stripped of their Islamic sanctity: the Dome became a church, while the mosque was repurposed as a palace for the king of Jerusalem. The

Christians called the Dome of the Rock the "Temple of the Lord" and they identified al-Aqsa with the Temple of Solomon, in tribute to its historic location. The magnetism of the site to men of the world who wished to embrace spiritual life survived the transition from Muslim to Christian rule intact: for it was here that Hugh of Payns and his small band of followers were allowed to lodge following the creation of their order in 1120. According to the writer known as Ernoul, this was the king's "most splendid" residence in the city.[32] The twelfth-century archbishop and chronicler William of Tyre explained that "because . . . they live next to the Temple of the Lord in the king's palace they are called the brothers of the Knighthood of the Temple."[33]

Despite these lodgings, the Templars could hardly have been said to live in luxury. In their earliest years at the Holy Sepulchre, they were dependent on charity, including handouts from the Hospitallers, who donated them their leftover food.[34] Their official recognition and housing on the Temple Mount did not much improve their material fortunes. According to the Welsh courtier and chronicler Walter Map, Hugh of Payns and his men lived there "with humble attire and spare diet," while Hugh used "persuasion, prayer and every means in his power" to induce "all such pilgrims as were men of arms either to surrender themselves for life to the service of the Lord in that place or at least to devote themselves thereto for a time."[35] The tax revenues of a few villages near Jerusalem were assigned to them by Baldwin II and Patriarch Warmund, "to cater for their food and clothing," but much of the first decade of the Templars' existence was eked out in penury, the small number of brothers dressed in secondhand clothes and not the distinctive uniforms they would later adopt.[36]

Their home was also far from perfect. "Large and wonderful" were the terms used by the chronicler Fulcher of Chartres to describe the basic structure of the repurposed al-Aqsa Mosque. But the lead that had lined its roof had been stripped and sold by King Baldwin I, and there had been no subsequent attempt to make repairs. "Because of our poverty [it] could not be maintained in the condition in which we found it," wrote Fulcher.[37] During the Christian conquest of Jerusalem in 1099, this had been the venue of one of the worst massacres of Muslim women and children. Their blood had run ankle deep throughout its halls. Now it was, in the words of one pilgrim who visited not long after Hugh of Payns's men set up home, "the dwelling of the new knights who guard Jerusalem."[38]

If these new knights were going to succeed in protecting Jerusalem's Christian inhabitants, pilgrims and territories from the many enemies who threatened them, they would need to grow: to build up numbers, resources and wealth. What was more, they would need an identity. To improve their fortunes, Hugh of Payns's men would have to look beyond their immediate surroundings and back to the world that had sent them to the Holy Land in the first place. They would have to appeal directly to the pope.

3

"A New Knighthood"

ONE CHRISTMAS EVE a few years before the fall of Jerusalem, a seven-year-old boy from Fontaines, in Burgundy, had a dream. As he slept he saw the Virgin Mary holding the Christ Child in her arms, as though he had been born that very moment. Bernard (known later as Bernard of Clairvaux, and later still simply as Saint Bernard) would grow up to be one of the greatest churchmen of his age: a champion of monastic reform, a renowned scholar, a bombastic and tireless letter writer, a brilliant preacher and an early patron and founding father of the Knights Templar.[1] His religious awakening would shape the direction of the Western Church in the first half of the twelfth century.

By 1126, when Hugh of Payns set off for France, Bernard was thirty-six years old. For twelve years he had been the abbot of his own recently founded monastery in Clairvaux ("clear valley") in the county of Champagne. The monastery sat in secluded, marshy ground watered by the river Aube, flanked by two shallow hills: one planted with vines and the other with crops. Here several dozen white-mantled Cistercian monks lived under Bernard's direction, following a strict, stripped-back monastic rule. The Cistercian Order had been formed in 1098, when a group of monks of the more popular Benedictine Order founded a new monastery at Cîteaux near Dijon to devote their lives to a purer form of religious life. The core Cistercian values were simple, ascetic existence, rigorous manual labor and isolated living far away from civilization. Cistercians contrasted sharply and deliberately with the black-clad brothers of a typical Benedictine monastery, who tended to indulge in fine food, preferred liturgical chanting to physical labor and filled their ornate chapels with fine art and artifacts. In contrast, the Cistercian monks under Bernard's care were committed to a life of obedience, prayer, scholarship, austerity and ceaseless toil at the abbey's flour mills, fields and fishponds. "Here is a spot that has much to delight the eye, to revive the weak spirit, to soothe the aching heart and to arouse to devotion all who seek the Lord," wrote one twelfth-century visitor to Clairvaux.[2] Yet this was also a deliberately sparse and testing environment, as the physical hardship of a life of meager sustenance was thought to encourage spiritual development and closeness to God. It suited Bernard perfectly.

The Cistercians were not the only men trying to reimagine religious life in Europe at this time. The twelfth century was one of the richest times of Christian renewal in the whole Middle Ages. Monasticism was exploding in popularity, and flowering with a diversity unseen since the early days of the Church. "O how innumerable a crowd of monks has by divine grace multiplied above all in our days," wrote one abbot in the 1130s. "It has covered almost the entire countryside of Gaul [i.e., France] and filled the towns, castles and fortresses."[3] This was more than rhetoric: it has been estimated that between the middle of the eleventh and the middle of the twelfth centuries the number of religious houses in many parts of Europe had expanded by 1000 percent.[4]

This great surge in monastic living corresponded to an energetic appetite for new ways to live, most of them centered on poverty, obedience and contemplation. Besides the Cistercians, the late eleventh and early twelfth centuries saw the establishment of the Carthusians (an order of hermits founded by Saint Bruno in 1084); Grandmontines (an extremely strict and poor order founded near Limoges around 1100); Tironensians (gray-clad and severely penitential brothers following the example of Saint Bernard of Thiron, who founded an abbey in 1109); Premonstratensians (established by Saint Norbert around 1120 to preach and serve ordinary parishioners in the community as "canons regular"); and many other orders, some enduring and others fleeting. Many of the religious orders, old and new, made provision for houses of women to live under their rule as nuns; there was also a growing trend of women becoming hermits or anchoresses, walled up for life in bare and remote cells. All of these allowed people to express their religious urges through their order: an all-consuming way of life governing what they wore, where they lived, what they ate and how they spoke—if they spoke.

Sometime before October 1126, Bernard of Clairvaux received a letter from King Baldwin II of Jerusalem.[5] In it the king wrote that yet another new religious group had been formed in the contested lands of the East, whose members had been "stirred by the Lord" for the defense of the crusader realm.[6] They were, wrote Baldwin, the *fratres Templarii*—the brothers of the Temple—and what they sought more than anything else was confirmation and a rule that would govern their lives. To that end he intended to send back two of his men to "obtain approval of their order from the pope." He hoped the pontiff would help them raise money and support, so that the Templars could better pursue the fight against "the enemies of the faith."[7] Baldwin urged Bernard to throw his weight behind this project by encouraging secular rulers across Europe to support the Templars, and lobbying the pope for formal recognition of the new order.

There was probably no one better in Europe to have asked to help. Bernard was a reformer, a powerful thinker and someone who understood what drove men to seek a new calling in life. More important, he was a master at extracting favors from the great and good. In hundreds of letters over the course of his long career, written in florid Latin and frequently at very great length, he flattered, supplicated, bullied and berated everyone from popes, kings, archbishops and abbots to runaway novices and would-be nuns doubting their vocation. He advocated causes as weighty as international war and papal schism, but was also quite happy to fight the causes of the humble and powerless. In one letter addressed to Pope Innocent II on behalf of a group of poor Cistercians, Bernard apologized for bothering Innocent when he was busy, then proceeded to lecture him on the business of being pope: "If you are faithful to the duty and traditions of the Apostolic See, you will not disregard the complaints of the poor."[8] On another occasion he wrote to a young virgin, Sophia, enjoining her at length to maintain her chastity, and inviting her to compare herself with other women who lived loosely and gave themselves over to finery instead of spiritual purity: "They are clothed in purple and fine linen, but their souls are in rags. Their bodies glitter with jewels but their lives are foul with vanity."[9] Bernard was a master of rhetoric and a friend of the powerful—a potent combination in any era.

Yet it was not just the nimble efficacy of Bernard's entreaties that made him such an appealing advocate. There were similarities between the still-developing Templar ideal and the Cistercian movement into which Bernard had thrown himself as a young man. Both were new spiritual organizations that placed poverty and obedience at their heart, rejecting earthly vanities in favor of hard physical work in the service of the Lord. And the Order of the Temple had close links, through its first members, to Champagne, the region of France that housed Clairvaux Abbey and where Bernard had spent most of his adult life.

So in 1126, when Bernard received King Baldwin's letter requesting the abbot's help, he looked favorably upon it. This was just as well, as the following year, in autumn 1127, the emmisaries promised by Baldwin arrived in Europe.[10] Among them was the first master of the Temple, Hugh of Payns.

✝

Hugh of Payns was sent west with a clear mission: to whip up support for the kingdom of the East. He did not go alone. In fact, he was one of several high-profile ambassadors from the Holy Land to visit Europe between 1127 and 1129, all aiming, in separate but connected ways, to strengthen links between the two blocs of Latin Christendom. One of these was William of Bures, King Baldwin II's royal constable, who had come to contract the marriage of Fulk, Count of Anjou, to King Baldwin's eldest daughter, Melisende: a union that promised to make Fulk heir to the sonless Baldwin's throne. The Count of Anjou was a perfectly good choice as future king: a wealthy widower, around thirty, pious but tough, and an experienced crusader who took a standing interest in the affairs of the East. He was said to maintain one hundred knights in Jerusalem at his own, no doubt considerable, expense. During his time in Outremer in the early 1120s he had met some of the first Templars. Ever since, he had paid them a modest but useful annual stipend of "thirty livres in the money of Anjou."[11]

Nevertheless, securing his agreement to become Baldwin's heir was a delicate political operation. It required Fulk to turn over his lands to his son, travel one thousand miles to meet a woman he had never set eyes on and take her as his wife, and embrace the most challenging military post in the Christian world. To sweeten the deal, William had brought with

him some truly magnificent gifts, including a fragment of the True Cross
and a decorated sword, which were to be presented to the cathedral in Le
Mans, at the heart of Fulk's territories.[12]

Hugh of Payns did not come bearing such impressive gifts, but his
task was just as urgent and, if anything, even more daunting. While William sought to cajole a single man into taking a crown, Hugh was tasked
with encouraging hundreds to part with their possessions and possibly
even their lives in exchange for a far more uncertain reward.

He was on a military recruiting tour, with one main objective. Back in
the kingdom of Jerusalem Baldwin II was planning a major assault on
Damascus, aiming to parlay a period of raiding that had begun late in
1125 into a full campaign of conquest. His hope was to permanently seize
the great city—a one-time seat of the Sunni caliphate—from its ruler,
the Turkic atabeg* Toghtekin.[13] Baldwin calculated that taking Damascus would require, in the words of William of Tyre, "the entire military
strength of the kingdom."[14] He foresaw the need for Western reinforcement; signing up more knights and experienced commanders to join the
campaign was Hugh's overriding aim.

Hugh's role as master of the Order of the Temple was a crucial factor
in his selection to lead such a prominent mission. The order was young
indeed, but it had already established itself as an elite military organization acting on behalf of the crusader states. The claim made in later years
that there were only nine Templars during the first nine years of the order's existence was romantic and numerologically pleasing, but false.[15]
Hugh was accompanied in Europe by at least five Templar brothers:
Godfrey of Saint Omer, Rolan, Payen of Montdidier, Geoffrey Bisol and
Archambaud of Saint-Amand.[16] This was evidently an arresting delegation, for they were granted audiences with some of the most powerful
men in northwest Europe.

Between October 1127 and the spring of 1129, Hugh of Payns and his
companions met two successive Counts of Flanders and the Count of

---

*Within the fractured Seljuq empire there were several parallel systems of political and
military office. The sultan was like a king. An emir was a rank below, who could exercise
personal office over a city or particular region. An atabeg was a regent-style governor, who
exercised power on behalf of an emir, if he was too young or weak to do so personally.

Blois, visited Fulk, Count of Anjou, and secured his agreement to help in the Damascus campaign and even tracked down Henry I, king of England and duke of Normandy, whom Hugh pressed for permission to raise funds across the Channel. Their encounter was recorded in the Anglo-Saxon Chronicle: "Hugh of the Knights Templars came from Jerusalem to the king in Normandy; and the king received him with great ceremony, and gave him great treasures of gold and silver, and sent him thereafter to England, where he was welcomed by all good men." The chronicler clearly judged the meeting a success. Hugh, he wrote, "was given treasures by all, and in Scotland too; and by him much wealth, entirely in gold and silver, was sent to Jerusalem."[17] The mission persuaded more people to go east and fight "than ever before since the time of the first crusade."[18] This was quite an achievement. Hugh of Payns and his fellow Templars were, in effect, preaching a crusade all of their own.[19] They had no formal backing from the pope, and contemporaries did not record them holding the sort of mass rallies of public cross taking that had characterized the First Crusade, but this direct appeal for reinforcement to fighting men of the West was extraordinarily successful. When Baldwin finally mounted his attack in 1129, the perception in Damascus was much the same. The Arab chronicler Ibn al-Qalanisi estimated that the Christian army was tens of thousands strong, thick with reinforcements from overseas.[20]

At the same time as he sought to round up an army to attack Damascus, Hugh of Payns was eager to expand the reach, wealth and membership of the Order of the Temple. Working through family networks and social ties—particularly around his home region of Champagne—he secured gifts of land, income from property, rights to feudal payments, gold, silver and—perhaps more valuable than anything else—promises of personal service. Dozens vowed that they would travel to the Holy Land and join the order, either temporarily or for life.

In October 1127 the Templars had been granted a house, grange and meadow at Barbonne, in western Champagne. At roughly the same time they were awarded an income drawn from feudal reliefs in Flanders. In the spring of 1128, while Hugh was in Anjou to witness Count Fulk taking the cross, the Templars secured land in the neighboring county of

Poitou. Donations were sent from as far afield as Noyon, a church north of Paris, and Toulouse, a day's ride from the Pyrenees.

It is worth noting that Hugh was not yet attempting to set up a Western branch of the fledgling order. His military concerns lay in the East yet his chief goal lay in building a network of patronage, capital and personal interest that would bridge the two thousand miles between the wealthy estates of central France and the dangerous plains and mountains of Syria and Palestine.[21]

One more purpose behind Hugh's journey could be satisfied neither by grants of wealth nor by pledges of military assistance. As King Baldwin II's letter of 1126 had intimated, what the Templars desired above all was confirmation by the pope of their legitimacy, and a formal rule to live by. In January 1129 a great ecumenical council gathered in Troyes, in Champagne—conveniently located just fifty miles northwest of that austere Cistercian monastery on the river Aube where Bernard of Clairvaux prayed and watched the energetic activities of his fellow countrymen with growing interest.

✝

The Council of Troyes formally assembled for its first session on Sunday, January 13, 1129. It was a meeting of friends and colleagues, mostly from the northeast of France. The seat of the Count of Champagne, Troyes was a prestigious commercial hub whose skyline was dominated by two great religious buildings: the Romanesque cathedral of Saint Peter and Saint Paul, and the Abbey of Saint Loup, a famously learned house of Augustinian canons. The city had, until recently, been the home of the great crusader Lord Hugh, Count of Champagne, who had donated the land for the foundation of the Abbey of Clairvaux. This was the self-same Hugh who, as a former overlord (and possibly relative) of Hugh of Payns, had resigned his title in 1125 and joined the Order of the Temple in Jerusalem. (Bernard of Clairvaux had written to commend him around the time of his abdication: "You from being a count have become a simple soldier, from being a rich man have become poor.")[22] When the council assembled in 1129 Hugh remained in the Holy Land, but it was his connections and wealth that had drawn together the master of the Temple and the abbot of Clairvaux.

The council was presided over by a papal legate, Matthew, bishop of Albano, representing Pope Honorius II. Twenty other churchmen attended: two archbishops, eleven bishops and seven abbots. Almost all were from Champagne or nearby Burgundy, as were the two leading noblemen present: Theobald, Count of Champagne, and William, Count of Nevers.[23] The majority of the abbots were Cistercians.

The two leading voices throughout the proceedings were Hugh of Payns and Bernard of Clairvaux. Hugh had called the gathering so that the Templars could be officially recognized and given a form of quasi-monastic rule. The record of the council, written by a scribe by the name of Jean Michel, outlined the procedure: "We heard in common chapter from the lips of the . . . Master, Brother Hugh of Payns; and according to the limitations of our understanding we praised what seemed to us good and beneficial, and eschewed what seemed wrong."[24]

This was, in other words, a drafting committee, engaged in a process of hearing, debating and amending the practices developed in Jerusalem during the first nine years of their existence. By the end of the council, Jean Michel had drafted in Latin a sixty-eight-point code of Templar conduct, later known as the Primitive (or Latin) Rule. This detailed the process by which knights of the order were to be selected and received, how they were to pray and which feast days they were to observe, what they should wear, eat and drink, where they should sleep, how they were to behave in public, and with whom they could—and could not—socialize.[25]

"In this religious order has flourished and is revitalized the order of knighthood," claimed the rule, praising all those who joined the Templars, willing to offer up their souls to God "for our salvation and the spread of the true faith." The notion that the Templars represented a new form of knighthood, which did not terrorize the weak, but dedicated itself to destroying evil, was one that Bernard of Clairvaux was developing at the time of the Council of Troyes, and which he would expound upon at length in the years to come. The Templars' new code bore the unmistakable stamp of his personal belief that knighthood could and should be reformed, Christianized, stripped of its earthly vanity and transformed into a calling of dignity, duty and godly purpose.

The rule started by addressing the practical issues of how a Templar brother could hope to square the prayer-bound life of a religious devotee with the rough-and-tumble life of a soldier in the saddle. Accepting that members were likely to spend much of their time on patrol or fighting in the field, rather than in the chapel contemplating the crucifix, the rule allowed a brother to substitute each daily church service that he missed for a set number of repetitions of the Lord's Prayer (or paternoster). Thirteen paternosters made up for missing the morning service of matins, nine for missing vespers in the evening, and seven for each of the daily sung prayers known as the canonical hours. This stripped-back version of the daily routine of monastic worship was designed to be achievable by noneducated laymen. Everyone, even the most illiterate peasant in France, knew his paternoster; by reducing holy duties to the most mundane repetition of the best-known prayer in Christendom, the Templars opened their pool of potential recruits to dedicated and talented men of any rank, and not just the rich and well schooled. The rule also made clear that there were two distinct categories of knights: those who signed up for life, having "abandoned their own wills," and those who agreed to join temporarily and fight "for a fixed term." The latter could easily satisfy the religious demands of the order with the bare minimum of formal religious training.

Reaction to the knightly stereotype pulsed through the proceedings at Troyes. Simplicity and equality were embraced. Templar knights were to wear habits of all white,* "which signifies purity and complete chastity."[26] Black or brown habits were prescribed for the lesser rank of Templar sergeants and squires—brothers who were sworn members of the order but did not carry the full rank or training of the Templar knight.

This was a far cry from the typical appearance of a twelfth-century warrior, who consciously advertised his status with colorful dress, rich fabrics and ornate accessories. To emphasize the point, many marks of

---

* The choice of white robes was one of the clearest Cistercian influences on the Templar Rule. The famous red cross would be added later, in 1139.

conventional knighthood were explicitly banned. "Robes should be without finery and without any show of pride," read the rule. "And if any brother out of a feeling of pride or arrogance wishes to have as his due a better and finer habit, let him be given the worst." Fur was forbidden. A linen shirt and a woolen blanket were permitted as protection against the extremes of temperature in the East, but otherwise outward decorations were to be scorned. A particularly violent proscription was made against trendy footwear, which in the early twelfth century could be quite flamboyant. "We prohibit pointed shoes and shoelaces and forbid any brother to wear them . . . for it is manifest and well known that these abominable things belong to pagans." The knight's lance was not to be adorned with a decorative cover. This austerity extended to every other aspect of horsemanship: "We utterly forbid any brother to have gold or silver on his bridle, nor on his stirrups nor on his spurs." The bags in which a knight carried his daily rations were to be made of plain linen or wool and an official called the draper was to ensure that brothers had their hair cut regularly and their beards and mustaches trimmed, "so that no excess may be noted on their bodies."*

Life within a Templar house was designed where possible to resemble that of a Cistercian monastery. Meals were communal and to be eaten in near silence, while a reading was given from the Bible. The rule accepted that the elaborate sign language monks used to ask for necessities while eating might not be known to Templar recruits, in which case "quietly and privately you should ask for what you need at table, with all humility and submission." Equal rations of food and wine were to be given to each brother and leftovers would be distributed to the poor. The numerous fast days of the Church calendar were to be observed, but allowances would be made for the needs of fighting men: meat was to be served three times a week, on Tuesdays, Thursdays and Saturdays. Should the schedule of annual fast days interrupt this rhythm, rations would be increased to make up for lost sustenance as soon as the fasting period was over.

It was recognized that the Templars were killers. "This armed

---

* Despite this, Templars wore their hair and beards in different styles according to the day: some images show them with full beards and others with long curly hair. An account by James of Vitry from the thirteenth century mentioned Templars with closely shaven heads.

company of knights may kill the enemies of the cross without sinning," stated the rule, neatly summing up the conclusion of centuries of experimental Christian philosophy, which had concluded that slaying humans who happened to be "unbelieving pagans" and "the enemies of the son of the Virgin Mary" was an act worthy of divine praise and not damnation. Otherwise, the Templars were expected to live in pious self-denial.

Three horses were permitted to each knight, along with one squire whom "the brother shall not beat." Hunting with hawks—a favorite pastime of warriors throughout Christendom—was forbidden, as was hunting with dogs. The only beasts Templars were permitted to kill were the mountain lions of the Holy Land. They were forbidden even to be in the company of hunting men, for the reason that "it is fitting for every religious man to go simply and humbly without laughing or talking too much."

Banned, too, was the company of women, which the rule scorned as "a dangerous thing, for by it the old devil has led man from the straight path to paradise . . . the flower of chastity is always [to be] maintained among you. . . . For this reason none of you may presume to kiss a woman, be it widow, young girl, mother, sister, aunt or any other. . . . The Knighthood of Christ should avoid at all costs the embraces of women, by which men have perished many times." Although married men were permitted to join the order, they were not allowed to wear the white cloak and wives were not supposed to join their husbands in Templar houses.

As if anticipating one natural consequence of this insistence on chastity, a further provision was made for knights who found themselves sharing a room in taverns while on Templar business. "If possible the house where they sleep and take lodging should be not without light at night, so that shadowy enemies may not lead them into wickedness, which God forbids them."

Finally, the order was to be ruled over by the master, advised by a council of "those brothers whom the Master knows will give wise and beneficial advice." Obedience to the master's commands was essential, and once orders were given, they were to be carried out "as though Christ himself had commanded it." It was in the master's power to examine and receive new recruits to the order, to distribute horses and armor among the brothers, to punish those who sinned or broke the rule and to use his discretion in enforcing the rule as he saw fit.

As time went on, the Templar Rule would expand to formidable length and complexity, adapting and developing as the order grew and changed. But with this first rule drawn up and approved under the authority of the papal legate in Troyes in January 1129, Hugh of Payns had achieved one of his principal goals in traveling to Europe. He had given his nascent organization a structure and a code of conduct by which to live. His next task was to make the Knights of the Temple famous, and to persuade the brothers themselves that they were doing the Lord's work.

+

At around the time Hugh of Payns was at the Council of Troyes, a man identifying himself as "Hugh the Sinner" (Hugh *Peccator*) prepared a letter addressed to "the soldiers of Christ in the Temple in Jerusalem."[27] Who exactly he was is uncertain, but it is tempting (and plausible) to identify him with Hugh of Payns himself. He certainly showed much the same concern for the furtherance of the Templar mission. The letter was inexpert but passionate. Some of its biblical allusions were mangled, others simply invented. Nevertheless, Hugh the Sinner implored his audience to one simple mission: to fight and win for the sake of Jesus Christ.

The devil, he wrote, was constantly trying to lure good men away from their good deeds. It was the duty of the Templars to resist Satan's wiles, to keep their faith in the order they had joined and to ignore the temptations that the world laid before them. They were not to "get drunk, fornicate, quarrel, backbite." The author was most worried that the Templars' morale was sagging in face of the hardship of their mission. "Stand firm and resist your adversary who is the lion and the serpent," he wrote. "Bear with patience what God has ordained for you." The duty of the Templar was not to seek lasting personal fame, but to serve the order.

At around the same time a much longer tract appeared, which also spoke directly to the order, spelling out its special place in the world and the providential importance of its mission. In this case its authorship was undisputed, and esteemed: it was sent by Bernard of Clairvaux.

"The book to the Knights of the Temple, in praise of the new knighthood" (*Liber ad milites templi de laude novae militia*—now usually referred to as *De Laude*) was written at some point between the founding of the order and 1136. Its content suggests that Bernard began work on it around the time of the Council of Troyes in 1129. The book is addressed directly to Hugh of Payns—"my dear Hugh"—whom Bernard says "asked me not once or twice but three times to write a few words of exhortation for you and your comrades."[28]

"A new kind of knighthood seems recently to have appeared on the earth," he began. "It indefatigably wages a twofold combat, against flesh and blood and against spiritual hosts of evil in the heavens."[29] To fight and die in the name of the Lord was the ultimate sacrifice. Bernard emphasized the profound difference between homicide—the sin of killing a man—and malecide—the act of killing evil itself, which God would consider a noble deed. Armed with this ingenious (if somewhat shaky) theological distinction, the Knights of the Temple could take on the very highest duty: more than simply being bodyguards for pilgrims, they were the defenders of the Holy Land itself. "March confidently then, you knights," Bernard wrote, "and with a stalwart heart repel the foes of the cross of Christ."

Just as the Rule of the Templars railed against the traditional trappings of secular knights, so, too, did *De Laude*, which was drenched in Cistercian values. Long hair, decorated armor, painted shields and saddles, gold spurs, billowing tunics, long sleeves, dice, chess, falconry and entertainments including jesters, bards and magicians were all dismissed with a sneer. "Are these the trappings of a warrior or the trinkets of a woman?"[30] Bernard praised instead the life of the new, ascetic, godly knight of the Temple: disciplined and chaste, his face stained by dust and sun, practical, egalitarian, well spoken and busy. These men lived for the sole purpose of destroying the faithless and casting out "the workers of iniquity . . . from the city of the Lord."[31] Although they lived quietly they would give battle like lions. "They set their minds on fighting to win rather than on parading for show," riding strong, swift horses rather than dappled show ponies and seeking to be "formidable rather than flamboyant." Thus, Bernard wrote, the new knights could be seen as the saviors of Jerusalem; an army true to the spirit of the Maccabees of ancient Judea, who had waged a war against massively superior forces to liberate the

Holy City from foreign occupation. "This is the help sent to you by the Holy One!"

This paean to the character and purpose of the Templars occupied the first four chapters of *De Laude*. The remainder—a further nine chapters—was a guided tour of the sites of the Holy Land that the Templars had been assembled to defend. It begins with the Temple itself—"adorned with weapons rather than jewels"—and includes succinct descriptions of Bethlehem, Nazareth, the Mount of Olives, the river Jordan, the Holy Sepulchre and the villages of Bethphage and Bethany—popular pilgrimage spots within a day's ride of Jerusalem. Bernard never traveled to Jerusalem in person—to him, Clairvaux Abbey was the real center of all spirituality—so his physical descriptions of the Holy Land relied on details gleaned from travelers and pilgrims.

Each chapter was effectively a short sermon.[32] Had it been read aloud or recited from memory at the relevant holy site, it would have provided inspiration, encouragement and insight to those who found themselves there. A knight of the Temple guarding a procession of pilgrims on the road to Bethlehem would be both practically and spiritually equipped for the task. He would be able to explain in reasonably learned terms the significance of each holy site to the civilians who traveled beside him. And should he find himself quaking inwardly for fear of ambush, he could steel himself with the words Bernard had written about the town, reflecting that Bethlehem was "the house of bread," where Christ, "the living bread come down from heaven [was] born of the Virgin."[33] Likewise in Nazareth, the momentarily disheartened Templar could cheer himself by recalling another one of Bernard's aphorisms, reflecting that he was walking on the very spot where "the infant God . . . grew to maturity, as the fruit matures within the flower."[34]

Hugh of Payns had asked Bernard to write "a few words of exhortation" designed to lift the spirits of men on the front line of combat. He had been tasked with giving "moral, rather than material, support" to the new order.[35] No one had thought harder about the Templars' curious fusion of the roles of monk and knight, and no one was better suited to putting into words the spirit of this potent new order. But Bernard was not the only one thinking seriously about the Templars. Far away from the Holy Land another patron was thinking about how he could help support the newly founded order. His name was Alfonso, king of Aragón, and he was at the forefront of the struggle against Islam—not battling Seljuqs and Fatimids in the Holy Land, but fighting the Moors of southern Spain, in the war known as the Reconquista.

4

"Every Good Gift"

I N July 1134, Alfonso the Battler, king of Aragón, set up camp outside the city of Fraga and commanded his servants to bring him his relics. He had quite an impressive collection. Over the course of a long and colorful career the sixty-one-year-old king had acquired fragments of the bodies or belongings of the Virgin Mary, several apostles, a few early Christian martyrs and assorted other saints, all of which were housed in small ivory boxes leafed with gold or silver and studded with precious gems. His finest relic of all was a piece of timber said to have come from the cross on which Jesus was crucified, which had been carved into a small crucifix and was kept in a jewel-encrusted ark made of solid gold. Alfonso had stolen it from a monastery in León, on the pilgrimage route to Santiago de Compostela.[1]

It was Alfonso's habit to keep his relics close by at all times. These shards of sainthood had seen plenty of action, as he had spent almost his entire adult life in the field, fighting with great success and little discrimination both the Christian princes whose territories neighbored his own and the Muslims who occupied much of the southern Iberian Peninsula. During most of that time the relics had been part of his baggage train, transported with the tent that served as his portable chapel. Now the priests brought the relics out, and before these precious flakes of wood, bone and leathery skin, Alfonso swore a violent oath.

Fraga lay on the banks of the river Cinca. This was frontier land, where Christian Europe butted up against al-Andalus, the Muslim states that had occupied most of southern Spain ever since the armies of the Umayyad caliphate had crossed the Strait of Gibraltar in the eighth century. For generations Christian and Muslim people here had rubbed shoulders under a shifting, multiethnic patchwork of kingdoms and emirates, which alternated between pragmatic coexistence and brutal warfare. Since the late tenth century, however, there had been a hardening of religious differences on the peninsula, and the wars between the various kingdoms had taken on an increasingly sectarian nature, in which the Christian rulers of the north saw it as their common duty to push the forces of Islam back toward North Africa. This effort had been granted papal blessing in 1101 by Pope Paschal II, who forbade Spanish Christians to join the holy war in the East, telling them to "remain in your country fighting with all your strength against the Moabites and the Moors."[2] At the First Lateran Council in 1123 this command was repeated, and the wars against Muslims in Spain were given explicit parity with the wars in the Holy Land. People began to speak of the *via de Hispania*, the "way of Spain," by which the Christians might ultimately open a sea route to Jerusalem from liberated ports in Spain or even a land route through North Africa and Egypt. The campaigns to erode al-Andalus became an official second theater in a much grander war whose ultimate goal was the conquest of the Holy Land.[3] Alfonso was an enthusiastic subscriber to this view of the world.

Fraga was in Muslim hands. The citizens had asked Alfonso via intermediaries to lift his siege, accept their surrender and allow the people to depart peacefully. Alfonso had been warned that if he did not do so, then a large relieving army of Muslim warriors would come and destroy him. This only increased his appetite for a fight. With God and the saints as his witnesses he now declared that there would be no mercy. "He planned to capture the city and kill the entire Moorish noble class," wrote one Christian chronicler. "He wanted their wives and children as prisoners, and . . . to confiscate all their riches."[4]

The two hundred heavily laden camels that swayed into view beside the banks of the nearby river Cinca on the morning of Tuesday, July 17, might have given the king of Aragón pause for thought. The great, lumbering pack beasts and their drivers were part of a large Muslim army led by the emir of Murcia and Valencia: a "brave warrior" by the name of Yahya ibn Ghaniya, better known to the Christians as Abengenia.[5] His army included forces from other regional Muslim strongholds such as Córdoba and Lérida, and it was heavily reinforced with men, animals and provisions sent from the Almoravid empire in North Africa—the real center of power in the Western Islamic world, with its capital in Marrakesh. The Almoravids were an exotic and dangerous enemy, their military leaders famed for the desert veil they wore at all times, covering their noses and mouths and leaving only their eyes on show. According to one estimate they had sent ten thousand men to Fraga. Even allowing for exaggeration, the forces now confronting Alfonso were plainly very large.[6]

The column of camels approaching the city walls were laden with relief supplies for the citizens. Alfonso ordered his kinsman, Bernard, Count of Laon, to lead an attack and bring back loot. Bernard demurred, suggesting a more cautious strategy. Alfonso flew into a rage, berating his cousin and calling him a coward. It was a fatal mistake.

When the Aragónese forces moved to confront the Muslim convoy, the camels and their military guard turned tail and fled. The Christians pursued but found themselves drawn into a trap. The rest of Ibn Ghaniya's army, which had been divided into four more columns, moved forward and encircled them, and without delay "began the attack with spears, arrows, stones and other missiles."[7] Meanwhile, the citizens surged out of the city gates. "Men and women, young and old" all fell on Alfonso's camp. The men massacred the noncombatant Christians, while the women led a general plunder, robbing the tents of food, equipment, weapons and siege engines.[8] Most humiliating, the Muslim plunderers stripped bare Alfonso's chapel, stealing his golden ark and leaving the holy tent "torn completely to the ground."[9]

The battle was a rout. Several bishops and abbots were killed, along with dozens of the best knights in Aragón and most of the army's leaders. Virtually all the members of Alfonso's household were captured and his entire infantry bodyguard of seven hundred soldiers was slain. In all his decades of warfare, during which Alfonso had fought battles and sieges from Bayonne to Granada, he had never suffered such a devastating defeat. He slashed and hacked away fiercely on the edge of the battlefield, but the effort was futile, and he was eventually persuaded to escape with a small cadre of knights. Together they fled west to Saragossa, then turned north toward the foothills of the Pyrenees and the beautiful Romanesque monastery of San Juan de la Peña, where Alfonso's father was buried. The warrior king was going home.

Alfonso died on Friday, September 7, 1134, most likely of wounds sustained at Fraga, although Christian and Muslim chroniclers attributed the cause of death to grief. The Reconquista had lost one of its most fearsome and energetic champions. But if fate had taken away one leader, it had brought on his tail a new wave of fighters who would shift the entire direction of the conflict.

Alfonso died as he had lived, austere in spirit and narrowly focused on deeds of war. As befitted a man who slept on his shield every night and believed "it is proper for a fighting man to associate with men and not with women," he never fathered a child.[10] In his will, written three years before his death, the king named as his principal heirs three orders based in Jerusalem: the Canons of the Holy Sepulchre, the Knights Hospitaller and the Templars, whom his will described as "the Temple of the Lord with its knights who strive to defend the name of Christianity."[11] To these three entities, Alfonso declared, "I bequeath . . . my whole kingdom, as well as the lordship I have in my kingdom, the sovereignty and rights I have over all the population of my land, clergy and laity, bishops, abbots, canons, monks, magnates, knights, burgesses, peasants, merchants, men and women, small and great, rich and poor, also Jews and Saracens."

Just five years after the Council of Troyes had given them a formal rule, the Templars had been granted a third part of an entire kingdom. This was quite a coup. It also set a course for their future. First, it meant that for the next two centuries the Templars would have a part in the Reconquista. Second, it demonstrated the spirit of ostentatious generosity toward crusading and crusaders that was growing across Europe—without which the whole concept of the military orders would have failed.

+

When Hugh of Payns returned to Jerusalem he did so with the fame of his young order firmly established. But despite his promises to his patrons in France and England he did not throw the order immediately into extensive military campaigning. The Templars' involvement in the attack on Damascus of 1129—an assault he had heavily advertised on his recruitment tour—was hardly promising. According to one account, the Christian forces conducted themselves "very imprudently and . . . beyond the bounds of military discipline."[12] Baldwin II's army approached the city in the autumn but he unwisely divided his forces. They were ambushed and then scattered by dreadful weather, slain by the defenders of the city amid thick fog and heavy rain. (The verdict back in the West was scathing. The author of the Anglo-Saxon Chronicle judged that the recruits sold on a glorious new crusade had been "pitiably duped.")[13]

Over the next ten years the Templars appear to have taken part in just two other significant actions. In 1137 eighteen of their knights were among those besieged alongside Fulk of Anjou in the castle of Montferrand, near Homs in the county of Tripoli. (By this time Fulk was king of Jerusalem, having succeeded Baldwin II on his death in 1131.) Two years later another ignominious engagement took place, this time in the kingdom of Jerusalem, near Hebron. Several Templars had joined a Christian army that engaged a large band of "wicked robbers and bandits." It was a rash and disorganized skirmish that ended in disarray, with the Christians fleeing across rocky, pathless plains and falling in dispiriting numbers. "Some perished by the sword, and others were hurled headlong from precipices," wrote the chronicler William of Tyre.[14]

In its early years the order did not make a habit of joining these sorts of actions. The Templars at this stage were seen as best suited to the important duty of castle guard. In 1136 they were awarded the job of garrisoning fortresses overlooking the dangerous passes in the Amanus Mountains, near Antioch. This was a major strategic responsibility: the Amanus passes were the key routes into Syria from Asia Minor, and controlling them was vital to the security of the county of Edessa and principality of Antioch, as well as the safety of pilgrims coming to Jerusalem overland.

On May 24, 1136, Hugh of Payns died. No contemporary chronicler mentioned the circumstances of his passing. (The date is known only because it was officially commemorated in the years that followed.) What is perhaps most notable is that the order he created outlived him without crisis. The rule granted at Troyes was silent on the way of appointing a new master, but later additions made it clear that it was done by election, in a chapter meeting at which the most senior Templars from both East and West were summoned to vote. Hugh's successor was Robert of Craon (also known as Robert Burgundio), a shrewd nobleman from Poitou who enjoyed close links to the new king Fulk of Jerusalem. One chronicler called him "a distinguished knight, valiant in arms, noble both according to the flesh and by nature."[15] At the time of Hugh's death Robert was serving as the order's seneschal, a title taken from the royal household for a steward with extensive administrative duties. Robert was a devoted member of the order, who had abandoned a fiancée at home in 1125 to travel to the Holy Land and fight. Like Hugh, he traveled regularly between Jerusalem and the West, and as master, he spent most of his time soliciting donations from wealthy benefactors in southern France and settling the ongoing legal disputes over Alfonso I's will in Aragón.[16] He had particular success building on the links between the order and the papal court in Rome.

On March 29, 1139, during one of Robert of Craon's visits to France and Italy, Pope Innocent II issued a bull (an official letter under a papal seal made from lead, for which the Latin word was *bulla*) addressed to the Templars. Like all papal bulls, this one was known by the first words of its text, *Omne Datum Optimum* ("Every good gift"), a quotation from the Epistle of James.*

Omne Datum Optimum granted the Templars a range of extraordinary privileges. The pope praised the knights who had joined the order for transforming themselves from "children of wrath" into listeners who have abandoned worldly pomp and personal possessions.[17] He then confirmed Knights of the Temple in their right to "always bear on your chest the sign of the life-giving cross"—a symbol that, when emblazoned in red on the Templar knights' white mantles, came to be an iconic uniform.

Innocent's support of the Templars made sense. He had been helped through a major political crisis between 1130 and 1138 by Bernard of Clairvaux. The papacy had fallen into schism and Bernard had backed Innocent's claim over that of the antipope Anacletus II. When the schism was settled in Innocent's favor, he had every reason to return the favor by showering the Order of the Temple with spiritual bounty. Even so, *Omne Datum Optimum* was exceptionally generous.

The bull placed the Templars "under the protection and tutelage of the Holy See for all time to come." Robert of Craon and his successors were to answer to no one but the pope: they were made explicitly independent across Christendom from the authority of kings and patriarchs, barons

---

* "Every good gift and every perfect gift is from above, and cometh down from the Father of lights, with whom is no variableness, neither shadow of turning" (James 1:17).

and bishops, and their customs were sweepingly declared to be free from the meddling of "any ecclesiastical or secular person." The rule drawn up at Troyes was confirmed, and Templars were designated "defenders of the Catholic Church and attackers of the enemies of Christ," a license so broad as to be effectively all-encompassing.

The Templars were guaranteed the right to be ruled by a master drawn from their own number and were exempted from paying tithes—the taxes routinely collected by the Church from its flock—while being permitted to take tithes from those who lived on land they owned. This income was to be reserved exclusively for their own use. They could appoint their own private priests to administer the "sacraments and divine offices," ignoring the authority of local bishops, and could build oratories—private chapels— at Templar houses, where brothers could be buried. Templar priests were answerable to their master—a highly unusual state of affairs, as their master, while sworn to obey the rule, did not himself have to be ordained.

Together these grants gave the Templars enviable privilege, independence and autonomy. (The Hospitallers, who had expanded from their medical and pastoral role to support a military wing from around 1120, did not have their rule confirmed by the pope until 1153, though they too were busy building up a network of property and favor in Europe to support their mission in the Holy Land.) The Templars were further protected by the ultimate papal sanction: anyone who harassed them would be excommunicated, forbidden "to partake of the most holy body and blood of our Lord, Jesus Christ," and sentenced to "suffer severe punishment" at the Final Judgment. This was a very serious threat, since according to ancient Church texts the punishments scheduled to greet the faithless and disobedient on the Day of Apocalypse included being burned in a vast pit of pitch and brimstone, hung by their eyebrows over a lake of fire and gnawed through the belly by a writhing mass of worms.[18]

The Templars' excellent relations with the papacy would continue well into the middle of the twelfth century. Celestine II, who held office for six months between Innocent's death in the autumn of 1143 and his own in March of the following year, issued on January 9, 1144, a bull entitled *Milites Templi* (Knights of the Temple), which granted all who joined them relief from penance and a guaranteed Christian burial. The Templars were also allowed once a year to open churches that had been

placed under interdict and to hold services there, at which they could collect donations. (Interdict was a severe sentence of earthly limbo, which
took the form of church closure, usually imposed when a local ruler had
fallen out with Rome; it could only be lifted by the pope or his direct
representatives.) Finally, Pope Eugene III, a Cistercian abbot and protégé
of Bernard of Clairvaux, who held office from February 1145 until July
1153, drew up a third bull, known as *Militia Dei* (the Knighthood of God),
which reconfirmed the Templars' right to appoint their own priests and
build their own private oratories in which they could hold services free
from the dangers that might arise should they "mingle with crowds of
men and meet women on the occasion of going to church."[19] Framed this
way, it sounded as if Eugene's purpose was to relieve the Templars from
the burden of mixing with women and the grubby poor. But this masked
a valuable financial privilege. Templar oratories were permitted to collect
tithes and charge fees for burying the dead—even when these were established in the jurisdictions of other churchmen. Beyond this, they did not
have to pass any of the wealth they collected to their local bishop, archbishop or abbot. This seemingly innocuous privilege would allow them,
in time, to amass untold riches.

+

The Templar seal, used to authenticate charters and documents, was a
wax disk showing two brothers riding the same horse, a reminder of their
desire to live in holy poverty. Yet, ironically, by committing to live in penury the Templars became rich. Their task of protecting pilgrims in the
Holy Land, and their philosophy of godly violence twinned with austere
personal virtue, had brought them patronage from on high. And as the
mighty fell in, so did the lesser men and women of Christendom, who
swelled the Templars' coffers with bequests of land, property, buildings,
feudal income, service and personal possessions.

The most devoted and able-bodied men could join the order, make
their vows, travel to the East and confront the forces of Islam in person,
either to fight as knights or to support the order's operations in some
other capacity, as chaplains, servants or sergeants, sworn brothers who
wore dark robes and performed vital noncombat functions.

But life in the saddle on the roads between Jerusalem and Jaffa was not possible or desirable for everyone. Some chose therefore to associate themselves with the order by offering gifts of their possessions. These could be as meager as a crate of firewood, an old cloak, a sword or a coat of chain mail, or as lavish as a whole estate, a church or a large sum of cash. They often came from those who had no means of joining the holy war in person. In 1133 and 1134, Lauretta, a woman from Douzens (north of the Pyrenees, between Carcassone and Narbonne), donated land, feudal rights and the labor of her tenants to the Templars, "who fight with courage for the faith against the threatening Saracens who are constantly trying to destroy the law of God and the faithful who serve it."[20] An obituary book from a Templar church in Reims begun a few decades later listed all the donations of individuals and the dates on which they were to be remembered by the brothers. It commemorated people like "Sibylla, niece of Thierry Strabo: she gave to this church a third of her vineyard" and "Baldwin Ovis, for whose anniversary mass his wife lady Pontia gave to this church one stall in the cloth market."[21]

Taken together, the things given by a generous West—money, horses, clothes, weapons—to support action in the East, provided what was known in Latin as the Templars' *responsio*. One third of the profits made in each Templar house were sent to the front line, where the order needed them most.

Donations came principally from four areas: the northern French territories above the Loire (the region of the *langue d'oïl*), the southern French counties around Provence (the *langue d'oc*), England and Spain. In order to manage the properties and gifts they received, and to coordinate the process of funneling the income to the Holy Land, Western Europe was organized under the authority of senior officials with responsibility for their own regions. Small grants of land would be parceled up into larger estates, overseen by a series of monastic-style houses known as preceptories or commanderies.* This land was either leased out, farmed for crops or grazed according to its location. Some of the income sustained the estate itself; profits funded the order. Many of these preceptories

---

* The terms "commandery" and "preceptory" can be used largely interchangeably, as can the ranks of the officers who oversaw them, known as either commanders or preceptors.

would have been hard to distinguish from a regular Cistercian monastery: staffed by a handful of sergeants, with a roster of servants doing menial work to support them.

In some houses women might be found, and not just as servants: occasionally husbands and wives joined the order together as associate members, meaning they could share aspects of Templar life, but had not taken the vows of poverty, chastity and obedience. From time to time particularly wealthy women were even appointed as preceptors and put in charge of the houses to which they had donated—though whether they actually took up their positions or appointed male deputies is not certain, as the Templar Rule was clear about the necessity of strict segregation between the sexes to avoid temptation. Templar houses in the Spanish kingdoms were particularly prone to bending their rules and allowing women to join the order as associates and even full sisters, perhaps because women had much greater freedom to dispose of their own property.[22]

Unlike most monasteries, Templar houses were linked together in a coherent hierarchy and answerable to a regional command structure. In the late 1120s one Hugh of Rigaud held responsibility for accepting grants in Provence, Aragón and Toulouse. He held the title of "procurator," suggesting the role of business agent.[23] Other early procurators included Hugh of Argentein in England, and Payen of Montdidier, responsible for the order's activities in northern France.

The great and good did not always need to be directly involved in holy war to see the benefit of patronizing the Templars. The order made large gains in England in the 1130s, profiting from a bloody conflict (now known as the Anarchy) that engulfed the kingdom following the death of King Henry I in 1135. Henry died without a legitimate male heir, and his daughter, Matilda, waged war against her cousin Stephen of Blois to secure the succession. Both sides had good reason to favor the Templars. Matilda was married to Geoffrey Plantagenet, Count of Anjou, King Fulk of Jerusalem's eldest son, while Stephen's home county of Blois neighbored Champagne, the crucible of Templar recruitment and ideology. Stephen's father had been a hero of the First Crusade, and his wife was a niece of Baldwin I. Stephen and Matilda vied openly to prove themselves the order's most generous benefactors. In return they hoped for political support and spiritual insurance as the Templars promised to pray for their good fortune and immortal souls.

During Hugh of Payns's tour of England in 1128, the order had estab-
lished a house in London known as the "Old" Temple, near Holborn.[24]
During the Anarchy a torrent of other royal gifts followed, including
land and property in Oxfordshire, Hertfordshire, Essex, Bedfordshire,
Lincolnshire, Berkshire and Sussex. In 1137 Stephen's wife gave the Templars the wealthy and well-connected manor of Cressing, in Essex (now
Temple Cressing), to which Stephen later added nearby land in Witham.[25]
In time this grant would become the basis for a rich and busy estate with
scores of tenant families working the land, a sprawling network of monastic houses, kitchens and farm buildings, their labor filling two vast
thirteenth-century grain-storage sheds, the Wheat Barn and the Barley
Barn, which still stand today.

Across the Channel the story was much the same. The Templars built
up vast networks of property in Champagne, Blois, Brittany, Aquitaine,
Toulouse and Provence, establishing commanderies to fix their local
presence. Dozens of Templar houses sprang up from the Gulf of Genoa
to the new Atlantic kingdom of Portugal, which was also being clawed out
of Islamic hands and resettled by Christians under the self-proclaimed
first king of Portugal, Afonso I Henriques. During the 1140s, Afonso
Henriques cleared the valley of the lower Tagus, eventually conquering
as far south as Lisbon, where the river empties into the Atlantic Ocean.
As early as 1128 Afonso Henriques described himself as a brother (con-
frater) of the Templars.[26] He placed several magnificent strongholds in
Templar hands, including a castle at Almourol and a sprawling fortress
at Soure, with long turreted walls and a vantage point over the countryside leading down to the Atlantic coast. In April 1147 he issued a charter
diverting the revenues of every church in the region of his castle at Santarém into Templar hands, "for the . . . knights and their successors to
have and to hold with perpetual rights so that no clergy or layperson may
make any claim in them."[27] Later he swapped this with the Templars for
a superb castle in Cera and allowed them to found a new town for their
headquarters, which they called Tomar. Knitting the Templars into the
affairs of his new kingdom brought security and prestige. It was also a
practical way of colonizing and garrisoning newly won land.

With every such advance, and each gift they received, the Templars'
wealth increased, their ability to pursue the Holy War grew and their

fame spread. Although he may not have realized it, Alfonso the Battler, king of Aragón, had been a pioneer in a movement that would change the face of crusading.*

✝

Over the course of a life spent fighting Muslims, Alfonso had given plenty of thought to the idea of a military order. Indeed, he had tried twice to start one of his own. In 1122 he had established the Confraternity (or Brotherhood) of Belchite, named for and centered on a frontier castle town some twenty miles from Saragossa. Tax exempt and permitted to hold whatever booty they could take from Islamic hands, knights who chose to offer their services at Belchite swore to maintain undying and implacable hostility toward "the pagans" and never to make peace with them.[28] Six years later Alfonso founded another order in an entirely new city called Monreal del Campo, built from scratch and endowed with revenues and freedoms that were explicitly modeled on those granted to the Templars.

Neither the Order of Belchite nor that of Monreal del Campo ever really took root. They did not seek or gain the same papal privileges as the Templars, and their sphere of operations never expanded beyond the immediate borderlands that they were tasked with keeping safe. But it was still significant that Alfonso had attempted to inject into his own skirmishes with Islamic foes features of the struggle that was taking place in the kingdom of Jerusalem. By the 1130s the war on the Iberian Peninsula had gained the political and spiritual status of a crusade. It

---

* The same was not quite true elsewhere in the Spanish kingdoms. In Castile the Templars were shunted aside before they could gain a real foothold. For a few years they held the castle of Calatrava, but this was returned to the Crown in 1158. At this point the rulers of Castile began to show a preference for their own native military orders, beginning with the founding of the Order of Calatrava by a Cistercian monk called Raymond of Fitero in 1163. Three years later in León the Order of Alcántara (also known as the Order of San Julián of Pereiro) was established, and around the same time the Order of Santiago sprang up, devoting itself to the protection of pilgrims on their way to one of the holiest sites in the West, the shrine of Santiago de Compostela in Galicia. These orders were more closely dependent on the realms in which they had been established, and never burst the borders to become truly international organizations like the Templars and Hospitallers.

Templar Properties in Western Europe
✝ Around the Second Crusade, ca. 1147 ✝

SCOTLAND

NORWAY

North Sea

Dublin

IRELAND

WALES

ENGLAND

SHIPLEY

GUITING Oxford

CRESSING

LONDON

Thames R.

WITHAM

GERMANY

Cologne

Atlantic Ocean

Rouen BEAUVAIS

LAON

NORMANDY

Paris CHAMPAGNE

Rhine R.

HOLY

BRITTANY

Seine R.

SENS

MARMOUTIER

Danube R.

0 Miles   200   400

ORLEANS

ROMAN

0 Kilometers   400

NANTES

BLOIS

ANJOU

LA ROCHELLE

FRANCE

EMPIRE

Bordeaux

Lyon

BURGUNDY

Venice

Compostela

Oviedo

LEON

AQUITAINE

RICHERENCHES

Genoa

ITALY

Leon

Burgos

NAVARRE

TOULOUSE

PROVENCE

AVIGNON

ALBENGA

SIENA

Pamplona

ARAGON

BRAGA

&

CASTILE

Monzon

Corbins

PORTUGAL

SOURE

Salamanca

Madrid

Zaragoza

Ebro R.

MONGAY

CORSICA

Rome

CERA

Tagus R.

BELCHITE

CHALAMERA

Lérida

Toledo

REMOLINS

BARBARÁ

Lisbon

ALMOURAL

SANTAREM

Tortosa

SARDINIA

AL·ANDALUS

BALEARIC
ISLANDS

Mediterranean Sea

ALMORAVID EMPIRE

✚ TEMPLAR PROPERTIES

Almoravid Empire

© 2017 Jeffrey L. Ward

was perhaps only natural that it should resemble a crusade in organization, too.

Certainly in the 1130s and 1140s the Templars flooded into Spain. They never took command of Aragón, for Alfonso's eccentric will was contested and a conventional political solution found to the succession crisis it provoked. (Put briefly, if not simply: Alfonso's brother, a Benedictine monk, was taken out of holy orders and married to the sister of the Duke of Aquitaine; the resulting daughter was married as an infant to the Count of Barcelona, Ramon Berenguer IV; Alfonso's brother, Ramiro, retired back to the cloister and Ramon Berenguer took control of Aragón, merging the kingdom permanently with his own territories.) All the same, the order did profit very handsomely from their place in Alfonso's last testament. As part of the final settlement, made in 1143 between Ramon Berenguer IV and Robert of Craon, the Templars received a formidable grant of income and the custody of six important castles, along with the lands that were subject to those castles' rule. Several of these were splendid properties and they would become even more so under Templar stewardship.

The sunbaked hilltop fortress at Monzón, proudly built by the eleventh-century Arab rulers of Saragossa to be all but siegeproof, was redeveloped under Templar ownership to include new defensive walls and towers, stables and barracks. It was one link in a chain of frontier castles—Mongay, Chalamera, Barbará, Remolins and Belchite—that were now placed into Templar hands to be managed, garrisoned and maintained. Since this was an expensive task, the Templars in Aragón were richly endowed. They were promised 10 percent of the kingdom's royal revenues, cash to the value of one thousand *solidi* (an antiquated but valuable gold coin) payable by the citizens of Saragossa, exemption from any taxes levied by the Aragónese kings and the right to one fifth of any plunder they could acquire fighting unbelievers.

This was not quite a third of the kingdom, but it was a fortune all the same, and far more than was received by the Hospitallers, who were deprived of their share of the will and given only small territorial awards as compensation (as were the Canons of the Holy Sepulchre).[29] Of course, the castles and income were not given simply to enrich the Order of the

Temple. The responsibility of maintaining border fortresses meant that the Templars now had a direct stake in the Iberian crusades. The charter confirming the Templars' rights to these castles in Aragón, written in Ramon Berenguer's name, explained that the purpose of enriching and empowering the Order of the Temple was "to establish a militia in the power of the heavenly army to defend the Western Church in Spain, to crush, defeat and drive out the race of the Moors . . . after the fashion of the Temple of Solomon in Jerusalem which protects the Eastern Church."[30] The Templars provided a small but reliable contingent to every army Ramon Berenguer raised, a service much appreciated by the king, who could rely on them to muster quickly and serve in his army for as long as required. They would help the king besiege the city of Tortosa in 1148, Lérida in 1149 and the castle at Miravet in 1152. In return, they could expect him to listen to their advice—Ramon Berenguer promised the Aragónese Templars that he would never make peace with his Muslim enemies without consulting them first.[31] Although the Templars' political influence waxed and waned according to their relationship with the king's successors over the generations, they would be a prominent presence in Aragón for more than a century to come. It may well be that Alfonso, cunning to the last, intended precisely that.

Across the Latin West the Templars' reputation was rising. Their property portfolio was growing explosively. Their leaders had proven themselves politically adept, befriending Christian kings from England to Jerusalem, currying favor with three different popes and inspiring men as temperamentally different as Alfonso I of Aragón and Bernard of Clairvaux to throw their weight behind the order. The Templars were efficiently organized in a pyramid of houses answerable to regional masters and ultimately to the grand master in Jerusalem. When challenged, they stood up robustly for their rights.

Not yet three decades had passed since the first master of the Temple had petitioned at the Council of Nablus for his ragtag band to be given official recognition, a place to sleep and some charitable donations to keep them going day to day. By the late 1140s, the Templars were famous all over the Christian world.

But fame alone was not enough. The Templars were, after all, a band of holy knights. They were fighting men: warriors whose reason for being was to protect or to kill. And in 1147 the time for killing was upon them. Half a century after the original Western charge on the Holy Land, the Roman Church was preparing to sponsor another massive and combined military assault on the East. It became known as the Second Crusade, and this time the Templars were at its heart.

PART II

Soldiers

1144–1187

They were the fiercest fighters of all the Franks.

—Ibn al-Athir

5

"A Tournament Between Heaven and Hell"

I MAD AL-DIN ZENGI toured the mine that his sappers had dug beneath the northern walls of Edessa and declared himself pleased.[1] The men had been working for four weeks, and the tunnel now extended into the "belly of the earth," its dirt walls held up with strong wooden beams and its mouth protected by Zengi's siege catapults, known as mangonels, which kept the city's few defenders—a rabble of cobblers, bakers, shopkeepers and priests—pinned down behind barricades, avoiding a constant bombardment of heavy stones. Alongside the boulders flew arrows: according to one Muslim chronicler, the air was so thick with missiles that even the birds stayed away.[2]

Zengi was a difficult man to satisfy. At sixty the atabeg of Mosul and Aleppo was still good-looking, with dark, sunbaked skin, graying hair and striking eyes. One admirer called him "the bravest man in the world"; another told of his extraordinary prowess with a bow and arrow, honed by countless hours spent hunting everything from gazelles to hyenas.[3] Yet even his admirers recognized that he was a vicious individual, whose military success sprang from a lifelong reputation as a butcher and brute of the most despicable severity. Zengi was casually inventive in the violence he directed toward enemies, subordinates and intimates alike. He crucified his own troops for marching out of line and trampling crops. If his military commanders irked him he either killed or banished them and castrated their children. A fit of pique directed at one of his wives ended with her being summarily divorced and dragged to a stable block to be raped by his grooms while he watched.[4] William of Tyre thought him "a very wicked man and a most cruel persecutor of the Christians" and "a monster who abhorred the name of a Christian as he would a pestilence."[5] In short, Zengi was one of the most terrifying military leaders in the whole of the theater of Islamic and Christian conflict. It was just as well for his sappers that they could dig straight.

Having finished his assessment of the mine, Zengi announced that he had no complaints. He returned to ground level and offered his congratulations to the engineers waiting outside for his instruction. Set fire to the struts, he told them. The flames would finish the job.

Edessa was a jewel in the Christian East. The county was the most northerly of the crusader states, and the city one of the first places captured during the First Crusade. It lay a long way inland: an outpost of Frankish rule beyond the banks of the river Euphrates, deep inside territory otherwise controlled by the Seljuqs. The city's population was a cosmopolitan blend of Greek and Armenian Christians and a relatively small ruling class of Franks, whose homes, shops and bejeweled churches were "surrounded by a massive wall and protected by lofty towers."[6] Edessa was further blessed by its possession of the holy shrine of the apostles Saint Thomas ("Doubting" Thomas) and Saint Thaddeus, among dozens of other precious relics.

Less fortunately, Edessa was ruled by Count Joscelin II, a short, thickset, swarthy man with bulging eyes, a large nose and smallpox scars all over his face. Joscelin was a mediocre military campaigner, a drinker and womanizer. All the same, had he been in Edessa Zengi would most likely have left the city alone. But on December 23, 1144, Joscelin was out of town visiting his castle at Turbessel, several days' ride west across the Euphrates, along with the majority of his mercenary troops. The great stone fortifications he had relied upon to secure the city in his absence were now creaking as Zengi's forces hammered against them.

A well-dug mine beneath a vulnerable stretch of wall was a very difficult thing to counter. The art of sapping was a specialist task, associated at one time with experts from Persia, who understood the specific requirements of bringing down heavy stone fortifications.[7] When Zengi's men set the timbers alight, the wood—which had been deliberately smeared with grease, tar and sulphur—quickly collapsed and the tunnel that it supported caved in.[8] Above it, a large section of the stonework near the city portal known as the Gate of the Hours lost its foundations. The mortar holding it together cracked, and then the whole edifice gave way. A large gap of one hundred cubits (around one hundred and fifty feet) opened, and Zengi's forces rushed over the rubble and put the city to the sword.

Zengi's men concentrated on murdering Franks rather than Armenians, but otherwise made little distinction between their victims. "Neither age, condition, nor sex was spared," wrote William of Tyre.[9] Six thousand men, women and children were killed on the first day of the sack. As panic gripped Edessa's civilians, they stampeded for the citadel in the middle of the city. But this only led to more deaths, for in the crush of people running for their lives, dozens were trampled. Hugo, archbishop of Edessa, under whose watch the government had been left, was cut to pieces with an ax.

Zengi's men tore through the streets, spending Christmas Day "pillaging, slaying, capturing, ravishing and looting" until "their hands were filled with such quantities of money, furnishings, animals, booty and captives as rejoiced their spirits and gladdened their hearts."[10] It was said that they took ten thousand children prisoners, for sale into slavery.[11] Finally, on December 26 their leader ordered the terror to cease, commanded his men to start rebuilding the city's defenses and went on his way. Edessa, one of the four great cities of the Latin kingdom of the East, a proud totem of God's love for the Franks, was back in Islamic hands. The shock would reverberate through the whole of Christendom.

✝

In 1147 the Templars' house in Paris was under construction, just outside the northeastern stretch of the city walls on a patch of swampy land that is now the chic neighborhood of Le Marais. It was given to the order by the pious French king Louis VII. Like many of his noblemen, Louis saw plenty to admire in the Templars and regularly made gifts to the order. (In 1143 and 1144 he assigned them the proceeds of rents levied on Paris's money changers.)[12] In time the Paris Temple would become one of the most astonishing urban fortresses in the West, its vast four-turreted central tower, the donjon soaring over the skyline, advertising the order's wealth and military prowess. In 1147, however, the Temple was still in the early stages of development. The marshes, watered by the Seine and its tributaries, were being drained in order to make them habitable. There was much still to do.

Over Easter one hundred and thirty Templar knights assembled in the city—among them Everard of Bretuil, Theodoric Waleran and

Baldwin Calderon—drawn there as part of a swell of powerful crusading men who had come to show their support for a movement that had been building ever since Edessa's fall thirty months earlier.[13] They would have stood out unmistakably from the crowds. Their white mantles were striking enough, and now a red cross could also be seen emblazoned across their uniforms. There would have been at least an equal number of dark-cloaked Templar sergeants and still more servants and support staff around them, giving the impression that a private army was in town, of a size that could ordinarily only have been raised by the greatest lords in Europe.

At the center of the Second Crusade, and overseeing events in Paris, were two men of great repute: Pope Eugene III, a former Cistercian monk and friend of Bernard of Clairvaux; and King Louis VII, whose personal piety was such a hallmark of his kingship that his wife, the fiercely intelligent southern duchess Eleanor of Aquitaine, sometimes wondered if she had married a monk and not a king. Eugene had invoked his supreme spiritual authority to call for a new crusade. Louis had agreed to fight it.

The sight of the pope and the king of France side by side in Paris made a deep impression on observers. The monk, crusader and chronicler Odo of Deuil, who saw them together at his home abbey of Saint-Denis on Easter Day (on which occasion the pope blessed a gigantic, golden, jewel-encrusted crucifix known as "The True Cross of the Lord Surpassing All and Every Pearl"), called it a "double marvel" to see "the king and apostolic father as pilgrims."[14] The crusading movement had not lacked for Western noblemen to join its ranks, whether as permanent leaders or warriors who lent their swords to the effort for a limited tour of duty, but no monarch had thus far been tempted to leave his kingdom to do the Lord's work, with the exception of Sigurd of Norway, who had sailed to Jerusalem in 1107. Forty years on, all that was about to change. Better yet, it was not only Louis who had agreed to go crusading: his promise had been matched by another of Europe's most significant rulers, Conrad III, king of the Germans.*

That Western Europe's two foremost kings should decide to go on

---

* The king of the Germans, also known as king of the Romans, was a ruler elected by the nobles and princes of the semiautonomous states of greater Germany.

crusade was a mighty commitment of royal power. This more than an-swered Pope Eugene's call to arms, issued in December 1145 (and reissued in March 1146) in the form of a bull known as *Quantum Praedecessores*. In this missive, written for mass popular consumption, Eugene had called for the "greater men and nobles" to prepare for war and "strive so to op-pose the multitude of the infidels, who rejoice at the time in a victory gained over us, and so to defend the oriental church." His orders had been enthusiastically transmitted by Bernard of Clairvaux. Growing old, painfully thin and frequently ill due to his insistence on fasting to the point of starvation, Bernard had nonetheless traveled ceaselessly through-out the kingdoms of the West, haranguing their leaders to support the new war effort. It had taken nearly three years, but in the weeks follow-ing Easter 1147, the mission to revenge Edessa's fall was finally ready to depart.

The Templars who had celebrated Easter in Paris most likely left with the rest of Louis's army on June 11, following a dramatic ceremony in the Gothic abbey church of Saint-Denis: the king approached the pope be-fore the gold-plated high altar, knelt to kiss a silver reliquary containing the remains of the abbey's patron saint, and received his pilgrim's purse, along with a blessing from the Holy Father. Tears were shed and prayers recited by the crowd who had come to see the king leave, and with good reason. Not for fifty years had there been such crusading fervor in the West.

Large armies with great lords at their head were, however, no guaran-tee of success, particularly on a testing land journey over several thou-sand miles. Little by little, as Louis's forces made their way east, it became clear that what was billed as an army was in fact little more than a very large, pious but incompetent rabble. Were it not for the Knights of the Temple, it is likely they would never have made it within sight of Syria at all.

+

Pope Eugene's crusading bull *Quantum Praedecessores*, which had been preached throughout 1146 and 1147 to ecstatic crowds far and wide across Western Christendom, and which justified attacks on non-Christians in the Near East, Iberia and (in a new addition to the movement) pagan areas around the Baltic Sea, bore a few striking similarities to the texts of both the Templar Rule and Bernard of Clairvaux's *De Laude*. Formally addressed to Louis VII, it made direct reference to the First Crusade, assuring its audience that "it will be seen as a great token of nobility and uprightness if those things acquired by the efforts of your fathers are vigorously defended." But Eugene also pointed out that those who took up the cross and went to "fight for the Lord" should "not care for precious clothes or elegant appearance or dogs or hawks or other things that are signs of lasciviousness." Furthermore, "those who decide to begin so holy a work ought to pay no attention to multicolored clothes or minivers [an expensive fur] or gilded or silvered arms."[15] Zealous Christians had been whipped into a frenzy of adventure for more than eighteen months, but it would not do to be too showy about it. They were to advance on the kingdom of Jerusalem as poor pilgrims, pride vanquished from their hearts and decoration stripped from their bridles.

Given Eugene's background as a Cistercian monk, his attitude in this regard was fairly predictable. Nevertheless, he could not have known or imagined just how much like the Templars his Christian soldiers of the Second Crusade would have to become.

Although the armies of the faithful set out confidently and cheerfully, their experience on the road quickly soured their spirits. Both Louis VII and Conrad III chose to march to Edessa overland, along the route followed by the first crusaders: a march through Bulgaria and across Greek lands, stopping at Constantinople, the capital of the Byzantine Empire, regarded by its inhabitants and many others besides as the greatest city in the world. From there they planned to cross hostile Seljuq territory in Asia Minor before finally making their way by either ship or foot to the crusader principality of Antioch. Others—including nobles from Flanders and England—preferred to reach the Levant exclusively by ship, stopping by the ports of the western Mediterranean and engaging the Muslims of al-Andalus on their way. (This contingent took part in the Portuguese king Afonso Henriques' conquest of Lisbon in 1147.) Both romantic and practical considerations influenced the French and German kings' decision to take the land route: there was a wish to walk in the footsteps of the first crusaders, and ships were expensive. But ultimately it proved calamitous.

To avoid tensions between parties, the two kings staggered their departures. Conrad left Nuremberg at the end of May, heading initially for Constantinople. Perhaps inevitably, since Conrad was effectively leading a mass migration consisting of some thirty-five thousand fighting men and a very large number of noncombatant pilgrims, trouble dogged him.[16] Feeding so many mouths was extremely challenging; maintaining order as the Germans encountered foreigners who were not thrilled at their presence was even harder. As Conrad's crusaders made their way through Greek territory, violent skirmishes broke out in towns, marketplaces and even around monasteries. In September, while the army camped at Choirobacchoi, to the west of Constantinople, they were hit by flash floods, which seriously depleted their numbers. Once they arrived outside the walls of Constantinople itself, it became plain that the Byzantine emperor Manuel Comnenus was an unwilling host.

Fifty years previously the armies of the First Crusade had arrived in response to a plea for help from Manuel's grandfather, Alexius I Comnenus, who had begged the Latin West to help him in his war against the Seljuqs. There had been no such request on this occasion. Indeed, the Byzantine emperor was positively irked by the thought of the Latin crusaders making further gains in Syria, not least around Antioch, which he thought was rightfully part of his own empire. His main desire seems to have been to see the king of the Germans and his ill-disciplined rabble over the Bosphorus and into Asia Minor as soon as decency permitted, and to be done with them.

He was rewarded in the first part of this wish, but not the second. The Germans crossed the Bosphorus, divided their men between troops and pilgrims and in mid-October struck out southeast by two diverging routes toward Antioch. By November they had all retreated to Constantinople and its environs: hungry, sick and bloody. Attempting to cross the high, arid plains around Dorylaeum, where Byzantine territory gave way to hostile Seljuq country, the crusaders had been set upon by fast, lightly armed and lethal horsemen-archers firing arrows from the saddle. William of Tyre described the lightning raids in which these hellish enemies specialized: "The Turks . . . charged en masse; while still at a distance they let fly countless showers of arrows which fell like hail upon the horses and their riders and brought death and wounds from afar. When the Christians tried to pursue them, the Turks turned and fled upon the horses and thus escaped the swords of their foe."[17] King Conrad was badly hurt in one of these assaults. His army limped back to Christian territory to meet up with King Louis VII and his army.

The second, French wave of the crusade arrived in Constantinople just days after the Germans had left, on October 4, 1147. The French received a slightly warmer welcome than the Germans, thanks in part to the diplomatic efforts of Everard of Barres, master of the Temple in France, who had been sent ahead on a diplomatic mission. The gates of Constantinople duly swung open to afford King Louis and his more respectable retainers a ceremonial welcome. In the words of Odo of Deuil, who chronicled the French crusade in colorful detail, "all its nobles and wealthy men, clerics as well as lay people, trooped out to meet the king and received him with due honor."[18] Behind the pageantry, however, lurked mutual suspicion. The Greeks were disgusted by the rude barbarians from the West; the Franks despised the spineless obsequies of their hosts. Odo of Deuil considered that "when [the Greeks] are afraid, they become despicable in their excessive debasement and when they have the upper hand they are arrogant in their severe violence to those subjected to them." Later he went further: "Constantinople is arrogant in her wealth, treacherous in her practices, corrupt in her faith."[19]

Louis VII had done his best to instill some basic discipline on the tens of thousands of his followers who lacked the Templars' military training. Sadly, like Conrad, he found the task beyond him. Outside his realm, his ability to issue commands was much reduced; outside his own personal guard at the core of his much larger army, Louis was able to exercise leadership only by advising, instructing and attempting to influence a council of nobles.[20] Petty crime and scrapping were almost impossible to prevent. "The king frequently punished offenders by cutting off their ears, hands and feet, but he could not check the folly of the whole group," lamented Odo of Deuil. Outside Constantinople, Louis's men quarreled with the

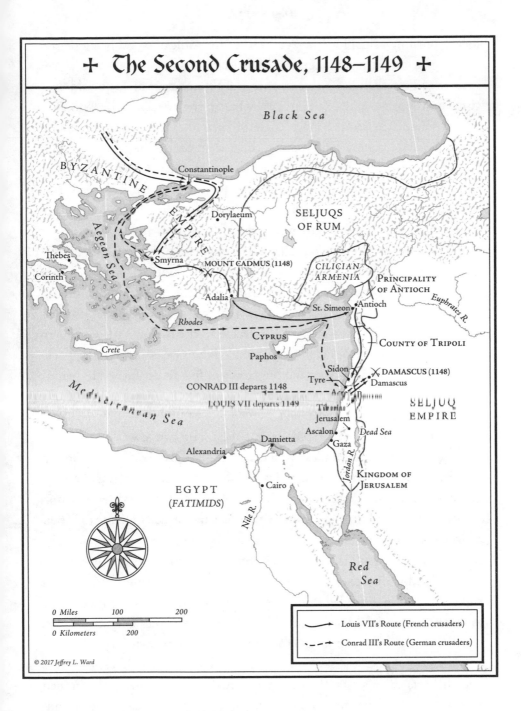

✠ The Second Crusade, 1148–1149 ✠

Black Sea

BYZANTINE

Constantinople

EMPIRE

Dorylaeum

SELJUQS
OF RUM

Thebes

Aegean Sea

Smyrna

MOUNT CADMUS (1148)

CILICIAN
ARMENIA

PRINCIPALITY
OF ANTIOCH

Corinth

Adalia

St. Simeon

Antioch

Euphrates R.

Rhodes

CYPRUS

COUNTY OF TRIPOLI

Crete

Paphos

Sidon

×DAMASCUS (1148)

Mediterranean Sea

CONRAD III departs 1148

Tyre

Damascus

LOUIS VII departs 1149

Acre

SELJUQ
EMPIRE

Tiberias

Jerusalem

Ascalon

Dead Sea

Damietta

Gaza

Alexandria

EGYPT
(FATIMIDS)

Cairo

Nile R.

Jordan R.

KINGDOM OF
JERUSALEM

*Red
Sea*

0 Miles   100   200

0 Kilometers   200

→ Louis VII's Route (French crusaders)

- -→ Conrad III's Route (German crusaders)

© 2017 Jeffrey L. Ward

locals, burning valuable olive trees "either for want of wood or by reason of arrogance and the drunkenness of fools."[21]

It was in both sides' interests that the French crusaders should continue on toward Edessa. But once they began their journey through Asia Minor toward Seljuq territory, their indiscipline had even more awful consequences. Having followed the coast road on the first stage of their journey between Nicomedia and Ephesus, in early January 1148 they turned inland and headed for Adalia on the south coast. The road took them through wild and inhospitable country, littered with the corpses of German soldiers who had fallen the previous autumn and lay still unburied. After several days, on January 8 it brought them to the difficult upland terrain of Mount Cadmus: "an accursed mountain," wrote Odo of Deuil, "steep and rocky," which demanded that the long train of animals, wagons, foot soldiers and horsemen traverse "a ridge so lofty that its summit seemed to touch heaven and the stream in the hollow valley below to descend into hell."[22] Rocks fell from above. When weak and hungry packhorses lost their footing they fell hundreds of feet to be dashed to pieces, dragging to their deaths anyone they hit on the way. Worse still, Turkish outriders had been spotted ahead.

Trying to guide a vast rabble over a mountain range was a task quite beyond Louis VII's capabilities as a commander. Disastrously, he allowed his army to separate and cross the peak of Mount Cadmus in three staggered groups. It was a gift to his enemies. Louis's rear guard remained in camp at the foot of the mountain, while the vanguard set off ahead. Their orders were to make an ascent before stopping to spend the night near the top, but their vanguard's captains ignored commands, crested the summit and descended the other side to pitch their tents on lower ground. Out of sight and poorly defended, the large baggage train containing food, tents and other essentials, accompanied by pilgrims, servants and attendants, was left to make the mountain crossing entirely on its own.

A baggage train was slow moving and vulnerable at the best of times, and this was the opening the Turks who had been shadowing the French were waiting for. They fell on the convoy and butchered its unarmed minders. Odo of Deuil later recorded the panic he felt as the Turks "thrust and slashed, and the defenseless crowd fled or fell like sheep. Thence rose a cry that pierced even to heaven."

The screams of terror carried down the mountain and Louis and a relief force from the rear guard dashed to rescue their companions. The battle that ensued was a desperate affair, in which Louis himself was nearly killed: he only escaped a rush by Turkish attackers by scrambling up a rock covered in tree roots and battering back his assailants with his sword until they tired of the pursuit and rode away. He rejoined his men once night had fallen, having come to them "in the silence of midnight, without a guide."[23] The French fatalities were considerable and the injury to their pride greater still; after a week skirting enemy territory, they had fared nearly as badly as the Germans. Ibn al-Qalanisi, writing in Damascus, recorded that in Syria "fresh reports of [Frankish] losses and of the destruction of their numbers were constantly arriving until the end of the year 542"; in the Christian calendar this was the late spring of 1148.[24] Something would have to change, or annihilation beckoned.

The Templars marching with Louis, far better trained for the reality of combat in the East than their comrades, came through the debacle on Mount Cadmus in remarkably good shape. While most of Louis's troops and horses were starving in the absence of their plundered baggage train and its vital provisions, the Templars had conserved their possessions. Although the main body of troops were prone to disobedience and panic, they had spent the march helping those around them survive the Turkish assault. Perhaps most important, the Templar contingent was led by the French master Everard of Barres, whom Louis trusted.

Now Everard's influence with the king and the manifest superiority of his men to the rest of the army transformed the entire expedition. King Louis did something quite astonishing: he signed over effective command of the entire mission to the Templar knights, allowing them to reorganize the military structure, take control of training and tactics and—most extraordinary of all—to temporarily enlist into the order every person in the vast royal following, from the meanest pilgrim to the mightiest knight. Suddenly the Templars were no longer a small but competent unit within the larger French army of the Second Crusade: they were effectively its leaders, and every man who followed them was, for a few weeks at least, a brother.

Odo of Deuil recorded that the king admired the Templars' example and ability, and wished for their spirit to be mapped onto the rest of his army so that "even if hunger should weaken them, unity of spirit would also strengthen them." He got far more than the spread of good cheer. Odo recorded in detail the steps the Templars took to drag the crusaders up from the desolation in which the massacre on Mount Cadmus had left them.

"By common consent, it was decided that during this dangerous period all should establish fraternity with the Templars, rich and poor taking oath that they would not flee the field and that they would obey in every respect the officers assigned them by the Templars."[25] A Templar by the name of Gilbert was given overall field command. The ordinary French knights were formed into divisions of fifty, each one commanded by a single Templar who reported to Gilbert. Straightaway the new command began drilling the troops in the art of fighting the Turks.

One of the most important duties for any Templar knight or sergeant, spelled out explicitly in the rule, was obedience. The rule stated: "No brother should fight or rest according to his own will, but according to the orders of the Master, to whom all should submit."[26] Holding formation was—and always has been—a first principle of competent military conduct, but in the panic on Mount Cadmus, what poor orders had been given were ignored, and many soldiers had run or fought as they saw fit. That had to change. In taking an oath of fraternity to the Templars, each of Louis's pilgrim warriors now accepted that it was his sworn duty to obey Gilbert and his deputies: to stand firm or take cover as they were told. This was more authority than Louis VII had ever been able to exert over his army and its effects were immediately felt.

The crusaders were also given a crash course in Turkish tactics and how to counter them. Mounted archers were deadly but predictable: their methods had been refined with great success over thousands of years, and they relied on the swift ambush raids that Odo of Deuil had seen firsthand and recorded in awestruck detail. Round-helmeted riders with quivers of feathered arrows slung at their waists would appear suddenly before the enemy and charge.[27] At the last minute they would tug their horses' reins, wheel and retreat. As they left, they would fire volleys of arrows, leaving the enemy shocked, bleeding and confused. These attacks would come in waves, with riders disappearing behind a shower of lethal shafts, changing horses and returning to mount a fresh assault. The horsemen were astonishingly skilled, capable of controlling with one or no hands beautifully trained steeds weighing eight or nine hundred pounds, stringing and drawing a heavy bow at a gallop and firing with mortal accuracy from over and around their horse's neck, head and flanks.[28] They worked in small, mobile groups, arriving one after the other and maintaining constant pressure. When they needed to fight at close quarters, the riders slung their bows across their backs and swung swords or jabbed spears, although this was risky when fighting the Franks, who tended to favor heavier armor than the Turks and were generally more at home with conventional hand-to-hand combat.

These were, without doubt, fierce and daunting enemies, who thrived on creating terror and panic. But they were not invincible, as Gilbert the Templar and his captains taught their newly enlisted companions. The key was to maintain discipline in the face of ambush for long enough to organize a counterattack. Odo of Deuil recalled the Templars' strategy: "Our men were commanded to endure the attacks of the enemies, until they received an order; and to withdraw immediately when recalled. . . . When they had learned this, they were also taught the order of the march, so that a person in front would not rush to the rear and the guards on the flanks would not fall into disorder. . . . Those whom nature or fortune had made foot soldiers . . . were drawn up at the very rear in order to oppose the enemies' arrows with their bows."[29]

This was no great tactical innovation. Indeed, the fact that basic troop positioning and adherence to officers' orders had to be taught to Louis's followers as though they were green youths being instructed in the first principles of combat illustrates just how woefully unprepared the crusaders had been to begin with.[30] All the same, with a little structure and the firm direction of their new commanders the crusader army descended from the mountains and rejoiced at reaching lower ground.

A triumphant song composed around 1146 to rally men to Louis's crusade had advertised the mission to rescue Edessa in rapturous terms, proclaiming, "God has organized a tournament between Hell and Heaven." (*Deus ad un turnei enpris / Entre Enfern e Pareïs*.)[31] This tournament continued when the crusaders marched in their new ranks toward Adalia on the south coast of Asia Minor. They were still the better part of a fortnight from the port, and would be hassled by the Turks virtually every step of the way.

The first test came as the army attempted to pass a wetland in which two rivers, their banks thick and slippery with mud, flowed a mile apart. Crossing the first river was difficult enough. Some of the horses, weak with hunger, sank into the mire and had to be pulled out by hand, a tiring task for men who were half starving themselves.

The road to the second river led the army between two high crags, perfect snipers' positions: anyone standing at the top of either crag could shoot at the crusader army as it passed slowly below. The army's new leadership was alert to the danger. Knights were sent up to hold the crags, in a race with the Turks. Each side secured one. In a brief standoff the Turks tried to intimidate their opponents with a show of contemptuous defiance. Odo of Deuil says they "plucked hair from their heads and threw it onto the ground, and by this sign, we were told, they indicated that they could not be dislodged from the spot by any kind of fear."[32] This time however, the crusaders intended to use not fear, but steel. The road between the crags was blockaded and a force of foot soldiers was instructed to rush the Turkish position. Numbers won out, and soon the Turks were fleeing the crag with Christian troops in lively pursuit. As they descended to the mudflats below they were cut down. Odo of Deuil rejoiced, re-marking that the unbelievers "found death and a grave in a place suited to their filthy natures."[33]

Morale was boosted by this victory, and with it the army marched on to Adalia, reaching the city by January 20. Conditions remained punish-ing: horses died by the roadside, where they were either left to rot or carved up for what scraps of meat remained on their exhausted bones. As the stock of beasts dwindled, the men were forced to abandon the packs, tents and armor they could not carry on their own backs. When the army came to a halt and made camp outside Adalia, disease began to tear through the ranks, its progress undoubtedly hastened by the weakened state of the half-nourished troops, who found the citizens of Adalia charging ex-tortionate prices for much-needed food.

The winter's snow and storms came, and a contrary wind blew for five weeks, preventing the crusaders from leaving the city by ship. But the army was now at least competently drilled and capable of protecting itself. Three Turkish attacks on the camp outside the walls of Adalia were beaten back, including one in which Templars rode in disguise among a group of other knights to chase away the enemy. They had decided early that they would rather keep their chargers alive and go hungry themselves, and the sacrifice now paid off: the sight of so many apparently well-fed horses beneath Christian knights convinced the Turks that the crusaders had managed to resupply, and they retreated.

Somehow, when spring came, the crusaders were still alive, having survived one of the most grueling marches imaginable. The land route into Syria was another forty days on foot, and there was some debate about whether it would be more righteous to stay faithful to the footsteps of their predecessors, or to take the more expensive but shorter option of crossing by ship to Antioch. After much deliberation and excruciating negotiation with the sailors and shipowners of Adalia, who pumped every piece of silver they could from their stricken guests, Louis departed in the first wave of sea crossings. His men straggled along behind him: some finding passage by boat, and the rest attempting to march. Others, according to Odo of Deuil, simply gave up on their promises to reach the kingdom of Jerusalem, and accepted alms and safe passage back through Asia Minor as enfeebled prisoners of a band of Turks.

The Templars had suffered the same privations as the rest of Louis's army. But without the self-discipline, levelheadedness, resourcefulness and commitment to the cause that they had shown, the French king's crusade might never have made it much past Constantinople. As it was, in early March, Louis disembarked in Antioch and prepared for the next phase of the plan to save Edessa. Once again, the Templars would be heavily involved.

6

"The Mill of War"

Louis VII reached the Holy Land by the port of St. Symeon at the mouth of the river Orontes, realizing that he was broke.[1] Quite beside the blood that had been spilled and the many wounds to his pride, the financial costs the king had incurred on his long journey from Paris to Antioch had exhausted his budget for the glorious pilgrimage. His men had been milked by the Greeks of Constantinople and Adalia, who saw their desperation and sold them food and passage at exorbitant prices. The prospect of now beginning a series of military offensives against Muslim-held cities was more than the king's coffers could bear. Fortunately Louis was still attended by Everard of Barres, a man personally invested in the French branch of the crusade. It was to Everard that he now turned for help.

The French needed a very large loan, and he hoped Everard would fix it. It was no secret that the Templars, although individually committed to a life of poverty, had already grown very rich. They knew the land and the people of the Latin East and were well placed to raise money either by drawing on their own resources or by cajoling others into supporting the cause. Perhaps most important, they had a sworn duty to protect pilgrims. In this case that could be interpreted as bailing out a crusader king. On May 10, 1148, Everard of Barres left Louis in Antioch and traveled south to Acre to gather funds.

The amount he raised, partly from the Templars' own treasury and partly by mortgaging their properties, was extraordinary. Later in the year Louis wrote to the regents he had left to govern France in his absence and asked them to find thirty thousand Paris pounds (livres parisis) and two thousand marks of silver to repay his debt to the Templars.* This was equivalent to half or more of the annual revenues of the French

---

* A mark was an accounting unit equal to two thirds of a pound, so in this case 1,333.33 livres parisis.

Crown.[2] In a letter to Abbot Suger of Saint-Denis, one of the regents, Louis wrote that he would not have been able to make his journey to the Holy Land without the assistance he had received in all matters from the brothers of the Order of the Temple, and that the order had nearly bankrupted itself to sustain him and his mission.[3] Assuming there was a kernel of truth to this, and that it was more than simple rhetoric to cast the Templars in a favorable light, it was clear that the order had gone to great lengths to protect the French king from embarrassment and prop up the faltering crusade effort.

Louis was not the only Western crusader king looking to the Templars for help in the spring of 1148. Conrad III had also made his way to the Holy Land following a chastening experience in and around Constantinople, sailing first to Acre, before traveling south to Jerusalem, where he stayed at the Templars' formidable headquarters on the site of the converted al-Aqsa Mosque.

By the time of Conrad's visit the mosque had been given over entirely to the Templars, and repairs and improvements were well underway. One chronicler now called it "the richest" building in Jerusalem.[4] It was still a vast, elegant rectangular building topped with a dome, its frontal façade dominated by large arched doors behind a high porch. But around it were a number of new outbuildings in various stages of completion: a hall and cloister to the west and working buildings to the east.[5] A smaller mosque to one side had been converted into a chapel—a fact noted by the well-bred Syrian poet and diplomat Usama ibn Munqidh—and plans were afoot for a vast new church to reflect the growing status of the order.

The urbane and erudite Ibn Munqidh, who lived to the age of ninety-three and had an unparalleled perspective on the turbulent first century of the crusades, regarded the Templars as his friends, despite their religious differences. He recorded that whenever he visited the al-Aqsa Mosque, the knights would be sure to clear their chapel so that he could pray facing Mecca. He noted this fact, it must be said, in the context of a longer anecdote illustrating the stupidity, barbarity and coarseness of the other Franks—he could not write about non-Templar Christians without uttering oaths such as "God curse them!" and "Almighty God is greater than the infidels' concept of him!"[6]

A sprawling stable block ran below the compound, built into the platform covering the Temple Mount. It was said that the stalls had been
constructed by Solomon himself—although in all likelihood they dated
back to the reign of Herod, at the time of Christ's birth. One writer
claimed they could hold two thousand horses and fifteen hundred camels; another more excitable visitor suggested the capacity was more like
ten thousand.

Conrad arrived in Jerusalem in time for Easter. His half brother, Otto,
bishop of Freising, wrote that he entered the city "amid great jubilation
on the part of clergy and people and was received with much honor." In a
sign of the respect afforded to the German king the brothers arranged
for his traveling companion, Frederick of Bogen, who died shortly after
arriving in the city, to be buried in their private cemetery near the Temple walls.

Conrad spent much of his time in Jerusalem in Templar company.
Otto of Freising noted that he went on a tour of the venerable sites, "visiting the holy places everywhere."[7] The Templars must have insisted on
providing their services. For all that they were evolving into a combat
brigade, the brothers were still at root members of an organization that
offered security and guidance on the pilgrim trail.

Alongside this itinerary of prayer and celebration, Conrad planned for
the forthcoming war in the north. Jerusalem had a new king, Baldwin III,
who had succeeded his father Fulk I on his death in 1143. Now aged seventeen, well educated and with an easy aristocratic bearing, Baldwin had
been ruling for three years alongside his mother, Melisende, and was
chafing to lead a major military expedition. In Otto of Freising's words,
the emperor therefore agreed, with the young king, the city's Latin patriarch "and the Knights of the Temple to lead an army into Syria about the
following July to take Damascus."[8]

+

Damascus was indisputably one of the jewels of the Muslim world and
the most significant city in southern Syria. The tenth-century Arab geographer known as al-Muqaddasi described it as one of the "brides of the

world," a town "crisscrossed by streams and encircled by [fruit] trees," blessed by the presence of the finest mosques anywhere on earth. The Great Mosque, founded under Umayyad rule in the seventh century, was an immense, lavishly decorated building, its walls covered in marble and gilded mosaics, which was reputed to have cost "eighteen mule loads of gold" to build. It was considered by the faithful to be the fourth-holiest site in the world after Mecca, Medina and Jerusalem: so pure that spiders never span their webs in its corners.[9]

Although a large clay citadel stood alongside the mosque, providing Damascus's defensive hub, the city walls were relatively small and weak. Miles of orchards surrounded the city on every side, dense thickets of fruit trees walled off into small plots navigable only along single-track paths. These were awkward obstacles to be sure, but not impossible to surmount. So on the face of it Damascus seemed a feasible target for Christian conquest. Seizing control of Damascus might represent a triumph on the scale of the capture of Acre and even Jerusalem.

Yet Damascus was not Edessa, the city whose plight had prompted the raising of the Second Crusade. It was not mentioned in Pope Eugene's *Quantum Praedecessores* and was not the city whose salvation had been preached across the West by Bernard of Clairvaux. Its defenses may have been largely composed of fruit trees rather than huge walls that required sapping, but it was no easy target. This had been proven as recently as 1129, when King Baldwin II had failed to take the city, a defeat greeted with contempt and indignation in the West. Moreover, in 1148 its governor, Mu'in ad-Din Unur, was technically an ally of the kingdom of Jerusalem, with which he shared a common enemy in the aggressively expansionist Zengi. To divert the whole focus of the Second Crusade away from Edessa and on to Damascus was a bold and apparently abrupt change of focus, in which the Templars clearly had a hand.

Many things had changed in the three and a half years since Edessa's fall in 1144. For one thing, Zengi was dead. The old tyrant had been murdered in his bed in September 1146: attacked by an unhappy servant while he was passed out drunk and left to suffer a slow and painful end.[10] Zengi had been succeeded by his two sons, the younger of whom, Nur al-Din, was if anything even more belligerent than his father. As the new governor of Aleppo, Nur al-Din was determined to keep his boot pressed firmly on the throats of the Christians in the county of Edessa, and to extend his reach farther south into the neighboring principality of Antioch.

According to the Damascus-based chronicler Ibn al-Athir, Nur al-Din, aged thirty when the crusaders gathered on the outskirts of his city, was "tall and swarthy in stature. He had no beard, except for on his chin, and he had a wide forehead. He was a handsome man with charming eyes. His dominion extended very much . . . the fame of his good rule and justice encompassed the world."[11] His name meant Light (Nur) of the Faith (al-Din).

This was a more generous assessment than the crusaders would have allowed. Under Nur al-Din, Edessa had been subjected to another horrible massacre, in response to a failed liberation attempt by its ousted leader, Count Joscelin II. The city's defenses were destroyed and its remaining Christian population either killed or enslaved. It was now too late for the crusaders to save any souls in Edessa. To complicate matters, Nural-Din had countered the Christian alliance pursued by Damascus's governor, Unur, by sealing his own treaty with the city. Nur al-Din had married Unur's daughter, and the rulers of Aleppo and Damascus began to present an increasingly united front against the Franks. So by the summer of 1148 it made a great deal more sense to attempt to break a dangerous partnership than to chase a losing cause in Edessa. Another option was to try to take Ascalon, a port held by the Fatimids, some thirty miles south of Jaffa, but since this was about as far removed from the initial purpose of the Second Crusade as was possible, it was rejected.[12]

On Thursday, June 24, 1148, the feast day of Saint John the Baptist, the town of Palmarea, near Acre, was filled with more or less every important person in the Latin East. King Conrad, King Louis and the eighteen-year-old King Baldwin III of Jerusalem were all present, along with Baldwin's mother and coruler Queen Melisende. A plethora of noble dignitaries from East and West were accompanied by an impressive cast of princes of the Church, including the patriarch of Jerusalem, two archbishops and a papal legate. Alongside these grandees sat the masters of the Hospitallers and the Templars, Raymond of Puy and Robert of Craon, now among the leading decision makers in the crusader kingdoms. The purpose of the meeting (often called the Council of Acre) was to come to an agreement on the target of the forthcoming military action. William of Tyre recorded that a serious debate broke out about the adoption of a Damascene policy: "Opinions of diverse factions were offered and arguments pro and con presented."[13]

Yet if we can believe Otto of Freising's account, the matter was all but predecided. Once Louis had agreed that the policy was sensible, the only matter to be discussed was "when and where the army should be mustered."[14] Confidence was high. According to one Muslim writer from the target city, their "malicious hearts were so confident of capturing it that they had already planned out the division of its estates and districts."

The conquest of Damascus would not prove quite so simple.

✝

Ibn Jubayr, a Spanish Muslim traveler who visited Damascus in the late twelfth century, described the city as incomparably lush: "The paradise of the Orient . . . perfumed flower gardens breathe life into the soul . . . gardens encircle it like the halo around the moon . . . its green oasis stretches as far as the eye can see, and wherever you look on its four sides its ripe fruits hold the gaze."[15] But on Saturday, July 24, 1148, as the combined troops of the crusader army began to hack through this fertile wooded belt, they did not find it quite so inviting.

William of Tyre described the tense, claustrophobic approach to Damascus as the armies of the three Christian kings picked their way, often in single file, through the narrow orchard paths on the outskirts of the city. The tracks they used were "wide enough to allow gardeners and caretakers to pass through them with pack animals that carry the fruit to the city," he wrote, but for a large body of troops dragging weapons and the machinery of war, leading oxen and camels hauling a huge baggage train, they were dangerously inadequate. Defenders hid between the trees, leaping out to attack the soldiers as they passed, or took aim from the top of watchtowers dotted here and there to guard the orchards from trespassers. "From these vantage points they kept up a constant downpour of arrows and other missiles," he wrote. Mud walls hid men carrying lances, who spied on the invaders through peepholes, waiting for the best moment to spear their enemy from the side. The crusaders advanced in "peril of instant death," William wrote. "From every direction there was equal danger."[16]

Despite these ambushes, the sheer weight of numbers and determination was on the Christians' side. They forced a path through the orchards, demolishing walls and barricades set up to stall their path. Hacking their way between the trees they finally came to the banks of the river Barada, which passed under Damascus's city walls.

A delegation had assembled on the banks of the river, lined up with catapults and archers to defend the city gates. But a furious direct charge by Conrad's German cavalry scattered this first force: knights leapt from their horses and ran forward with their swords swinging. Conrad himself fought in the fray with noted success: it was said he savaged one Turkish knight so grievously that he cut off the man's head, left shoulder, arm and part of his torso with a single blow. Soon the river leading through the western suburbs of Damascus was secured and the crusaders began digging in, erecting their own barricades with trees felled from the orchards. "The mill of war," observed the Damascus chronicler Ibn al-Qalanisi, "ceased not to grind."[17]

The crusader armies had set out so confident of a swift triumph that they had not brought siege engines, or provisions to last more than a few days. It was calculated that fruit plundered from the orchards and water drawn from the river would sustain them, and that the maximum time needed to break the city would be a fortnight. The Christians had not reckoned on the ferocity of the Muslim defense, nor on the fact that almost as soon as their armies approached the city walls, reports began arriving of relieving forces making their way imminently to the crusader camp. "Large numbers of bowmen" rode in from the Biqa Valley, east of Beirut, to harass the besiegers, while forces from within the city started to bombard the Franks' positions "with the swiftness of hawks swooping on mountain partridges."[18]

What happened next would be a matter of debate for years to come. On Tuesday, July 27, observers peering out from the city watchtowers saw the crusader camp fall strangely silent. Occasional sallies of horse or foot soldiers were repelled with a hail of lances and arrows, but for the most part the siege had fallen still. "It was thought," wrote Ibn al-Qalanisi, "that they were planning a ruse and preparing a stratagem."

In this he was quite correct. The three kings leading the siege were taking counsel, and coming to a bold and highly controversial decision. Abruptly, and to many perplexingly, it was decided to abandon the offensive on the western side of the city and to move instead to a new position in the southeast, where intelligence suggested that the orchards were thinner, the walls weaker and victory would be faster. Rumors of several large relieving forces seem to have spooked the Frankish leadership to the point of being willing to gamble heavily on a switch in strategy to force a rapid victory.[19] Their hard-won positions were abandoned and the entire army moved east. As it transpired, this was a disastrous move.

Although he was not himself present at the siege of Damascus, William of Tyre interviewed as many veterans as he could, and he painted a bleak picture of events.[20] The removal of the armies caused widespread grumbling, soon amply justified by events. On arriving at their new position, the Franks found it perfectly well defended and not at all an open door to conquest. There were no orchards, it was true, but all this meant in practice was that the besieging army now went hungry. Any possibility of returning to the west side of the city had immediately been cut off, for having seen the Franks move, the city's defenders had rushed to barricade the roads with huge rocks and felled trees, guarded by archers. The Christians could no longer go forward, for the army was not provisioned for long enough to effect a successful siege, and neither could they go back. The possibility of an attack from relieving forces grew by the hour. Somehow, the Franks had thrown away their most promising military position in years.

The leading lords assembled for a conference and concluded, after a poisonous discussion in which accusations of treachery were flung around, that the only sensible strategy was to pack up and go home. It was almost unbearably humiliating. Men had traveled thousands of miles, enduring disease, starvation, shipwreck, ambush and poverty, in the hopes of following in the footsteps of the first crusaders and winning a string of magnificent victories in the name of the Lord. But in the end, the eastern thrust of the Second Crusade had turned out to be nothing more than a four-day hike through a booby-trapped fruit field, a few isolated skirmishes and an impotent retreat. "Our people," wrote William of Tyre drily, "returned without glory."[21]

✝

The Templars had invested a great deal in the Second Crusade. They had marched Louis VII through Asia Minor and propped him up with enormous loans. They had taken Conrad III in and provided him with protection and their considered military advice. Together with the master of the Hospitallers, Robert of Craon had backed the plan to attack Damascus rather than Edessa. Their reward for all this was vanishingly slight.

After Damascus the Frankish kings briefly considered an assault on Ascalon, but it came to nothing. Conrad left the Holy Land in September 1148. Louis stayed for seven more months, celebrating Easter in Jerusalem before going home to France in late April. And then the recriminations began.

The consensus among the Frankish chroniclers was that their masters could not possibly have failed so roundly unless they had been in some way betrayed. It was a matter of accepted fact that someone had sabotaged the campaign—that was how Conrad III himself explained the disaster, although he could not pinpoint the source of the treachery. Various people were suspected: one name thrown around was that of the crusader Lord Thierry, Count of Flanders, who was thought to have coveted the lordship of Damascus for himself, arousing a jealousy among his peers that persuaded them to deliberately hobble the whole mission just to thwart him. Others said that an Eastern lord called Elinandus of Tiberias had accepted a massive bribe—paid in fake treasure—to persuade his superiors to change tactics. Even King Baldwin and his mother were suspected, as men sought an earthly explanation for a military travesty that could only otherwise be attributed to the wrath of a capricious God.

The Templars, too, came under suspicion. An English polemicist and bureaucrat, John of Salisbury, who served as ambassador at the papal court, expressly blamed the order for its part in the debacle, although he could not quite say what it had done. He was no supporter of the

Templars, whose privileges he considered to be actively dangerous to the Church, but he was plugged tightly into the gossip of the papal court under Eugene III, where tongues were wagging, and the Templars were upon them.

There is no evidence to suggest that this was anything more than slander. The Templars had done their job with as much diligence and devotion as anyone could reasonably have asked of them. Their purpose was to protect pilgrims—and their role in escorting, defending, training, financing, advising and fighting alongside the pilgrims of the Second Crusade represented the highest possible demonstration of duty. They had risked their lives and courted bankruptcy in order to prop up the efforts of the crusader armies, which were at times negligently, even suicidally, led. To blame them for the failure of the crusade was in one sense deeply ungrateful. Yet it also showed just how intimately the Templars were now associated with the fortunes of the Holy Land and the defense of the Christian settlements there. In three decades they had become almost synonymous with the kingdom of God that had been carved out of the Islamic Near East. This was to be both their highest honor and their greatest curse.

7

"The Godforsaken Tower"

THE WRECKED TOWN of Gaza lay silent and empty. It had once been among the finest cities of the Near East: a stopping point on the coastal road from Syria through Palestine to Egypt, made rich by a thriving market and renowned for its mosques, churches and massive, airy houses built in marble.[1] But in 1149 only its natural wells and reservoirs remained to indicate that this was once a place where people of many religions had thrived. War had swept through the elegant streets and emptied Gaza, seemingly for good. "It was now in ruins," wrote William of Tyre, "and entirely uninhabited."[2] Its vacant and shattered buildings bore out the words of one of the city's finest native poets, Abu Ishaq al-Ghazzi: "The past is gone. . . . You have but the moment in which you exist."[3]

In the winter of 1149–50 Gaza began to stir. Spades broke the earth to dig new foundations, and stonemasons cut blocks for new fortifications. The city—or a significant part of it—was rising once again. On a hill in the center of the broken town a new castle was being erected, "notable for its wall and towers." This was not just an act of urban regeneration. It was part of an aggressive new military strategy being pursued in the far south of the crusader kingdom, with the Templars at its heart. For as the new castle was erected, the brothers were being earmarked to serve as both its guardians and its beneficiaries.

That winter was an unsettled moment for the Knights of the Temple. Robert of Craon died on January 13, 1149, and in his place was elected Everard of Barres, the master in France who had served King Louis VII so diligently during the debacle of the Second Crusade. Everard was clearly a competent financier and an adept diplomat, but his heart lay in France. Like Robert of Craon, he saw more value in representing the order among its sponsors in Europe than serving in a full-time military role in Jerusalem, not least because of the sheer scale of the credit the order had extended to the French Crown.

94

Everard returned to Paris when the royal ships set sail in the spring of 1149. He left in charge Andrew of Montbard, a middle-aged knight who had served the Templars since at least 1130. One of eight children from a noble family in Burgundy, two of his brothers were Cistercian monks at Cîteaux.[4] He was an uncle of Bernard of Clairvaux, although a few years younger, whom he regularly apprised by letter of the Temple's successes and hardships in the land of the Lord. Andrew once likened his work to that of an ant, but his humility masked considerable military talent.[5] During his time with the order, he had risen to the office of seneschal. He was the man who had ultimate responsibility for the Templar flag, the *confanon bauçant* or piebald banner: a simple black-and-white standard that was raised on the battlefield by another officer, the marshal, for the Templars to fight around, and which could not be lowered unless every knight on the field was dead.* Andrew of Montbard knew the politics of the Latin East well and diligently reported events to friends back home.

Unfortunately, almost as soon as Master Everard had left for Paris, Andrew of Montbard was sending letters after him, reporting on the deaths of many brothers in defense of a blood spattered piebald.

On June 29, a disastrous battle at Inab, near Antioch, saw an army under Prince Raymond of Antioch obliterated by forces led by Zengi's son Nur al-Din, the atabeg of Aleppo. Raymond was a controversial character, to say the least. Since traveling from Poitiers to claim Antioch by marriage to its nine-year-old heiress, he had fallen out with the king of Sicily, the Byzantine emperor and Antioch's patriarch. He was rumored to have seriously offended Louis VII by behaving rather too chivalrously toward Louis's wife, Eleanor of Aquitaine, who happened to be his niece. The battle of Inab marked the end of Raymond's colorful progress. He was captured on the battlefield and beheaded. Nur al-Din sent his head to the Sunni caliph in Baghdad as a trophy.

It fell upon the kingdom of Jerusalem to stem further losses. Baldwin III and his mother, Queen Melisende, asked the Templars to help

---

* When at camp the piebald banner identified the location of the seneschal. During battle, it was the Templars' marshal rather than the seneschal who physically raised and carried the flag and who organized its protection. See Judith M. Upton-Ward, trans. and ed., *The Rule of the Templars: The French Text of the Rule of the Order of the Knights Templar* (Woodbridge, Suffolk, UK: Boydell Press, 1992).

prevent Nur al-Din's armies from seeing in the crisis of Raymond's death an opportunity to march on the city of Antioch. The Templars had immediately joined the king's army, providing one hundred and twenty knights and approximately one thousand "well-armed squires and sergeants." Then they raced north, wrote Andrew, borrowing on the way seven thousand Acre bezants* and one thousand Jerusalem bezants to fund their campaign.[6]

They reached Antioch, but were immediately pinned down by Muslim soldiers arriving from Iconium (modern-day Konya, in Turkey) and Khorosan (in Persia). Now they were in desperate straits and required urgent resupply and reinforcement. "We are writing to ask you to return to us in haste with no delay," Andrew told Everard. "You will never have a better reason for coming back nor could your return ever be more welcome to God, more useful to our house and the land of Jerusalem. . . . Many in our army are dead, which is why we need you to come to us with those brothers and sergeants you know to be fit for the task. No matter how quickly you come we do not think you will find us alive, but come without delay; that is our wish, our message and our request. . . . Venerable father, sell everything you can and bring the proceeds to us yourself so that we may live on. Farewell."

Andrew of Montbard's letter gave a bleak picture of the military situation in Antioch as the Franks tried to resist a buoyant Nur al-Din. It also summed up much of the reality of life for the Templars in the kingdom of Jerusalem. They were expected to provide rapid-response military support wherever the enemy struck throughout the three remaining crusader states of Jerusalem, Tripoli and Antioch.

It was in the context of this wide-ranging duty that the Templars had begun to be regularly granted fortresses from which they could police the more vulnerable areas subject to Latin rule. One such was then being built on the hilltop in Gaza. "When it was entirely finished in all its parts," wrote William of Tyre, "it was committed by general consent to the Knights of the Temple, to be held by them in perpetuity together

---

*Bezants were the high-value gold coins of the crusader kingdom, minted in imitation of the Arabic *dinar* and the Greek *hyperpyron*.

with all the adjacent district. This charge the brothers, brave and valiant warriors, have faithfully and wisely guarded."[7]

This was high praise from William of Tyre. An erudite Latin scholar born in Jerusalem around 1130, and a second-generation crusader schooled within sight of the Templar palace at the cathedral school attached to the Church of the Holy Sepulchre, William had finished his education in Paris and Bologna—the two leading universities in Europe—before returning to the East to pursue a career in the Church. He eventually rose to become archdeacon and finally archbishop of Tyre—a spiritual rank second only to the patriarch of Antioch. A friend of kings, a gossip and a significant political player in his own right, William of Tyre wrote several epic histories, including an account of Islam since the time of the Prophet Muhammad. From around 1170 he composed a massive Latin chronicle of the Christian East called *A History of Deeds Done Beyond the Sea*—its title making it evident that it was designed for consumption in the learned circles of European courts and universities.

William shared with other Western churchmen a gingerness toward the whole concept of the military orders. He particularly distrusted the Templars and he seldom missed an opportunity in his chronicle to cast doubt on their motives. In the case of Gaza, however, facts were facts: almost as soon as the Templars took possession of the castle, they beat back a Fatimid attack so effectively that no further assaults were made. The castle was effectively the first line of defense in the southernmost reaches of the kingdom of Jerusalem: an outpost of Latin influence before the coast turned uniformly hostile. The order knew the job that was expected of it in Gaza, and they did it well.

+

The new castle at Gaza was not built for its views. It was built to serve a specific policy of extending Christian influence south. Gaza lay at the extreme southwest of the Latins' territories: south of Jaffa, Jerusalem, and, most important of all, Ascalon, a heavily fortified town still loyal to the Fatimids. Ascalon was an Islamic forward base on the windswept coastal road, from which assaults could be launched into Christian territory. It was also a bulwark against any advance into Egypt by the kings of

Jerusalem. Conquering Ascalon promised greater safety and the possibility of consolidating Christian influence in the direction of the Sinai
Peninsula. A march on Ascalon had been considered but rejected by the
armies of the Second Crusade both before and after the failure of the
siege of Damascus, but there was now a growing sense that the city could,
and should, be taken. Three years had passed before the young king Baldwin III could put that idea into full effect, preoccupied as he was by a
power struggle with his mother, who did not wish to relinquish control
she had exercised during her son's minority. But the new fortress suggested a move on Ascalon was at last under way.

The Templars' presence in Gaza isolated Ascalon from Egypt, making the
coast road unsafe and unsuitable for Fatimid troops. The only way the
Shi'a caliph in Cairo could send reinforcements to the city was by sea: a
serious inconvenience as the city did not have a protected harbor, but
only a sandy beach that made landings difficult except in very calm weather.[8]
The fortress at Gaza completed a containing circle of castles around Ascalon, under construction for a decade and a half.

About twenty-five miles across the plains east of Ascalon lay Bethgibelin, a medium-sized fortress built around 1136 and given to the
Knights Hospitaller.[9] A short distance north of Bethgibelin were two
more castles built to defend the kingdom's southern borderlands: Ibelin
and Blanchegarde, built in 1141 and 1142 respectively. Individually and collectively they were unsubtle statements of Frankish power, signaling the
Christians' intent to choke Ascalon slowly, with a noose made of stone.

✝

On January 25, 1153, a flag bearing the sign of the cross flew outside the
turreted walls of Ascalon, which swept in a great crescent guarding the
landward side of the heavily militarized coastal city. The flag advertised
the arrival of the twenty-two-year-old King Baldwin III and an excited
Christian army, whose members were busy swearing oaths to harm the
defenders of Ascalon as much as they could.[10] The leadership of the army,
a massive delegation of princes, lords, high churchmen and experienced
soldiers, surveyed the imposing edifice before them as their men pitched

tents in a circular camp, subdivided into various quarters, each loyal to a different lord. Amid this bloodthirsty crowd was a sizable delegation of Templars.

The city was a formidable sight. Built in a natural basin on sandy ground planted with vines and fruit trees, its walls were lit by the winter's sunshine during the day, while at night the masonry flickered by the flames of glass oil lamps, allowing watchful sentries to peer down at anyone who approached the four fortified gatehouses. The largest of these, known as the Jerusalem Gate, spoke in its angry architecture to the wariness of Ascalon's citizens: lofty towers rose high above a barbican with a series of smaller interior gates defending a winding passageway that led to the main entrance.

The Templars who assembled with the royal army had a new master, Bernard of Tremelay. He was the order's fourth since its inception, and owed his position to the retirement of Everard of Barres, who gave up his post at some point after April 1152, deciding to forgo a military life in favor of quiet monastic contemplation alongside an aging Bernard of Clairvaux. By this point Bernard was in physical decline, unable to stomach anything more than tiny portions of liquefied food, his legs so swollen and painful that at times he could not even sit up to write, let alone walk. He died on August 20, 1153: "A ready spirit," as he put it, "in a weak body." Everard lived another quarter century in the peaceful surroundings of the abbey, and was still around to see the Templar patron achieve sainthood in 1174.[11]

Bernard of Tremelay, who like so many early Templars was from Burgundy, near Dijon, was not a tested leader. When he brought his delegation of Templars to Ascalon at the end of January he had been master for less than a year. But what he lacked in experience he made up for in bravery and belligerence. He was about to lead his brothers into their most daring military engagement since the order had been formed. On January 25, 1153, the great siege of Ascalon was about to begin: a decisive struggle to bring the mighty Fatimid city under Christian control. It was an "arduous and almost impossible feat," wrote William of Tyre. Almost, but not quite.

The first two months of the siege were slow and inconclusive. The citizens of Ascalon outnumbered the Franks outside by two to one. They were well trained, well stocked, and highly motivated to resist, for in William of Tyre's words, "They were fighting for their wives and children, and what is more important, for liberty itself."[12] Yet while they could resist, they could not counterattack. From the towers and ramparts, lookouts might have reported that Baldwin III's camp resembled a bristling satellite city—heavily protected against any potential relief force and so well established it even had its own marketplace. The view from the shore was even less promising: a small fleet of fifteen galleys commanded by Gerard of Sidon blockaded the approach to Ascalon by water. Daily skirmishing took place around the city, favoring first one side and then the other; but the overall state of the conflict was a stalemate.

Then, around Easter, which fell that year on April 19, events began to swing in the Latins' favor. As spring calmed the sea routes from Europe the annual influx of shipborne pilgrims came to visit Jerusalem. This was not a crusading force armed for war, but it was still a valuable boost of pious Christians and boats at precisely the time when military reinforcements were needed.

On hearing of the pilgrims' arrival, Baldwin III sent orders that no one who entered his kingdom was to be permitted to leave, and anyone who joined the army at Ascalon would receive payment for their part in "a labor so acceptable to God." More important, the king forcibly impounded every ship that landed in his ports and diverted them all to the waters around Ascalon. Day after day the Christians' manpower increased. "Great was the joy in camp, and hope of winning the victory was unbounded," wrote William of Tyre. "Among the enemy, on the contrary, grief and anxiety prevailed ever more and more."

The sailors who heeded King Baldwin's instructions to sail south might have expected to be ordered to join a naval blockade. Instead, when they arrived their ships were beached, the masts cut off and the hulls stripped down to the beams. They were paid a handsome fee for the loss of their vessels, and the timber was handed over to workmen who used it to build siege engines. These included rock-throwing catapults and mobile shelters to protect sappers while they attempted to dig out the earthen embankments holding up the thick city walls. One weapon in particular would decide the fate of Ascalon for the next three decades. It was a giant structure, as tall as the walls, composed of long wooden beams supporting fighting platforms, all covered in a fireproof shell made of animal hides stretched over a wicker frame. Its purpose was to allow Frankish knights to climb up to the level of the battlements and kill defenders on an even plane. Siege warfare was a hallmark of European confrontation, and the structure built at Ascalon was clearly of a very high standard. Its construction was known as far away as Damascus, where the chronicler Ibn al-Qalanisi wrote about it with a combination of disgust and grudging admiration. The Franks had reduced Ascalon "to sore straits," he said, "by bringing up to its assault the Godforsaken tower, in the midst of a great host (may God defend it from their malice)."[13]

The Templars, led by Master Bernard of Tremelay, must have observed the construction of the siege tower carefully. When it was ready, and had been dragged into position alongside a carefully selected point in the walls of the city, the Templars positioned themselves in the vicinity of what was now the focal point of intense daily fighting, much of it taking place high above the ground.[14] Baldwin's catapults slammed rocks into the city's walls, while on the top of their formidable tower, men at arms battled the resisting soldiers in hand-to-hand combat and shot arrows at panicked citizens running through the streets below. Out at sea, an Egyptian fleet of seventy galleys had arrived with favorable winds blowing up from the south, scattering Gerard of Sidon's now hopelessly outnumbered naval blockade. But this was now incidental to what was taking place on the battlements on the land side.

By mid-August the siege of Ascalon had been under way for more than six months. Morale within the city was plummeting. So long as Baldwin's army could use its tower, it held the advantage; relief by sea was useful, but the city could only be fully rescued by driving back the besiegers on land. The leading citizens took counsel and resolved to do anything they could to destroy the tower. The only way they could see to do this was to somehow build a fire that was so hot it could destroy the thick hides protecting its timber skeleton. The men and women of Ascalon were put to work collecting "dry wood and other material suitable for kindling," wrote William of Tyre. "There seemed to be no other hope."

During the night of Saturday, August 15, the plan was put into action. Every piece of fuel that had been rounded up was carried to the wall nearest the tower and dumped over the side. Little by little a pyre was built in the gap separating the tower from the masonry. When it had risen high enough, pitch and oil were poured on top. Then a flame was dropped and the bonfire began.

The breeze that had carried the ships along the Levantine coast blew in toward Ascalon from the sea. Over the course of the night, however, it abruptly changed direction, and a brisk wind began to come in from the east, behind the Christian armies. For the people of Ascalon this was a disaster. The swift breeze fanned the flames at the base of Baldwin's tower, causing them to leap hungrily upward. And as they grew, the flames blew against the city wall, superheating stones and mortar that had already been weakened by months of pelting from the Franks' trebuchets.

As dawn approached on Sunday the siege tower still stood. But the wall could take no more. The hot stone cracked, and as the first light of dawn crept up behind the besiegers, "an entire portion of the wall . . . crumbled entirely with a noise that roused the whole army." The rubble roared as it collapsed, and men on both sides scrambled from sleep, grasping their weapons. As they did so, there was another crash. Tumbling stones had ploughed into the base of the siege tower, cracking the wooden ship masts that formed its vertical struts. They shattered, and the terrible machine wobbled, almost throwing off watchmen who were perched on its balconies. But it did not fall. Before it, Ascalon now lay open.

Bernard of Tremelay and his fellow Templars were either camped close to the tower, or more alert during the early dawn than their Christian comrades—or possibly both. As soon as they heard the sound of the wall crunching into the base of the tower they were up at arms, hurtling toward the breach in the wall. Bernard took personal command of his men.

"The Franks (God curse them) are the most cautious of all men in war," wrote Usama ibn Munqidh, who spent four months fighting running battles against Christian raiding parties in the countryside around Ascalon during the years immediately before the great siege.[15] The Templars that day were anything but. As dust from the collapsed hole settled, some forty knights pushed past the siege tower, climbed over the stricken wall and headed into the city. Then, wrote Ibn al-Qalanisi, "they rushed into the town, and a great host were killed on both sides."[16]

What prompted Bernard of Tremelay to give the order that only his own men should storm the breach in Ascalon's walls? He must surely have expected support from the rest of the army behind them. What is certain is that it was the last significant decision he ever made. Inside a city that had been under siege for six months, the Templars found themselves outnumbered by desperate men. The citizens picked up their weapons and moved in. Others dragged beams of wood toward the hole in the wall and started building barricades. The Templars were trapped. Even if there had been an escape route, their rule forbade them from fleeing the battlefield. Their fate was sealed.

Blocked into a hostile city with no chance of retreat or rescue, the Templars were massacred. None was taken for ransom—not even their master. This was unusual for such high-value prisoners. It spoke to the fearsome reputation the Templars held among their enemies and the pent-up fear and desperation of citizens who had been pinned down under enemy assault for half the year. No amount of wealth or booty was worth the lives of forty of the ablest Christian soldiers in the region, who had presented themselves unsupported for the taking. No detailed record of the fight between the citizens of Ascalon and the Knights of the Temple survives, but at the end of it, every single one of the Templars was dead.

It would take another week of fighting before the inhabitants of Ascalon could be forced back from defending their patched-up wall and agreed to hand over their city to Christian rule and sue for peace. On Saturday, August 22, Baldwin III's standard was raised over the highest tower in the city. But it had come at a high cost: the final battle had been fought with the butchered bodies of the forty dead Knights of the Temple dangling from the ropes hoisted high up on the city walls.

✝

Bernard of Tremelay was succeeded as master by the pious and literary seneschal Andrew of Montbard, who served for two years, until 1156. Although the loss of forty brothers was a serious depletion in the order's fighting manpower, as an organization the Templars were not fatally damaged. Recruiting new men was always possible thanks to the burgeoning network in Europe, particularly around their traditional heartlands of

Burgundy, Champagne and Poitou. They remained in possession of the castle at Gaza and were an important military element in the kingdom of Jerusalem's security policy. In the far north Templar knights still manned castles guarding the passes through the Amanus Mountains, but the hostility prompted in some by the siege of Ascalon illustrated the ambivalence with which the Templars were increasingly viewed.

William of Tyre was scorching in his disdain, ascribing the worst and basest motives to Bernard for ordering a suicide mission. The Christian custom in battle, he explained, was that plunder belonged to the plunderer. So, he argued, faced with the chance to make the first foray into Ascalon, the Templars decided that they should be the only looters allowed in, reserving the spoils of victory to themselves. "Out of cupidity, they refused to allow their comrades to share in the booty," he wrote. "Therefore they alone justly suffered the peril of death."[17]

Could this be true? William was writing in hindsight, by which point he had developed a firm distrust of the order's independence and occasional disregard for royal orders. Yet in his long and detailed history of the Christian kingdom of Jerusalem he had also extended praise for the order's robust defense of Gaza, and reported other episodes with relative equanimity. Plainly, there was a genuine feeling among his sources that Bernard of Tremelay's behavior at Ascalon had been foolish at best and at worst simply greedy.

No other writer covered the events in such depth, making William of Tyre's judgment hard to interrogate. The secrets of Bernard of Tremelay's heart left the earth as his corpse was hoisted above the crumbling walls of the city into which he had led his men. But could he really have imagined he could defeat an entire city with just forty men?

In 1154 the Templars remained a vital component in the kingdom of Jerusalem's military capability. Other than at Ascalon they maintained their discipline on the field, their rule insisting that commands were to be obeyed unerringly and that martyrdom was preferable to flight. Yet at the same time it also seems clear that while obedience and discipline within their own command structure was tight, the same was not necessarily true when it came to fighting with others. Templars owed allegiance to no one but God, the master and the pope. Neither kings nor patriarchs had any formal command over them, and though their able services were sought and willingly given, in the end the Templars were ultimately free from any effective oversight. They defended the idea of Christendom and the honor of Christ, but how they did so was technically a matter for their own instinct and judgment.[18] For the most part, this made them an extremely agile and useful elite fighting force. At times, however, their independence made them dangerous, and they came to be suspected as much as they were admired by the secular rulers with whom they had to share the field of combat.

8

"Power and Riches"

THE VIZIER'S SON had escaped from Egypt, but people had been trying to kill him ever since. In the early hours of Saturday, May 29, 1154, he fled Cairo, leaving through the massive, fortified, rectangular towers of the city's Victory Gate with a small party of family members, their few remaining friends and as much treasure as they could carry from the royal palace. For the eight days that followed they were harassed relentlessly by nomadic Arab tribesmen armed with bows and swords, who chased their little convoy as it hurried toward the dusty hills flanking the Valley of Moses, near the ancient city of Petra. They were heading north to take refuge in Damascus, where Nur al-Din might protect them, but their chances of arriving there unharmed seemed distressingly remote. Every hour of daylight brought a fresh round of attacks.[1]

The vizier's son was called Nasr al-Din. He and his father, known as Abbas, had good reason to run. Behind them they left Cairo spattered in blood. Days earlier the two men had successfully conspired to kill the Fatimid caliph, al-Zafir, as revenge for his attempt to remove Abbas from his post. The assassination had triggered the violent deaths of several of the caliph's brothers, a steward of the royal household, at least one man-servant and a substantial number of Egyptian soldiers.

This was not the first murder that Abbas and Nasr al-Din had committed, but it was certainly the most spectacular. Abbas was the caliph's chief minister, the highest political position in the land. Nasr al-Din, meanwhile, was the caliph's best friend, confidant and, so the rumors went, lover: an extremely handsome young man with whom the caliph spent his days carousing in the palace and nights roaming the city streets in disguise.[2]

The killing of the caliph had been arranged in order to extend the father's power and erase the son's mounting notoriety as a sodomite. In the end it achieved neither. The caliph was lured at night to Nasr al-Din's house, near Cairo's sword market, and cut to pieces before being thrown down a well. The following day the palace was gorily purged—but even by the Fatimids' bloody standards, this was a step too far. Al-Zafir was the supreme spiritual and political leader of the dynasty to which every Ismaeli Shi'ite in the world owed their allegiance: a man, in the words of William of Tyre, whom "the Egyptians are accustomed to cherish and revere as a supreme divinity."[3] His death sparked rioting in the streets of Cairo and invited the governor of Upper Egypt, Talai ibn Ruzzik, to march on the city and proclaim a military takeover. Instead of seizing command of the caliphate, Abbas and Nasr al-Din had been forced to run for their lives.

Abbas was not happy about the manner in which they had been compelled to leave Cairo. For one thing, his horoscope had warned him against leaving town on a Friday. His consternation was well placed, for on June 7, as his party made their way through the desert outpost of al-Muwaylih, having finally (or at least momentarily) outrun their Arab pursuers, they were ambushed by a party of Christians.

To the Templars and their companions, the sight of Nasr al-Din and Abbas's caravan train was undoubtedly alluring. Usama ibn Munqidh, the cultured Syrian man of letters, had been in Cairo as a guest of the vizier at the time of the bloodbath and had been forced to take flight with the killers. He was riding with Nasr al-Din and later recalled that their group included horses, camels, slaves, wives and treasure looted from the palace. Nasr al-Din's horse was beautifully tacked, with a valuable quilted saddlecloth embroidered with nearly a pound of gold thread.[4] These were not just important Muslims, they were juicy prey, loaded down with booty, and the Christian patrolmen fell upon them with glee.

Usama ibn Munqidh described the ensuing confrontation as a battle, but it seems rather to have been more of a trouncing. Some of the Egyptians were butchered; others were captured and relieved of their treasure and their wives. Templars on patrol were formidable opponents: organized, well drilled and merciless. Those who could run from the onslaught did so, bolting for the hills and leaving their spare horses to gallop away wild. It was a wise choice. When the dust cleared, Abbas lay dead, along with another of his sons, Husam al-Mulk. Nasr al-Din was swept up and led away as a prisoner, probably to Gaza, the closest Templar castle. The family's fall had been swift and painful. Back in Cairo the new vizier, Ibn Ruzzik, was recovering the corpse of the murdered caliph and preparing to give him a decent burial.[5]

Nasr al-Din's encounter with the Templars was sensational enough to be spoken about in England, where the acidic court chronicler and arch-deacon of Oxford Walter Map recorded a lively account of the young man's scandalous adventures.[6] Map took special interest in the Templars' role, as did William of Tyre. Both men heard and recorded versions of the same story: having been ambushed and then imprisoned by the Templars, Nasr al-Din responded not by resenting his captors, but by seeking to impress them. It was said that while he was in prison he turned to the Frankish faith, asking "to be reborn in Christ," and imploring his guards to teach him the Western alphabet and the first tenets of Christian belief.[7]

Neither of the two most informed Islamic chroniclers mentioned this supposed conversion, and Walter Map's account involves such an obvi-ously embroidered, didactic and romantic version of the tale that it is hard to know what if any part is based on fact. Nevertheless, the essential version of the story as it reached Europe in the later 1150s held that when Nasr al-Din was taken into Templar custody he proceeded to renounce his faith with the ambition of saving his neck.

Unfortunately he had badly miscalculated, as he so often did. The Templars were not a missionary organization. They may have been God's soldiers, but their purpose was not to bring enemies into the loving arms of Christ; it was to fight and kill them. They scorned those of their own number who flirted with abandoning the faith, even under duress. (A Templar brother known as Roger the German who was captured fight-ing near Gaza around this time was forced by his Muslim captors to raise his finger and recite the *shahada*, "There is no god but God, Muhammad is his prophet." On his release Roger was expelled from the order.)[8] More than this the Templars were pragmatists. Their mission was lofty, but the world in which they operated was messy. In the context of the long war they were fighting, Nasr al-Din was not a potential soul saved so much as a wanted man and a valuable prisoner.

The politics of Fatimid Egypt were well known to those who lived and operated in the region, and Nasr al-Din's captors quickly realized there were men in Cairo who would wish to bring him to account: men who were prepared to pay handsomely for the prospect of revenge. To the Templars, this fact outweighed all others. So after holding Nasr al-Din for "a long time," they opened negotiations to sell him back to his enemies.[9] A price of sixty thousand pieces of gold was agreed and after only a short delay Nasr al-Din was collected by Ibn Ruzzik's agents and taken back to the scene of his crimes, shackled and caged and carried through the desert by camel.

The chronicler Ibn al-Athir wrote that Nasr al-Din remained silent for the duration of his journey back to Cairo. Only when faced with the city gates did he open his mouth, reciting a short verse reflecting on his misfortunes: "Yes, we were once living there but / Accidents of fate and stumbling chance destroyed us."[10] Walter Map wrote that Nasr al-Din clung boldly to his newfound Christian beliefs, and ended his days tied to a stake and shot to death with arrows. Map was a man whose pen kept up with his colorful imagination, and in telling this story he deliberately echoed the hagiographies of Saint Edmund the Martyr and Saint Sebastian. Other writers agreed that Nasr al-Din was taken by a mob of citizens and ripped apart before his broken corpse was hung from a cross on the huge, round stone towers of Cairo's Zuwayla Gate. "The people literally tore him to pieces bit by bit with their teeth," wrote William of Tyre.[11] Whatever his fate, few would have been sorry to see him go.

+

By the middle of the 1150s the Templars had spread far and wide across the Latin Christian states in the Holy Land. They were a relatively small force—perhaps fewer than one thousand knights in the three remaining crusader states, although their numbers were multiplied by several times as many sergeants and auxiliary troops in the form of Syrian light horsemen, or turcopoles, whom the order hired as mercenaries in time of need. They had plenty to keep them busy. Letters and chronicles of the time made casual reference to the Templars' business: a raid here, a skirmish there, men lost in battle or imprisoned in enemy jails, battalions provided to royal armies for military adventure and prisoners taken to raise valuable funds for the order's ongoing mission. A letter written in 1157 to Pope Adrian IV was typical. After a passage bemoaning the capture of a number of knights, including the master, Bertrand of Blancfort, the letter went on to describe in cheerful terms a raid that the Templars had conducted on a Muslim wedding party. Two hundred and thirty "pagans" had been put to flight, the pope was proudly told. He was assured that every one of them was either taken prisoner or "slain by the sword." Despite the gratuitous violence described (or perhaps because of it) the letter opened by hailing the Templars as the new Maccabees, defenders of those living under or being persecuted by the infidel.[12]

The center of operations—the seat of the master, seneschal, marshal and draper—remained the Temple complex in Jerusalem. By the mid-twelfth century the order had made it well and truly their own. A sense of the Temple's grandeur was captured by Theoderic, an intrepid German pilgrim who humbly described himself as "the dung of all monks," who visited the Holy Land between 1169 and 1174. In his account of his journey Theoderic described the Templars' headquarters, which he called the Palace of Solomon, in considerable detail, and his account gives one of the most vivid snapshots of its appearance:

> Like a church it is oblong and supported by pillars, and also at the end of the sanctuary it rises up to a circular roof, large and round and also like a church. This and all its neighboring buildings have come into the possession of the Templar soldiers. They are garrisoned in these and other buildings belonging to them. And with stores of arms, clothing and food they are always ready to guard the province and defend it. Below them they have stables once erected by King Solomon. They are next to the palace and their structure is remarkably complex. . . . A single shot from a crossbow would hardly reach from one end of this building to the other, either in length or breadth.
>
> Above them the area is full of houses, dwellings and outbuildings for every kind of purpose, and it is full of walking places, lawns, council chambers, porches, consistories and supplies of water in splendid cisterns. Below it is equally full of wash rooms, stores, grain rooms, stores for wood and other kind of domestic stores.
>
> On the west, the Templars have built a new house, whose height, length and breadth, and all its cellars and refectories, staircase and roof, are far beyond the custom of this land. Indeed, its roof is so

high, that, if I were to mention how high it is, those who listen would hardly believe me. . . . There too they have founded on the edge of the outer court a new church of magnificent size and workmanship.[13]

The Temple was not the only thing about the order that impressed Theoderic during his travels. "It is not easy for anyone to know how much power and riches the Templars have," he wrote. "For almost all the cities and villages, which were once frequent in Judea and had been destroyed by the Romans, they and the Hospitallers have captured, and they have built castles everywhere and garrisoned them with soldiers. This is in addition to a great many properties they are known to possess in lands abroad."[14]

One of the very first things pilgrims saw on arriving in the Holy Land were the Templar castles on the road from Jaffa to Jerusalem. Two of the most prominent among them were Castel Arnald, constructed by the patriarch and citizens of Jerusalem in the early 1130s (during the reign of King Fulk) and handed over to the Templars shortly afterward, which protected a point where the road narrowed as it entered the mountains; and Toron des Chevaliers (also called Latrun), which guarded another mountain pass. European travelers would have noticed that these differed sharply from the castles they knew from home, where a central tower built on a mound of earth called a motte was usually enclosed by a perimeter wall, forming an area called a bailey, in which outbuildings were placed. In the East, Templars tended to build or garrison enclosed, heavily defended courtyards with practical rooms such as refectories, chapels, chapter houses and sleeping quarters built directly into the walls. These thick and functional walls surrounded a courtyard that was both a cloister and a training ground.[15]

Smaller Templar outposts could be found to the east of the Holy City on the road to the river Jordan, where Jesus was baptized and pilgrims traveled in large numbers to bathe and pray. Particularly notable on this highway was a tiny but striking tower, about thirty feet on each side, known as Maldoim, or "the Red Cistern."[16] Wherever pilgrims went, the Templars went, too. Wherever the order built, they often marked their properties with a distinctive logo, carved into the stone: a triangular shield with an upside-down T bisecting its top half.[17] Fortresses and watchtowers bearing this distinctive logo could be found guarding the routes throughout the kingdom of Jerusalem, county of Tripoli and principality of Antioch.

The ports of Haifa and Acre were, like Jaffa, popular disembarking points for pilgrims. The Templars had a house in Acre close to the seashore, which Theoderic thought "very large and beautiful." Since Acre was much larger and more centrally located on the coast than Jaffa, this was becoming the order's most important supply point, where shipments of men, money and equipment would arrive from European ports.[18] Outside the walls of the city, Templar castles could be found at notorious danger spots. Where the coastal road below Haifa narrowed to a pass that was vulnerable to attack by brigands, the order maintained a tower on a sandstone ridge known as Destroit (Districtum), in reference to the strait through which the road wound. Further inland, placed strategically on the intersection between the roads connecting Jerusalem with Tiberias and Acre with Baisan, was a larger fortification called La Fève (or al-Fule). This was a sophisticated and well-provisioned outpost: Theoderic noted that it was built on a natural pool, from which a mechanical wheel was used to draw water.[19]

La Fève, taken over around 1172, was one of the biggest castles raised in the twelfth century. At a hundred yards by one hundred and thirty yards, it could hold hundreds of troops and horses: an ideal place to gather men ahead of battles and to police a road that ran off to four major crusader-held cities. In the 1180s an Arab writer would call La Fève "the best castle and the most fortified, the fullest of men and munitions and the best provided."[20] Hyperbole was also lavished on Le Chastellet, built at enormous expense high upstream on the river Jordan, above the Sea of Galilee. Arab rulers cast envious glances at this menacing enclosure, noting that its walls, built from great stone slabs, were more than twenty feet thick.[21]

In the county of Tripoli, the Templars manned one of their mightiest castles anywhere in the world, directly abutting the shore and the town wall in the small coastal settlement of Tortosa. The order was invited to build at Tortosa by William, bishop of Tripoli, in response to devastating raids by Nur al-Din. Although the castle was damaged by an earthquake

✝ Templar Castles in the Latin East ✝

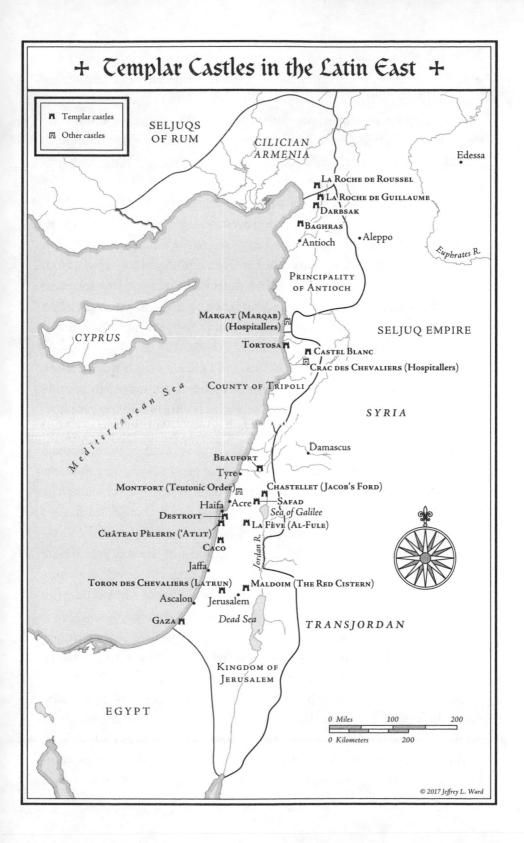

Legend:
- ♦ Templar castles
- ♠ Other castles

SELJUQS OF RUM

CILICIAN ARMENIA

Edessa

La Roche de Roussel
La Roche de Guillaume
Darbsak

Baghras
Antioch
Aleppo

PRINCIPALITY OF ANTIOCH

Euphrates R.

CYPRUS

Margat (Marqab) (Hospitallers)

Tortosa

Castel Blanc
Crac des Chevaliers (Hospitallers)

SELJUQ EMPIRE

SYRIA

COUNTY OF TRIPOLI

Mediterranean Sea

Damascus

Beaufort
Tyre
Montfort (Teutonic Order)
Haifa · Acre
Destroit
Château Pèlerin ('Atlit)
Caco
Jaffa

Chastellet (Jacob's Ford)
Safad
Sea of Galilee
La Fève (Al-Fule)
Jordan R.

Toron des Chevaliers (Latrun)
Ascalon
Gaza
Jerusalem
Maldoim (The Red Cistern)

Dead Sea

TRANSJORDAN

KINGDOM OF JERUSALEM

EGYPT

0 Miles 100 200
0 Kilometers 200

in the early thirteenth century, it remained a fortification of intimidating scale and heft, with eleven towers built into a double wall, giving it the appearance of a crown. Along with Tortosa came rights in the nearby tiny island of Ru'ad (Arwad); some way inland lay another ominously massive fortress, Castel Blanc (Safita), which belonged to the order from around the same time, in the early 1150s.

As Edessa had fallen before the Second Crusade and had not been recovered, the crusaders' northernmost possessions were in Antioch, itself under regular attack. Here the Templars' main focus was their watch duty in the Amanus Mountains. The brothers monitored foot traffic from mountainside towers at Baghras, Darbsak and La Roche de Roissol, peering through arrow slits in the fortifications and ensuring that the right sort of visitors made it through the mountains without molestation, and the wrong sort did not.

Together, this grid of castles and towers defended both the northern and southern hinterlands of the Latin states, and attempted to provide some measure of security at the most sensitive points in between. A small elite force of several hundred knights inhabited these fortifications, backed up by a larger number of sergeants, support staff, hired mercenaries, servants and slaves. All of them were ultimately supplied by the large and growing infrastructure of Templar houses in Europe, which by the 1170s was turning the Order of the Temple into a global organization.

Meanwhile, in Aragón, Castile-León, Navarre and Portugal the Templars were busy knitting themselves into the fabric of the holy war. By the late 1150s they had been established in the Spanish peninsula for three decades, and had built up a large portfolio of fortresses and properties granted to them by the monarchs fighting the Reconquista.

The most enthusiastic patron in the region was Afonso Henriques, Count of Portugal, who had as a young man declared himself a brother to the Templars, suggesting that he had at some time formally become an associate member of the order. He was generous with his gifts. The first castle the Templars held in Portugal was their fortress at Soure, which, as we have seen, the ambitious ruler had bestowed on them as early as 1128, in the first decade of their existence. Soon the order was adding to it. During the 1140s Afonso Henriques had fought his way south, reclaiming Muslim territory around the valley of the river Tagus. In 1144 the local Templars helped him attack the town of Santarém, a former Roman settlement that had been under Islamic rule since the eighth century. Afonso Henriques put an end to that, conquering the city and expelling its Muslim population. For their help in this assault the Templars were awarded the proceeds of all the churches in the newly Christianized town.

Three years later they traded Santarém for an even greater prize. Between July and October 1147, a Portuguese army assisted by seaborne troops from England, Scotland, Frisia, Normandy and Flanders heading for the Second Crusade in a fleet of more than one hundred and fifty ships descended on Lisbon, besieging it for seventeen weeks, smashing the city's walls and gates with battering rams, siege towers and trebuchets, then running amok in the streets for several days and massacring the garrison of the citadel in contempt of an oath they had sworn to let the men live.

The conquest of Lisbon was a huge boon for Afonso Henriques. Within a decade he had managed to secure for Portugal the status of a kingdom. To assert his Christian credentials he created a bishopric in Lisbon, endowing it with the churches in Santarém that he had awarded to the Templars. This was not the slight it seemed: as compensation the new king gave the Portuguese Templars the fortress of Cera and the right to found the town of Tomar, to use as their religious headquarters. Gifts continued to flow well into the thirteenth century. In Aragón the order was also thriving. By 1143 Alfonso's eventual successor, Ramon Berenguer IV, had come to terms with the Templars in the matter of their recompense for giving up their claim to one third of the kingdom. The order was secure in a string of vast fortresses, perhaps the finest of which was Monzón, a Muslim-built hilltop stronghold by the river Cinca that was all but siegeproof, and which the Templars extended until it was the equal of any castle in the Holy Land. The order was fighting in his armies, laying siege to cities and castles on Ramon's behalf and being generously recompensed for their troubles, in the form of estates and properties that both supported their local war efforts and contributed to the Templars' wider, institutional wealth. Crusading in the Spanish peninsula was every bit as much a combined effort between military orders and kings as it was in the more famous outposts of the east. It had its own regional flavor and relations between individual rulers and masters varied according to politics, personality, and circumstances. All the same, as crusading matured from the Atlantic to the Dead Sea, it was clear to the middle of the twelfth century that the Templars were at the heart of it.

9

"Troubles in the Two Lands"

KING AMALRIC OF JERUSALEM was a struggler. He spoke with a stammer, which made eloquent conversation a chore. He ate sparingly yet still grew so fat that his blubbery pectorals hung down to his waist like an old woman's pendulous breasts.[1] He found it hard to charm his courtiers, who thought him taciturn and devoid of small talk, and consistently lost his pious battle to resist the sin of fornication, sharing his bed with married and unmarried women alike.

Most of all Amalric struggled with the infernally complex demands of ruling Jerusalem: holding together the disparate Christian lands of the East in the face of increasingly sustained attack from his enemies, who were gathering force under the regional leadership of Nur al-Din. This was a fight waged on several fronts, against adversaries in Egypt and Syria who were gradually finding coherence, confidence and purpose. Amalric was a competent king: one Muslim writer admired his "bravery and subtle cunning, the likes of which the Franks had not seen since they appeared in Syria."[2] But during the decade he governed Jerusalem his kingdom grew steadily less stable, and at times this brought him into open conflict not only with the Muslim rulers of Syria and Egypt, but with his own men.

When Amalric was crowned king on February 18, 1163, he was twenty-seven years old. His brother Baldwin III was eight days dead, having succumbed at the age of thirty-three to a bout of fever and dysentery that had worn him down over several months. William of Tyre suspected foul play, blaming a Syrian Christian doctor from Antioch named Barac for giving Baldwin toxic health pills. Experiments after the king's death appeared to back this up, for the pills, when mixed with bread, were potent enough to kill a dog. Whatever the case, the king died in Beirut and a solemn procession brought him home to Jerusalem for burial. Both Baldwin's funeral and Amalric's coronation took place at the Church of the Holy Sepulchre.

The transition in kingship unsettled the Christian barons of the Holy

Land. Baldwin had married a thirteen-year-old, Agnes of Courtenay, a few years earlier. She was only seventeen at the time of his death, and had borne no children. There was not much to dispute in Amalric's succession. All the same, there were grumblings among the major lords of the realm about his fitness for the job. When the new king wrote to Louis VII seven weeks after his coronation, boasting that his accession had been tranquil and well supported, he was slightly glossing over the ambivalent reception he had received from some of his peers.[3] He was more truthful in his admission that the troubles facing his newly inherited kingdom were severe, and that "Christendom in the East is greatly depleted and under more pressure than usual."[4] Earthquakes had damaged castles and other buildings in Antioch over the previous summer, and Nur al-Din's forces were now threatening to raze everything that nature had failed to destroy. Reynald of Châtillon, Prince of Antioch, one of the toughest nobles ever to arrive in the Latin states and a brutally firm ruler of his principality, had been taken prisoner and was rotting in Nur al-Din's dungeons. Christian authority in the north was crumbling, while Nur al-Din's power was increasing. The fearsome atabeg was beginning to close in on his ultimate strategic goal: uniting all of Syria under his rule, then taking over Egypt by fomenting a coup against the Fatimid rulers of Cairo, or conquering it outright.

Throughout the 1140s and 1150s Nur al-Din had steadily expanded his authority out of Aleppo and into neighboring cities and states. He claimed the overlordship of Mosul in 1149, following the death of his brother; in 1154 he ousted the ruler of Damascus. The lands that once made up the county of Edessa were all subdued and under his control by 1164. For the first time since the crusaders had arrived in the Holy Land, Syria was united, while Fatimid Egypt was nearly bankrupt. It had been paying tributes to the Christian kings of Jerusalem ever since the fall of Ascalon in 1153, and the randomness of dynastic succession meant that it was ruled by a series of weak, young caliphs. It was ripe for conquest.

The connection of Egypt and Syria was as worrying a prospect for the Christians as it was an enticing one to Nur al-Din. Joining the two states would encircle the Christian coastal territories with a common enemy in the north, south and east. The fracture that had for decades pitted Sunni Seljuq Turks against Shi'ite Fatimid Egyptians was crucial to the crusaders'

ability to carve out and maintain their kingdom. It was widely understood to be the duty of every Christian king of Jerusalem, Amalric included, to see that this did not happen.

In 1163 the master of the Temple was Bertrand of Blancfort, a toughened
veteran of the wars of the East. Bertrand had been elected as the sixth Templar master in 1156, following the death of Andrew of Montbard. He had
provided military assistance to Baldwin III on several occasions and at great
personal cost. In June 1157 he was caught up in a humiliating military defeat
at Banyas in Antioch. In the course of this ambush, Baldwin had been
forced to run away from the battlefield and many prominent Franks had
been taken prisoner, including the king's marshal, Odo of Saint-Amand, the
powerful Lord Hugh of Ibelin and Bertrand himself.

William of Tyre described Bertrand as a "religious and God-fearing
man."[5] His experience as a prisoner of Nur al-Din suggests he was also a
man hardened by war. After the defeat at Banyas, Bertrand had been
taken to Damascus as part of a shameful convoy. Knights were tethered
two to a camel. Each camel bore an unfurled banner decorated with the
scalps of dead men, hanging from the lance by their hair. Prisoners of the
highest status like Bertrand were permitted to ride alone on horseback
in their mail vests and helmets, but they too were forced to carry a grisly
standard as they rode.[6] Bertrand was held prisoner in Damascus until 1159.
When Amalric was crowned king of Jerusalem he had been out of prison
for nearly four years. He was committed to placing the Order of the Temple at the service of the crown of Jerusalem, but he was wary of putting his
men forward to fight a combined force they had no hope of defeating.

The Templars' first clash with Nur al-Din was surprisingly successful.
In the autumn of 1163 information reached the Christians that Nur
al-Din was resting his armies at La Boquée (Buqaia) in the county of
Tripoli. An ambush was planned, apparently at the instigation of two
high-ranking lords from the West: Godfrey Martel, brother of the Count
of Angoulême, and Hugh "le Brun" of Lusignan, both of whom were visiting the Holy Land on pilgrimage.

Godfrey and Hugh were men of considerable status. It is highly likely
that they had been in contact with Bertrand of Blancfort from the moment of their arrival. Certainly by the autumn they knew the Templars
in Tripoli, for when they attacked Nur al-Din at La Boquée, Godfrey

and Hugh chose as their commander in the field a Templar knight of high rank and serious repute. His name was Gilbert of Lacy.

In 1163 Gilbert of Lacy was the preceptor, or regional commander, of the Templars in the county of Tripoli. Probably in his fifties, he had spent much of his adult life in England, picking his way through the turbulent politics of the Anarchy. He had sided with Henry I's daughter and named heir, the Empress Matilda, in her bitter succession struggle against her cousin King Stephen. One chronicle of the time, known as the *Gesta Stephani*, called Gilbert "crafty and sharp," saying he was "careful and painstaking in every action of war."[7]

What was more, Gilbert had a long history of involvement with the Templars. During the Anarchy he had donated a manor to the order at Guiting, a valuable, fertile spot between Gloucester and Oxford in the low, green Cotswold hills. When the fighting was over and Matilda's son had been crowned King Henry II, Gilbert had judged his political career to be complete. In 1158 he had resigned his lands to his son and joined the order. He was a high-status recruit: a nobleman, a warrior and a charitable Christian prepared to abandon the comforts of life at home to lead the armies of the faithful. Two years later he was in Paris as a member of a Templar delegation that stood as guarantors of a peace between the new English king and Louis VII of France. (The extensive continental lands held by the Plantagenet kings of England made for near-constant disputes with the rulers of France.) For an active soldier, though, there was only one place to be. By 1162 Gilbert had traveled to the Holy Land and taken command of the Templars at Tripoli, and he was now leading the ambush on Nur al-Din's forces at La Boquée.

The raid caught Nur al-Din's forces totally unawares. "Many of his men were made prisoners, and still more perished by the sword," wrote William of Tyre. "In despair of his life he fled in utter confusion. All the baggage and even his sword were abandoned. . . . But the Christians, laden with spoils and manifold riches, returned victorious to their own land."[8] The triumphalism of William of Tyre's account reflects the success of the ambush. But in truth it was only a small setback for Nur al-Din.

In 1164 the Templars were once again involved in a direct assault on Muslim forces. This time the focus was in the south. Almost as soon as Amalric was crowned he began planning for a series of campaigns against

Egypt, launching his first attack within months of his coronation. Like Nur al-Din he recognized the Fatimids' weakness and aimed to take advantage of a bitter power struggle taking place in Cairo between the vizier, known as Shawar, and a portly, flamboyant Kurdish general called Shirkuh, portly and flamboyant, with cataracts in his eyes, who was attempting to foment rebellion and overthrow the Egyptian government on behalf of Nur al-Din. Amalric was aware that Egypt was a very wealthy land, which could provide lucrative plunder as well as a source of territory to be offered as reward to loyal noblemen who served the Crown well. He saw that security around Ascalon and Gaza would be much improved if the crusader kings could lay claim to the Nile Delta cities farther down the coast, such as Damietta, Rosetta and Alexandria. He also knew trade links with the rest of the Mediterranean would be considerably boosted if any or all of these could be taken.[9]

+

The Templars joined Amalric's second march against Egypt in July 1164. The king headed toward the edge of the Nile Delta and besieged Shirkuh in the ancient city of Bilbays. Amalric and his supporters devoted several months to the siege, managing to drive out Shirkuh and claim a financial reward from Shawar for their efforts, but by October they nevertheless had to withdraw without making any important territorial gains. Worse, while they were throwing their efforts into war in the south, Nur al-Din had taken the opportunity to attack them in the north. As soon as Amalric left for Egypt, Nur al-Din charged deep into Antioch and on August 10 he engaged a very large Christian force led by Raymond III, Count of Tripoli, and Bohemond III, Prince of Antioch, at the battle of Artah. The Christian army was said to have included twelve thousand infantry and six hundred knights, of whom more than sixty were Templars, but this time Nur al-Din had the upper hand. He destroyed the crusaders' army, killed a huge number of knights, took all of their leaders prisoner, then marched on through Antioch and seized the important coastal city of Banyas. Here was an important lesson for Amalric. The Christians could either attack Egypt or defend their territories from Nur al-Din's aggression in the north; they struggled when they attempted to do both.

Bertrand of Blancfort saw this all clearly. Like his predecessors he wrote letters and sent envoys to Louis VII of France, hoping to excite him about the prospect of leading another crusade. In October and November 1164 the master sent two letters outlining the uncomfortable drawbacks of fighting on two fronts in the Holy Land at the same time. This was more than a matter of military theory. At Artah the Templars had lost sixty knights, many more sergeants and a great number of Syrian turcopoles, whom they hired to bolster their numbers in the field. These were significant numbers of men who would be costly to replace. Only seven Templars had escaped.

"Most serene king, the troubles in the two lands of Antioch and Jerusalem are too numerous to enumerate," Bertrand wrote in his first letter. He followed up a month later, complaining about the miseries inflicted by Nur al-Din while he had been occupied in Egypt. "Although our king Amalric is great and magnificent, thanks to God," wrote Bertrand, "he cannot organize a fourfold army to defend Antioch, Tripoli, Jerusalem and Babylon [i.e., Egypt] . . . but Nur al-Din can attack all four at one and the same time if he so desires."[10] Bertrand demonstrated a stark understanding of the calculus of warfare in the East. It was largely about numbers. Nur al-Din had them. The Franks, for the most part, did not.

Here, then, were the first signs of a breach between the expectations of the king and the capabilities of an overstretched military order. Bertrand concluded his letters to Louis by telling him that he was sending a personal messenger to explain what he could not put in writing. This messenger, Walter Brisebarre, was "honest and careful in God's business and has been involved in these events from beginning to end." Was this a coded way of telling the king that he could expect a truth less varnished from his messenger than he was prepared to put in writing? We cannot know. Yet it was clear in the autumn of 1164 that while the Templars were prepared to assist Amalric, their master had reservations about the prospect of lasting success while he was on the throne.

✝

On January 30, 1167, Amalric marched out of Ascalon once more on his way to Egypt. This time the Latin army was on a mission to halt another assault on Cairo by Shirkuh, aimed at expelling the Fatimids from the city. Amalric was riding south at Shawar's request, having been offered an enormous bounty as the price of success. In return for Christian assistance, Shawar had promised to pay the king of Jerusalem 400,000 dinars. By weight this was roughly 3,750 pounds of solid gold. With strategic necessity now allied to the promise of cold, hard cash, Amalric and his men were prepared to endure the hardships of a desert march, through whirlwinds so thick with sand that it was impossible to do anything but dismount from one's horse and lie down until the blinding, abrasive storms raged themselves out.[11] They were also prepared to disregard the fact that Egypt was in a state of acute internal chaos, and in no position to pay the fanciful sum its vizier had promised.

Once again the Templars rode alongside the king, although this time the mood must have been strained, as the previous year Amalric had hanged twelve of the order's brothers in a fit of rage. In 1166 a high-status nobleman and royal associate called Philip of Nablus* had joined the order following the death of his wife, donating a significant number of land-holdings in Transjordan for the Templars' use. Transjordan (also known by its French name, Oultrejourdain) was a highly volatile region on the fringes of Egypt, over which Amalric and Nur al-Din were vying for control.[12] Such a major transfer of property in a sensitive part of the kingdom had to be signed off by the king. Amalric had agreed but he regretted his decision almost immediately.

One of the assets Philip brought to the order was a fortified desert cave. Amalric gave the Templars specific instructions that it was to be defended at all costs but straightaway the order had lost it to Shirkuh's men. In William of Tyre's short and hostile account of the episode, there is a distinct whiff of treachery. According to his chronicle (informed and slanted by his close personal relationship to Amalric, who employed him as tutor to his son), a Muslim force attacked the cave, and the king duly raised "a goodly company of knights" to travel down the river Jordan and fight them off. Before they arrived, however, news reached them that the Templars had surrendered. "Disconcerted and infuriated . . . the king caused about twelve of the Templars responsible for the surrender to be hanged from a gallows."[13]

---

* Philip of Nablus was a future master of the order, holding command from 1169 to 1171.

Nevertheless, the Templars supported the campaign of 1167 and rode with the royal army. An inconclusive clash, known as the battle of al-Bebein, occurred on March 18 some distance south of Cairo. Amalric's army of Christian knights, backed by a contingent of "worthless and effeminate Egyptians" whom William of Tyre called "a hindrance and not a help," were ranged against Shirkuh's much larger forces, whose heavy cavalry numbered in the thousands.[14] The battle broke up in confusion, with casualties on both sides.

Amalric pushed on. Following Shirkuh, he marched back down the Nile Delta, heading northwest, and besieged the famous maritime city of Alexandria, blockading it with a fleet and bombarding it with trebuchets from the land. The siege of Alexandria was abandoned only when Shirkuh sued for peace, agreeing to leave Egypt and to accept that Shawar would remain as vizier at Cairo, with a Christian garrison controlling Alexandria. In the short term this seemed a reasonably successful outcome. But within a year, the peace had collapsed, further poisoning relations between the king and the Templars.

+

In 1164 a Templar knight called Geoffrey Fulcher had made his way east from Paris and landed at Acre. Geoffrey was the preceptor of Jerusalem, a veteran of twenty years who traveled extensively between Europe and the Latin states and had close links with Louis VII of France. As a favor to the French king, Geoffrey had spent his first months back in the Holy Land riding around the pilgrim sites, touching each with a ring. He sent the ring back as a present to the king in Paris, along with letters bemoaning the military disasters that had afflicted the kingdom of Jerusalem, and begging for more men and resources.

Three years later, in 1167, Geoffrey had ridden across the desert on the campaign into Egypt. He was chosen by King Amalric as a leading envoy sent to extract from Shawar firm promises that payment would be rendered for the Christian intervention. Geoffrey rode into Cairo with Hugh of Caesarea, a lord who had been born in the kingdom of Jerusalem, and their experiences in the palace were truly dazzling.

As vizier of Fatimid Egypt, Shawar served under the caliph al-Adid, a young man of about sixteen or seventeen who had endured a dreadfully turbulent childhood. His father had been murdered by Nasr al-Din and Abbas, and his older brother, al-Fa'iz, had ruled briefly before dying as a child. Al-Adid had become caliph in 1160, aged around eleven, but Shawar wielded practical power on his behalf. Although this seemed to suit the caliph, who one Christian chronicler thought led "a decadent life among his girls," supposedly keeping a different concubine for each day of the year, al-Adid was nevertheless revered among his people, who believed he held the sacred power to make the Nile flood.[15]

The Latins were acutely aware of the caliph's prestige, and in treating with the Fatimids they were concerned to extract concessions and guarantees not only from the vizier but also from his master. For this reason, Geoffrey Fulcher and Hugh of Caesarea were sent to Cairo to meet with al-Adid himself and see to it that he would guarantee the promises Shawar had made. Their instructions were that only the caliph's personal word and handshake would do. Their mission took them on an adventure to the heart of the Fatimid caliphate: a place few men and only a handful of Western-born Christians would ever see.

Geoffrey and Hugh called the splendor they had seen on their way to the inner sanctum "unique and after a fashion unfamiliar to our world."[16] To enter the palace complex, they later told William of Tyre, they were led down dark, narrow passageways, hemmed in on all sides by dozens of bodyguards armed with swords. At each doorway stood large sentries, who saluted the vizier enthusiastically as he passed. Led by the palace's chief eunuch, they walked in wonder through vast courtyards surrounded by walkways, marble columns and sparkling fish pools where exotic birds sang strange songs. Eventually they came to the caliph's chamber, which was hung with curtains embroidered in pearls. They watched Shawar throw himself three times to the floor at the base of a golden throne and kiss the handsome, sparsely bearded young man's feet, while privy councillors and eunuchs looked on from the wings.

The Templar preceptor, incongruous amid all this bowing and scraping in his stark white uniform emblazoned with a red cross, offered the caliph none of this genuflection. Quite the opposite. He looked on as Hugh spoke to the leader of the Shi'ite world as though he were a slippery hawker in the Caesarea bazaar. Ignoring the eunuchs and the fawning officials, Hugh browbeat al-Adid into repeating, word by word, the terms of King Amalric's deal with Shawar, before demanding that it be symbolically honored by an ungloved handshake.

The caliph's flunkies stared in astonishment, but al-Adid performed his duty and sent Geoffrey and Hugh on their way. A military and political pact between the Fatimid ruler and the Christian states had been sealed with the most intimate ritual the young caliph may ever have performed. Its validity rested in large part on a handshake between a caliph and a Templar. But would the caliph stand by his word? And equally important, would the king of Jerusalem?

The deep personal investment of the Templars in the pact and their holdings in Gaza must have been factors the following year when relations with the king hit a new low. In October 1168, giving little warning even to his closest confidants, Amalric reneged on his agreement with Shawar, "mustered the forces of his realm and went down into Egypt."[17] He carried out a lightning siege at Bilbays, butchering the civilians, then headed straight for Cairo, at which point he camped outside the gates of the city and waited for the vizier to make him another large offer to leave.

The offer came: this time it was two million pieces of gold—a sum so vast it was almost laughable. Amalric withdrew his troops, put out his hand and waited for the money to start raining. It was a calamitous error.

Had Bertrand of Blancfort or Geoffrey Fulcher been present, perhaps they might have cautioned Amalric to place less trust in the vizier and think twice before undermining their agreement with the caliph. On this occasion, though, they were not consulted. They had opted to have nothing to do with this foolish and impolitic mission, which broke an agreement they had brokered in good faith. They had firmly declined to join the invasion: a serious snub to the king, and one that can only have been made after a great deal of reflection and prayer.

While the king of Jerusalem sat and waited for the first installment of his golden ransom, Shawar contacted his former enemy, Nur al-Din, and begged his assistance in driving off the greedy Franks. Shirkuh was duly packed off for Cairo, gathering a large army along the way. He managed to elude Amalric in the field and placed his own troops in front of Cairo in such numbers that it became plain there was no hope for the Christians of driving them away. By January 2, 1169, Amalric realized he had no choice but to break camp and return to Jerusalem. He had not collected two million gold pieces. He had not conquered Cairo. He had merely slaughtered the civilian inhabitants of a Nile Delta city, sat around for a few weeks and gone home.

This was only the beginning of his troubles. Once Amalric had left Egypt, Shirkuh took the simple, deadly step that he had awaited all along. He invited Shawar for a friendly parlay in his tent outside Cairo. At the appointed time for the meeting he slipped away and went for a walk along the water. Shawar arrived, expecting a convivial discussion. Instead, he found Shirkuh's men waiting to kill him. They fell on him, wrestled him to the floor, stabbed him several times and cut his head off. Shirkuh returned from his walk, sent word to the caliph that he wished to visit him in Cairo and marched in, announcing himself the new vizier. After little more than a heartbeat and the severing of a head, Egypt had fallen into Nur al-Din's hands. Its annexation by Sunni Syria was under way and the days of the Fatimid caliphs, who had sat in their exotic palaces in Cairo for more than two hundred and fifty years, were about to draw abruptly to an end. The Templars' worst fears had been realized. They faced encirclement by a unified and emboldened enemy. It was much as Bertrand of Blancfort and the preceptor Geoffrey Fulcher had predicted in their doom-laden letters to France.

And this was not all. Within months, the resurgent forces of Islam would have a new leader more dangerous than Nur al-Din, wilier than Shirkuh and no less ferocious than Zengi. He would cause the Franks in general, and the Templars in particular, more trouble than they had experienced in seven decades of occupation. To his admirers he was "one of the great heroes, mighty in spirit, strong in courage and of great firmness, terrified of nothing."[18] To those who suffered the worst of his wrath he was "the rod of [the Lord's] fury," sent "to rage and exterminate the obstinate people."[19]

His name was Saladin.

10

"Tears of Fire"

THE DUST KICKED UP by the march of Saladin's massive army was enough to turn the brightest morning into a shadowy, dusklike gloom. "At times the earth groaned under the squadrons," wrote his admiring secretary Imad al-Din, "and the heavens received with joy the particles of dust." In full flight it must have been a truly daunting sight: twelve thousand professional cavalrymen galloping ahead of three times as many volunteers. Saladin's close associates boasted among themselves that when the Franks of Jerusalem (whom they regarded as a "pollution" and "the filth of the dregs of humanity") received word that the horde was approaching, they would quake in terror and wish "that they had never been born."[1]

During the decade that followed the fall of Cairo, Salah al-Din Yusuf ibn Ayyub, a charismatic, politically agile, relentlessly ambitious and extraordinarily self-assured soldier, made himself the preeminent leader in the Islamic world and the founder of a dynasty of sultans known as the Ayyubids, after Saladin's father. Saladin had been a leading commander on Shirkuh's Egyptian campaigns, not least because he was the old man's nephew. But the circumstances of his birth did not alone account for his successes, and before long the nephew had overtaken his uncle's achievements. Within a year of the city's capitulation Shirkuh came down with a quinsy—a serious abscess in his throat brought on by an enthusiastic session of gorging on rich meats. He died abruptly on March 22, 1169, and Saladin seized control.[2] He swiftly switched the city's allegiance from the Shi'ite Fatimid caliph al-Adid to the Sunni Abbasid caliph in Baghdad, then began a campaign that aimed to bring every major Islamic territory in Egypt, Syria and Mesopotamia under his personal command.

Naturally, Saladin's ambition brought him many enemies, among them Nur al-Din, who had sponsored Shirkuh's coup in Egypt and who saw himself, not some upstart Kurd, as the man who was destined to rule Syria and Egypt together. Saladin had other ideas. Through a combination of incisive military leadership, relentless campaigning, sheer personal charisma and a healthy dose of good fortune, between 1169 and 1177 Saladin expanded his range of influence out of Egypt to become the most important threat to other Muslim rulers in Aleppo, Damascus and Mosul. In 1171, on the death of al-Adid, the Fatimid caliphate was formally abolished. Saladin then set about consolidating Sunni rule under his own direction across Egypt.

Attempts to kill him by stealth, plot or on the battlefield all failed. Nur al-Din died in 1174, and Saladin immediately stepped into his shoes. He first forced his way into Damascus, organizing a swift coup against those trying to press the claim for leadership of Nur al-Din's eleven-year-old son. He had the boy removed from the city and then married Nur al-Din's widow to give himself a veneer of legitimacy. Having secured Damascus, the following year he launched a campaign against Nur al-Din's family and followers farther north, defeating them decisively in battle and gaining the towns of Homs and Hama. Respectful entreaties to the Abbasid caliph in Baghdad now paid off, and in recognition of his rising reputation and conquests he was granted the title "sultan of Egypt and Syria" in 1175. In the late 1170s he continued to press Nur al-Din's relatives and former associates in Aleppo (which eventually fell to him in 1182) and Mosul (which eluded him). By the start of the 1180s he was unquestionably the dominant figure across the Islamic Levant.

Saladin rooted his claims for authority on a carefully manufactured image of himself as the true defender of the faith, whose commitment to jihad trumped that of all others. A generous, pious, witty and (relatively) humane ruler, he was also an extraordinarily resourceful judge of men and their motivations, whose character as much as his deeds left a deep impression on those around him. His close followers Ibn Shaddad and Imad al-Din, who wrote detailed accounts of Saladin's life and achievements, seldom had to strain their pens or their imaginations in search of encomia for their master.

Central to their praise was Saladin's boundless desire to face down directly the accursed Franks who occupied Jerusalem and held sway in the lands of Tripoli and Antioch. "The Jihad, his love and passion for it, had taken a mighty hold on his heart and all his being, so much so that he talked of nothing else, thought of nothing but the means to pursue it, was concerned only with its manpower and had a fondness only for those who spoke of it and encouraged it," wrote Ibn Shaddad.[3] This was more than simple piety. Saladin's greatest insight, which directed much of his career, was the understanding that fostering unity in the fragile Islamic world (and cementing his personal authority over it) could best be achieved by rallying his fellow Muslims under the banner of holy war against an unbelieving enemy.

Saladin's naked ambition for conquest and his powerful anti-Christian sentiment pulled him inevitably toward war with the Latin kingdom. The only real surprise was that it took him the better part of a decade to make his first move. But when it came, the Templars were among the first ranks lined up against him.

✝

Following Saladin's seizure of power in Egypt in 1169, relations between the Templars and the king of Jerusalem were fraught. Bertrand of Blanc-fort died that year, and the order's central convent elected Philip of Nab-lus as his successor. Philip may well have been imposed on the Templars at the king's request, although it is equally possible that his election was a deliberate move on the part of the order to repair relations with the Crown. Either way, it was successful in the short term, for under Philip's command the Templars returned to Egypt, accompanying a (futile) royal invasion. But Philip's loyalty to the Crown outweighed his commitment to the order. By 1171 he had resigned his post to lead a royal embassy to the Byzantine emperor Manuel Comnenus in Constantinople. On his way to the imperial court he died.

Philip was succeeded by another apparent Amalric loyalist, Odo of Saint-Amand, who had also seen royal service as the marshal of Jerusalem—a top-ranking post in the king's military command. Presum-ably the desired effect of Odo's election was to keep the Temple in line with royal policy. This time it was less successful. Odo's actions as leader suggested an aggressive, impulsive temperament, and he came quickly to value the independence of the order above any obligation to serve as Amalric's puppet.

The first crisis of Odo's leadership involved a mysterious splinter Shi'ite sect called the Assassins, whose members practiced the art of spectacular public murder. The Assassins' headquarters were at Alamut Castle in Persia, but from the 1130s they also held pockets of territory in the mountains of Syria and occupied a number of castles between the county of Tripoli and principality of Antioch, high in the Nosairi Mountains. By Amalric's reign, William of Tyre believed there to be sixty thousand Assassins, whose ten fortresses were supplied by the taxes of all the villages nearby. The Assassins probably derived their name from their fondness for hashish, which they used before launching terrorist attacks on major public figures in the Near and Middle East. "If there happens to be a prince who has incurred the hatred or distrust of this people the chief places a dagger in the hand of one or several of his followers," wrote William of Tyre; "those thus designated hasten away at once, regardless of the consequences of the deed or the probability of personal escape."[4] Writing later, the German chronicler Oliver of Paderborn heard that "the Assassins and their chief, the Old Man of the Mountain, had the custom of casting knives against the Christians to cut off the lives of those who care for the business of Christianity."[5] In truth the Assassins were more concerned with other Muslim leaders, which was why Amalric sought a peaceful accommodation with them against their common Sunni enemies in Syria and Egypt.

To that end, in 1173 the Old Man of the Mountain sent an envoy to Amalric's court. The envoy was known as Abdallah, and according to the heavily slanted report given by William of Tyre, he was "wise and eloquent, skilled in counsel and fully instructed in the doctrine of his master."[6] But Abdallah's eloquence was not at all to the liking of the Templars, as one of the deals he had been sent to propose would have ended a lucrative source of income to the order.

The Assassins and the Templars were near neighbors and knew each other well. The Templars' large castle at Tortosa was very close to the Assassins' strongholds in the Nosairi Mountains. The nearest of these, La Coible (Qala'at al-Khawabi) was little more than five miles away from Templar territory. This was not a mortal threat in itself: the Assassins did not generally bother to target the order, as Templars were by their

nature replaceable, and individual brothers mattered far less than the order as a whole.[7] In fact, they paid the Templars some two thousand gold
bezants every year to be left alone. Canceling this arrangement was
thought by William of Tyre to be high on Abdallah's list of negotiating
points, and he found Amalric willing to concede the issue for the sake of
broader security. The king proposed a deal and sent the Assassin back into
the mountains under armed guard, with letters of protection to finalize
terms with his leader.

William of Tyre recorded what happened next. "Under the escort and
the guide . . . provided by the king, Abdallah had already passed through
Tripoli and was about to enter his own land," he wrote. But as Abdallah
approached the mountains, he was ambushed. Walter of Mesnil, a Templar knight recognizable by the fact that he had only one eye, along with
other unnamed accomplices in Templar uniform, "rushed the party with
drawn swords and killed the envoy."[8]

The news of this appalling treachery sent Amalric into a fury. He
summoned his barons and ranted to them that "the royal authority seemed
to be put to naught and undeserved infamy [was] brought upon the good
faith and constancy of the Christian profession."[9] He sent two barons,
named by William of Tyre as Saher of Mamedunc and Godechaux of
Turout, to "demand from the master of the Templars . . . that satisfaction
be rendered to the king and the entire realm for this sacrilegious outrage." He wanted Walter of Mesnil's one-eyed head on a platter.

Unfortunately, Odo refused to cooperate. He claimed it was a matter
of internal discipline, most likely pointing to the papal bulls granted in
the 1140s, which placed the order outside royal jurisdiction and made it
answerable only to the pope. Odo said he would impose penance on Walter and send him to Rome for judgment. "He forbade anyone, on the part
of the pope, to lay violent hands on the brother," wrote William of Tyre,
noting that the master also "added other remarks, dictated by the spirit
of overweening arrogance with which he was possessed." These must
have been fairly full-blooded if William, who enjoyed sprinkling his
chronicle with colorful anecdote wherever possible, deemed them unfit
for public consumption.

The expectation that Odo would be a pliable Templar master thus died together with Abdallah. Amalric eventually arrested Walter of Mesnil when he sent two knights to confront the master at Sidon: they pulled Walter out of the Templar house where he was being kept and dragged him in chains to Tyre, where he was left to rot in a royal dungeon. Yet that was as much as the king dared do. Somehow he restrained himself from imposing harsher measures on the order at large, exercising moderation that William of Tyre found surprising.[10] Instead, relations were left to smolder. The Templars remained committed to the defense of the Latin states, but it was a role they performed on their own terms, with a fierce sense of independence from royal oversight.

In 1179 there was an attempt, at a general synod of the Western Church in Rome known as the Third Lateran Council, to put checks on the military orders' freedom from authority and oversight, in the religious sphere if not the military and diplomatic. (It is possible, although not proven, that William of Tyre himself led this effort; he attended the council as archbishop of Tyre and representative of the Eastern states.) The truth was that the Templars and Hospitallers performed an increasingly essential role that no one wished to hamper unduly. And this would become starkly apparent in the 1180s, as the threat posed by Saladin grew, making it more evident every day that internal divisions were less important than the simple struggle for survival.

+

In December 1177 a messenger staggered north from Jerusalem heading to the castle of Harim, near Aleppo. He was "mutilated and lacerated," bloodied, weak and barely alive, but he clutched a precious cargo: an open letter to all the Christian faithful, describing events that had taken place a few weeks previously, between Ramla and Ibelin at a place called Mont Gisard (Tell al-Safiya). It was written by Raymond, the acting master of the Hospital in Jerusalem, where medical facilities had been stretched to the limit. This was a serious matter in itself. The Hospital was as palatial as the Temple: situated directly opposite the Church of the Holy Sepulchre, it had eleven wards and between one and two thousand beds for the sick and wounded.[11] It took a major crisis to overwhelm this institution—and that was exactly what Raymond's letter described. A Christian army including many Templars and Hospitallers had clashed with a force of Saladin's warriors. Thousands had been killed on both sides, and many who survived were now gravely injured, their wounds being patched up by the brothers of the Hospital and their souls by the prayers of the faithful. "Marvelous are the works of the Lord," wrote the Hospitaller. "Blessed is he who is not shocked by them."[12]

The battle of Mont Gisard was the first major armed showdown between Saladin and a Christian army and its timing was no accident. The kingdom of Jerusalem had been weakened in 1174 by the sudden death of King Amalric from dysentery he contracted during a siege at Banyas. The jolt caused by Amalric's death was made very much more serious by his succession. His son, Baldwin, was thirteen years old. He was also suffering from leprosy—a grim, devastating disease that began with numbness in his limbs as a child and which would advance to cause him great pain, grotesque disfigurement, blindness and long periods of incapacity. Leprosy was a relatively common curse of the Latin kingdom: so well known that the leper hospital situated just outside Jerusalem had been incorporated as the Order of Saint Lazarus in the 1140s and its volunteers had taken on military functions in the manner of the Hospitallers and Templars. There was little the order could do beyond offer palliative care as over a period of years the bacteria numbed the sufferer's extremities and secondary infections caused fingers, toes and parts of the face to rot, lesions to appear all over the body and the eyesight and respiratory system to fail. The only uncertainty was how long it would take the victim to die.

For three years Saladin watched the leper king Baldwin IV struggle to take control of his kingdom, while he himself secured his position as sultan of Syria and Egypt and maneuvered against Nur al-Din's partisans in Aleppo and Mosul. By 1177 he was ready to test the strength of the crusader states. In the late summer he assembled a large army in Egypt, marched into Frankish territory, bypassed a small Christian army scrambled to stall him at Ascalon and advanced rapidly toward Jerusalem itself, burning homes and villages as he went. King Baldwin IV, sick and scarcely able to lead in person, was supported by a number of high-ranking Christian lords, including the pugnacious former Prince of Antioch, Reynald of Châtillon, whose decade and a half of captivity in Aleppo had only fostered an unbreakable desire to make war on the forces of Islam. In November 1177 Reynald had recruited Master Odo of Saint-Amand and eighty Templar knights on the king's behalf, and together they sallied out of Gaza on a mission to pursue Saladin's massive army and force it out of the kingdom and back to Egypt by whatever means possible.

The Templars riding in battle formation were a formidable sight. Their original Latin Rule had by now been expanded with dozens more clauses composed in French, which spoke not to religious routine but to the hard business of fighting on the plains and mountain passes of Syria and Palestine. Templar hierarchy was strictly defined, with the master supported by officers including the seneschal, who was his second-in-command, the marshal, who played a leading role when the Templars rode in the field, and regional commanders, the preceptors, with responsibility in individual cities or lands. The turcopolier was responsible for recruiting and organizing Syrian-born light cavalry. The draper was a quartermaster, ensuring that the knights and sergeants were properly equipped with the weapons, armor, uniforms, bedding, camping equipment and everything else they needed in the field.

Discipline was valued above all else. The knights rode behind their piebald flag and their rule laid out strict mandates for behavior when camping, riding in a column in the field or launching an attack. Templars were bound by their vow of obedience: to God, to the rule and to their military superiors.

Templar knights were forbidden to load baggage or saddle their horses without an explicit order from the marshal. When any such order was given, the brothers were expected to respond with a brisk affirmative, "De par Dieu!" meaning "On behalf of God!" before straightaway doing their duty. On the march the knights rode in columns while their squires walked in front, carrying their lances. On night marches the whole column proceeded in near-total silence, and even during daylight hours only very necessary discussions were permitted. Leaving one's place in the column was discouraged. During combat, breaking ranks was utterly forbidden for any reason except to help a fellow brother whose life was in immediate peril. The brothers rode wordlessly and determinedly onto the battlefield, breaking their silence only when the trumpet blast ordering a charge was sounded: then they would ride together while singing Psalm 115.[13]

> Not to us, Lord, not to us,
> But to your name be the glory,
> Because of your love and faithfulness.

To scatter or flee in the face of danger was considered a disgrace. Any brother who did so would have his horse taken from him and would be marched back to camp on foot—a particularly humiliating punishment for a knight, since his whole martial identity rested on his horsemanship and ability in the saddle. Even a brother who was maimed to the point of incapacity was forbidden to leave his squadron without express permission from his commander. Retreat from the battlefield was prohibited until the army in which the Templars were fighting was defeated and the piebald banner lay on the ground, its bearers dead around it.

This willingness to be the last men standing was what made the Templars such a valuable component in any army assembled by the kings of Jerusalem. It was why the late Amalric had allowed them such latitude, despite the order's defiance of his authority and policy. And it was why Amalric's son, the leper king Baldwin IV, and Reynald of Châtillon took eighty of the Gaza Templars to Mont Gisard when Saladin's armies were spotted there in the winter of 1177.

Judging by an account written by the thirteenth-century scholar and chronicler Abu Shama, Saladin's army was not expecting much resistance from the Franks. The sultan allowed his soldiers to fan out across the countryside, pillaging villages rather than holding together. "Fortune was against them," noted Abu Shama grimly, and he was not mistaken.[14] The Latin army, bearing before them the Jerusalem fragment of the True Cross—their most holy relic—appeared unexpectedly and bore down on the Muslims in the manner they knew best: the heavy cavalry charge, in which horsemen threw themselves headlong at the enemy with each mail-clad warrior deployed as fast and as hard as was possible. Performed properly, this was a dreadful sight and Muslim armies were traditionally poor at defending against it. The Frankish knights were heavily outnumbered, but they came at Saladin's men with righteous fury.

Abu Shama waxed poetic in his account of the Frankish charge: "Agile as wolves, barking like dogs . . . they attacked en masse, like the burning of the flame."[15] They picked their moment beautifully, waiting for Saladin to attempt a tactical rearrangement of the troops he had close to hand: attacking with purpose at a moment of confusion.[16] A hard fight ensued. Saladin's nephew and emir (or noble commander) Taqi al-Din "fought valiantly with the sword and the lance," but around him men were falling by the hundred. "Many of his brave officers found martyrdom," wrote Abu Shama, "and went to taste the joys of the eternal home."[17]

Saladin fought surrounded by his elite personal bodyguard of Mamluks: slave soldiers abducted from the Asian steppe and raised as warriors from childhood, who wore yellow silk over their breastplates, matching the sultan's battle dress of the same color. "Always surrounding their lord, they endeavor with one accord to protect him from harm, and they cling to him even unto death," wrote William of Tyre.[18] Like the Templars, these men were defined by their dedication to self-sacrifice, supreme martial training and refusal to leave the battlefield, even when faced with overwhelming defeat. "It often happens that while the rest make good their escape by flight, nearly all the Mamluks fall."[19]

Mont Gisard saw a great slaughter of Mamluks. Those who sought to flee the battlefield were chased for miles across a treacherous marsh known as the Swamp of Starlings, flinging away their armor and weapons to make a faster escape. One hundred valuable breastplates were collected by the Frankish trophy hunters who picked over the battle site after the fighting was done. Saladin escaped death but he was humiliated and suffered a miserable journey back to his base in Egypt, battered by vile winter weather, his men pining for their lost friends and abandoned food and drink, and his caravans robbed by Bedouin tribesmen on the road to Cairo. It was one of the worst military defeats Saladin ever suffered, and it lived with him for many years: an indignity that demanded revenge.[20]

The eighty Templars of Gaza who fought at Mont Gisard shared in the glory of a bloody victory, which the acting master of the Hospitallers reported as "a happy victory over an incalculable horde of Saracens."[21] Few knew that they had also contributed to the triumph by means of cunning of the first order. Two sons of Saladin's nephew Taqi al-Din were present at the battle. One of them, Ahmad, "a very handsome youth" who had only just come into a full beard, managed to shoot a Latin knight with an arrow but was killed shortly thereafter, attempting a second charge on enemy lines.[22] The second, whom Abu Shama named as "Chahinchah," had a rather more complicated story. Prior to the battle he was approached by an agent in Damascus who was secretly working for the Templars. This covert asset had managed to convince Chahinchah that in return for a pledge of allegiance King Baldwin was prepared to install him as ruler of Cairo in his great-uncle's place.

Despite the obvious improbability that the leper king would be in a position to turn Saladin out of Egypt, let alone control its succession, this plot had proceeded some way and the Damascus agent had presented the duped son with forged documents seeming to authorize his coming over to the Christian side. Chahinchah had agreed to a personal meeting, but was only led up the garden path. He was taken to a "solitary place" and handed over to the Templars, who chained him up and took him away as a captive. He was held by the order for more than seven years and eventually used to leverage the release of Christian prisoners from Saladin's own dungeons. For all their well-publicized military competence, the Templars also brought sophisticated intelligence to the theater of conflict. In 1177 they made use of both in helping peg back Saladin as he made his first serious probe into the Frankish kingdom.

But the sultan of Syria and Egypt was a not a man accustomed to swallowing defeat.

✝

A new crusader castle was under construction on a hillside beyond the river Jordan, between Huleh and Lake Tiberias, in a place called Jacob's Ford. Ground was struck in October 1178 on the order of the king of Jerusalem, and in the six months that followed foundations were dropped and walls "of marvelous thickness and adequate height" had begun to

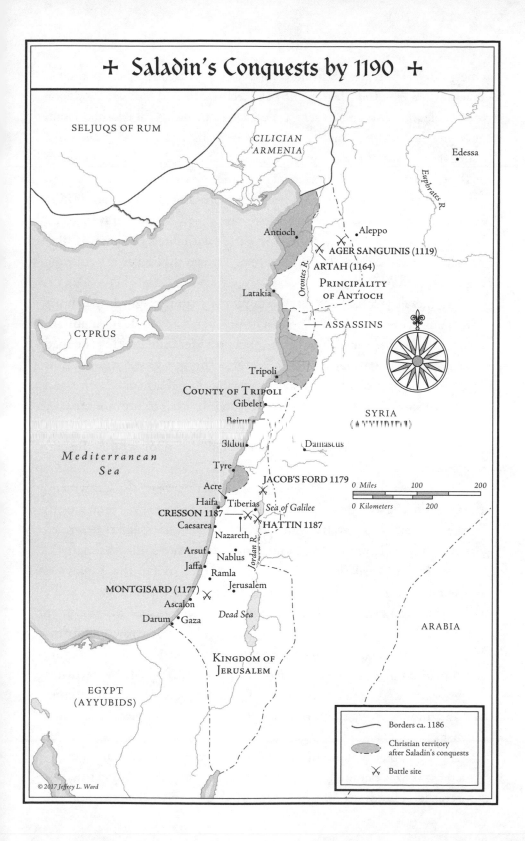

✝ Saladin's Conquests by 1190 ✝

SELJUQS OF RUM

CILICIAN ARMENIA

Edessa

Euphrates R.

Antioch

Aleppo

✗ AGER SANGUINIS (1119)

ARTAH (1164)

Latakia

PRINCIPALITY OF ANTIOCH

Orontes R.

✝ ASSASSINS

CYPRUS

Tripoli

COUNTY OF TRIPOLI

Gibelet

SYRIA (AYYUBID)

Beirut

Mediterranean Sea

Sidon

Damascus

Tyre

Acre

JACOB'S FORD 1179

Haifa

Tiberias

Sea of Galilee

CRESSON 1187 ✗

Caesarea

Nazareth

HATTIN 1187

Arsuf

Nablus

Jordan R.

Jaffa

Ramla

MONTGISARD (1177) ✗

Jerusalem

Ascalon

Dead Sea

Darum • Gaza

ARABIA

KINGDOM OF JERUSALEM

EGYPT (AYYUBIDS)

0 Miles	100	200
0 Kilometers	200	

Borders ca. 1186

Christian territory after Saladin's conquests

✗ Battle site

© 2017 Jeffrey L. Ward

emerge.[23] The position of this new fortress was both strategic and divine. It was where the Old Testament patriarch Jacob had stopped to divide his people into two bands, sent a message to his vengeful brother, Esau, and wrestled with an angel of God, who dislocated his hip.[24] Muslims called it the Ford of Lamentations, and held it in just as much veneration as the Christians. To this ancient significance was added a more practical value: Jacob's Ford was an important river crossing on the road linking Acre and Damascus, and was part of the much longer caravan route known as the Via Maris, connecting Egypt with Mesopotamia. It ultimately formed the critical central stage of a global trading artery running from China to Morocco.

The pass at Jacob's Ford was a troublesome spot, plagued by bandits and highwaymen, who launched lightning raids from their mountain hideout above the Zebulon Valley, robbing travelers and making the road near unpassable without a military escort. The new castle would allow for a permanent protective garrison, securing the passage of pilgrims and traders through Christian Palestine. It also promised to provide security from potential attacks out of Damascus, which lay just a day's march away—a particularly pressing need in the light of Saladin's foray the previous year.

The castle at Jacob's Ford was a joint project between the Crown and the Order of the Temple. Throughout the winter of 1178–79 stonemasons worked on raising the walls, while patrols of Frankish soldiers defended the road and hillsides from bandits, ambushing and killing as many as they could. By April 1179 the castle was coming along: three quarters of the foundations had been dug, a perimeter wall with five gates and a single tower built and an oven and a water cistern installed. Workmen continued busily toiling with spades, hoes and wheelbarrows, shuttling back and forth between large piles of stone, lime and pebble.[25] As other parts of the kingdom were in need of attention, Baldwin IV returned to Jerusalem and handed the half-built fortress over to Odo of Saint-Amand and the Knights of the Temple to defend, complete, adapt and furnish.

There was plenty more work for them to oversee: a second, outer perimeter wall was planned, as was a moat and gatehouses connecting two courtyards. Hundreds of workmen lived alongside the knights and sergeants who formed the military garrison: masons, architects, black-smiths, sword makers, armorers and Muslim prisoners, who were put to work as laborers.[26] Some fifteen hundred men were camped around the fortress complex. The order was able to fund this huge operation, which included building as well as defending the finished castle, thanks to the financial rights it had been granted in the land around it. If the castle at Jacob's Ford was not structurally complete, it was at least amply provided for and ready to begin serving its purpose.[27]

Within weeks of the raising of the piebald banner over the castle, its partial defenses were tested. The construction could scarcely have been concealed from Saladin, who rightly viewed the fortress as a provocative attempt to shift the balance of power in the region between Christian Acre and Muslim Damascus, and a basic affront to religious propriety: the infidels were building on ground that was held sacred to all good Muslims. Almost as soon as King Baldwin and his entourage left Jacob's Ford, Saladin brought an army to Banyas—well within striking distance of the castle and in the laconic words of Ibn al-Athir, he "remained a while and dispatched raids into Frankish territory."[28] Ibn al-Athir heard that the sultan made an offer of sixty thousand dinars for the castle to be demolished peacefully. The offer was rebuffed.[29] So in the days leading up to Trinity Sunday, May 27, 1179, he prepared to compel the Templars to abandon the castle by force.

According to William of Tyre, Saladin moved troops to the castle walls and "without intermission sent forth dense showers of arrows and harassed the besieged within its walls with repeated assaults."[30] This was an exploratory mission, and it ended after only a few days when a Templar called Renier of Mareuil shot an arrow from behind the dusty, unfinished battlements and managed to fatally wound one of Saladin's most senior emirs. Saladin withdrew. But he did not stay away for long.

Realizing that they could not leave Odo and the Templars to defend the building site indefinitely, Baldwin's council scrambled to get troops back to Jacob's Ford via Tiberias. Marching through the countryside surrounding Banyas they could see smoke rising everywhere from villages burned by the sultan's army. Urgent action was needed.

On Sunday, June 9, the king's cavalry split from the foot soldiers accompanying them. The horsemen riding ahead of the rest of the army encountered a group of Saladin's forces out on a plundering expedition and bested them in a skirmish. Both sides fell back. The Latin knights pursued the scattered plunderers for several miles, but before long they ran into Saladin himself with a far more substantial body of men. Suddenly, fortunes were reversed. After a brief attempt to stand and fight, the Latins now found themselves fleeing for their lives. Some scattered into the mountains, others made for the nearby castle of Beaufort. King Baldwin IV, who was carried with the army, was helped to safety by his personal bodyguard, but around two hundred and seventy Christian horsemen were captured and taken prisoner. Disastrously for the Templars, this included their master, Odo of Saint-Amand.

Odo had spent time in prison before, having been locked up in Damascus in the days of Nur al-Din along with Bertrand of Blancfort. William of Tyre held him in particular contempt, deliberately misquoting the book of Job to describe him as "a wicked man, haughty and arrogant, in whose nostrils dwelt the spirit of fury."[31] Without being very specific about the nature of Odo's mistakes, William blamed him for the rout and wrote that "many people laid at his door the loss and never-dying shame of this disaster."[32] In truth Odo was hardly alone in his failings. Ibn al-Athir noted that the other prisoners taken at Jacob's Ford included Balian of Ibelin, "the highest-ranking Frank after the king," as well as Hugh of Galilee, lord of Tiberias, the master of the Hospitallers "and other notorious knights and despots." The prisoners were taken from the battlefield as Saladin returned to Banyas, many to face long and miserable spells awaiting ransom.

For Odo of Saint-Amand, this was the last taste of freedom he would enjoy. "Within the year he died a captive in a squalid prison, mourned by no one," wrote William of Tyre. Imad al-Din was even less sympathetic: "The master of the Templars went from his prison cell to the dungeon of hell."[33] The order later reclaimed his body in exchange for a Muslim leader whom they were keeping prisoner. It was a sorry end for the eighth master of the order.

Imad al-Din recorded Saladin's reaction when he first learned that a fortress was being built at Jacob's Ford. The exact words are more likely a literary invention than direct, reported speech, but they capture his characteristically matter-of-fact approach to wartime leadership. "To those who told him that the castle, when constructed, would control weak points on the Muslim frontier and make safe passage very difficult, Saladin replied 'Let them finish and we will then go and destroy it from top to bottom so that no trace of it remains.'"[34] At the end of the summer of 1179 that is precisely what he set out to do.

Saladin's men arrived from Banyas on Friday, August 24, with all the tools for a siege. They brought trebuchets capable of battering the fortress with large stones, cut trees for timber and stripped vines from the ground to build protective shields to keep the trebuchet operators safe from crossbow bolts aimed from the castle walls.[35] They also bought ladders, digging equipment and fire.

Knowing that reinforcements were likely to arrive quickly, Saladin planned for an attack that would last no more than a week. The siege began around 5 P.M. with a full-blooded assault on a barbican (a fortified outer gatehouse) close by the main castle walls. Professional soldiers were accompanied by enthusiastic hangers-on, who had joined up for excitement, booty, the glory of jihad or all three. According to Ibn al-Athir, "The fighting was furious and intense. One of the common people in a ragged shirt climbed the barbican of the fort and fought on the wall when he reached the top. Others of his comrades followed him. They were joined by the troops and the barbican was taken."[36] By now it was nightfall, and Muslim guards were stationed at the newly taken barbican to watch for any unexpected attack. Fires were lit outside each of the castle's entrance points to ensure that no one could pass in or out unnoticed.

Hemmed in, the Templars inside the castle decided to lock down their position and remain behind the walls, a good twenty feet thick, to await relief. They had no shortage of food and arms, and could sit for weeks if required. As they settled in for rescue, they must have expected to hear the hellish thud of a trebuchet bombardment beginning. But instead came another, equally discouraging sound: the scrape of shovels as a gang of Aleppan miners began to dig a tunnel under the fortress's single great tower in the hope of collapsing it.

For two days the miners dug, until they had produced a tunnel some twenty yards below ground and around three yards wide. This was deemed sufficient to bring down the tower. The wooden props inside were duly set ablaze. But nothing happened. The great beast of a tower simply stood there. As Monday morning dawned, Saladin directed his entire supporting workforce to the task of putting out the fires inside the mine: a dinar was offered to every person who brought a pail of water to throw into the tunnel.

By Tuesday, word had arrived that relief was on the way. The Templars inside the fortress had only to wait a few days and they could be hopeful that the besiegers would be driven off.

Saladin was also aware of time pressing, and he sent his miners back into their charred tunnel to dig as they had never dug before. For two more days they labored, widening and deepening the shaft beneath the tower. On Wednesday night fires were lit again, and this time the subterranean turbulence was more than the vast walls of the tower could bear. As the sun came up on Thursday morning a section collapsed to wild applause outside.[37] Saladin's gleeful men rushed in. Baldwin's relieving army was still several hours' ride away and what had seemed like a straightforward waiting game was now a last stand.

Behind the collapsed wall the Templars had piled wooden barricades and tents. When the tower fell, a draft of scorching air was sucked into the fortress, searing everything and everyone it touched and starting a fire that spread panic through the castle.[38] Saladin's men rushed in, capturing the most valuable Christians and slaughtering without mercy any Muslim apostates and mercenary archers they could lay their hands on.

True to the spirit of their rule, the Templar knights did not go meekly into the hands of their enemies. Saladin's chancellor al-Qadi al-Fadil sent a lavishly overwrought letter to the Sunni caliph in Baghdad describing the suicidal battle fought amid the wreckage of the burning fortress. He described "tears of fire" falling from the crumbling tower and gave his pen full flight in conjuring the horror he had seen. "The purple shades of darkness were replaced by a pomegranate crimson," he wrote. "It seemed like the dawn filled the night, and the sky was lit by other fires than those of the east and west. . . . The fiery breath devoured men and stone, and a sinister voice of catastrophe cried, 'I am talking to you neighbor! Listen to me!' . . . The infidels cried, 'Truly, it is a terrible thing!'"[39]

There was more than poetry in al-Fadil's letter, for he recorded the final moments of the Templar commander as the burning battlements were overrun: "The prince who commanded the place witnessed its destruction and the disasters befalling his friends and companions. When the flames arrived at his side, he threw himself into a hole full of fire without fearing the flames. In burning, he was soon thrown into the other furnace [i.e., hell]."

By the afternoon of Thursday, August 30, the fortress at Jacob's Ford had been taken and the ground lay littered with hundreds of arrows, pathetically abandoned tools and the twisted bodies of the dead, some with their heads split open with sword blows, some with their limbs hacked off. Horses, mules and donkeys that had not died during the assault were rounded up and taken, as were one thousand mail coats from the armory. Some bodies were left for carrion. Others were thrown into the water cistern: a foolish indignity, given the outbreak of disease that swiftly followed in the sultan's army.[40] Once the castle had been stripped of anything worth looting, Saladin fulfilled the dire promise he had made. He stayed in the area until October, by which time "he had demolished the fort and razed it to the ground."[41]

The defeat at Mont Gisard had been well and truly avenged. One Muslim writer of the time called the castle at Jacob's Ford "a nest of misfortune."[42] The poet al-Nashw ibn Nafadha crowed:

> The destruction of the Franks came speedily,
> Now is the time to smash their crosses.
> Had the time of their death not been near,
> They would not have built the House of Lamentations.[43]

Searching for a cause to which to attribute the disaster, William of Tyre looked to the general sinfulness of the Latins. He concluded his description of the debacle at Jacob's Ford with a passage from the psalms: "The Lord their God has departed from them," he wrote in despair.[44]

For a time, it seemed that he was right.

"Woe to You, Jerusalem!"

OR SEVERAL YEARS, the Holy Land simmered. After Mont Gisard and Jacob's Ford, both Saladin and the Franks needed time to recover, repair and consolidate. In the spring of 1180 a two-year truce was agreed, allowing the sultan to concentrate on cementing his power in Aleppo and Mosul and the Franks to deal with the crisis of leadership that spilled out from the declining health of King Baldwin IV. As with all great affairs in the crusader states, the Templars were tightly involved.

First came the eternally difficult task of drumming up support in the West for the underfunded East. The military orders, thanks to their international infrastructure linking profit-making Western houses with the fighting units in Outremer, were a natural conduit for diplomatic relations between the two halves of Christendom. So in 1180 a delegation of Templars was sent to Pope Alexander III in Rome to lobby for the pronouncement of a new crusade. Alexander was not a blind champion of the military orders. In the previous year he had presided over the Third Lateran Council, whose edicts had specifically admonished the Templars and Hospitallers for ignoring the authority of bishops and collecting tithes for their own use, but the brothers who made their way to Rome in 1180 were nonetheless successful in convincing the pope of their great need and hardship.[1] He therefore agreed to throw his weight behind the calls for a new crusade led by one or more of the great kings of the day. The Templar delegation passed his appeal for military assistance jointly to the aging king of England, Henry II, and a new, young king of France, Philip II (later known as "Philip Augustus").[2] The fifteen-year-old inherited his crown in September 1180 after Louis VII died of a stroke, aged sixty. But the turbulence of such a great transition made it hard to direct either king's attention toward the Holy Land. A third great crusade was not yet to be forthcoming.

Although the Templar mission to Rome did not ignite a new crusade, the order did not just sit back and accept their new situation. In

Jerusalem it undertook a bold change in its own leadership. While Odo of Saint-Amand languished in his prison cell the order had no functioning master. Robert Fraisnel assumed the title of "grand preceptor," but he could not be elected as master while Odo lived.[3] Then, when Odo died in prison in 1180 and and his post fell vacant, the Templars of the central convent chose not to promote Robert Fraisnel or indeed any other brother in the East. Instead they voted to hand the leadership to Arnold of Torrolla, an elderly and experienced knight who had spent much of his long career leading the armies of Christ in Aragón. Arnold had been master of Spain and Provence since 1167, proving himself remarkably successful at attracting sponsorship and enriching the order in a difficult corner of Christendom.[4] He had established a reputation beyond his own field of command, for to elect a man of Catalonia to lead the knights in Jerusalem, Tripoli, Antioch and everywhere else besides showed an extraordinary degree of faith in his talent. It also suggested an awareness that the order needed to take advantage of its role as an international organization. In light of the tormented relationship between the Crown and the order under Odo's leadership, Arnold's election was a thoughtful attempt to steer the Templars back to their primary duties and away from disruptive meddling in domestic politics.

It took Arnold more than a year to travel east and take up his post. He began by shaking up the senior leadership. Robert Fraisnel was moved out of his position as grand preceptor and replaced by Girbert Eral, likely a native of Aragón.[5] One of Arnold's first missions was to mediate a dispute between the prince and patriarch of Antioch, a diplomatic effort he shared with Roger of Moulins, the experienced and cautious master of the Hospitallers. Settling disputes between bickering factions of Franks was no doubt wearying work but he must have known it was nothing compared to the challenges that lay ahead.[6]

As soon as the temporary peace with Saladin expired in 1182, a new series of tit-for-tat campaigns began, with the major tussles for control around two important commercial routes: the caravan roads between Egypt and Damascus that cut through Transjordan; and the disputed territory near Galilee around the Via Maris. Saladin framed his attacks on Christian territory and possessions in the language of jihad, for his claim to supremacy in Cairo, Damascus, Mosul and Aleppo rested on his self-hewn image as the scourge of the infidel. Certain Frankish lords played up gleefully to the stereotype he perpetuated. The worst offender was Reynald of Châtillon, who, having given up the title of Prince of Antioch, was now lord of Kerak and remained a dominant political figure in the Christian states. In 1183 Reynald took a flotilla on a looting expedition along the eastern coast of the Red Sea and into the Hijaz—the most holy province of Arabia—inciting rumors that he intended to invade Mecca and Medina and steal the body of Muhammad. Saladin never forgave him for this insolence.

In the early years of his rule, Saladin had spent much more time fighting Muslims who objected to his rule than he had attacking Christians. But in 1182 that began to change.[7] With peace officially broken, he invaded the Christian territories twice in two consecutive summers. In the high summer of 1182 he marched an army across the river Jordan and through Frankish lands south of the Sea of Galilee. Then he tried and failed to besiege Beirut by sea. The following summer the sultan was back, menacing similar territory. A very large Latin army was assembled to repel him, led by Guy of Lusignan, who had married Baldwin IV's sister, Sibylla, and was wielding ever more influence in the kingdom. By refusing to give battle and drawing the Muslims into a running skirmish around La Fève, Guy exhausted Saladin's patience and provisions and forced him to abandon the engagement: a clever tactic, but one that earned him harsh accusations of cowardice from his opponents, including the powerful Raymond, Count of Tripoli. This criticism stung him deeply.

In the heat of 1183, with Saladin's armies now at the fringes of Frankish territory and Baldwin rapidly falling into total incapacity, there were more things to worry about than Guy of Lusignan's hurt feelings. Baldwin's leprosy had rendered him childless, and a decision about the future rule of Jerusalem was badly needed. After some deliberation, the king named as his heir another Baldwin: the infant son of his sister, Sibylla, and her first husband, William of Montferrat. On November 20, 1183, the child was crowned co-king in the Church of the Holy Sepulchre in Jerusalem in a farcical scene described by William of Tyre. The barons of the Holy Land swore their allegiance to the five-year-old Baldwin V, but William wrote that many of them felt deeply uneasy about the fact that although the kingdom now had two monarchs, "since both were hampered, one by disease and the other by youth, [the coronation] was wholly useless."[8]

For precisely this reason the resolution of the succession did little to stabilize the political situation in Jerusalem. Indeed, its main effect was to worsen existing tensions between two of the most powerful noblemen in the realm. On one side was the young king's stepfather, Guy of Lusignan; on the other Raymond, Count of Tripoli, who had served on several occasions as regent, had presided over the young king Baldwin V's coronation and expected to be afforded the preeminence befitting his status. Guy and Raymond's mutual loathing opened a fissure in Frankish politics at an already fragile time, and it would have devastating consequences for the kingdom they both thought it their duty to defend. In May 1185 Baldwin IV died, blind, bedridden and in agony. He was just twenty-four. He was buried beside his father in the Church of the Holy Sepulchre, and seven-year-old Baldwin V was now king in his own right. This solved nothing, least of all the poisonous rivalry between Guy of Lusignan and Raymond of Tripoli, who was appointed to serve as regent for the underage monarch.

The succession of a child not old enough to lift a sword, let alone swing it in anger, had a direct impact on the Order of the Temple. In 1184, with the leprous Baldwin IV nearing the grave, and royal authority accelerating toward a major crisis, Arnold of Torroja's diplomatic skills were called into service on another mission to the West. The aim this time was to persuade a capable adult ruler from one of the great European realms to come east and assume the crown of Jerusalem by election. The Templar embassy of 1180 had failed to entice either Henry II of England or Philip II of France to come to the kingdom's aid. Now the master of the Temple himself traveled back, accompanied by Eraclius, patriarch of Jerusalem, and Roger of Moulins, master of the Hospitallers. Their intention was to implore the monarchs to help prevent a catastrophe in the East: to prove themselves truly Christian kings who would come to the aid of Christ's city and his people in their direst hour of need.

The mission was a failure. In the first place, Henry and Philip had too much at stake in their own realms to risk resigning their crowns. Both were sympathetic but refused the overtures. And it came at a high cost.

Arnold of Torrolla did not even make it to their royal courts, for during the long expedition—an arduous sea and land journey of more than one thousand miles—the master died. The order was compelled to elect its third leader in four years.

The choice they made was fateful. Arnold's replacement, Gerard of Ridefort, a headstrong soldier very new to the order, threw himself with far more energy into the struggles and turmoil of the Holy Land. But as he did so, he, his fellow Templars and the whole kingdom of Jerusalem were hurtling headlong toward their direst moment.

+

Gerard of Ridefort had come to the East from Flanders, or northwest France, arriving by 1175. He knew Arabic and had experience in the highest echelons of secular service, having served Raymond, Count of Tripoli, and been named a royal marshal under Baldwin IV but his introduction to the order of the Temple was the indirect result of a fit of pique: he had fallen out catastrophically with Raymond over a disputed marriage deal. In 1179 the count had promised to marry Gerard to the next eligible daughter of one of his vassals to come onto the marriage market. But when an heiress did become available, Raymond welched on the deal and instead sold the hand of Gerard's intended bride (the daughter of the lord of Botron) to a Pisan merchant called Plebanus, who was prepared literally to pay the girl's weight in gold. Gerard was deeply insulted, believing his honor to have been impugned. The whole situation was made worse by the fact that French-speaking parts of Christendom had little but contempt for Italians. Gerard left Raymond's court in a fury. He entered King Baldwin's service and then, after recovering from a period of illness, joined the Templars. It is possible he was quite seriously ill and that he had sworn a holy oath to join the order if the Lord allowed him to recover. In any case, Templar life suited him, and once he had taken the white mantle, Gerard was rapidly promoted. By 1183 he was serving as seneschal.[9] As second-in-command he was an obvious candidate for promotion to master when Arnold of Torrolla died in 1184. But his selection turned out to be highly controversial.

Almost from the moment he was elected, Gerard divided opinion, thanks to a penchant for bold political action that all too often spilled into rashness. To one writer Gerard was a "happy man!"—a blessed and glorious soldier who devoted his life to martial deeds in the name of Christ. In this view his defining characteristics were his chivalric pride and utter refusal to take a backward step, even when his life was in peril.[10]

Others saw him differently: perceiving not a maverick with the heart of a lion but a grudge-bearing hothead who encouraged others to share his own rash inclinations and led many good soldiers to their deaths.[11] Which view best described Gerard is not easy to say. Certainly he showed none of the instinctive caution that had characterized the conservative military policies of Bertrand of Blancfort, nor the diplomatic subtlety of Arnold of Torrolla, and his temperament led him and the order too often into trouble. Then again, Gerard lived and led in even less easy times. The route to heaven in the 1180s did not seem to be open to the timid.

In late August 1186 King Baldwin V died at Acre. He was only eight, and had reigned as sole king for little more than a year. The Templars escorted the boy's corpse back to Jersualem, where he was laid to rest beside his royal uncle and grandfather in the Church of the Holy Sepulchre in a small but lavishly appointed tomb intricately decorated with acanthus flowers, an image of Christ flanked by angels and small, carved images of dead baby birds.[12] The beauty of the small boy's resting place could not obscure the fact that the kingdom was now entering a genuine crisis of succession.

When young Baldwin V became king, it had been agreed that in the event of his death the next king of Jerusalem should be chosen by a panel that would include the most illustrious rulers in Western Christendom: the pope, the kings of England and France and the Holy Roman Emperor. This high-minded principle looked back to the successful selection of Fulk of Anjou. In theory it had much to recommend it, notwithstanding the fact that none of the electors saw fit to take on the job themselves. Relying on the lottery of succession by birth and familial precedence had landed the kingdom with a leper and a child king; this was no way to defend the holiest realm on earth. Unfortunately, in August 1186, when Baldwin died, the notion of an election was abandoned in favor of a ruthless power grab: a coup that was enabled and to an extent orchestrated by Gerard of Ridefort.

The regency of Jerusalem had been contested for several years between Raymond, Count of Tripoli, and Guy of Lusignan. Baldwin's death provided the opportunity for Sibylla and Guy to settle the rivalry for good and in Gerard they found a willing and uniquely well-placed ally. The Templar master had neither forgotten nor forgiven Count Raymond for the insult he had dealt him by selling off his rightful wife for a pot of gold. Moreover, he had a vital hand in releasing the regal paraphernalia that was essential to Jerusalem's royal ritual.

Rather than wait months for a decision to be ground out by international power brokers, Sibylla, Guy and Gerard decided to pursue Sibylla's personal claim to her father's throne—which meant setting aside the rival claim of her younger sister, Isabella. They convinced Eraclius, patriarch of Jerusalem, to carry out the coronation ceremony before anyone could act to stop them. As a sop to their enemies, they promised that Sibylla would divorce Guy and take a new husband of her own choosing.

A coup of this speed and audacity required practical help, for it relied on Sibylla being able to lay her hands on the sacred treasure required for her coronation. The treasury containing the royal jewels and regalia of Jerusalem could only be opened using three separate keys at the same time. One was held by the patriarch of Jerusalem, another by the master of the Hospital, Roger of Moulins, and the third was in the possession of the master of the Temple.

Gerard and Patriarch Eraclius backed Sibylla's bid for the crown, but Roger of Moulins was far less sure. Gerard concluded that the best way to reason with him was the most direct. On Tuesday, November 11, 1186, with the gates of Jerusalem closed to bar their enemies from entering the city, Gerard and his allies went to Roger's quarters in the Jerusalem Hospital and harangued him, demanding that he hand over his key and submit to the inevitable transfer of power. Roger refused. It was only after a physical confrontation between the two masters that the Hospitaller finally agreed to release his key, which he petulantly threw into the courtyard rather than handing it over civilly.

The coronation could now proceed. As the man who had literally collected the crown from the jewel house, Gerard of Ridefort had a prime position at the ceremony, and he could scarcely contain his glee. When the crown was placed on Sibylla's head he was close to the altar, and he was even closer to Sibylla's devious intentions. After she had been crowned, the new queen was asked whom she intended to take as her king in place of the divisive Guy of Lusignan, who was scheduled very shortly to be divorced from her. To the shock of many gathered in the Holy Sepulchre, she called Guy himself forward, commanded him to kneel before her and placed a second crown on his head.

At her shoulder Gerard of Ridefort put his own hand on Guy's crown and helped settle it. As he did so, he was heard to mutter with satisfaction, "This crown is well worth the marriage of Botron," in reference to the bride that Raymond had taken from him. The Templar master was now the kingmaker. He soon found his place among a hawkish faction at court, constantly advocating aggression as a guiding principle of government, directed toward both the forces of Islam and enemies closer to home. It would turn out to be a deadly combination.

✝

On the night of April 30, 1187, lookouts in Nazareth spotted a number of Saladin's armed men heading past the town on a reconnaissance mission directed at the fortified town of Sephoria (Saffuriya), a few miles to the northwest. With its large square stone castle and the remains of a Roman amphitheater, Sephoria had been earmarked as an assembly point for a Christian defensive army raised by the new king to resist Saladin's increasingly determined forays into the kingdom. For several years the sight of Muslim armies marching through Latin territory, burning crops as they went, had become more and more common, and now here again were the Saracens, a long way over the river Jordan and marching through the heartlands of Christian country.

Guy and Sibylla's controversial accession in the autumn of the previous year had been justified as a means of improving the security of the Latin kingdom. Quite the opposite had followed. The woeful dilapidation of Frankish royal power in the years since King Amalric's death and the confused state of the kingdom would have emboldened any ruler with designs on their lands, but Saladin's bolder forays were also a reflection of his evolving personal attitude toward the Franks. In the early 1180s he had been content to launch periodic raids into specific disputed regions. After 1186 his vision expanded and he began to regard the Latins of the

East not simply as rivals with whom to tussle but as an existential enemy to be cleansed from the earth. Saladin had forged a career by carefully cultivating an image as a purifying zealot, for whom jihad meant everything. He was bound at some point to follow through with his rhetoric. The sultan also fell extremely ill in late 1185: "His life was despaired of and a rumor went round that he had died," wrote his biographer and counselor Ibn Shaddad.[13] Survival seems to have inspired in him a heartfelt desire to destroy his enemies at any cost.

During the winter of 1186–87 the factions supporting King Guy and his rival Raymond of Tripoli were spiraling toward civil war. Raymond's disgruntlement at Guy's naked power grab had evolved into a full-blown attempt to replace the joint monarchs with a pair of his own choosing: Humphrey of Toron and his wife, Isabella—Sibylla's sister. In order to protect himself while he plotted this coup d'état, Raymond had taken the defiant, near-senseless step of making a personal truce with Saladin, allowing him to carry out exploratory missions on his territory. It was under the terms of this agreement that Saladin was allowed to send seven thousand men marching past Nazareth on the last day of April 1187. The force was led by his trusted and experienced Turkish emir, Muzaffar al-Din (also known as Gökböri, or the Blue Wolf). The old soldier shared command with Saladin's trusted son and heir, known as al-Afdal.

Gerard of Ridefort was close to Nazareth on the evening of April 30 as part of a delegation traveling north from Jerusalem to Tiberias with the aim of bringing Raymond to terms with the king. The Templar master had been urging an armed strike on the dissenting count to bring him into line. Guy had resisted and instead a peace conference was scheduled to take place in early May in Tiberias. Gerard was on his way there in the company of Roger of Moulins and Josias, archbishop of Tyre, together with their respective entourages. They planned to collect the powerful lord Balian of Ibelin at the Templar castle of La Fève, from where they would all go on to Tiberias and attempt to bring Raymond as calmly as possible to his senses. As it transpired, they would never get there.

When Gerard of Ridefort learned that Raymond had allowed Saladin's men the freedom to roam across his territory, the master's most combative instincts were stirred. Nazareth was not subject to Raymond's lordship, and its people were not bound by the truce he had negotiated.

Gerard took a hard interpretation of his mandate as leader of the Templars: it was his duty to defend the land.[14] He sent to the nearest Templar garrison at Caco (Qaqun), summoning eighty of the knight-brothers to his side. Roger of Moulins followed gingerly, raising ten Hospitallers, and a further forty knights retained by the king joined them.[15] Instead of continuing to La Fève and Tiberias, they all now made for Nazareth with the aim of tracking down the sultan's forces and putting them to flight.

One hundred and forty knights (the original party and their reinforcements) was a respectably large force considering its hasty muster, but it was dwarfed by the seven thousand men Saladin's generals had under their command. On the morning of May 1 the disparity became horribly apparent as the Templars tracked down al-Afdal and his men to a wooded area at the Springs of Cresson, a natural fountain not far from Nazareth.[16] Gerard now had with him nearly a full complement of the Templars' highest officials: the seneschal Urs of Alneto, the one-time grand preceptor Robert Fraisnel, who was now serving as marshal of the Temple, and the respected brother James of Maillé.[17] They assessed the scene with Roger of Moulins and all decided that a discreet withdrawal was their only option—all, that is, but Gerard of Ridefort.

"Gerard was an energetic knight, but impetuous and rash." This was the verdict of the German chronicler Oliver of Paderborn when describing the Templar master's conduct at the Springs of Cresson.[18] Even given the advantage of a surprise attack, it was vain to believe that a few hundred men fighting against thousands would lead to anything but annihilation. Gerard insisted it was the Christians' duty to charge, "in a desire to defend Christ's inheritance."[19] He taunted the Hospitaller master and James of Maillé for their reticence, sneering that they were cowards.[20]

The English chronicler Ralph of Coggeshall, describing the scene from afar, put into Gerard's mouth a long and florid speech, in which he praised the Templars' disdain for "vain and perishable things" and argued that they were the true inheritors of the Maccabees, who had fought for "the church, the law and the inheritance of the Crucified One."[21] In other words, the red crosses on their white mantles positively demanded that they stand and fight. Ralph of Coggeshall almost certainly conjured the words from his imagination, but he captured Gerard's extreme approach to the norms of twelfth-century chivalry and the idealized mind-set of the order more generally.

Everyone who wore the red cross had sworn to serve the order until the end of his life, to be obedient to the master and to "help to conquer, with the strength and power that God has given you, the Holy Land of Jerusalem."[22] Every single Templar at Cresson had at one stage in his life replied, "Yes, sire, if it please God," when asked if he was prepared to do those things. Now was the time to make good on that promise. Instructed by Gerard to ride against an army perhaps twenty times larger than theirs, they had no choice but to obey. The men crossed themselves. They shouted together, "Christ is our life and death is our reward."

Then they rode madly toward al-Afdal and his horde.[23]

When Bernard of Clairvaux had written his manifesto for the new knighthood in the 1120s, he had implored Templars faced with mortal danger to say to themselves: "Whether we live or die, we belong to the Lord."[24] He told them that going willingly to their deaths in Christ's name was a sure path to salvation. Of course, it was one thing for Bernard to write this, theorizing a thousand miles from the Holy Land and glorifying in a martyrdom he would never himself experience. It was quite another for a band of ninety Templars, called from their castle and told to attack against impossible odds, to swallow down their fear and do it. Yet they did. Each man spurred his horse forward, and the battle fought at Cresson would live long in the crusader mythology.

The cold truth was that of the one hundred and forty knights who rode at the Saracens, some of them Templars and others merely carried along in the madness, only a handful escaped alive. Gerard of Ridefort, who ordered the charge, was badly wounded in the fighting but eventually left the battlefield, accompanied by three of his companions. Fifty to sixty knights died in a shower of their own gore; the rest were taken away to imprisonment and enslavement at Saladin's pleasure. Roger of Moulins, the master of the Hospitallers, who had joined the fray reluctantly, was beheaded, as was the Templar marshal Robert Fraisnel and (it seems) the seneschal, Urs.[25] They did not go to their deaths easily: the Mosuli chronicler Ibn al-Athir wrote that it was "a battle fit to turn black hair gray."[26] Nevertheless, as Ralph of Coggeshall put it, "Cruel death consumed nearly all."[27] The Templars and their companions had sought the crown of martyrdom, and they had found it. So had the master of the Hospitallers along with a number of his own brothers, and a large number of citizens of Nazareth, who had been following the company of knights at a distance, hoping for plunder, only to be set upon by Muslim riders as they fled for home.

Perhaps in tribute to the heedlessness of the charge, saintly legends soon sprang up concerning the conduct of those who had died at Cresson. James of Maillé's death was transformed into a Christian folktale and held up as an example of the idealized crusader, gloriously and joyously embracing martyrdom. According to the author of a contemporary chronicle, he stood alone when almost all his companions had been killed, "surrounded by enemy troops and almost abandoned by human aid, but when he saw so many thousands running toward him from all directions he strengthened his resolve and courageously undertook the battle, one man against all."[28] According to this telling, James's enemies were so won over by the Templar's bravery that they urged him to lay down his weapons and surrender so that they could spare his life. He ignored them and continued fighting until "at long last, crushed rather than conquered by spears, stones and lances, he sank to the ground and joyfully passed to heaven with the martyr's crown." Later it was said that James's white horse and uniform had convinced Saladin's men that he was a manifestation of Saint George, "the Knight in Shining Armor, the protector of the Christians," and that they had been overjoyed when they had finally killed him.

They may have killed the man, but they could not kill the legend. Once cold and stiff and abandoned to the elements, James's corpse became a source of holy relics. Some placed dust on the body and then sprinkled it on their own heads, hoping that it would infect them with the dead man's valor. One man cut off his genitals "and kept them safely for begetting children so that even when dead, the man's members—if such a thing were possible—would produce an heir with courage as great as his."[29]

For every holy trinket harvested from James of Maillé's body, ten were taken from his butchered comrades by Saladin's soldiers. Gerard of Ridefort wrote to the pope to inform him of the doleful defeat at Cresson, complaining that he had "suffered serious losses of horses and arms, quite apart from the loss of men," and advising the Holy Father that "the evil race of pagans is inflamed to attack the . . . land more strongly than usual in accordance with the purposes of its iniquity."[30] He did not mention the fact that as Saladin's army had retreated, it had borne dozens of dead Templars' heads before them on their lances.

+

Less than two months after Cresson, on Saturday, June 27, 1187, Saladin crossed the river Jordan again a few miles south of the Sea of Galilee. This time he brought thirty thousand men, roughly half of whom were cavalry. They had spent several weeks at Ashtara, assembling their numbers, performing military drills and reviewing battlefield tactics. This was no longer an exploratory expedition. It was an all-out invasion: the long-promised strike to rub out the Christian kingdom of Jerusalem.

As the sultan had made no secret of his intentions, King Guy of Jerusalem had been able to rally his forces. In the aftermath of the battle of Cresson, he had sent out a message calling on every able-bodied Christian man in the East to take up arms and join him in defending the kingdom. This was known as the arrière-ban—a general levy—and its promulgation was a sign of existential danger. Castles were emptied almost entirely of their garrisons, so that "no man remained in the cities or the villages or the castles who was able to go to war."[31] The military orders were called up along with every available secular knight. Thousands of mercenaries were hired to supplement the infantry and provide expert light cavalry. The cost of this was borne by a windfall fund paid to the Church by Henry II as penance for his role in the murder of Thomas Becket in Canterbury Cathedral in December 1170. The funds were intended to pay for a new crusade, and held for safekeeping by the Templars, who chose to release them in this hour of emergency. One chronicler reported that Gerard of Ridefort, ever looking to settle a score, gladly released the treasure, "to combat the Saracens and to revenge the dishonor and damage that they had done to him."[32] All told, Guy's army probably numbered at least twenty thousand men, of whom twelve hundred were knights, including several hundred white-mantled Templars, representing perhaps one third of the whole of the order's elite fighting force in the crusader states. They mustered at the secure base of Sephoria, where they could be provisioned and watered to meet the coming attack. "It was a limitless crowd, innumerable as the sands of the desert," wrote Imad al-Din.[33] The True Cross, carried before every Christian army of such a size, was brought out to offer Christ's protection.

Imad al-Din reckoned that the Franks knew they were threatened by an apocalyptic war: "The whole of the forces of Islam against all of infidelity," and he was correct.[34] After the debacle of Cresson a fragile peace had been struck between the king and Raymond of Tripoli—but Guy's war council was far from united and many among them (including the Templar master) still considered Raymond an untrustworthy traitor. When Saladin's advance across the river became known, the council's personal animosities and divided approach to warfare quickly surfaced.

Guy's instinctive reaction when faced with a hostile army was to stall, play for time and wear the enemy out without bringing them to battle, where he would be forced to face the inevitable lottery of field combat. Despite having assembled one of the largest armies in the history of the Christian kingdom, this was his inclination in July 1187. Saladin's army was undoubtedly massive, but it was far from unified: "As divided in place of origin, rites and name as they were united in their determination to destroy the Holy Land," wrote one Frankish author of the time.[35] Guy's favored strategy was to avoid meeting Saladin long enough for his coalition to collapse and his army to begin to disintegrate.

This was exactly the posture that Saladin wished to goad his opponent into abandoning. Fatefully it was an approach to warfare that was little in favor with some of the men around the king. As regent he had been mocked for his failure to fight when Saladin had raided Jerusalem in 1183, and he was susceptible to advice that promised to make up for this past humiliation.

On July 2, 1187, Saladin marched his army to Tiberias at first light and laid the city under siege. The townsmen had neither the appetite nor the capability to resist and their town was soon plundered and set on fire. The garrison held out, but this too presented a problem: Raymond of Tripoli's wife, Eschiva, was trapped inside and now risked falling into

Saladin's hands. It was unlikely that she would be mistreated, but if she were taken prisoner the ransom would be vast and the dishonor considerable.

To Raymond's credit, he set aside his concern for his town and his wife and urged the king to hold firm and not be drawn into a battle on Saladin's terms. He insisted that it was better to ransom his wife than to be coaxed into a trap. But Gerard of Ridefort was consumed by the same mood of righteous belligerence as he had been eight weeks earlier at Cresson, and along with the new master of the Hospitallers, Armenguad of Asp, he advised precisely the opposite.[36] One French source gave Gerard a spirited speech in which he asked in disgust whether the king was really going to listen to the advice of a traitor, and told him his royal honor depended on advancing.[37] Given Gerard's previous vindictiveness and propensity for extremism, this seems plausible. It was, however, scandalously poor strategy. Caught between the uncertainty of battle and the promise of a bloodless but shameful defeat, Guy took the Templar master's advice and decided to attack. He was walking into a trap. As Saladin himself later put it, "Dawn was about to break on the night of unbelief."[38]

On the morning of July 3 the Knights of the Temple assembled in the rear guard of King Guy's vast army as it moved out of Sephoria and ground its way down the old Roman road running east toward Tiberias. It was, said Ibn al-Athir, "high summer and extremely hot," and there were real practical difficulties presented by marching armed men through the desert.[39] The brothers had long experience fighting in these conditions, but they could not avoid thirst, and like the rest of Guy's army relied on natural springs to replenish their supplies of water. By noon the army stopped at the town of Turan, which had a fountain, although it was barely adequate to cool the throats of twenty thousand men together with their horses and pack beasts. Ahead of them lay an arid wasteland, across which Saladin had sent outriders to fill in every well and block every spring they could find. His own army was supplied from the rear by camel trains bringing water up from the Sea of Galilee. He was determined not to allow the crusaders the same comfort.

The folly of Gerard of Ridefort's words now became plain. To advance past Turan meant riding into territory where the army would weaken through simple dehydration with every hour that passed. But having committed to the strategy, Guy would not now change his mind. The Templars in the rear guard, led by Gerard and his second-in-command, the order's seneschal Terricus, followed as the army ground its way further toward Tiberias. As they rode, the Templars set to work, repelling skirmishing parties sent out from the bulk of Saladin's forces, who had themselves changed position, marching to Kafr Sabt and halting in anticipation of the Latins' arrival.

According to stories told by Templar brothers in the months and years to come, a deep unease now settled over Guy's troops. It was said that as they marched, the king's chamberlain looked at the scorching midsummer sky above them and watched an eagle soar over the royal army, holding in its talons a crossbow with seven bolts (representing the seven deadly sins) and "crying out in a terrible voice: 'Woe to you, Jerusalem!'"[40] Ahead of them, Saladin waited.

As soon as Guy's army left Turan, the sultan's nephew Taqi al-Din and Muzaffar al-Din scrambled to take the town, cutting off the possibility of retreat and any hope of maintaining a water supply from the rear. They were, in Saladin's words, "unable to flee and not allowed to stay."[41] Harrassed and moving hopelessly toward a rocky, exposed, dust-dry plateau, the Christian army was now surrounded. They had marched all day at a painfully slow pace and eventually stumbled to a halt, forced to camp a waterless night, with the enemy hemming them in so closely that they could hear troops talking to them in the darkness. "If a cat had fled from the Christian host it could not have escaped without the Saracens taking it," wrote one well-informed source.[42] Cries of "*Allahu Akbar*" (God is great) and "*La 'ilaha 'illa-llah*" (There is no god but God) haunted the Christians as they spent a miserable night under the stars. To the northeast loomed the twin rocky mounds of an extinct volcano known as the Horns of Hattin. Below them was a village with a spring, but the route toward it was blocked. There was nothing for the Franks to do but to lie in the dark and suffer.

At dawn they rose and armed themselves, expecting an onslaught. Cruelly but brilliantly, Saladin prolonged their torture by letting them

stumble onward a little longer toward the Horns of Hattin. Then he ordered his men to set alight the desert scrub. Plumes of smoke filled the
air, rasping at parched throats and providing, Saladin hoped, an image of
an awaiting hell. Finally, when the plain was thick with acrid wood smoke
he gave the command to his archers to nock their bows. They drew and
released. The arrows filled the air "like a swarm of locusts." Infantry and
horses started falling.

Half blind, hot, tired, weak and under fire, discipline began to sag. A
counterattack was essential so, according to a letter written by a merchant in Acre who heard reports filtered back from the battle, Guy
turned to the Templars and asked them to lead the attack on the tormentors. "He gave orders for the master and the knights of the Temple to
begin hostilities. . . . Attacking like strong lions the knights of the Temple killed part of the enemy and caused the rest to retreat."[43]

Terricus, the seneschal, found himself alongside Raymond of Tripoli,
who was commanding the vanguard. With them was Reynald of Sidon,
leading the rear guard, and Balian of Ibelin. Together the four men led a
targeted charge at the part of Saladin's army commanded by Taqi al-Din.
But instead of holding position to take the attack, Taqi al-Din instructed
his men simply to part as the horsemen barreled toward them, allowing
them to fly through the lines untouched. Once they had passed, his infantry closed ranks once more, blocking the route back. Four of the most
senior Christian leaders on the battlefield were now cut off from the rest
of the men whom they were supposed to be commanding. With little
other option, they spurred their horses and fled. In his open letter to all
Templar brethren of the West some days after the battle, Terricus felt
compelled to explain that it was only "with great difficulty that . . . we
ourselves managed to escape that dreadful field."[44]

The army they left behind was now heartily demoralized, crippled by
thirst, weary and exhausted. But they were not yet defeated. "They understood that they would only be saved from death by facing it boldly," wrote
Ibn al-Athir, "so they carried out successive charges, which almost drove the
Muslims from their positions despite their numbers. . . . However, the
Franks did not charge and retire without suffering losses. . . . The Muslims surrounded them as a circle encloses its central point."[45]

The fighting continued throughout the afternoon. Despite the heat it was a brutal contest. Saladin himself recounted in grisly and poetic terms the ferocity with which his men attacked the Franks: "The eyes of the spears were directed at their hearts. . . . Rivers of swords sought out their livers. . . . The horses' hooves massed dust clouds for them; showers of arrows, shooting out sparks were sent down on them, merged together by the thunder of neighing horses, with the lightning of polished swords flashing alongside them."[46]

The Frankish army now broke up. According to Ibn Shaddad, "one group fled and was pursued by our Muslim heroes. Not one of them survived."[47] King Guy and his knights prepared to make a final stand.

The king and a group of knights, likely including Gerard of Ridefort and his Templars, had managed to scramble up to the Horns of Hattin, where the ruins of Iron Age and Bronze Age fortifications offered some natural protection. Reaching the higher ground, the thirsty, weary men would have been able to look down in agony at the great, unreachable expanse of cool water that was the Sea of Galilee. Making the position briefly defensible, they erected King Guy's bright red royal tent. Into it hurried the bishop of Acre, carrying with him the one thing that the Latins hoped could save them: a jeweled casket holding the fragment of the True Cross, on which Christ had suffered and died. It had to be defended at any cost.

From his command position, Saladin watched Guy's tent being pitched and the Christians preparing to defend their king and their holy relic. Alongside him was his son al-Afdal, who later recounted to Ibn al-Athir the tense moments that followed. The sultan knew that the enemy's cavalry would fight with every last scrap of its remaining strength. The men were cornered, and they were arranging themselves for an assault on the one part of the Muslim army that could turn impending defeat into victory: Saladin and his bodyguard of Mamluks. The sultan was, said his son, "overcome by grief and his complexion pale."[48]

Younger and less experienced, al-Afdal could not understand his father's trepidation. As each Christian charge from Guy's tent was beaten backward, al-Afdal whooped with joy, and shouted, "We have beaten them!"

"My father rounded on me," he later recalled. "He said: 'Be quiet! We have not beaten them until that tent falls.'"

Just as Saladin uttered those words, the two men saw Guy's red tent finally overwhelmed. The king and the True Cross were taken. The battle was over. "The sultan dismounted, prostrated himself in thanks to God Almighty and wept for joy."[49]

+

The blood-streaked battlefield at Hattin was marked by two monuments: a dome erected on Saladin's instructions, known as the Qubbat al-Nasr (Dome of Victory), and a widespread scattering of human bones, which were lying in fleshless piles all across the plain when Ibn al-Athir visited the site a year later. The sultan boasted of having overseen the slaughter of forty thousand men in battle.[50]

Those who survived the battle of Hattin were at Saladin's mercy, to be executed or imprisoned as their position dictated. Many were led away into captivity and sold into slavery. Ibn Shaddad heard of one gleeful Muslim combatant leading away thirty Christian soldiers tied together with a tent rope.[51] The price of slaves in the markets of Damascus plummeted due to oversupply. But some captives merited more than a few bezants in the public auctions. Gerard of Ridefort and several hundred Templars and Hospitallers were among those taken alive from the battlefield, in an astonishing parade of illustrious prisoners that included King Guy, Reynald of Châtillon, Humphrey of Toron (his stepson) and many others. A newsletter sent to Archumbald, master of the Hospitallers in Italy, lamented that more than one thousand "of the better men were captured and killed, with the result that no more than two hundred of the knights or foot soldiers got away."[52]

On the evening of July 4 King Guy and Reynald of Châtillon were brought before Saladin, who was by then sitting in splendor in the porchway of his royal tent. The sultan comforted the parched, defeated and terrified king and gave him a cup of iced julep (rosewater) to quench his thirst. This was both a kindness between rulers and a display of hospitality that in the Arab tradition implied that the king's life was now safe under Saladin's protection. When Guy handed the cup to Reynald, Saladin's demeanor shifted; he informed Reynald through a translator that he had not offered him the drink, and that he was therefore not yet safe. The two men were sent away to eat and find their lodgings, then brought back to the sultan's presence. Guy was seated within the pavilion and forced to watch as Reynald was confronted face-to-face by Saladin, who had sworn an oath to be revenged upon him for an attack he had made on a Muslim caravan and for his pirate raids on the Hijaz back in 1183.

Saladin harangued the one-time Prince of Antioch for his irreligion, treachery and impertinence, calling him names and rehearsing his many misdeeds. He told him that the only way he could save his life was by converting to Islam—an offer he knew Reynald would refuse. When the grandstanding was over the sultan stood, drew his scimitar and brought it sweeping down into the gnarled veteran's neck. His intention was to take Reynald's head off, but in his excitement Saladin missed his mark, cutting one of his arms off at the shoulder. Reynald fell and servants rushed in, dragged the bleeding man from the tent and finished him off.[53] Saladin looked to Guy and reassured him that he was safe from harm. It cannot have filled the terrified king with much confidence.

Reynald's death was a matter of personal vengeance for Saladin: the fulfilment of a deadly oath and a grudge held for years. His treatment of the Templars, however, was a matter of cold political and military calculation. The knights of the order, along with their Hospitaller counterparts, had fought with great distinction at Hattin, as was noted by more than one Muslim correspondent. Saladin had no intention of letting them fight another day. "They were the fiercest fighters of all the Franks," wrote Ibn al-Athir, and their zealous commitment to holy war was a pillar of the Latin states' defenses.[54] Just as he had wiped the Templar castle at Jacob's Ford from the face of the earth, now he set about eradicating his prisoners.

Imad al-Din reported that Saladin wished to "purify the land of these two unclean orders, whose practices are useless, who never give up their hostility and who have no use as slaves. The one and the other are the worst of the infidels."[55] A fat fee of fifty dinars per prisoner was offered to any Muslim who would bring a knight of the Temple or Hospital to the sultan. "He ordered that each would have his head cut off and be erased from the land of the living," wrote Imad al-Din.[56]

A call went out to members of Saladin's clerical entourage to carry out the sentence. Volunteers were drawn from Sufi mystics, lawyers, scholars and ascetics, many of whom had never carried out such a deed in their lives. "Each of them asked the favor of executing a prisoner, drew his sword and rolled up his sleeve," recounted Imad al-Din. Saladin's soldiers and emirs lined up beside him to watch the grotesque carnival. Then the brothers of the Temple and of the Hospital were beheaded one by one. Some of the amateurs cut swiftly and cleanly and were applauded. Others hacked away with blunt blades. "Others were ridiculous and had to be replaced," wrote Imad al-Din. All the while Saladin sat and smiled, his grin contrasting with the bleak scowls of the Christian brothers ending their days before him, butchered like sheep.

"Not one of the Templars survived," wrote Saladin in his triumphant letter recounting his victory at Hattin. He was not totally accurate. A few years later a Templar knight turned up in Acre claiming not only to have escaped the field at Hattin, but to have made off with the True Cross and buried it for safekeeping, although he subsequently forgot where he had put it.[57] Gerard of Rideford, meanwhile, was spared the bungled cleaving of the Sufis. He was held for a time in a Damascus prison before being ransomed back to the order at painfully high cost. Terricus led the order until Gerard's release. When he assessed the human cost of the events that summer, he calculated that between the Springs of Cresson and the Horns of Hattin, two hundred and ninety knights had been lost: a huge swath of the Templars' manpower in the East. This was only a fraction of the thousands of other men who had gone down with them, victims of the master's thirst for martyrdom, which seemed to embrace everyone but himself.

Hattin was a humiliating military defeat, a spiritual disaster and the beginning of the end for the Latin kingdom of Jerusalem. By stripping the castles and towns of the Christian littoral of anyone who was capable of fighting and marching them into the hellmouth at Hattin, King Guy had left the realm horribly vulnerable to a rapid assault, which was what Saladin now immediately undertook. In the three months after Hattin, his men swarmed over the leaderless Frankish lands like ants. In rapid succession they overran Tiberias and Acre, Sidon and Beirut, Haifa and Caesarea. Nazareth and Bethlehem were lost and dozens more towns and castles fell, with only a handful of the greatest inland fortresses managing to hold out. Jerusalem's port, Jaffa, was taken. Ascalon, won after such a struggle in the 1150s, was gone by September, as were Darum and Lydda. By the autumn every major stronghold in the kingdom of Jerusalem had been lost, with the exceptions of Tyre and Jerusalem itself. On September 20 Saladin arrived before the Holy City, ready to finish what he had begun.

Jerusalem was by then in no position to hold its walls. Balian of Ibelin commanded a pathetic garrison composed of a handful of merchants and every male over the age of sixteen, who had been knighted for the purposes of mounting an honorable defense. It was completely inadequate. Saladin put his catapults and sappers to work immediately and after nine grim days in which the women of the city wept and shaved their children's heads as penance for their sins, a breach was made. Balian of Ibelin sued for peace and on September 30 the city formally surrendered on the condition of a peaceful transfer of power with no massacres, and a forty-day amnesty for Christian citizens to buy their freedom before facing enslavement.

Saladin made his formal entry to Jerusalem on Friday, October 2, the anniversary of Muhammad's Night Journey, when the Prophet had traveled with the angel Gabriel to what was now the Dome of the Rock on the place the Christians called Temple Mount. Straightaway Saladin sent men up the great golden Dome. They tore down the cross that had been erected on it and, according to a letter sent to England by Terricus, dragged it around the city for two days, ceremonially beating it for the people of the city to see.

Next they moved into the Templars' headquarters in al-Aqsa Mosque. "The Aqsa mosque was filled with pigs and filth," wrote Imad al-Din, "and obstructed with buildings from the time of the infidel, this race of perdition, unjust and criminal."[58] The sultan's forces duly set to work purifying it, knocking down walls and buildings that had been put up during the Templars' tenancy, and washing the entire building from bottom to top with rosewater. On October 9, Friday prayers rang out in four directions from the Temple Mount, and a sermon was preached by an imam from Damascus, Ibn al-Zaki, celebrating the works of Saladin and calling on all Muslims to continue the jihad.

Fifty Templars who were evicted from their headquarters were allowed to form a guard to escort Christian refugees out of Jerusalem to settle wherever they could find a safe new home. Most made for the coastal city of Tyre, which was holding out as a bastion of Latin defiance. The brothers divided themselves into a vanguard and rear guard of twenty-five knights each and marched the bedraggled citizens north, every step carrying them farther away from the city of Christ's Passion, into hostile and dangerous country.[59] It was a pitiful reversal of everything the order stood for.

Sixty-eight years had passed since Hugh of Payns and his fellow knights had gathered around the Holy Sepulchre to imagine into existence a new order that would defend the Holy City and protect its Christian pilgrims. It had taken Saladin less than fifteen weeks to massacre its members, imprison their master, seize their castles, overrun the holy sites they had sworn to protect and turn almost everything the order stood for into dust.

It was hard to avoid the conclusion that God had abandoned his soldiers.

PART III

Bankers

1189–1260

"Come out, heavily or lightly armed, and fight for God's cause with your money and your lives."

Ibn Wasil, quoting Qur'an 9:41[1]

12

"The Pursuit of Fortune"

THE INTERNATIONAL HEADQUARTERS of the Order of the Temple, once a vast palace in Jerusalem, was now a tent on Mount Toron, surrounded by other tents billeting the great and good of the Christian Holy Land.[1] From their humble beginnings, the Templars were humble once more: dozens of their castles lost, hundreds of men dead and their mission in disarray. The brothers took pride in their ability to seek out and endure humiliating hardship.[2] Between 1187 and 1189, however, humility and hardship had been thrust upon them. There was no avoiding the evidence of their demise: from their vantage point high on Mount Toron, one hundred and twenty feet above sea level, they could look down to Acre and be reminded daily of everything they had lost.

The rooftops of Acre were a tightly packed jumble of workshops, houses, churches, fortified towers and commercial properties clustered around a central citadel, bordered to the south and west by the sea and encircled on the landward side by a strong stone wall, beyond which stretched a sandy plain. Acre was one of the largest ports in the Holy Land: the leading commercial harbor on the coast. The city had dazzled the Spanish writer and traveler Ibn Jubayr, inspiring him to quote from the Qur'an when he recorded that "Acre is the capital of the Frankish cities in Syria [and] the unloading place of 'ships reared aloft in the seas like mountains.'" Although Ibn Jubayr deplored the stinking streets, filthy with rubbish and excrement, and railed against the conversion of ancient mosques into Christian places of worship, he went so far as to say that "in its greatness [it] resembles Constantinople."[3]

At the time of Ibn Jubayr's visit, in the autumn of 1184, before the tumult of Hattin, this magnificent city had been among the most important Christian strongholds in Outremer. Now, in the autumn of 1189, it was occupied by the armies of Islam, as was virtually every other once-Christian settlement below the Sea of Galilee, with the exception of Tripoli and the impregnable island fortress of Tyre. Friday prayers rang out in the place of church bells, and Muslim guards peered suspiciously from the towers punctuating Acre's stone defenses. There was plenty to occupy their attention, for in the summer of 1189 a coalition of Christian troops had begun to assemble, massing forces outside the walls of Acre with one simple aim: to take it back.

Among the Templar brothers living beneath canvas on Mount Toron was Gerard of Ridefort. For nearly a year after Hattin he had been held in a Damascus prison cell, but in June 1189 he had been released as part of a bargain struck between Saladin and King Guy. The king was set loose in exchange for the surrender of Ascalon and he was allowed to choose ten knights to accompany him. The list he came up with included one of his brothers, Aimery of Lusignan, and Gerard of Ridefort, master of the Templars. The tariff for Gerard's liberty was set high: the order was forced to give up its castle at Gaza. That it did so spoke more to their sense of honor than to military strategy, for while masters were replaceable, Gaza was not. An expensively assembled military hub controlling the routes between Egypt and the Palestinian coast was now in Muslim hands. It was a heavy price to pay.

Still, what was done was done, and Gerard was free. When he returned to power he displaced the acting leader Terricus, who disappeared from the central hierarchy of the order for nearly ten years, perhaps feeling that in surviving Hattin and helping to deal with the aftermath, his duty had been done. Gerard was quick to revert to his customary leadership style: belligerence whatever the cost. There was plenty to animate him. Looking down from Mount Toron toward occupied Acre he would have recognized the Templars' large palace in the southwestern quarter of the city, now home to a lawyer friend of Saladin's by the name of Issa el-Hakkari. Its loss was intolerable.

Both the Hospitallers and the Templars had kept fine properties in Acre, as befitted their status in the Holy Land. The Hospitallers' house was in the city, while the Templar house was built on a squat spit of land jutting out into the Mediterranean near an L-shaped seawall that sheltered ships at anchor in the inner harbor. The German pilgrim Theoderic wrote that the house was "very large and beautiful," referring perhaps to the large Romanesque arches punctuating its formidable stone walls.[4] But it was more than beautiful. Thanks to its prime location in the busiest merchant stronghold, it was the order's most important commercial hub in the East. The Templars' commercial interests in Acre were overseen by a high-ranking sergeant known as the commander (or preceptor) of the shipyard, and it was through him that the principal supplies of goods, munitions and manpower from the West reached the Latin states.[5]

Large underground tunnels had been dug, running nearly four hundred yards from the palace cellars, beneath the Pisan quarter to the city's customs house, known as the Court of the Chain. Here clerics sat on stone benches spread with blankets, accounting for revenue received using pens dipped in ebony inkstands ornamented in gold.[6] To ensure a secure passage to and from this gilded countinghouse the order had built a sophisticated transit shaft, which split at one point into two parallel tunnels, overlooked by a guardroom cut into the rock, where a sergeant brother could sit and look through a metal grille to monitor the traffic passing below.[7]

To the north of the main palace, in a suburb known as Montmusard, were two more areas belonging to the order: the "Templar quarter" and a large block of stables. Taken together, the brothers' possessions in Acre were substantially larger than those in Jerusalem. Now all were in enemy hands. The lawyer Issa el-Hakkari had been given everything: their "houses, farms, land . . . crops and other property."[8] Under his management the main palace had been augmented with a large tower that protruded insolently above the city skyline, a visible provocation to Gerard of Ridefort and his comrades on Mount Toron.*

In the first week of October the Templars had been outside Acre for five weeks. Gerard had had a hand in bringing them there. Fresh out of jail he had surveyed the wreckage of the Christian kingdom and urged on the king a policy of decisive action to strike back at Saladin. The losses of the battle of Hattin, Jerusalem and the True Cross had startled the Christian realms of the West into action and it was well known that the kings of England and France, the Holy Roman Emperor Frederick Barbarossa, Philip II of France and many other illustrious nobles were planning a

---

* It would have been only slight consolation for Gerard to see that the Hospitallers' house, with its apartments, church and wards for treating the sick, had been converted by Saladin into a school.

massive crusade—the biggest since 1096. Accompanied by the king's brother Aimery of Lusignan, he had argued that it would be disgraceful if these monarchs arrived and found the king of Jerusalem idle in his eviscerated realm. "It is much better that they should find that you have besieged a city," the two men urged.[9] Guy, always susceptible when his honor was impugned, had agreed.

The city he had settled on was Acre. A royal army, rounded up from the remaining rumps of Frankish territory in Antioch and around Tyre, eventually arrived there on August 29, 1189. Initially there were six hundred knights, including a modest delegation of Templars, but the numbers had grown significantly. On the last day of August several boats full of Pisan troops had disembarked south of the city and set up camp on the beach. Ten days later fifty more ships had arrived, carrying thousands of Danish and Frisian crusaders commanded by the famous Flemish knight and nobleman James of Avesnes, one of the most respected and feared military leaders in northern Europe. In late September Guy's enemy, the Pisan nobleman Conrad of Montferrat, who was agitating to replace Guy as king, had brought one thousand knights and twenty thousand infantry up from Tyre. Personal squabbles notwithstanding, this was now a very large Frankish force, capable of blockading Acre from the sea and manning a partial encirclement by land.

In response, Saladin had come to Acre with a sizable army of his own. Just as the Christian army surrounded the city, so his troops took up positions in an even wider semicircle, with a command post on a hill of its own, known as Tell al-'Ayyadiya. From the first weeks of September the two sides skirmished with each other: Saladin's men sought to maintain supply lines into Acre through weak spots in the Latins' land blockade and ambushed foraging parties, while Guy's men worked to keep them at bay. These were little more than exploratory jousts, but numbers on both sides were swelling, and all were well aware that they were moving toward a massive siege at Acre. The result would be either a brake on Saladin's conquest of the Christian Holy Land, or another chapter in the sorry story of the Latin states' slide toward oblivion.

On the evening of October 3 the Frankish commanders decided to make their first move against Saladin's growing army. According to Ibn al-Athir's chronicle, King Guy realized that although the sultan had a large force with him at Acre, many of his best troops were scattered in other important regions of his large dominions: some to the north in Antioch, others defending the Egyptian ports of Alexandria and Damietta, others watching carefully over the Christian city of Tyre to repel any possible attack on that front. There would be no better time to launch an assault on the army outside Acre, to cut supplies to the Muslims who were pinned down within the city walls. Guy ordered his army to prepare for a large maneuver the following day.

On the morning of October 4, "like a plague of locusts, creeping across the face of the earth," the Christian army assembled at the foot of Mount Toron and advanced across the plain at walking pace toward Saladin's base on Tell al-'Ayyadiya. The lighter infantry, armed with bows and crossbows, preceded "the main strength of the army . . . a brilliant sight with their horses and arms and various insignia."[10] Behind them came the elite mounted units: the royal guard, the Hospitallers led by their master Armenguad of Asp, and the Templars led by Gerard of Ridefort.

Carrying the black-and-white banner at the head of the company of brothers making their way across the dusty plain of Acre that morning was their recently appointed marshal, Geoffrey Morin.[11] Previously the commander of the Templar house at Tyre, Geoffrey had been promoted to his new office shortly before Master Gerard's release from prison.[12] According to the protocols laid down in the rule, Geoffrey rode with a personal guard of five to ten white-mantled knights, one of whom carried a spare banner, in case the marshal's was damaged or torn in battle.[13] He was the most important Templar on the battlefield after Gerard, and the whole order grouped themselves around him.

The piebald banner was one of many flags flying as the large Christian army advanced. And when it drew within charging distance of Saladin's army, the piebald took the lead. A signal went up and the infantry stopped marching. They parted in two, and out of the gap came the heavy cavalry, charging as one toward the enemy. Unwilling to stand in the way of barreling horsemen, the troops stationed in front of Saladin's base camp fell back, leaving the way to the royal tent open. Saladin went with them, and the Franks immediately fell on the defenseless positions, slicing through guy ropes, plundering what they could and killing anyone who stood in their way. The dead included the Muslim governor of Jerusalem,

Saladin's chamberlain Khalil al-Hakkari, and a noted poet and scholar, Ibn Rawaha.[14] According to one account of the battle, Saladin's own tent was briefly seized by the Count of Bar, a crusader who had recently arrived from the West, although it was apparently not destroyed.[15]

"The knights of the Temple, who are second to none in renown and devoted to slaughter, had already charged through all the enemy lines," wrote an approving Christian chronicler. "If the rest . . . had pressed on after them and pursued the enemy with equal enthusiasm, that day they would have won a happy victory over the city and the war. But the Templars went too far in their pursuit of fortune and their own inclinations."[16] Not for the first time under Gerard of Ridefort's leadership, boldness gave way to recklessness.

As Saladin's army retreated and the Templars and their accompanying knights scooped up the booty left behind, no one noticed that a large party of armed citizens had crept out of an undefended gate in Acre and made their way around the back of battlefield, joining up with some of the sultan's troops who had initially retreated from the camp. Quietly they moved toward the place where the black-and-white flag advertised the Templars' location. Then, without warning, they attacked.

Looking back, the Templars now realized they were isolated from the rest of the cavalry, which was busy engaging Saladin's right flank. This meant they were now vulnerable to assault from all sides and cut off from any easy communication with their fellow Franks. They attempted to fight their way back to the field, but it was impossible. They were encircled. The only thing to do was to rally together and fight.

One chronicler had Gerard of Ridefort deliver a rousing speech as he assessed the grave trouble into which he had once again led his comrades. "Urged by his companions to flee so that he would not perish, he replied: 'Never! It would be shame and scandal for the Templars. I would be said to have saved my life by running away and leaving my fellow-knights to be slaughtered!'"[17] This was literary invention but still it spoke to the master's principled refusal to back away from danger. This was what had taken him hurtling toward seven thousand men at the Springs of Cresson, and crawling across the smoke-choked, bloodstained scrubland below the Horns of Hattin. He had escaped from both of those disasters, but he would not escape the plains of Acre.

As blades flashed, horses fell and men died in panic, Gerard and his men were overrun. "The swords of God overwhelmed them from every side and not one of them escaped," wrote Ibn al-Athir. "Most were killed and the rest were taken prisoner. Among them was the master of the Templars whom Saladin had captured and freed."[18] This time there would be no prison, no ransom and no mercy. Gerard was summarily executed on the battlefield. "He fell slain with the slain," observed the Christian author of a chronicle known as the *Itinerarium Peregrinorum*.[19] Somewhere behind him the piebald banner, the last, proud symbol of Templar resistance, was wobbling above its beleaguered defenders. Eventually it, too, fell, collapsing to the ground in the lifeless hands of Geoffrey Morin.

October 4, 1189, was another dreadful day for the Latin warriors of the Holy Land. As the Templars were steadily butchered, the rest of the army was dissolving. Animals ran wild and men lost their nerve. "They put the enemy to flight, and were then conquered and fled back themselves," wrote a Christian chronicler, in disgust.[20] Only a desperate rear guard organized by King Guy's brother Geoffrey of Lusignan prevented the capture of Mount Toron. After several hours of fighting, the battle drew to an exhausted close. The Franks had been beaten again. Around fifteen hundred men were lost, and others staggered back to camp so disfigured by their injuries that their friends could not recognize them. Saladin's men gathered up the bodies of their victims and dumped them into the nearby rivers. As the corpses rotted, the water ran foul. For those who remained alive outside Acre, it was clear that a long and terrible siege lay ahead. The promised reinforcements could not come soon enough for the Holy Land's beleaguered defenders—nor, indeed, for the ragtag, leaderless rump of Templar knights who stared down from Mount Toron at their former palace and wondered if they would ever again see their flag raised above its roof.

✝

A horribly injured sailor staggered through the packs of soldiers swarming outside the walls of Acre on his way to tell his sorry tale. It was June 11, 1191, and for the last four days the unlucky seaman had been held prisoner and tortured by a band of foreign invaders, who plucked him from the sea following a naval battle, leaving his shipmates flailing hopelessly in the waters all around him.[21] The wretched man would have been better off drowning, for although alive he had been cruelly mutilated and sent to the citizens of Acre as an example of what happened to those who defied the armies of God.

The sailor was in one sense just another victim of the siege of Acre, which by June 1191 had been going for twenty-two months, claiming hundreds of lives through violent clashes on land and at sea, malnutrition and disease. Yet he was also a grisly symbol of something bigger. His grotesque injuries had been inflicted on him to advertise the arrival of a dangerous new player in the war against Saladin. This newcomer was "wise and experienced in warfare and his coming had a dread and frightening effect on the hearts of the Muslims," wrote Ibn Shaddad.[22] His great-grandfather was King Fulk I of Jerusalem, but he himself was the king of England, one of the fiercest fighters of his generation and a supporter of the Templars. He was tall, well proportioned and charismatic, with striking gold-red hair and an arm that seemed to have been made to swing a sword. History would know him as Richard Coeur-de-Lion: the Lionheart.

Famous men had been arriving in Acre throughout the spring, among them the king of France, Philip Augustus, who landed on April 20 with six large ships, surrounded by his leading nobles and thousands of enthusiastic crusaders, causing Ibn Shaddad to admit that he was "a great man and respected leader, one of their great kings to whom all present in the army would be obedient."[23] Richard trailed Philip by several weeks, and was one of the last to arrive. But what the English king lacked in punctuality, he more than made up for with the sheer force of his personality. Ibn Shaddad lavished his highest praise on Richard, writing that he was "a mighty warrior of great courage and strong in purpose. He had much experience of fighting and was intrepid in battle." He further noted that athough he was, in the crusaders' eyes, "below the king of France in royal status," he was "richer and more renowned for martial skill and courage."[24]

Richard had taken the cross in 1187 while still a prince, inflamed like almost every young soldier of his age by the devastating news from Hattin. Instability in the West, including a deadly quarrel with his dying father, King Henry II, meant that it had taken Richard four years to make good on his oath to travel east and do battle for Jerusalem.* But his halting preparation had eventually produced a spectacular crusading force. One hundred and fifty ships set off from Portsmouth and sailed more than two thousand miles via Lisbon, Sicily and Cyprus, collecting Richard in southern Italy. Their progress had been a bloody spree. Lisbon was sacked and Sicily invaded. Cyprus was conquered and Richard had had the Byzantine governor, Isaac Comnenus, arrested and clapped in silver manacles for having the impertinence to oppose his landing. None of this was very pious, but it lacquered Richard's reputation as a decisive military commander of the sort sadly lacking among the Latins of the Holy Land since the death of King Baldwin III. The king of England arrived at Acre bearing ships, money, horses, weapons, cloth, food and men. Most of all, he came carrying the hopes of the Christian world on his shoulders.

Richard's arrival was an important boost to the Templars' morale and manpower. The months that followed the defeat of October 4, 1189, were gloomy. There was such a dearth of senior brothers left in the East that the order's central convent was either unable or unwilling to elect a suitable candidate to replace Gerard of Ridefort as master. For a few months command was assumed by a brother known in documents simply as "W."[25] He was a chaplain brother: one of the order's private priests, who wore black robes like a sergeant and the distinctive ceremonial gloves that were the privilege of ordained members. W. was apparently a devout and educated brother, but he was not a warrior.

In 1190 temporary cover had come in the form of two of the West's most senior brothers, who replaced W. and shared a brief joint command. The first, Amio of Ays, was a Burgundian intellectual with family ties to Provence, who took up the post of seneschal. Amio had previously visited Outremer in the late 1160s, during the reign of King Amalric, but he had not settled, instead going on to build his reputation in Paris, managing business transactions on behalf of the more financially motivated

---

* Henry II died a miserable death on July 6, 1189, with his two sons, Richard and John, in rebellion against him.

Templars of France. He was successful enough at this to be appointed master of the West, the most senior posting outside the Holy Land. But at heart Amio was nothing like his brothers in the kingdom of Jerusalem. His main job in Paris was managing a network of agricultural estates, negotiating land and property deals with churches and abbeys and ensuring that proper standards of religious observance were maintained in Templar houses under his supervision. His chief hobbyhorse, expressed regularly in the documents he witnessed and sealed, was a desire for "perpetual peace." This platitude was enough to sustain a very successful career in a land where Templars were religious servants first and soldiers second. In the Holy Land, however, peacemongers like Amio were in short supply and even shorter demand.

Fortunately, Amio was joined in 1190 by Girbert Eral, a former confidant of the late master Arnold of Torrolla, under whom he had briefly served as the order's preceptor. Since 1184 Girbert had been master of the Temple in Spain and Provence. The Iberian Peninsula was still a live theater of war: in the mid-twelfth century an Islamic revolution in North Africa and southern Spain had seen the Almoravid dynasty replaced by a severe and murderous Sunni regime known as the Almohads, whose leaders declared themselves caliphs and sought to push back against Christian advances on the peninsula. In the year Girbert was appointed as master in Spain and Provence a huge siege had taken place at the castle of Santarém, close to the Templars' Portuguese headquarters at Tomar. Portuguese forces had battered back an Almohad besieging army and killed the caliph Abu Ya'qub Yusuf with a poisoned arrow. Exposure to this sort of grinding conflict meant Girbert was rather more attuned to strife and bloodshed than his thoughtful, peace-loving comrade. He was well suited to the East. In 1190 Girbert once again took up the role of preceptor, and together he and Amio shepherded the order through a troubled year.

The Templars' fighting staff had been gutted by Saladin, but Amio and Girbert's arrival showed that the order was able to absorb near-mortal blows in the Holy Land and rebuild their numbers in relatively short order. In May 1191 Amio left his post and returned to Paris, to be replaced by Roric of La Courtine. The change came not a moment too soon: Richard landed at Acre several weeks later, on June 8, carried on a wave of exuberant belligerence that would call for the Templars' full involvement. It was as well for Amio that he had left before the trouble began.

The crusading force Richard had brought with him from his royal lands in England, and his French holdings of Normandy, Anjou and Aquitaine, had been planned and executed on a grand scale. He arrived in Acre with his fleet expanded to nearly two hundred ships, a huge personal army, many powerful and experienced noble supporters and a mountain of gold, raised by selling political offices, lordships and property back in England. He also brought experienced and trusted military advisers, whom he had come to know and rely upon during the thirty-three years of his life, more than half of which had been spent on military campaigns in and around Poitou, which Richard first ruled as count when he was fifteen years old.

One of these, Robert of Sablé, numbered among Richard's most important feudal vassals and allies. Robert held a large swath of land around Le Mans, the Plantagenet family heartlands, and had been deeply involved in Richard's preparations for crusade in Anjou and Normandy over the spring and summer of 1190.[26] He was one the king's three admirals, and as well as commanding a large division of the royal fleet he had served as an ambassador when the army had overwintered in Sicily. He also sat on an official committee responsible for dividing up the possessions of crusaders who died on the journey. Richard trusted him deeply. Not long after his arrival at Acre Richard ordered Robert to take his vows as a Templar knight, whereupon the order promptly elected Robert of Sablé as their new master.

Richard was not the first king to cajole the Templars into appointing a master of his own choosing: Everard of Barres had been a trusted servant of King Louis VII, and Philip of Nablus and Odo of Saint-Amand were both effectively creations of King Amalric. But never had a master so obviously and purposefully been parachuted into position by a visiting monarch. Co-opting the military orders by splicing their leadership into his own command structure was an important plank of Richard's crusading strategy. The English king had also brought with him a new Hospitaller master, Garnier of Nablus, who was prior of the Hospital in England, and Robert Anglicanus, an Englishman who was appointed treasurer of the Hospital in 1192.[27] For the Templars and for the kingdom of Jerusalem, this policy would have a long-lasting effect.

✝

For a month an abominable torrent of stone was hurled against the walls of Acre. The huge crusader army commanded by Richard the Lionheart and Philip Augustus were pelting the city's towers and fortifications with trebuchets built to the latest designs. Richard owned four, the Count of Flanders two and the Duke of Burgundy one. Philip Augustus possessed a particularly ingenious array of siege weapons, including a huge catapult he had nicknamed *Malvoisine* ("Bad Neighbor") and several mobile engines that could be pushed up against the walls to allow hand-to-hand fighting on the battlements. Philip himself sat in a wooden hide close by the city, aiming his crossbow at soldiers high above him, and avoiding the incendiary devices loaded with Greek fire that were hurled in his direction. The Templars manned a powerful trebuchet of their own, as did the Hospitallers; public conscription among the ordinary pilgrims who had joined the crusader army had paid for another, which they christened "God's Stone-thrower." Below the ground sappers clawed at the foundations of Acre's towers, while the great battery of heavy artillery smashed the beleagured citizens from the air. Morale inside Acre had been collapsing for some time, and with the steady bombardment throughout June and July it reached a nadir. "The defenders' spirits sank when they stared death in the face," wrote Ibn Shaddad.[28]

Saladin's army remained camped around Tell al-'Ayyadiya, from where they communicated with the frightened townspeople by beating drums and sending swimmers between the ships in the harbor carrying messages around their necks. Largely, though, they were helpless. The crusaders numbered around twenty-five thousand and they had dug in their positions behind ditches and earthworks. When Saladin's forces attempted to assault the Latin ranks, they were driven back by men—and women—wielding bows, swords, daggers, lances, double-headed axes and clubs studded with iron teeth.[29] Both King Richard and King Philip had been ill with a disease—probably scurvy—that made their hair and nails fall out, but Richard had remained defiant, and insisted on being carried out from his tent each day on a stretcher to shoot crossbow bolts at defenders patrolling the walls.

By the first week of July the townspeople of Acre had all but given up. Their walls were breached in several places, they were running short on supplies and they feared a massacre if the city fell by storm. They decided to sue for peace. Negotiations were overseen on the Latin side by a delegation that included the new master of the Hospitallers, Richard's companion Garnier of Nablus. Despite Saladin's known hostility to any peace process, a surrender was agreed, by which the city would be given up, 200,000 gold dinars paid in compensation, more than fifteen hundred Christian prisoners released and the True Cross that was lost at Hattin given back. The sultan reluctantly approved the terms and on July 12 the gates of Acre were flung open. The crusaders piled in, and, at midday, the onlooking Ibn Shaddad was depressed to see "the banners of unbelief" raised above Acre's rooftops.[30] Richard took up residence in the citadel, and Philip Augustus and his entourage were accommodated as guests of the Templars, restored at last to their spectacular house by the docks. The French royal flag was hoisted on the Templars' new tower, added during the tenancy of Issa el-Hakkari. The piebald banner would have to wait. Still, after four years in the wilderness, the Templars once again had a home.

They also had a purpose. The battle of Acre marked the end of King Philip's crusade: he considered that he had fulfilled his vows and set off for Paris, eager to escape the Lionheart, who had repeatedly belittled him during the crusade and broken an agreement to marry Philip's sister. One of the French king's leading nobles, the Count of Flanders, had died at Acre and Philip wished to stake the Crown's claim on the richest parts of his inheritance. He headed back to France, leaving the Holy Land to fend for itself. King Richard, by contrast, was only just getting started.

He began with a mass march down the coast, with the aim of retaking as many ports and settlements as possible between Acre and Ascalon—including Haifa, Destroit, Caesarea, Arsuf and Jaffa—before turning inland and heading for Jerusalem itself. Of course this was easier said that done. A long foot campaign was liable to collapse into indiscipline, given the logistical demands of provisioning tens of thousands of men, and the certainty of harassment by Saladin's agile, lightly armored horsemen.

The experience of the Second Crusade, with its awful slog through Asia Minor, suggested that the military orders would be essential to providing security and discipline on the move, so in the late summer and early autumn of 1191, they were asked to deploy in exactly that capacity. There was no time for the Templars to sit and enjoy their restoration. On Tuesday, August 20, Richard summarily massacred around twenty-six hundred Muslim prisoners on the plain of Acre, citing Saladin's failure to make good on his promise to return the True Cross and pay 100,000 dinars of the fee agreed at the city's surrender. Two days later his crusader army had packed up camp and was on the move.

The huge column snaked its way slowly south, tracked on its right-hand side by a fleet of ships hugging the coast. The Templars rode rear guard, watchful and alert as they followed in the distance Richard's war banner depicting a giant dragon, which was being wheeled along on a cart.[31] Their job was to repel raiding parties swooping down from the mountains, whose assaults were occasionally heavy enough to force the whole convoy to a standstill. By day they endured heat exhaustion and dodged the arrows shot by riders determined to revenge the merciless slaughter of family members and friends outside Acre. By night they lay in the dark listening to the crusaders chant pilgrim prayers into the blackness and enduring swarms of giant tarantulas that crawled into the camp and bit anyone not alert enough to scare them away.

Little by little they ground their way south. Muslim garrisons abandoned the towns ahead of them, destroying what they could before they left. On Tuesday, August 27, the crusaders left Haifa. On Sunday, September 1, they were passing out of Caesarea. Two days after this they fended off a full-blooded assault during which the Templars lost a large number of horses as their tormentors rode behind them raining down javelins and arrows. After the attackers had been beaten back, a huge pile of dead horses was made and "the common people made a great commotion as they struggled greedily to buy the meat, which was not cheap." Fights broke out among the ranks in the scrabble to buy horseflesh. "Flavored with hunger rather than sauce . . . it was delicious," wrote one wry observer.[32]

By September 5 the army had reached the forest of Arsuf, the last significant landmark on the road to Jaffa. They were relieved to find that contrary to rumors the enemy had not set fire to the woodland to prevent them from passing. Once they had traversed the woods they set up camp, and Richard requested a parlay with Saladin. The sultan deferred to his brother al-Adil (known to the crusaders as Saphadin), who had instructions to spin out discussions as long as he could in anticipation of mounted reinforcements. Bad-tempered talks soon broke up, with al-Adil scornfully rejecting Richard's demand for the return of all Christian lands lost since 1187. Meanwhile, Christian scouts reported that a large enemy force was forming up ahead, ready for battle. "Their army covered the whole face of the earth all around and was beyond numbering," recorded one writer.[33]

On the morning of September 7 Richard ordered his army to rise at dawn and don their armor in readiness for an immediate assault. Then he divided the crusaders into twelve squadrons, which were proportionally arranged into five battalions and lined up with one flank by the sea. Reversing positions from the march, the Templars under Robert of Sablé were now in the front line, and the Hospitallers in the rear. Their goal was to avoid being pinned down, to keep moving, as they had done since the departure from Acre. They hoped to hold their formation and fight on the move until they reached higher terrain up ahead that could be taken for a fortified camping ground. It was a tactic that depended on a high dose of self-belief and, above all, discipline, which was why the Templars were placed in the lead.

Around 9 A.M. the crusaders were charged by a wave of Muslim soldiers assembled from far across Saladin's empire: Bedouins carrying round shields and bows, black Africans on foot and, behind them, Turkish cavalry, whose deadly gallop was accompanied by a cacophony of trumpets, clarions, horns, flutes, rattles, cymbals and high-pitched war cries. Behind it all, from the direction of Saladin's personal guard, a drum could be heard, beating relentlessly.[34]

Rather than attacking the Templars in the vanguard, Saladin's men flanked the crusader army and concentrated on fighting the Hospitallers at the rear. Protected by a thick cascade of arrow shot, they hurtled into the Christian lines, swinging swords and jagged cudgels. Richard's instructions were for the whole army to remain firm and withstand the waves of attack, waiting for a prearranged signal of six trumpet blasts to start their own cavalry surge. But needled by the oppressive heat and the pressure of a sustained attack, the Hospitallers lost their discipline and charged early. It could have brought disaster, but Richard and the rest of the Frankish command kept order for long enough to coordinate the horse assault they had planned. As the trumpets sounded, all along the crusader lines infantry parted and knights flew out. The timing was perfect: three charges was all it took to send both flanks of Saladin's army scattering in disarray. Despondent and angry, the sultan withdrew, consoling himself by beheading a handful of captives.

The battle of Arsuf was another splendid victory for Richard. The Templars had played their part, helping to maintain the army's shape under fierce pressure. After the battle was over, the king conferred on them a somber honor: a deputation of Templar and Hospitaller brothers, guarded by Syrian turcopoles, were sent back to the area where the bulk of the fighting had taken place to search for the body of James of Avesnes. The famous Flemish knight and nobleman had gone missing during the violence and he was feared dead. Once again, the Templars did their duty, scouring the field of battle until they found him, reportedly surrounded by the headless corpses of fifteen Muslim fighters, "his face so smeared with congealed blood that they could hardly recognize him until it had been washed with water." The brothers bore his lifeless body back to camp, where it was buried amid great lamentation, with full military honor.[35]

If Saladin and his emirs had underestimated Richard before, the siege of Acre and battle at Arsuf now convinced them to amend their thinking. As the crusaders pushed steadily south, the sultan sent word ahead to Ascalon, instructing its Muslim population to destroy the city's defenses, burn their houses, shops and granaries, pack up their homes and leave. He preferred to ruin the great coastal city himself than allow it to fall as Acre had and risk its being used once again as a Christian base from which to threaten Egyptian shipping and launch raids on the roads to Cairo. Released from duty, troops defending Ascalon were redeployed: "The strength of the Muslim forces was preserved for the protection of Jerusalem," wrote Ibn Shaddad.[36]

By mid-October the crusader army had reached Jaffa. The march the Templars had shepherded down the coast had been remarkably successful, retaking a valuable clutch of towns and securing a morale-boosting victory in battle without devastating casualties. Now attention on both sides turned to Jerusalem. Diplomatic exchanges between Richard and Saladin via the sultan's brother stressed the sanctity of the city to both sides. Richard promised that the Christians would fight to the very last man to win it back, although he also hinted that the return of the Holy Cross might mollify him in the meantime. Saladin retorted by reminding him that the Temple Mount and the Dome of the Rock were the places where Muhammad had encountered angels. He said his inclination was to destroy the Cross, an act that would be pleasing to God, but that he was holding on to it for a while in case it proved useful in some way in the future. The closest the sides came to a settlement was an extraordinary proposal by which all Christian settlements on the west bank of the river Jordan would be handed over into the trust of the Templars and Hospitallers, under the ultimate rule of a joint monarchy to be created in Jerusalem with the marriage of al-Adil to Richard's sister Joanna. This was a farsighted proposal but rather before its time; it foundered on Joanna's indignant refusal to consider joining her flesh with a Muslim, and al-Adil's corresponding lack of interest in converting to Christianity.[37]

As it transpired, this high-minded but futile exchange was as close as Richard and the warriors of the Third Crusade ever came to Jerusalem. In December a large force of pilgrims and soldiers set out on the road inland from Jaffa in the hope of storming the city and visiting the Holy Sepulchre, "for they had an indescribable yearning to see the city of Jerusalem and complete their pilgrimage."[38] Abysmal weather broke up the expedition, as heavy winds and rain killed pack animals, rusted armor and rotted perishable food. The crowd made it as far as Betenoble (Bayt-Nuba), on the road from Ramla, from where Jerusalem loomed tantalizingly in the distance. But as their destination crept closer, Richard's advisers grew warier as to the wisdom of attempting to besiege the most heavily defended city in the Holy Land, for which Saladin had made it plain he would fight to the death.

According to a Christian chronicle, the Templars and Hospitallers counseled Richard in the strongest terms against attempting to storm Jerusalem, arguing that he lacked the numbers required to besiege the city while also fighting a relieving force, and that even if they succeeded, they would find themselves helpless to hold what they had won. Richard was commanding an army of pilgrims, whose express intention was to see the Holy Sepulchre and get straight back to the West, where many had left unattended families, estates and business interests. Unless the men among them joined the military orders en masse—an impossible prospect—they could not be expected to dig in for the difficult and potentially lifelong mission of holding Jerusalem, along with every other recaptured town west of the Jordan. It would be far better, they argued, to concentrate on the more realistic task of rebuilding Ascalon.

After some deliberation, Richard agreed. He turned his army around and headed back to the coast. Groans of misery greeted the announcement of his decision, but Richard's mind was made up. His thoughts were beginning to turn to England and to his vast patrimonial lands in northern and western France. Over Easter 1192 a steady stream of reports began to arrive from home, telling him that his kingdom was under threat from Philip Augustus, who was conspiring with Richard's devious younger brother, John. The king was also suffering from recurring bouts of illness and becoming increasingly bogged down in the labyrinthine politics of the Latin states. Once Easter had passed he found himself implicated in the violent death of the Pisan magnate Conrad of Montferrat, who had managed to sideline Guy of Lusignan after the death of Queen Sibylla in 1190. Conrad had had himself elected as the nominal king of Jerusalem, only to be murdered by Assassins at Acre on April 28, 1192, three short days after his formal acceptance of the crown.

This was not the sort of business for which Richard had traveled to the East. In June he agreed to have one more tilt at Jerusalem, but once again, having reached Betenoble the Templars and Hospitallers convinced him that it was folly to go any farther. After an aborted plan to invade Egypt, on September 2, 1192, Richard agreed to a three-year truce with Saladin, which froze territorial gains as they stood and granted Christian pilgrims unmolested access to pray at the Holy Sepulchre in Jerusalem. Five and a half weeks later, on October 9, Richard boarded his ship at Acre and set out for home. As his galley left the harbor, those on board would have been able to see the towers of the Templar house receding behind them. For some in the king's company the sight may have had a special poignancy. According to one account, Richard attempted to travel back to England incognito, disguised in Templar uniform and surrounded by a bodyguard composed of Templar brothers.[39] If so, this was hardly surprising. The Knights of the Temple had been with him all the way. They meant to remain with him until the end.

✛

Richard's journey home was almost as eventful as his crusade. He had made several dangerous enemies during his time in the East, among them Duke Leopold V of Austria, whom he had insulted and humiliated during the division of spoils after the fall of Acre. A white-mantled Templar disguise was not sufficient to keep the Lionheart from falling into Leopold's hands when he was shipwrecked in the Adriatic several weeks after leaving Acre. Richard would spend nearly eighteen months in prison at Trifels Castle, held hostage by Leopold's overlord Henry VI, the Holy Roman Emperor, who demanded—and received—a ransom of 100,000 pounds for his release, a sum roughly equivalent to the cost of an entire crusade.

None of this, however, could detract from the general sense that Richard the Lionheart had saved the Franks of Outremer. He had arrived in the Holy Land as a new king with everything to prove. He left as a living legend: hated by some, revered by others, feared by all. His name would quickly become synonymous with the Christians' desire to win back Jerusalem at any cost. Fifty years after his death, Muslim mothers were said to quiet their unruly children by saying, "Hush! Or I will send king Richard of England to you."[40]

Saladin, nearing the end of his life, was deeply struck by his opponent's chivalry and military skill, and with good reason. Brutal as Richard could be, he was an inspirational commander who valued martial skill, religious zeal and discipline, and knew how to deploy them to best effect. This had direct implications for the Templars. Richard's pragmatic decision to bind both military orders into his direct sphere of influence had helped secure his victory. His deployment of the Templars for the purposes they were created and his willingness to heed their advice restored stability and pride to the order following Gerard of Ridefort's impetuous and disaster-strewn administration. Robert of Sablé died in 1193, a year after Richard's departure, but his appointment had been an unqualified success, providing purpose and discipline at a moment of crisis. This mattered just as much back in England as it did in Outremer, as the order continued to enjoy the patronage of the Crown.

There was one more, very tangible way in which Richard had altered the world in which the Templars operated. During the king's final year in the Holy Land, he and his protégé Robert of Sablé struck a short-lived deal that would have long and quite unforeseen consequences for the order. It centered upon the island of Cyprus, which Richard had conquered from the Byzantine governor Isaac Comnenus shortly before he sailed into Acre in 1191. Having taken the island, Richard needed some way to run it. He alighted on the idea of selling it to the Templars.

In 1191 this made a good deal of sense: the order had lost dozens of castles and towers to Saladin's conquests and no longer had a permanent base; Master Robert, the man authorized to make such a decision, was Richard's creation, and the order, although depleted in manpower, was still cash rich from its steadily growing estates in the West. The two men agreed on a fee of 100,000 gold dinars. The Templars advanced the king a down payment of 40,000 and sent twenty knight-brothers and around one hundred other fighting men, commanded by brother Reynald Bochart, to rule Cyprus from the citadel in Nicosia, the largest city in the center of the island.

Bochart found on Cyprus a population that was unwilling to be ruled. One chronicle recorded that the order ruled as though all the island's inhabitants were serfs, and that they in turn "could not bear the indignities the Templars inflicted on them." Most likely this meant that the order attempted to levy stiff taxes to raise the sixty thousand bezants they still owed the king of England. Whatever the case, in April 1192, while Richard was negotiating Jerusalem's fate with Saladin and al-Adil, a major rebellion broke out on Cyprus. The castle at Nicosia was besieged and on Easter Sunday, of all days, the Templars were forced to fight their way out with cavalry charges that left blood running in the streets and trickling into the river Pedieos.[41] They then rode out into the fields and mountains on a punitive rampage of waste and death. Bochart and his men had failed and the order had overreached. Richard was prevailed upon to dispose of Cyprus in some other way.

His solution was to transfer the island to Guy of Lusignan. In exchange he asked Guy to compensate the Templars for their losses and to assume the remainder of their debt. Guy was adrift following the death of Sibylla and the subsequent loss of his crown. Marginalized by Conrad of Montferrat in a poisonous factional conflict, there was a certain attraction in removing him from the Latin mainland. Guy had been present when Richard first conquered Cyprus, and he was willing to hold it as a fiefdom of Richard's Western empire. Installing him in place of the Templars was a solution that suited everyone. Guy was once more a king, Richard was rid of an island he had conquered but did not want, and the Order of the Temple could retain valuable, revenue-generating estates on Cyprus without the onerous responsibility of political rule.

13

"Nowhere in Poverty"

EOFFREY FITZ STEPHEN'S new book looked splendid. Nearly one hundred sheets of parchment, carefully cut and assembled by one of London's finest bookbinders, were delicately stitched into a pair of small beech-wood boards, each covered in soft brown leather. Weird and wonderful decorations were stamped on the leather: lions and herons, legendary winged snake-dragons known as wyverns, tiny flowers and intricate leaves. Between them all was a picture of the biblical king David, sitting cross-legged with his crown on his head, playing a harp. Metal clasps held the book closed and a little tab of parchment poked out from the base of its spine, so Fitz Stephen could pull it from the shelf at his leisure, and inspect its tight, neat lines of clerical handwriting.

When he did so, row upon row of abbreviated Latin script leaped off the page to form a pleasing image of a flourishing business, of which Fitz Stephen was the chief executive officer. This was not a large volume, but it was an incredibly valuable one—a census of landed property that was like a private Domesday Book.* It described in minute detail all the possessions of the Order of the Temple in England, where Fitz Stephen was the master.[1] The pages listed the many fine things that fell under his care: manor houses and homesteads, sheep farms and water mills, churches, markets, forests and fairs, sprawling estates and isolated villages where dozens of men worked in serfdom, owing compulsory field work during harvest season to the order in return for their own small plots of land. This was a property portfolio accumulated over more than half a century from pious donations and smart business deals. It included hundreds of interests scattered across England: from Connerton, in the far southwest of Cornwall, to Linthorpe, a sparse hamlet in the far northeast at the

---

* The Domesday Book was a huge survey of property and people in England and Wales, carried out on the orders of William the Conqueror twenty years after the Norman Conquest in 1066.

mouth of the river Tees, where a century and a half earlier Vikings had still landed their longships. Between these two extremes Templar properties could be found in almost every county of England. Some were truly magnificent—such as the vast manor at Cressing in Essex, or the wealthy preceptory at Bruer in Lincolnshire, where a graceful compound of buildings spilled outward around another large, round-naved church. Others were ordinary city houses rented out to tenants, or simple and unglamorous patches of farmland in the quiet countryside. The power of all these properties lay in their combination, for together this was a proud and profitable empire.

Besides being the master of the Templars in England, Fitz Stephen was a well-connected aristocratic figure of high social standing who counted among his friends bishops and abbots, princes and kings. He had taken charge of the order toward the end of king Henry II's reign, around 1180, and his leadership over the decade that followed was something of a coming-of-age period for the order in England. For two generations there had been Templar houses in the realm, populated by brothers praying and working on behalf of their benefactors and their warrior colleagues in the East. Under Fitz Stephen, however, the English Templars had cemented their special status as a favored order whose services were seen as indispensable by the Crown.

Knights of the Temple had been mixed up in England's great affairs of the realm almost since Hugh of Payns's visit in the 1120s. During the the Anarchy, both sides had sought Templar favor. In 1153, when the Anarchy was resolved by a treaty granting the English Crown to the future Henry II, a Templar knight by the name of Oto (probably the master) was an official witness. Templar knights had subsequently been seconded to the king's court, where they worked as diplomats, a role in which the international nature of the order gave them a certain neutrality and mutual acceptability. When Henry arranged a complex marriage deal between one of his infant daughters and the son of the French king Louis VII, three Templar knights had taken delivery of the castles forming part of the child bride's dowry. In 1164, when Henry quarreled with Thomas Becket, his truculent archbishop of Canterbury, the then master of the English Temple, Richard of Hastings, helped mediate. When Henry's loose and angry words resulted in Becket's murder before the

altar of Canterbury Cathedral in December 1170, and the king was forced
to pay a large fine in penance, he deposited it with the Order of the Temple, who sent the money east to be spent on troops for the Hattin campaign. Henry had appointed a Templar, Brother Roger, as his almoner—the
man responsible for ensuring that charity was distributed to the poor on
the king's behalf. His barons followed suit, including the glamorous
knight turned statesman William Marshal, who also appointed a brother
as his almoner and would take Templar vows on his deathbed in 1219.[2] England's Templar masters—men like Richard of Hastings and Geoffrey
Fitz Stephen—were drawn from well-to-do dynasties whose sons were
used to going into ministerial service for the Crown. The work they did on
the king's behalf made the order a visible and reliable part of public life.

Fitz Stephen ran the order from a plush London headquarters, whose
grandeur reflected the esteem in which the English Templars were held
and the wealth this allowed them to amass. Originally they occupied the
"Old" Temple in the London suburb of Holborn, to the northwest of the
thick-walled square mile of the City. In 1161 this valuable piece of real estate was sold to the bishop of Lincoln and the Templars' central convent
moved half a mile or so south, where the brothers built the "New" Temple at a fashionable riverside address on Fleet Street. Here they had access to the busy waterways of the Thames, useful when the fastest way to
travel to and from the City was by boat. On the road side, the New Temple was perched directly on the main thoroughfare connecting the mer-
cantile heart of the City with Westminster, where the palace and the
towering abbey were a hub for royal and religious business.

Fitz Stephen's predecessors had constructed a large monastic compound, with halls for the brothers who lived there, stables, a cemetery and
an orchard. An earth-and-stone wall ran around the perimeter, and at the
heart of it all was a round-naved church built from Caen stone—limestone
quarried in Normandy, envied across northern Europe as the finest building material that money could buy. The circular nave of the New Temple
Church almost gleamed as the sun moved over it. The architecture was
devout and purposeful: its shape deliberately echoed the Holy Sepulchre
in Jerusalem, a reminder of the crusading mission of the Temple, and an
implicit boast of the order's wealth and global reach. It was also competi-
tive. At the same time as the Templars were building their round church

at the New Temple, the Hospitallers were constructing a round church in their base at Clerkenwell, to the northwest of London.[3]

The year 1185 had been a golden one for the English Templars in their new headquarters. First, the compilation of Geoffrey Fitz Stephen's inquest into Templar possessions had begun: commissioners sent reports of diligent investigations the length and breadth of the country back to the New Temple for sifting, sorting and transcribing on the pages of the master's beautifully ornamented record book. On top of this, Eraclius, patriarch of Jerusalem, had visited England.* As one of the greatest churchmen on earth, Eraclius's presence in London was a marvel in itself. Although his considerable powers of persuasion had failed to convince Henry II to take up the throne of Jerusalem, Eraclius nevertheless contributed fruitfully to the English branch of the Templars by consecrating their round church at the New Temple. This honor would only have been bettered if the pope himself had left Rome to bestow his blessing.

Finally, in 1185 Henry II had begun to use the New Temple as a treasury, effectively relying on the order as a bank of deposit. Coin, jewels and valuable trinkets were held at Fleet Street, making the New Temple a strongbox facility that complemented other nearby royal fortresses such as the Tower of London, a few miles to the east. The order had impressed Henry with the security of its buildings, and the king may also have appreciated the fact that the order had a permanent presence in almost every county of England, as well as most of the major realms of Western Europe. Throughout his reign Henry II paid close attention to centralizing mechanisms in government, using his royal sheriffs to project the will and financial policies of his government into the farthest localities. His decision to start using the Order of the Temple as a bank suggested that he saw their potential as a wide-ranging body that could help him in his mission.

In 1188, having heard the news from Hattin, Henry tasked the Templars with helping to collect a levy known as the Saladin tithe: a tax to raise emergency funds for a new crusade. With their intimate ties to the

---

* This was the embassy that left Jerusalem in 1184, on which Master Arnold of Torrolla died.

cause and their infrastructure all over England, the Templars were perfectly placed to go about collecting this money, and Henry trusted them to do it. Fitz Stephen had cause to discipline one unscrupulous brother, Gilbert of Ogerstan, who was caught skimming a personal profit from his tax collections, contravening the stern Templar rules against brothers having any money of their own. Otherwise their role seems to have been a success, for as the years passed and Henry's crown passed to his successors, the Templars grew in status and royal favor.

Henry's son Richard was instrumental in the Templars' resurgence as a military force in the Holy Land. He was no less admiring of the order in his own kingdom: in the brief months between his accession as king and his departure for Acre, Richard had issued charters granting, confirming and formally guaranteeing the Templars' possessions all over England and Wales, and exempting them from a whole raft of royal taxes imposed on landholders across the kingdom. Indeed, not only were they exempted from the Crown's routine impositions on local communities to support law and order, or for the repair of roads and bridges, or for garrisoning royal castles; they were also awarded a special grant of a mark of silver (i.e., two thirds of a pound, or 160 pence) to be paid annually to the order by every sheriff in England.[4] Their value to the king was so high that he was prepared to allow the Templars near-total immunity from the ordinary demands of royal government and taxation.

Having returned to England by way of captivity in Germany, Richard spent most of the rest of his reign fighting Philip Augustus over his landholdings in Normandy, Anjou and Aquitaine. He died suddenly and shockingly in 1199: contracting blood poisoning after being hit by a crossbow bolt while besieging a castle in Châlus. But the cozy relationship between Templars and English kings would continue under Richard's unlucky and generally despised brother and successor King John. The Templars were one of the few powerful groups in England whom John did not offend or alienate. He relied on them for day-to-day loans, and stayed at the New Temple for important festivals like Easter. The Templars stood by him for more than five years when he quarreled with the pope and England was placed under interdict; and when John was forced in June 1215 to grant his subjects the famous charter of liberties known as

Magna Carta, Brother Eymeric, then master of the order in England, was among its official witnesses, his name placed appropriately after the archbishops, bishops and abbots who also testified to the charter's sealing, but before all the secular magnates.[5]

Not everyone in England was impressed by this cozy relationship between the Plantagenet kings and the Knights of the Temple. A contemporary of Geoffrey Fitz Stephen's at the court of Henry II, the clerk, chronicler and wit Walter Map, devoted several pages of his long book, *Courtiers' Trifles*, to a sketch of the Templars. Map knew of the Templars' origins under Hugh of Payns, a man to whom he referred with grudging approval as "no coward," a warrior with a "zeal for righteousness" who prescribed "chastity and sobriety to his order."[6] Map did not deny that "kings and princes came to think that the object of the Order of the Temple was good and its way of life honorable" and recognized that "by the help of popes and patriarchs" the Templars had been granted high blessing as "the defenders of Christendom" and "loaded . . . with immense wealth."[7] Yet he had his doubts. And when we consider that he was attached to the royal court, which traveled ceaselessly around England, Normandy, Maine and Poitou—all areas where one might stumble across a tract of Templar land or a thriving Templar house—it is possible to see why.

"Nowhere save in Jerusalem are they in poverty," Map wrote. Perhaps he was thinking of the omnipresence of Templar officials across the Plantagenet lands, with regional commanders in the duchies of Aquitaine and Normandy whose authority superseded the notional boundaries between different lordships. Henry II had struggled all his life to exercise rule across the turbulent territories of Gascony, Anjou and Brittany, all of which had different traditions of government and historical allegiance—yet a single Templar master (the master of Aquitaine) ruled over all three jurisdictions without apparent contradiction or difficulty, marshaling resources and collecting alms, rents and private taxes.[8] Equally Map may have had personal matters in mind. Not far from his birthplace in the Welsh borders stood the grand Templar house of Germany, built with a Holy Sepulchre–style round nave and sustained by two thousand acres of fertile Welsh farmland.[9] This was a very long way indeed from the ideal of Cistercian-style poverty that the order had once espoused.

Among Map's other grumbles was his objection to the inherent contradiction of the new knighthood, in which men "take the sword to protect Christendom, which Peter was forbidden to take to defend Christ." At root, he simply loathed the idea that the Holy City of Jerusalem was defended by homicidal knights. "There Peter was taught to ensue peace by patience: who taught these [Templars] to overcome force by violence I know not."[10]

In this Map was not alone. His contemporary John of Salisbury, a diplomat at the papal court in Rome, also believed that the basic tenet of Templar existence—the concept of the warrior bound by a religious oath—was an unholy contradiction. John despised the fact that the Templars were not subject to the proper authority of local bishops, and suspected them to be engaged in abominable sin: "When they convene in their lairs late at night, after speaking of virtue by day they shake their hips in nocturnal folly and exertion," he wrote.[11] Likewise, the learned abbot Isaac of l'Etoile, a Cistercian monk from Poitou, saw the Templars as a creeping perversion of the Cistercian ideal. Saint Bernard had praised the Templars as "a new knighthood." Isaac begged to differ. "A new monstrosity" was his verdict.[12]

Fortunately, this view was not shared by the pope or by any of the great Western monarchs who protected the order and made use of its services. For those who wielded power, the Templars combined martial prowess with spiritual prestige and global connections. For this reason, Templar knights were to be found among the inner circle of every pope after the accession of Alexander III in 1159, serving the Holy Father in his private rooms as chamberlain. Alexander III also employed a pair of Templars named Bernardo and Francone to look after his financial affairs: testament to the business know-how for which the order was becoming famous.[13]

In France and its vassal states the Templars were just as close—perhaps even closer—to the Crown. There had long been direct contact between the French king and Templar officials in the East—dating back to the Second Crusade. By the end of the twelfth century that relationship had deepened and brothers based at the massive Temple complex, just out-side the city walls, were ready visitors to the royal palace on the Île de la Cité. In 1202 a Templar brother called Haimard, a resident of the Paris Temple, was appointed treasurer to the Crown, an arrangement that benefited both parties equally. The Templars gained enormous prestige and political influence from the beginning of a tradition that would last for more than a century. France gained the most modern accounting sys-tem in Europe, consolidating all royal income and expenditure through a single set of books, allowing careful scrutiny and management on a scale seen nowhere among its neighbors.[14] The French king's heavy reliance on Templar expertise was mimicked by his subjects. Across the realm, men and women sought Templar help in raising loans, guarding treasure, keeping charters, treaties and wills, and transferring funds over long dis-tances.

As the order grew more famous and respected and useful to king and country, it was little surprise that its possessions flourished. In Marseille, on the Mediterranean coast, a lucrative dock was established, where in 1216 the Templars were granted special favored access to the harbor and allowed toll-free and unrestricted access for their ships. These went to provision their brothers in the East with horses, arms, coin and other supplies and also profited from taking pilgrims and merchants to the Holy Land. The Templars of Marseille were able to offer this valuable service because the order had started to commission and maintain its own vessels, rather than relying on the shipping magnates of Venice, Genoa and other Italian seafaring cities, who were traditionally domi-nant in maritime transport across the Mediterranean.

Templar properties and houses sprawled from north of Normandy to the Pyrenees. The order was well provided in their traditional heartland of Champagne, where successive counts had allowed the brethren ex-traordinary freedom to build up their interests. They were granted the right to hold properties and titles of any sort, stopping short only of full lordships. In busy merchant towns like Provins the Templars owned multiple houses and levied heavy taxes on local enterprises including ab-batoirs and tanneries, where animal hides were worked into leather. They took a slice of wool production and weaving; charged for mill use, oven space and permission to fish rivers; leased vineyards to winemakers and even owned a couple of fruit stalls in the town center. Their own, directly managed, lands yielded wine and cereal crops.[15] All over France the order was collecting rents and tolls, and making a profit on the fruits of their own estates. They were major feudal lords, and thousands of men and women lived in various forms of bonded servitude on Templar land, owing by ancient custom the sweat of the labor for a fixed number of days per year, or being compelled to present as rent in kind a fixed number of cows, chickens, crops or eggs.

This situation was replicated across the Christian West. In Italy, the Templar presence had spread rapidly throughout the peninsula as far south as Sicily, where there were major preceptories in Messina and throughout the island. In Aragón—where the Templars' long history stretched back to the days of Alfonso the Battler—the order owned manors, vineyards and olive groves as well as a portfolio of residential and commercial property. The charter register of the Templar house in Huesca, in northern Aragón, contains records of transactions by which the Templar brothers bought orchards, wineries, shops and houses. They received pious gifts that sometimes extended to every living possession of Christian penitents, who declared that they donated out of their "fear [of] the pains of hell and wish to see the joys of Paradise."[16] The brothers would pray regularly for the souls of those who made them their heirs—the better the gift, the more frequent the prayers.

Just as in France and England, this acquisition of land and property in Spain's Christian kingdoms went along with an elevated political profile. In Aragón this peaked in 1213 when a new king, James I, came to the throne as a five-year-old, following the death of his father, Peter II, on the battlefield. Young James was entrusted first to the care of the pope, but straightaway the Holy Father arranged for him to be raised by William of Montrodón, the master of the Templars in Spain and Provence. James was kept safe for four years from the bloody factional warfare that had killed his father, walled up at the impenetrable Templar fortress in Monzón: their massive hilltop castle compound protected by thick, red, angular stone walls and towers, inside which was a preceptory that more closely resembled a private city. When he reached the age of nine, James began slowly to be introduced to government in Zaragoza and the

Templars released him back to the world. James I was lukewarm about his time under Templar supervision, writing in his autobiography that while he was held there, his fathers' lands were mortgaged "to Jews and Saracens," and it ended up badly wasted. By the time he was nine years old, he recalled that he could not "be held any longer at Monzón, so greatly did we desire to leave."[17] But the order had performed a profoundly important duty. The fate of a king and a kingdom had been placed squarely in their hands and the fact that James grew up to be one of the most successful of the Reconquista kings was appropriate to his forma-tive years spent in the company of Templar knights.

As an adult, James I maintained his close links to the order, although he did not lavish them with the overt favoritism that they received in England and France. The war against the Almohads continued through-out most of his sixty-three-year reign, and the king proved himself one of the great crusader kings of the Western theater, relying heavily on both Templars and Hospitallers in his campaigns. With Templar en-couragement and a good deal of military help between 1229 and 1235 James conquered the islands of Mallorca, Menorca and Ibiza from the semi-independent Almohad ruler Abu-Yahya: a huge military undertak-ing that involved thousands of troops on both sides and protracted siege warfare. In the invasion of Mallorca the Templars provided around one hundred knights, several transport boats and plenty of strategic advice, for which they were rewarded with a share in the island as it was divided up between the many groups who helped conquer it—although this was not equal to the one fifth of all lands they helped conquer that had been promised to them in 1143 when Alfonso I's will was finally settled. Never-theless, the Templars of Aragón continued to assist the king in his war of Christian conquest: when he turned his attention to invading Valencia he had twenty Templar knights and a commander in his army. In 1238 James drove out the Moors of Valencia and began colonizing the sur-rounding area to form a new kingdom, with himself as king. The Tem-plars were handily rewarded, with a house in the city, gardens and farmland—although again their gains fell way below the one-fifth thresh-old they thought they had a right to expect.[18] The conquest of Valencia was also a mixed blessing for the order: its completion in 1244 meant that Aragón had sealed off its final frontier with the forces of Islam, reducing the urgency of their mission in the kingdom. Although the Templars kept command of some formidable castles, their role was set to diminish from its twelfth-century peak. They nevertheless remained a much more prominent presence in Aragón than elsewhere in the Spanish kingdoms, particularly Castile and León, where the smaller, native military orders were preferred to the supranational giants who owed their name and sent their wealth to the Temple and the Hospital in Jerusalem.

✠

Among the many princes and potentates in Christendom who did value the Templars, enrich them, use their services and inoculate them against the grumblings of the late-twelfth-century's waspish court writers and priggish abbots, few were so energetic in their support for the order as Pope Innocent III. Born Lotario dei Conte di Segni, Innocent assumed the papacy on January 8, 1198, before his fortieth birthday, and ruled over the Church with all the force of his outsized personality until his death in 1216. He was a great Church reformer, the scourge of those monarchs (like King John of England) who did not fully respect the authority of the Holy See, and a wholehearted advocate of the Church's militant mission in the East.

Encouragingly for the Christians, Saladin died at dawn on March 3, 1193, following a "bilious fever" that lasted for around a fortnight. He was fifty-five or fifty-six years old, and in his astonishing career he had changed the whole shape of politics in Syria and Egypt, establishing his Ayyubid dynasty and creating a legend that would live on for centuries. Saladin's biographer Ibn Shaddad wrote that "the world was overwhelmed by such a sense of loss as God alone could comprehend."[19]

That sentiment did not extend to Innocent III. Saladin had done more damage to the crusading movement than any other man—and he had died without ever fully loosening his grip on Jerusalem or returning the great relic of the True Cross that had been kept at the Holy Sepulchre and was once the pride of the Latin Church. Yet in death, he offered an opportunity for the Christian Church to take advantage of Ayyubid's confusion. During Saladin's lifetime he had divided up his empire into regional fiefdoms governed by various relatives: Saladin's eldest son, al-Afdal, managed the lands around Damascus; his second son, al-Aziz Uthman, held sway in Egypt; and his third son, Az-Zahir Ghazi, controlled Aleppo and northern Syria. The sultan's brother al-Adil was based at Kerak in the Transjordan. On Saladin's death this diffusion of power created a tussle for overall supremacy that would rumble on for many years to come.

With the Ayyubid empire momentarily in disarray, in 1202–4 Innocent III launched the Fourth Crusade, which sought to seize back the initiative. Unfortunately for Innocent it was a fiasco in which European troops and a Venetian fleet set out for the Holy Land but instead diverted to Constantinople, which they ruthlessly and greedily looted before installing a new Latin ruler, replacing the Byzantine Greek emperor Alexios III Angelos with the Count of Flanders, who assumed the imperial title as Baldwin I. The Ayyubids continued, in their familial rivalries, untroubled. However, despite this embarrassing failure, Innocent remained passionately concerned with the fate of the Latin Christians of the East and devoted to the idea that they might still win back Jerusalem. Moreover, Innocent saw the Templars in the East as manning the front line of the Holy Land's defense and, in common with the ruling class of the day, viewed their brothers in the West as invaluable administrators and diplomats.

Innocent III protected and patronized the order with great zeal. He used Templar brothers as tax collectors, granted the order new privileges and issued papal bulls reconfirming the general protections it had enjoyed for decades. He described members of the military orders as "men of character and prudence" and advised the clergy who went out preaching in favor of his ill-starred Fourth Crusade to always have a Templar and a Hospitaller brother with them.[20] Over the course of his papacy he reiterated the Templars' rights to collect tithes and immunity from tithes charged by other clergy. Innocent reaffirmed the Templars' right to build their own churches, forbade any other Christians from harming the brothers or their possessions and exhorted the order to examine closely their new recruits to avoid a weakening of the Templars' collective moral fiber. (This was an important issue after Hattin, when there was a pressing need for new men, which threatened to dilute the quality of recruitment.) He stepped in to overrule a sentence of excommunication on

Girbert Eral, the Spaniard who succeeded Robert of Sablé as master of the Templars in 1193—and threatened anathema against anyone who dared to disobey Templar commands. Taken together, this was a serious restatement of the order's privilege and power.

The Templars: ever present, capable and experienced in the business of fighting the enemies of Christ, were a useful manifestation of Innocent's vision of the Church militant. In turn, the pope was as good a patron as any of the secular kings of Christendom who had thus far made use of the order. By the time Innocent died in 1216 the Templars were stronger, richer and better connected than at any time in their history. It was true that most of their members and associates lived thousands of miles from the front line of the war against the Muslims of Syria and Egypt that had occupied the brothers in the East for close to one hundred years, and that even in Europe only a small number were militarily active against the Almohads. Few lived the life originally envisaged by Hugh of Payns and Saint Bernard. Nevertheless, all had a part to play in either funding or fighting in the crusades. While the Templars were diversifying out of military activity into banking, estate management and international diplomacy, the order had seldom been so central to the crusading movement as it would be in the years immediately following Innocent's death. With Saladin gone, things were stirring again in Outremer: a Fifth Crusade was planned, with its focus on Egypt and the merchant cities of the Nile Delta. This would be a massive undertaking, summoning men and matériel from all over Christendom and deploying it on an amphibious campaign in hostile territory. It would demand devotion, know-how and money. And who better to turn to for the planning, execution and cleanup of this extraordinary new adventure than the Order of the Temple?

14

"Damietta!"

A NORTH WIND BLEW down the coast as a steady stream of ships
cast off from harbor in a calm bay whose jetty lay in the shadow
of a huge new Templar castle. Château Pèlerin, named after the
volunteers who had helped build it, was as large as any other fortification
erected by the Christians of the Holy Land over the course of the past
hundred and twenty years. It sat perched on a rocky spit jutting into the
sea not far from Haifa, roughly halfway between Jaffa and Acre, the working capital of the Christian kingdom of Jerusalem. Six miles away was
Mount Tabor, which the Saracens, led by Saladin's brother al-Adil, had
recently taken and fortified with a military base. Château Pèlerin was conceived in part as a riposte to Mount Tabor—and it did its job well.

A state-of-the-art example of military hardware, Château Pèlerin
(also known as 'Atlit) had replaced the older complex nearby at Destroit,
erected decades earlier to guard the narrow coastal road at a point that
was vulnerable to brigand raids. Whereas Destroit was effectively a large
watchtower, Château Pèlerin was a palace barracks, providing garrison
space for thousands of troops and a harbor for Templar shipping. It included every feature of a military command center: a deep ditch protecting the landward entrance; inner defenses incorporating huge stone
blocks scavenged from an ancient Phoenician wall; a round church; a
dining hall designed to hold up to four thousand soldiers at a single sitting and internal staircases wide enough to allow a knight on horseback
to ride around the castle as he pleased.[1] It was equipped with ample dungeons, fit to hold prisoners of war, enemies of the order and wayward
brothers who had fallen foul of the order's increasingly detailed rule.
(Case studies of brothers imprisoned in chains at Château Pèlerin were
preserved, relating misdemeanors ranging from brawling and dressing in
secular clothing to illicit fondling at night.)[2] Château Pèlerin was a powerful statement of Christian reconstruction after the traumatic encounter with Saladin, its name a potent reminder of the Templars' chief

advantage as a fighting force: the fact that they were supplied and assisted by a seemingly endless stream of pious pilgrims. It had cost so much money to build, wrote one Christian writer, that "one wondered where it all came from."[3]

Aboard one of the ships setting off from the harbor in late May 1218 was William of Chartres, who had become master of the Templars following the death of Girbert Eral in 1201 and that of his successor, Philip of Plessis, in 1210. He traveled with Garin of Montaigu, master of the Hospitallers, and the marshals of both orders. Indeed, virtually the whole Templar central convent in the East was mobilizing, leaving behind only a skeleton crew of castellans and the officials directly responsible for maintaining commercial and shipping operations in Acre.

The military orders were traveling with the entire war machinery of the Latin East. Galleys loaded with weapons and armor accompanied passenger vessels carrying crusaders who had come to the Holy Land from Flanders, Austria and Hungary, and high-ranking churchmen including the patriarch of Jerusalem and the bishops of Acre, Nicosia and Bethlehem. With them too was the new king of Jerusalem, John of Brienne, a nobleman from Champagne who was administering the Eastern kingdom on behalf of his infant daughter Queen Isabella II. (John had taken a slightly complex path to kingship: he had married a granddaughter of Amalric known as Maria of Jerusalem, who had died in 1212, shortly after giving birth to Isabella, leaving John as regent.) Hundreds of ordinary pilgrims were setting sail, too, many of whom had already made a long journey from their homes in Bremen and Cologne, inspired to take crusader vows by the miraculous appearance of crosses blazing in the sky. The Fifth Crusade, first called by Pope Innocent III in 1213, had gripped the hearts of faithful northern Christians, and now those who had taken their vows and set out for the Holy Land were making the final leg of their journey to the city that had been selected for attack: Damietta, in the Nile Delta.

✝

At almost exactly the same time as one army was leaving Château Pèlerin in May 1218, another crusader fleet was unfurling its sails and heading for the Nile from the opposite direction: leaving the Atlantic coast of

Portugal, rounding the Algarve and making its way through the Strait of Gibraltar into the calmer, warmer waters of the Mediterranean. It comprised around eighty cogs—huge, oak-timbered ships powered by a single, large, square sail.[4] With this fleet was Peter of Montaigu, a long-serving Templar from a well-connected crusading family, who had risen through the ranks, serving as master for Spain and Provence, and latterly master in the West, making him the most senior brother outside the Holy Land. His brother, Garin of Montaigu, who had taken ship at Château Pèlerin, was master of the Hospitallers.*

Peter of Montaigu was a native of the Auvergne in southwest France, and despite having made his career in Europe rather than the East, he had seen plenty of godly warfare at first hand. On July 16, 1212, he had fought at the battle of Las Navas de Tolosa, in which a coalition of forces from the Spanish kingdoms of Aragón, Castile and Navarre had attacked a huge North African army led by the Almohad caliph Muhammad al-Nasir.

The turn of the thirteenth century had seen a revival of Muslim fortunes in southern Spain, as the Almohads had sought to reconquer lands taken from them by the steadily encroaching Christian kingdoms. In 1195, at the battle of Alarcos, the Almohad caliph al-Mansur inflicted a stinging defeat on an army commanded by Alfonso VIII of Castile. The Christians were driven from the battlefield and lost many castles and towns in the aftermath. The Spanish military orders who had taken part in the battle were rocked by the defeat: the Order of Santiago lost nineteen knights, including their master, and the Order of Calatrava two castles and an uncertain number of men.[5] These were not losses they could easily accommodate, nor could they simply brush off the humiliation of defeat. After much lobbying led by the military orders, Innocent III was persuaded in 1209 to grant the struggle against the Almohads full crusade status, aiding recruitment by allowing combatants to claim remission from sins for their involvement.

The battle of Las Navas de Tolosa was the culmination of this crusade. The kings of Castile, Navarre, Portugal and Aragón all took to the

---

* Two other Montaigu brothers also rose high in religious service, both based on Cyprus. Eustorg of Montaigu became archbishop of Nicosia, and Fulk of Montaigu bishop of Limassol.

field, along with the Templars, the orders of Santiago and Calatrava, and volunteers from France who had traveled to southern Spain, between Cordoba and Granada, for the express purpose of fighting the Almohads.

The Templars had fought in the rear guard at the battle, and Peter of Montaigu had witnessed the carnage that ensued as the Christians tore into the Muslim forces, chasing Muhammad al-Nasir (who had succeeded al-Mansur in 1199) from the field, his bodyguard of chained black African slaves failing to protect him from the devastating cavalry charges. The king of Castile crowed after the battle that the Christians had lost only twenty-five or thirty men, while they had killed one hundred thousand Muslims.[6] In fact, there were substantial losses on the Christian side, heavily borne by the military orders. The Templars lost their Portuguese master, and the master of the Order of Santiago also died. But it had been a morale-boosting victory and seemed to suggest that God was smiling once again on the Christians.

Now, six years later, Peter of Montaigu's ship was sailing away from the scene of another victory. Disappearing on the horizon was the shattered fortress of Alcácer do Sal (al-Qasr), some forty miles south of Lisbon, which had been placed under siege the previous autumn by a united force of Portuguese Christians and crusaders from Frisia and the Rhineland, who had battered it for months until its walls had finally come crashing down.

The enthusiastic assault had forced Alcácer's Muslim defenders to abandon it in October 1217: a victory heralded by yet another appearance of the Holy Cross in the night sky. The triumph owed much to the Spanish Templars, who had come en masse under their master Pedro Alvítiz to help with the siege.[7] "The Saracens were conquered through divine strength," wrote one chronicler. "One of their kings was killed and with him a great many were massacred or led into captivity."[8] This was just the sort of success that the Western crusaders hoped to replicate as they converged on the Egyptian coast.

+

"Damietta!" wrote the German churchman and historian Oliver of Paderborn, who had traveled from his home near Cologne to take part in the Fifth Crusade. "Renowned among kingdoms, most famous in the pride of Egypt, mistress of the sea."[9]

The city was rich, prosperous and busy: worth every syllable of this enthusiastic eulogy. To its west flowed one of the largest of the many waterways that formed the Nile Delta, where salt water mingled with freshwater that had come hundreds of miles from the Ethiopian highlands, and hungry crocodiles basked in the shallows.[10] On the eastern side of the city was the saltwater Lake Mansallah, long, shallow and full of fish. An abundant water supply meant that the city was surrounded by fertile farmland and villages, and the townsfolk amply stocked year-round with staple crops springing from the Nile's flood plain.[11] Yet Damietta was more than just the hub for riverside agriculture. It was one of the great port settlements of the region: convenient for traders from the flourishing Italian city-states of Genoa and Venice, and well connected to the coast towns of the Levant. With a fair wind a ship could travel from Acre to Damietta in less than a week. The opulent city of Cairo was in easy reach to the south. Damietta was a regular stopping point for merchant ships hugging the coast of the southern Mediterranean and a traditional hub for seafaring traders of the West to access the overland caravans heading east toward India and China, their camels and wagons loaded with exotic silks, spices, salt, gold, timber, oils, medicine and slaves.* Like Alexandria, across the delta, Damietta was an alluring prize, attacked with wearying regularity by the various imperial powers who had risen and fallen in the eastern Mediterranean during the previous five hundred years.

For the Christian soldiers gathering outside Damietta in 1218, traveling from England, Flanders, western France, the German principalities, Austria, Hungary and many other places besides, all of this wealth was

---

* In the late twelfth century an Arab customs official writing a tax manual recorded the goods that flowed through Egypt's port towns, noting that Damietta did a particularly good trade in poultry, grain and alum—an ingredient vital to textile production throughout Western Christendom. Egypt was also a source of exotic treasure robbed from the tombs of its ancient kings: besides gold and precious stones it was one of the only places in the world where pharmaceutical traders could obtain ground mummy dust—a prized ingredient in certain medieval medicines. See David Abulafia, *The Great Sea: A Human History of the Mediterranean* (Oxford: Oxford University Press, 2011), 297.

undoubtedly tantalizing. But so, too, was Egypt's spiritual lure. Damietta did not feature prominently in the life of Christ, but it was an entry
point to Egypt, the land where the Israelites had fled Babylon and roamed
the wilderness; where Moses had received the commandments; where
the Virgin Mary had cleaned Jesus' clothes in a holy spring. (The well in
question was a noted point on the pilgrim trail—where faithful Christians gathered to wash themselves on the feast of Epiphany, in a garden
full of balsam trees.) More than any of this, though, in the minds of
the crusaders of 1218 Damietta was the crucial first step to regaining Jerusalem.

Pope Innocent III preached the Fifth Crusade in 1213, but died on July 16,
1216, after a bracingly aggressive papacy in which he preached three crusades, excommunicated several princes and reasserted the might of
Rome. He did not live to see the armies he had called set off, so his mission was seen through by his successor Honorius III. An intelligent native of Rome who was in his midfifties when he was elected pope,
Honorius was not quite as bullish as Innocent, but he was committed
enough to crusading to divert a tenth of papal revenue for three years to
the project and to correspond vigorously with its various leaders—
including King Andrew of Hungary, Duke Leopold VI of Austria, the
patriarch of Jerusalem, the masters of the Templars and Hospitallers
and John of Brienne, titular king of Jerusalem.[12] There was no English
king involved, for John had died amid a civil war in 1216, leaving a child to
succeed him. Nor was Philip Augustus of France to be seen. But Honorius relentlessly petitioned his protégé, the king of the Germans, Frederick II Hohenstaufen, whom he had tutored as a child, to demand that
Frederick lead his own vast armies south and join in the attacks. The
pope had also ordered crusade processions throughout every city in
Christendom on the first Friday of every month, "so that every believer
could intercede in favor of the crusaders by prostrating humbly during
his prayer."[13]

    One thing Honorius did not do, however, was to involve himself in
military strategy. He felt this duty belonged to the princes and potentates who had stepped forward to lead the mission. It was partly for this
reason that a crusade originally called to restore Jerusalem to Christian

rule ended up being diverted to a trading post at the mouth of the Nile, two hundred miles from the Holy City.

The decision to attack Damietta rather than Jerusalem had been taken in Acre around October 1217 at a war council drawing together all the most senior crusaders from East and West. In a letter to Pope Honorius, the Templar Master William of Chartres had explained that Jerusalem could not be taken without first reducing the Saracens' ability to supply their armies in Palestine from the south and weakening the power of the Muslim ruler of Egypt, who by this stage was Saladin's nephew al-Kamil.[14]

The fact that there was yet another new sultan on whom to make war spoke to the continuing flux in the Ayyubid world. In the two decades following Saladin's death power had consolidated and then fractured once again. In 1201 his brother al-Adil had managed to assert his authority as sultan of Egypt and Syria, subduing opposition from Saladin's sons. But as al-Adil approached his death in 1218, the empire was split once again, this time between his own sons. Thus al-Kamil (known by the crusaders as Meledin) was installed in Cairo and slated to become the next sultan and ruler of the family; al-Mu'azzam (known as Coradin) held sway in Damascus; and a third brother, al-Ashraf, controlled Aleppo and northern Syria.

Damietta was the first point at which the crusaders aimed to test the enemy's new hierarchy. John of Brienne wrote that "through an invasion of the kingdom of Egypt, the Holy Land might be more easily liberated from infidel hands."[15] The Templar master appears to have approved of this strategy—he may well have been involved in pressing the case for it at the Acre conference. The Templars had played a significant part in planning the crusade, raising loans to help finance troop payments through the Temple in Paris under the guidance of the treasurer, Brother Haimard. It stood to reason that they would have a similarly critical role in the military action that followed.

+

The ships traveling from East and West converged on Damietta in the early summer of 1218. Those coming from Château Pèlerin reached the

Egyptian coast on May 30, only to find the German and Frisian fleet carrying Peter of Montaigu had already started disembarking. The crusaders established a bridgehead at the river mouth a short way upstream,
and began to survey the city's defenses.

Like any valuable jewel, Damietta was well guarded, protected by
three sets of turreted walls, each looming larger than the last. Twenty-
eight towers had been built into the walls, and moats dug between them
for extra security. Opposite the western wall of the city, in the middle of
the river, was an island, and on that island stood yet another tower to
which the citizens had attached a huge set of chains that could be raised
in moments of distress to prevent ships from entering the river through
its only viable channel.[16] Inside the city defenders were equipped with
every conceivable device for bludgeoning, burning or impaling anyone
foolhardy enough to face them down. One of their most potent weapons
was Greek fire: a sticky, naphtha-based inflammatory resin, which could
be sprayed from pipes or hurled, grenade style, in pots that shattered
on impact. Greek fire was almost impossible to extinguish. It was a
nasty and highly potent weapon to turn on soldiers attacking from the
water. Taken together, Damietta's defenses were as tough as any that a
crusading army had faced, and al-Kamil could be expected to send regular relieving sorties up from Cairo to hinder the course of the siege.
Serious planning, discipline and expertise would be required to breach
Damietta—all the more so as the attempt was set to begin in the heat of
the summer, where temperatures daily exceeded 110 degrees Fahrenheit
in the shade.

The crusaders' first task after setting up camp was to take the tower
on the island in the middle of the river—for without it the city was unbreakable. Having formally elected John of Brienne as their leader, they
set about the task with gusto. First came an enthusiastic trebuchet bar-
rage, which lasted for many days. Under cover of this bombardment, several of the most spirited and confident groups in the crusader armies
kitted out ships with ladders and wooden forecastles and attempted to
maneuver beside the chain tower and scale its walls. According to Oliver
of Paderborn, attack ships of this sort were fitted out by the Austrians,
Frisians, Germans and Hospitallers, and the Templars supplied at least
one ship. All failed. The Hospitallers' ladder was shattered, as was that

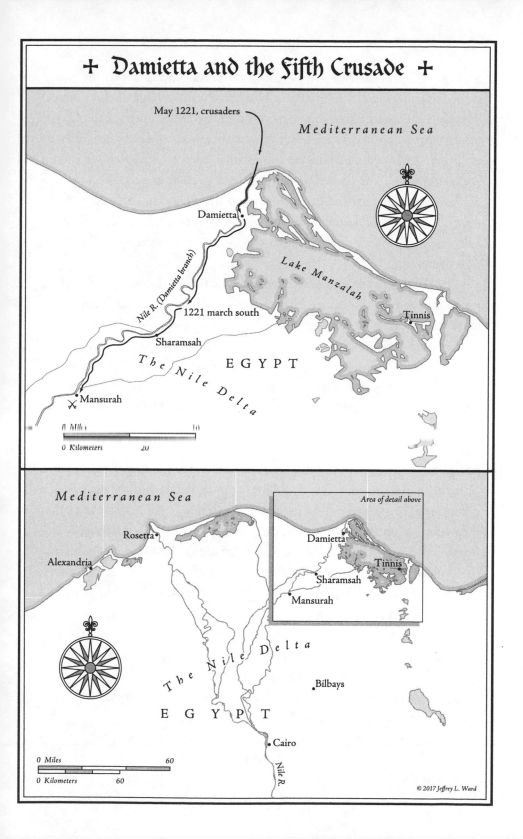

✠ Damietta and the Fifth Crusade ✠

May 1221, crusaders

Mediterranean Sea

Damietta

Nile R. (Damietta branch)

Lake Manzalah

1221 march south

Tinnis

Sharamsah

EGYPT

The Nile Delta

Mansurah

0 Miles 10

0 Kilometers 20

Mediterranean Sea

Rosetta

Alexandria

Area of detail above

Damietta

Tinnis

Sharamsah

Mansurah

The Nile Delta

EGYPT

Bilbays

Cairo

Nile R.

0 Miles 60

0 Kilometers 60

© 2017 Jeffrey L. Ward

on the Duke of Austria's ship, hurling warriors headlong into the water, where they drowned, "wounded in body to the advantage of their souls." The German and Frisian ships anchored in the river and tried to pelt the tower with an onboard catapult, but a counterblast of Greek fire lit both on fire and they limped back to base camp "pierced with arrows within and without."[17] The Templars built an armored ship protected by bulwarks, which they rowed directly next to the tower, in the midst of the fighting. "No small damage" was done to it, wrote Oliver of Paderborn.[18] Like their German and Hospitaller colleagues, they were forced to abandon the assault.

The crusaders continued to bombard the tower and bridge with their trebuchets, aiming to weaken the connection with the city. In the meantime, work began on shore, under Oliver of Paderborn's personal direction, to assemble an amphibious destroyer made from two ships lashed together, with four masts, a rotating bridge and a fireproof covering of animal hides. With this anchored in position, a second attempt to storm the tower began. Fierce fighting raged between the defenders of the chain tower and the soldiers stationed on what was effectively a floating fortress. On the shore the churchmen prayed loudly and venerated their finest relic: a chunk of the Holy Cross said to have been hacked from the larger relic lost to Saladin at Hattin.[19] Despite a violent catapult battle and the release of a great deal of Greek fire, for a long time neither side could blast the other into submission. But eventually, during one particularly intense assault on the afternoon of August 25, the Christians managed to leap from their platform and build a fire outside one of the tower's lower doors. Smoke and flames licked up through the upper stories, and the panicked defenders soon realized their situation was hopeless. Many threw themselves out of the small windows to escape the inferno and consequently drowned in the river. One hundred and twelve others surrendered to the Duke of Austria. "Our men gave thanks to God," wrote James of Vitry, bishop of Acre, who was present.[20] The first stage of the capture of Damietta was complete.

Shortly after this—amid fierce fighting in the last weeks of August—William of Chartres, the fourteenth master of the Temple, died, along with many other luminaries, including a bastard son of King John of

England. "More martyrs for Christ, more confessors of Christ, being de-livered from human cares at Damietta," sighed Oliver of Paderborn.[21] In William's place the order elected Peter of Montaigu, the Western master who had come to Egypt via Portugal and the siege of Alcácer. This was a good appointment: Peter was intelligent, experienced and reasoned in his judgments. It was also a notable one, as for the first time the masters of the Temple and the Hospital were siblings. Both orders had been built on top of networks of highborn French-speaking families, but few things symbolized the essentially aristocratic nature of their membership quite so clearly as the appointment of the Montaigu brothers as masters at the same time.

Although the Nile tower had been taken relatively quickly, success-fully tackling the defenses of Damietta itself was far trickier. The saffron-colored Ayyubid standard flew safely above the bristling walls, and months passed in inconclusive projectile bombardments and occasional skirmishes as defenders attacked the Christian camp. There was some cheer when news reached the camp that al-Adil had died on August 31. "Grown old with evil days and sickness," wrote Oliver of Paderborn, "he was buried in hell."[22] In practice, however, little changed. The vigorous young sultan al-Kamil was still alive and now in charge, and Damietta was still standing firm.

The Templars on the Fifth Crusade faced the same miseries as the rest of the army as winter approached. Conditions deteriorated quickly. Poor provisioning led to a mass outbreak of scurvy. Men limped around the siege camp with their lower legs in agony and their gums swollen up and rotting. Some crusaders left, having been away from home for a year, which they reckoned to be adequate fulfillment of their vows. Others arrived, but not all of these were entirely helpful. Leadership was particu-larly weakened by the appearance of the influential but divisive fifty-three-year-old Pelagius, bishop of Albano, a cardinal and legate sent by Pope Honorius who fancied himself, not entirely accurately, to be a mili-tary tactician as well as a curate of souls.

In late October the Templars' camp was raided early one morning by a large skirmishing party, resulting in a small cavalry battle in which more than five hundred men were killed. The following month the camp was lashed by a three-day storm, which swelled the river, washed away tents and smashed several ships at anchor into splinters. When things finally calmed down in early December, raids continued from the captured river tower. Oliver of Paderborn recorded one encounter in awe: having been sucked too close to Damietta's defensive barricades by the river's strong current, one of the Templars' ships was showered with stones and Greek fire, then surrounded by light enemy craft. Muslim soldiers fastened themselves to the vessel with grappling hooks, then scaled the high wooden sides and engaged in a hand-to-hand battle on deck. "When they had fought for a long time, the ship at last was pierced (whether by the enemy or by our own men we do not know) and sought the depths, drowning Egyptians with Christians, so that the top of the mast scarcely appeared above the water," Oliver wrote. He went on to liken the Templars who had died in the Nile to the Old Testament hero Samson. "So also those martyrs dragged into the abyss of the waters along with themselves more than they could have killed with their swords."[23]

Fighting continued through the winter and into the following spring, and still the triple walls of Damietta stood firm. The Templars' piebald banner could be spotted all over the war zone, joining dozens of others, including those of a relatively new German military order known as the Teutonic Order, which aimed to replicate the structure and achievements of the Templars. The Teutonic Order had its origins in Acre, where it was established as a German branch of the Hospitallers during the great siege of 1190–1191. At that time they ran medical services for German troops injured in the fighting, working under canvas salvaged from the sails of their ships. Like the Hospitallers, the Teutonic Order soon adopted a military role and by the early decades of the thirteenth century was established as the third great Christian military order of the crusading movement.[24]

By the summer of 1219 most clear-eyed observers could see that the Fifth Crusade was grinding toward a stalemate. The leadership had fallen to squabbling, and the general feeling was that only a massive surge of troops led by the German king Frederick II Hohenstaufen would allow a Christian triumph. But though he had promised the pope he would do so on multiple occasions, Frederick did not come. It seemed, wrote Oliver of

Paderborn, that Damietta would be delivered into the hands of the Christians "by divine power alone."[25]

That summer a peculiar man arrived at Damietta purporting to be just such an agent of godly intercession. Giovanni di Pietro di Bernadone was a merchant's son from the Italian region of Umbria who had experienced an epiphany after hearing a preacher describe how Christ had exhorted his followers to go out among God's people and bring forth the kingdom of heaven. According to the Gospel of Matthew, Jesus had told his apostles: "Heal the sick, raise the dead, cleanse those who have leprosy, drive out demons. Freely you have received; freely give. Do not get any gold or silver or copper to take with you in your belts—no bag for the journey or extra shirt or sandals or a staff. . . . Whatever town or village you enter, search there for some worthy person and stay at their house until you leave."[26] The young man had taken these words literally, and under the new name of Francis of Assisi* he had embraced a life of poverty, casting off the luxuries of his bourgeois upbringing to become a wandering beggar and preacher, clad in a rough gray habit. He completely rejected personal property and merriment and chose instead to walk barefoot around the Italian mountains, telling anyone who would listen that they ought to repent their sins or face God's wrath.

Francis soon developed a band of followers, and in 1209 he organized them as the Order of Friars Minor (also known as the Order of Lesser or Minor Brothers and, later, the Franciscans). The friars followed a plain and uncomplicated rule that Francis had developed on the basis of a few verses of the Gospels. Like the Templars, Francis and his fellows took vows of obedience, chastity and poverty. There, however, the similarities ended. Indeed, Saint Francis's appearance at Damietta in 1219 was a reminder of just how far the brothers fighting there had come from the way of life their founders had envisaged.

It was exactly a century since Hugh of Payns had established the Order of the Poor Knights of the Temple of Solomon in Jerusalem. Those one hundred years had seen the Templars transformed from indigent

---

* Assisi was the town of his birth, Francis a nickname supposedly given him in infancy by his father, meaning "Frenchman."

shepherds of the pilgrim roads, dependent on the charity of fellow pilgrims for their food and clothes, into a borderless, self-sustaining paramilitary group funded by large-scale estate management.

Francis of Assisi was not quite as guileless as he appeared—for one thing, he had managed to have his order blessed by Pope Innocent III. Yet his personal bearing was a striking counterpoint to that of the high-ranking officers of the Temple. Whereas Francis was a freewheeling, shoeless beggar, they were political players with contacts at the royal courts across Europe, property magnates whose estates stretched from Scotland to Sicily, crack soldiers who could afford to build gigantic amphibious bases in war zones and financial experts co-opted into the bureaucratic machinery of Christendom's leading kingdoms. Whereas Francis led his new order with nothing but a gray woolen smock thrown over his thin shoulders and the words of the apostles on his lips, Peter of Montaigu was entitled under the Rule of the Templars to four warhorses, up to four pack animals, a personal retinue including a chaplain, clerk, valet, sergeant, farrier, Saracen translator, turcopole and cook, a three-man bodyguard, a strongbox for keeping all his valuables and a private room for his own use within whichever Templar palace he was visiting.[27] The Templars were respected and valued throughout the Christian world, but they plainly could no longer be thought of as radical, uncompromising ascetics.

Upon arrival at Damietta, Francis put himself forward as a negotiator. He walked out of the Christian camp and presented himself to the nearby Egyptian army. There he demanded to see al-Kamil so that the new sultan could be shown the error of his faith. According to James of Vitry, the chronicler and bishop of Acre, Francis "preached to the Saracens for a few days but with little result."[28] The sultan politely refused his offer to perform a miraculous walk through fire as proof of God's favor, and sent the eccentric young man back to his own side. Only al-Kamil's good humor saved Francis from summary beheading, a fate many Templar brothers had met over the years.

✠

Since neither head-on assault nor the pleadings of a righteous friar had managed to reduce Damietta, the only thing for the crusading army to do was wait until the garrison inside the city was on the brink of starvation. This moment did not arrive until September 1219, by which time the siege had been under way for eighteen months. Reports reached Oliver of Paderborn of extreme hunger inside the city, accompanied by outbreaks of disease.[29] Envoys from al-Kamil offered a peace under which the Christians would leave Damietta, receiving in exchange "the kingdom of Jerusalem entirely," with the exception of castles at Kerak and Montréal in the Transjordan, which sat on the crucial land route connecting Egypt with Damascus.[30]

To many of the weary crusaders—particularly those from France, Germany and England—this sounded like a very good arrangement. Jerusalem was, after all, what they wanted. However, the legate Pelagius led a faction in favor of pushing on to take Damietta at all costs, arguing that since the Muslim occupiers of Jerusalem had destroyed the defenses of the Holy City, it would be impossible to hold, and to retreat now would be to fall into a trap and risk ending up with nothing at all. This argument was backed by the Montaigu brothers, and in the short term at least it transpired that they were right. Despite rancorous disagreement among the crusade leaders, the siege continued, and by November 1219 the city's defenders had weakened to the point of collapse. On November 5 an assault on the walls with ladders was successful, and the crusaders forced their way into the city, finding a ghastly sight when they entered: "streets strewn with the bodies of the dead, wasting away from pestilence and famine."[31] James of Vitry wrote that "the smell and the polluted air were too much for most people to bear."[32] Gold, silver, silks and slaves were plundered from shops and houses, while churchmen wandered the streets looking for surviving children, five hundred of whom they forcibly baptized into Christianity.

With the fall of Damietta al-Kamil withdrew up the Nile, leaving the crusaders to enjoy themselves. On November 23 they took the nearby fort town of Tanis, while the Templars set out to raid the coastal town of Burlus. According to Oliver of Paderborn, a two-day march "brought back many spoils—about one hundred camels and the same number of captives, horses, mules, oxen, and asses and goats, clothing and much household furniture," although it exhausted the Templars' horses, many of whom died of dehydration.[33] As they returned, members of the newer

Teutonic Order rode out to meet them. The difference in military capability between the two orders was on sharp display, for the Teutonic knights set out without crossbowmen and archers to defend their lines: they were set upon by a Muslim ambush party, and their preceptor, marshal and many other brothers were taken prisoner.

By the middle of the year 1220 the Templars had been on the outskirts of Damietta for more than two years, and were knitted as tightly into the fabric of a crusade as they ever had been. Ever since Innocent III had proclaimed the Fifth Crusade, Templar brothers had helped to collect the papal tax known as a twentieth. They sat on commissions alongside Hospitallers and local clergy to account for the money collected throughout the realms of Christendom, which was distributed on a regional basis to enable as many people as possible to join the crusade.[34]

A letter written by Pope Honorius to Pelagius on July 24 of that year illustrates just how deeply involved the Templars and Hospitallers had become in the basic infrastructure of financial transfers. Honorius was concerned that none of the crusade tax required for the front line of the war effort should reach Egypt via the Lateran, so that there could be no suggestion of papal corruption or misappropriation of funds. This was a noble aim, but one that required a decentralized means of moving money, as well as trustworthy and godly men with a presence in every realm involved in the crusade and the practical ability to move large amounts of coin and treasure securely. The Templars and Hospitallers and the new Teutonic Order were the ideal agents.

Honorius acknowledged in his letter that the military orders were indeed able to move impressive sums. He then listed some of the recent Templar transfers from Europe to Damietta: five thousand gold marks, paid directly from the papal chamber; thirteen thousand marks collected in England and conveyed by four Templars named as Hugh of Saint-George, John of Novill, Gerald of Soturririo and "Roger the Englishman from the village of Angles"; seventeen hundred and eleven marks raised in Hungary and delivered jointly with the Hungarian Hospitallers; another five thousand marks raised in England and moved through the Templar treasurer in Paris, Brother Haimard; six thousand ounces of gold collected in France and also routed via Haimard's office in Paris; a huge weight of coin from Spain and Portugal, which amounted to more than twenty-five thousand pieces of gold and more than five thousand pounds in assorted silver currencies.

These were significant transfers and a testament to the pope's faith in the Templars' probity and expertise. "Because we have been accustomed to send the tax and other money more frequently by means of the brothers of the Temple and the Hospital, we do not have other intermediaries in whom it might seem we could have greater trust," wrote Honorius. (He nonetheless asked Pelagius to remain vigilant and inform him the moment he suspected any funds were leaking as they were transported to Egypt.)[35] In letters sent elsewhere during the Fifth Crusade, Honorius maintained a similar position, warning his correspondents that they should disregard rumors of corruption or impropriety leveled against the orders, since "if the Templars and Hospitallers did not daily spend money for their sergeants, their crossbowmen and other necessary combatants … the army would be totally incapable of remaining at Damietta."[36]

✝

The Templars were playing a vital role in funding the crusade and defending the newly captured city of Damietta, but their concentration of men and resources in Egypt was starting to cause them problems elsewhere, not least back at Château Pèlerin, which by the late summer of 1220 was under attack by forces led by the sultan of Damascus, al-Kamil's brother al-Mu'azzam. Just as in the 1160s, the Templars were not able to fight successfully in Palestine and Egypt simultaneously.[37] In September 1220 Peter of Montaigu was back in Acre and able to describe the familiar predicament in a letter to his friend Nicholas, bishop of Elne, far away in the Pyrenees. Al-Mu'azzam was emboldened, he wrote wearily. "Finding that the cities of Acre and Tyre were not sufficiently supplied with knights and soldiers to oppose him, [he] continually did serious injury to those places both secretly and openly; besides this he often came and pitched his camp before our castle which is called the Pilgrims' [i.e., Château Pèlerin], doing us all kinds of injury; he also besieged and reduced the castle of Caesarea in Palestine."[38]

The situation in Damietta, on which Montaigu was also keeping a close eye, was growing increasingly confused, and major strategic disagreements were growing among the crusade leaders. Peter explained that higher up the Nile, al-Kamil was amassing a large army, which they ignored at their peril. "The legate and the clergy, desirous to advance the cause of the army of Christ, often and earnestly exhorted the people to make an attack on the infidels, but the nobles of the army, as well those of the transmarine provinces as those on our side of the water, thinking that the army was not sufficient for the defense of the aforesaid cities and castles . . . would not consent to this plan," Montaigu wrote. Saracen ships cruised off the Egyptian coast. Resources were being stretched. Intelligence from the East said the dangerous al-Ashraf, brother of al-Kamil and al-Mu'azzam, was consolidating power. He might soon set sight on one or more of Acre, Antioch, Tripoli or Egypt. If he did so, thought the Templar master, each "would be in the greatest danger, and if he were to lay siege to any one of our castles, we should in no wise be able to drive him away."[39]

In 1221 Peter of Montaigu returned to Egypt. He was there in June when al-Kamil made another bid for a brokered peace with the Christians, along much the same lines as the truce he had offered two years previously. Having seen at first hand the dangerous state of affairs in Palestine, the Templar master now urged acceptance. He was overruled. It was decided by Pelagius, John of Brienne and others that the time had come to move on the Egyptian army once and for all. Peter of Montaigu was voted down, so he agreed to support a drastic alternative: a march up the Nile to provoke the Egyptians into battle. This was a brave move but it was being made perilously late. While the crusaders had dithered the previous year, al-Kamil and his allies all over the region had been laying a trap. Now it was about to be sprung.

In a letter to Alan Martel, the Templar preceptor in England, Peter of Montaigu later described the disastrous march on al-Kamil's army.[40] On June 29, 1221, the Christian army emerged from their tent city outside Damietta and began to move upriver, accompanied by galleys. Ahead of them al-Kamil's army repeatedly fell back, abandoning their camp and refusing to engage. It seemed too good to be true. The crusaders pressed ahead eagerly, with the Templars riding rear guard, raiding villages as they went and aiming their crossbows at any Muslims who came into view. The chronicler Ibn al-Athir wrote that "they and everyone were

convinced that they were going to conquer Egypt."[41] Yet some were beginning to have their doubts. John of Brienne was nervous that the army
was advancing too deep into unfamiliar territory, and many of the men
plainly agreed with him. According to Montaigu, around ten thousand
abandoned the army without permission and disappeared.

Behind the crusaders, reinforcements sent by al-Kamil's brothers in
Syria were shadowing the Christians' march by foot and by boat. Worse
than this, the Nile was starting to rise. Despite having been in the region
for more than two years, the crusader army did not understand the complex network of natural and man-made water channels that fed into the
river. Nor did they properly comprehend the variable seasonal rhythms
of the waters, which rose sharply in late summer and generally overspilled
the river's banks, but had only flooded weakly during their short time in
Egypt. Al-Kamil knew the workings of the river all too well, and as the
crusaders worked their way into increasingly perilous terrain in late July,
his boats and soldiers continued to stalk them, blocking the river and
barring the way back to Damietta.

By August 10 the crusaders had stopped opposite the heavily fortified
camp at al-Mansurah, where the large Damietta branch of the Nile di-
verged from another branch, known as the Tanis. (The fort Tanis, near
Lake Mansallah, took its name from this section of the river.) They were
penned in at the V of the two waterways. They were also completely surrounded, for behind them the river was now blockaded, while Muslim
troops had taken up positions barring all overland paths beside and
around the river branches. Two weeks later, the Nile flooded and its waters washed away most of the crusaders' baggage train. "The army of
Christ lost its packhorses, equipment, saddlebags, carts and virtually all
its essential supplies in the swamps," wrote Peter of Montaigu.

This would have been bad enough, but al-Kamil now played his trump
card. To regulate the Nile's floodwaters, canals and channels had been
built by local farmers. The sultan ordered the sluice gates to be set so that
as much water as possible would rush toward the crusader position. The
land on which the army marched was turned into thick, soupy mud,
bringing the troops to a standstill. Even the Templars could not cope
with the panic that set in as frightened men tried to wade out of a great,

slick, sucking mire. The crusaders were caught, wrote Peter of Montaigu, "like fish in a net." Their march was over. On August 28 Pelagius realized there was nothing to do but surrender.

The sultan's generosity—apparently abundant in previous parlays—now evaporated. He summoned John of Brienne to his tent and informed the king of Jerusalem civilly but firmly that his men would all starve to death unless the Latins agreed to new peace terms: Damietta and the fort at Tanis were to be returned, and the armies occupying northern Egypt were to leave. Muslims enslaved in Acre and Tyre were to be freed. Eight years of peace was to be assured. It was an unconditional surrender. John had no choice but to agree.

Montaigu heard all of this and understood it well: he was part of a delegation sent back to Damietta to recount the humiliating news. At first the defeat was greeted with amazement. Next a riot broke out in which houses were destroyed. Then, despondently, the men holding Damietta prepared to leave. Upriver the army was beginning to make its way back, muddy, wet and hungry. They were saved from starvation during their slow and painful retreat only because al-Kamil, with the magnanimity of a man who had secured total victory, agreed to provide fifteen days' worth of bread to see them on their way, out of Egypt and back to the denuded kingdom of Jerusalem. As part of the protocol of surrender, John of Brienne and Pelagius submitted themselves to a short period of honorable captivity. This did not last long, and soon they were on their way back to Acre, trounced and spent. "Sympathize with us in our misfortune," wrote Montaigu to his colleague Alan Martel back in England, as he described all this in gloomy detail. "And offer us whatever aid you can."

The abrupt and highly embarrassing failure of the Fifth Crusade reflected badly on everyone involved. Yet again, vast amounts of money had been expended on attacking enemy positions with no permanent gain. Jerusalem remained in Muslim hands. Christian writers fell back on the usual gloomy explanations for this lamentable outcome: Peter of Montaigu wrote of "the disasters that befell us in the land of Egypt because of our sins."[42] Pope Honorius, understandably dismayed, focused much of his blame on Frederick II Hohenstaufen, whom he had consecrated as Holy Roman Emperor in 1220 on the absolute assurance that Frederick would return the favor by finally joining the crusade. Instead, Frederick had stalled, evaded and dodged his obligation, preferring to concentrate on the complex political problems attending his office as the most powerful ruler in the West. Many more years would pass before he would finally arrive in the East. But when he did, it had dramatic consequences for the Templars.

15

"Animosity and Hatred"

Peter of Montaigu fell to the ground and kissed the emperor's knees. Around him, soldiers and townspeople whooped in exaltation. It was September 1228 and the whole of Acre had come out to witness the arrival in the East of Frederick II Hohenstaufen, the most powerful prince of the West, backed by a fleet of seventy galleys and thousands of men.[1] Even the Egyptian sultan marked the occasion by sending the great visitor gifts of gold and silver, silks and jewels and a whole host of rare animals including camels, elephants, bears and monkeys. The Holy Land had received many distinguished guests over the years, but few were so illustrious as Frederick, the Holy Roman Emperor, a man of such singular gravitas and intellectual range that his admirers called him *stupor mundi*: the wonder of the world.

At first glance, admittedly, he did not look like much. Frederick was middlingly tall, balding, with a permanently ruddy face and poor eyesight. He was stocky limbed and fit but lacked the thick beard that signaled unquestionable manhood, even though he arrived in Acre in September 1228 a few months short of his thirty-fourth birthday. He had been a king his whole life: crowned as ruler of Sicily when he was two years old, recognized as king of the Germans when he was twenty-one and formally elected Holy Roman Emperor in 1220, at the age of twenty-six. Now he was adding a final piece to his dominions. He had sailed to Acre via Cyprus to lay claim to the position of king of Jerusalem and launch a crusade against the sultan who held the Holy City.

Collecting titles was one of Frederick's specialties, and the crown of Jerusalem had come to him by way of a wedding. In 1225 he had married John of Brienne's thirteen-year-old daughter, Isabella, the rightful queen of Jerusalem. As part of the deal Frederick had taken over her father's rights to act as titular ruler of the Latin kingdom. Three years later Isabella bore him a son, whom they named Conrad. Sadly for her, but somewhat fortuitously for Frederick, the girl promptly died of childbed fever, leaving Frederick holding a baby who was next in line to the throne. His crusade in 1228 was therefore a mission with two motives: to regain Jerusalem and lay claim to the Crown. In theory the kingdom was Conrad's, but technicality did not count for much in Frederick's opinion. He was determined to make himself the next Christian king of the Holy Land, and woe betide anyone who should stand in his way.

What he lacked in physical stature, Frederick amply made up for by the force of his personality. One writer who knew him admitted that he was "an adroit man, cunning, greedy, wanton, malicious, bad-tempered. But at times he was a worthy man, when he wished to reveal his good and courtly qualities, consoling, witty, delightful, hardworking. He could read, write, and sing and he could compose music and songs. . . . Also he could speak many different languages. . . . If he had been a good Catholic and loved God . . . he would have had few equals."[2] The accusation of godlessness was one that would dog him all his life, for he was said in private to scoff at all faiths, while in public he surrounded himself with exotic-looking servants drawn from the Muslim population of Sicily, as well as the more usual Christian retainers. Skepticism appears to have been one consequence of a curious and roving mind, which delighted in scientific discovery as much as artistic pleasure and the thrill of sports, particularly hunting with birds, about which he considered himself the foremost authority on earth.

Such, then, was the man whose knees Peter of Montaigu had bent to kiss. But Montaigu did not bow down in acknowledgment of the emperor's erudition. Rather, this was an act of cautious political accommodation between the Order of the Temple and the leader of the latest crusading mission to reach the East. Whatever Frederick's motives, he was most prestigious king to have visited since Richard the Lionheart thirty years earlier. The military orders had a duty to work with him as best they could, and had promised keep the peace between Frederick and John of Ibelin, lord of Beirut, a powerful local lord who was extremely suspicious of the emperor's arrival. Unfortunately for both the Templars and the emperor, Montaigu's genuflection was a sham. Within weeks relations between them had dissolved to the point of violence.

Frederick had not had much to do with the Templars of the Holy Land before his encounter with their master in Acre, but there was much in his personality and policies that augured badly. For a start, it was hard to avoid the notion that he was at heart unenthusiastic about the whole business of crusading, and perhaps with good reason. The task of managing so enormous and complex a political inheritance as the Holy Roman Empire did not allow much space for delving deeply into the affairs of Jerusalem, and what relatively slight experience the Hohenstaufen dynasty did have of the Eastern wars was deeply unpromising. Frederick's grandfather, Frederick I Barbarossa, had drowned in Asia Minor on his way to the Third Crusade, and his father, the emperor Henry VI, had made his most notable contribution by holding Richard the Lionheart hostage on his way home from Acre. Henry VI had ransomed Richard back to the English for 100,000 marks and promptly spent the majority of that gargantuan sum on conquering the kingdom of Sicily.[3]

Frederick's own reign had thrown up a number of reasons to warrant distrust. Templars and Hospitallers had a long-established presence on the island of Sicily, but during his minority they had been muscled aside by the recently formed Teutonic Order, which strove aggressively to gain preeminence over their longer-established counterparts. Some felt this to be actively dangerous, and a number of Sicilian knights had come to the East to join the Order of the Temple specifically to escape the emperor's ill will.[4]

One of his chief advisers was the master of the Teutonic Order, Hermann of Salza, an extremely capable politician who was highly respected by his men. Under Hermann's influence Frederick had granted the Teutonic Order in Sicily tax exemptions on all their Sicilian imports and exports, and formally approved their request for the same "liberties, customs and all the rights" as were enjoyed by the Templars and Hospitallers. In 1221 he successfully petitioned Pope Honorius III to secure the German brothers freedom from religious tax and oversight. And when he married Isabella II in 1225, becoming king of Jerusalem, he used his new powers to grant the Teutonic Order total immunity from all secular powers in the East.[5] All of this was bound to concern the Templars, whose whole model for success relied on the highest favor of Western kings and on their special status.

Finally, there was the fact of Frederick's notorious slipperiness. He had twice taken a vow to go on crusade: once in 1215, when he was crowned as king of the Germans, and again in 1220, when he was crowned emperor. It had taken him almost a decade to finally make his way to the Holy Land, and even then he came a full year late, claiming he had been ill. Eventually papal patience had snapped and, somewhat ironically, when Frederick finally arrived in Acre in September 1228 as a crusader he did so with the full wrath of the papacy blowing against him.

The chief reason for this change of attitude was that there had been a change of pope. Honorius III had died in March 1227 and been replaced by the elderly and strident Gregory IX. Crotchety but acute, Gregory's displeasure was easily aroused, and during the course of his papacy he aimed it at heretical students in Paris, pagans in the Baltic and even cats, whom he suspected of being incarnations of Satan. He established the Inquisition to root out heresy across Europe and enacted very severe measures to persecute Jews, including mass public burnings of the Talmud.

Before he got around to cats, heretics and Jews, however, Gregory turned his attention to the Holy Roman Emperor. His first significant act as pope was to excommunicate Frederick as punishment for his constant procrastination. In a papal bull annoucing his decision, he lambasted the emperor for "casting aside all fear of God, paying no reverence to Jesus Christ, and heeding little the censure of the Church," and railed against a man who had "abandoned the Christian army, left the Holy Land exposed to the infidels, despised the devotion of the people of Christ, and, to the disgrace of himself and Christianity, was enticed away to the usual pleasures of his kingdom."[6] The bull of excommunication arrived in Acre very shortly after the emperor did and its appearance shattered all pretense of good faith between Frederick and the Templars, as did the emperor's habit of launching into bitter diatribes about the unjust pope. The result was that within weeks of Peter of Montaigu's theatrical leg nuzzling, the order was at loggerheads with the most powerful secular ruler in the West, who was leading what came to be known as the Sixth Crusade.

The feud began in earnest with the emperor's decision to march south from Acre to Jaffa on November 15, so that he could parlay with the sultan of Egypt. Power in the Ayyubid world was tangled after al-Mu'azzam, the ruler of Damascus, died of dysentery on November 12, 1227, and was succeeded by his twenty-year-old son al-Nasir.[7] Preferring political consolidation to a happy family, al-Kamil attempted to overthrow his nephew and seize Damascus for himself. The trouble drew in a third family member, al-Ashraf, ruler of the Jazira, with the result that the Ayyubid empire of Egypt and Syria entered another difficult period of internal unrest.

Rightly sensing an opportunity, Frederick decided that he could make the most of the discord to regain some of the Christians' lost territories. He was undermanned and a full-on campaign of conquest against the Ayyubids was unrealistic. Still, a show of unity from across the Latin states might be enough to persuade al-Kamil to make concessions—perhaps even returning Jerusalem itself. From his experiences in Sicily, where Muslim and Christian culture intermingled, Frederick was better acquainted than any previous Western crusade leader with the characters and customs of the Islamic world, so much so that scurrilous tales abounded of his "enjoyment of living in the manner of the Saracens," including a taste for "dancing girls who also sang and juggled." Setting aside his personal predilections, he was confident that a show of force followed by a parlay for peace would be a fruitful strategy.[8]

The Templars and Hospitallers saw things differently. Allied with the acerbic and forceful patriarch of Jerusalem, Gerold of Lausanne, they refused to march with the rest of Frederick's army, arguing that it would be a disgrace for them to associate with a man who had been excommunicated from the Church. Pope Gregory's words on the matter were clear: "We order him to be strictly avoided by all." Peter of Montaigu and the new master of the Hospitallers, Bertrand of Thessy,* decided they would carry out their duty to the letter. They agreed to follow the army, but only at a distance of a day's march—enough to render them honorably present but practically useless.

Frederick was not a man accustomed to being thwarted. In response to the frustration of his wishes he took aim at Château Pèlerin, the Templars'

---

* Garin of Montaigu died before March 1, 1228, at Sidon.

massive coastal fortress south of Acre. This was one of the Templars' most spectacular and valuable possessions in Outremer, its importance to the order such that the master and many brothers had returned from Damietta to defend it from al-Mu'azzam during the Fifth Crusade.[9] It was also conveniently placed on the road between Acre and Jaffa. Frederick stopped before the castle and demanded that the Templars hand it over to him for occupation by his soldiers—by which he almost certainly meant that he intended to transfer it to the Teutonic Order.

Impasse was swiftly achieved. Frederick was angry with the Templars, but he was in no position to devote precious time and resources to storming a castle built to the highest military specifications by Christian pilgrims. In the opinion of one writer of the time, he was committing a "great treason" merely by entertaining the thought.[10] The Templars inside Château Pèlerin barricaded the doors against the emperor's men and simply waited for them to go away. Frederick backed down, but the rebuff had done enough to ensure his lasting fury. The Templars claimed thereafter that the emperor "wished to kill them" by treachery, while Frederick's contacts heard that the Templars were plotting to murder the emperor first.

Things were no better in the months that followed, as Frederick reached Jaffa and spent the winter pressing al-Kamil for an agreement by which the city of Jerusalem could be opened up to Christian worshippers once again. The emperor was a bully, but he was no fool, and he had assessed the Ayyubid position precisely. The family struggle over Damascus was al-Kamil's chief preoccupation, and the sultan saw a peace with the Christians as a considerable advantage to him. Frederick, for his part, had a natural ability to charm those he thought worth charming, and his sympathy with Islamic culture—"The emperor lived and dressed totally like a Saracen," wailed Patriarch Gerold—helped him to secure a peace on more favorable terms than any that had been achieved since the fall of Jerusalem in 1187.[11]

On February 18, 1229, al-Kamil formally agreed to give up the Holy City and the Holy Sepulchre to Christian governance in exchange for a ten-year truce. Both Christians and Muslims were to be allowed access to the city, and the Christians were to be recognized as the legitimate rulers of

Bethlehem, Nazareth, Sidon, Jaffa and Acre. The crusader kingdom, dismembered for more than four decades, was now partially restored. It included once more the entire stretch of coastline from Jaffa to Beirut, going inland in some places as far as the river Jordan. Some reconstruction would be allowed in Jerusalem, although the two sides took differing views as to whether that meant rebuilding the defensive walls the Ayyubids had razed a decade earlier, to prevent a Christian army from holding the city were it ever reconquered. This was not a reversal of all that had been done by Saladin, still less a repeat of the miraculous deeds done in 1099 during the First Crusade. All the same it was an astonishing achievement, which Frederick trumpeted in a letter to his young cousin Henry III, the Plantagenet king of England. "In these few days, by a miracle rather than by strength, that business has been brought to a conclusion which . . . many chiefs and rulers of the world . . . have never been able till now to accomplish by force," he wrote.[12] The German poet and crusader Freidank wondered, "What more can sinners desire, than the sepulchre and the Holy Cross?"[13] Many of Christ's faithful would have nodded in agreement. Even if the True Cross was not returned—having apparently vanished in Damascus—the Holy City was once again back under Christian occupation. The Templars, however, were unimpressed.

The most important place in Jerusalem to Christians was the Holy Sepulchre, for in that magnificent church lay the tomb of Christ, covered with a thick slab of marble and venerated by every pilgrim who came to the Holy Land. Certainly, regaining Jerusalem was an important as a matter of pride; and of course, like any other major city in the eastern Mediterranean, it had commercial benefits for Christian traders. The Sepulchre, though, mattered most. Yet for the Templars there was another very significant site: the al-Aqsa Mosque, which they called the Temple of Solomon, where their order had been created, and where it had been housed between 1119 and 1187. The Temple was their home, from which they had been exiled. Its return was a matter of profound and defining importance to their dignity as an order, but that had not factored into Frederick's negotiation.

"The Franks took over Jerusalem and the Muslims were outraged and thought it monstrous. This caused them to feel such weakness and pain as are beyond description," spat the chronicler Ibn al-Athir when he reported the deal struck between Frederick and al-Kamil.[14] In truth the loss of the city to the Christian heathens was not total, for it did not include the Temple Mount. To Muslims this was the Haram al-Sharif, containing the al-Aqsa Mosque and the Dome of the Rock: the holiest location in Islam after Mecca and Medina. When Saladin had conquered Jerusalem, he had pulled down the Templars' outbuildings around the mosque and cleansed the whole place with rosewater, restoring Qur'anic inscriptions and installing "incomparable marble," "gilded mosaics," "handsome Qur'an copies and fine reading stands."[15] To give back the mosque to the polluting Christians would have been quite unforgivable, which is why one of the key terms in Frederick and al-Kamil's peace deal was that it should remain under Muslim control, so that Muslim pilgrims could worship there unmolested and free of charge. There would be no reconstruction of the Templars' old quarters. The order would have to make do with other, less hallowed dwellings.

Templar holdings elsewhere were also limited by the terms of the treaty. A few properties on the road between Jerusalem and Jaffa were to be given back so that the brothers could oversee a safe, direct route from the sea to the city, but otherwise, in the words of Patriarch Gerold, "nor one foot of land was to be returned."[16] Château Blanc and Tortosa, two of their larger castles in the county of Tripoli, were to be left "in their own state"—in other words, not to be improved or upgraded.[17] By contrast, Hermann Salza's Teutonic Order was allowed under the treaty to continue building its own massive castle of Montfort, in the hills near Acre, where the German brothers had struck ground in 1227.

In fairness to Frederick, the deal he struck was not first and foremost a calculated snub to the Templars. The loss of Jerusalem was a serious business and it needed to be made palatable to the sultan. Yet there was enough in the terms of the agreement for the order to feel insulted, and plenty of grounds for suspicion that the emperor had made a truce not for the good of all the Franks of the East, but to secure his crown and protect his commercial interests, which relied on favorable trading conditions between Sicily and Jerusalem.[18] But what could they do? On March 17, 1229, Frederick worshipped at the Church of the Holy Sepulchre and, despite being excommunicated, took the crown of Jerusalem from on top of the altar and placed it on his own head. The master of the Teutonic Order, Hermann of Salza, justified his patron's behavior to the congregation once Frederick had left the building, reminding them that the emperor had achieved a truly historic thing. "It is almost impossible to describe the joy of the people," he later recalled.[19]

Certainly it was impossible to describe the joy of the Templars, for there was none. The waspishly anti-imperial chronicler Philip of Novare wrote that far from being the subject of general adulation, "the emperor was by now unpopular with all the people of Acre, [and] he was especially disliked by the Templars."[20] It did not take long for that dislike to boil up into open rebellion. Angry and with nothing to lose, the Templars mustered their forces in Acre, where, accompanied by Patriarch Gerold, they prepared to defy Frederick for daring to make such a hollow peace.

Although the Jerusalem agreement of 1229 was supposed to cool tensions between Christians and Muslims in the Holy Land for ten years, it had one glaring flaw. It was at root a contract between the emperor and the sultan, which could be read as a personal vouchsafe rather than something binding on all the princes and nobles of their shared faiths. It was no secret that both Frederick and al-Kamil were only passing through Palestine, and that both men soon planned to leave. He may have been the newly crowned king, but Frederick also had to mind his affairs in Germany and Italy, while al-Kamil had his own business in Cairo. And although al-Kamil had agreed to a truce, there was no indication that his relatives were prepared to sit back and embrace their Christian neighbors. Without the men who made it, the peace would mean nothing.

To highlight this point, the patriarch and Templars began raising troops to march first against Damascus and subsequently against Jerusalem, which they planned officially to claim in the name of the pope. Plainly this was an absurd idea, born out of venom and distrust rather than any sound military strategy; but personal animus had now set in and could not easily be put aside. The patriarch took to denouncing the emperor as a violent, fraudulent Antichrist, claiming that "from the sole of his foot to the top of his head no common sense would be found in him."[21] The emperor simply got angry.

Arriving in Acre shortly before Easter 1229, Frederick confronted the patriarch and told him to call off the Templars and the army he was raising. Gerold told the emperor that he did not do the bidding of excommunicates. In response an irate Frederick ordered the town criers of Acre to call together the population so that he could speak to them en masse. Then he laid out his case. "He addressed them and stated that which he desired: and in his address he complained much of the Temple," wrote Philip of Novare.[22] According to the patriarch's account, Frederick went rather further: "He began to complain bitterly of us, by heaping up false accusations. Then turning his remarks to the venerable master of the Temple, he publicly attempted to tarnish the reputation of the latter, by various vain speeches, seeking thus to throw upon others the responsibility for his own faults which were now manifest and adding at last that we were maintaining troops with the purpose of injuring him." Frederick ordered the Templars to leave Acre and announced that crossbowmen would be placed on the gatehouses so that once the brothers had departed, they would not be allowed back in. "Next he fortified with crossbows the churches and other elevated positions and especially those which commanded the communications between the Templars and ourselves," railed Gerold. "And you may be sure that he never showed as much animosity and hatred against the Saracens."[23]

As good as his word, the emperor now filled Acre with troops. To relieve his anger he also had a few friars whipped through the streets. The Templar house in Acre was placed under siege, imperial soldiers blockaded the patriarch's palace and for five days Acre was turned into a war zone. Frederick was already excommunicated, but for good measure the patriarch threatened to extend the punishment to anyone who "should aid the emperor with their advice or services against the Church, the Templars, the other monks of the Holy Land or the pilgrims."[24]

Frederick was now left with two options: to escalate or to retire. He chose the latter. News had reached him that his troubles in Sicily were beginning to outweigh those he was experiencing in Acre. The return of Jerusalem was his legacy to the Holy Land. It was time to go home.

As quickly as he was able, Frederick prepared to leave. He removed all the weapons he could from the armories of Acre and destroyed what could not be shipped, so that the Templars could not seize them for their own advantage. Imperial soldiers were stationed in the garrison and the Teutonic Order overlooked the city from their slowly expanding castle of Montfort. Frederick appointed deputies known as *baillis* to run the kingdom of Jerusalem and Cyprus, to which he had also attempted to stake a claim during his visit. He wrote letters back to his most illustrious contacts in the West putting across his side of events. Then on May 1, 1229, he hurried down to Acre's docks to take ship for Italy.

As he went, said Philip of Novare, delighting in the opportunity to demean the emperor whom he loathed, "the butchers and the old people of the street, who were most ill disposed, ran alongside him and pelted him with tripe and bits of meat."[25] Frederick II Hohenstaufen, who had come to the Holy Land with kisses raining upon his knees, departed it with offal hanging from his shoulders. It was a miserable way to go.

+

Frederick II's crusade may have been fraught by ill feeling among the crusaders, and have left behind a lingering factional divide between the emperor's supporters and a baronial party led by the noble Ibelin family and the Templars, but the deal struck with the sultan resulted in a period of overall security for the Latin states that long outlasted the emperor's departure. The restoration of Christian territories, begun with the Third Crusade, had been moved forward significantly by the emperor's brief visit. The existential danger posed by Saladin three decades earlier had now long receded.

From Jaffa in the south, a long stretch of the coast was once again under Frankish control—with the unbroken run of Christian holdings extending through Acre and Tyre as far north as Tortosa and Margat in the county of Tripoli. Beyond that the principality of Antioch, although much reduced from its twelfth-century peak, was still a viable political entity, while Cyprus was ruled by kings of the Lusignan family, despite Frederick's attempts to sideline them and take the island for himself.

At the end of the 1230s further waves of foreign crusaders arrived in the Holy Land, led by Richard, Earl of Cornwall, the brother of Henry III of England, and Theobald of Champagne, the poet-king of Navarre.[26] These missions, known collectively as the Barons' Crusade, built on Frederick's territorial gains, wrestling back former Christian holdings including the castles of Beaufort, Belvoir, Safad and Tiberias in the north, and Ascalon in the south. They even paved the way for the Christians to take further control in Jerusalem: in 1241 Muslim access to the city was restricted and Christians were readmitted to the Temple Mount, a situation that lasted for three years, until the arrival of marauding Khwarizmian Turks in August 1244. This was a particularly miraculous achievement, described with pride in one newsletter from Templar high command to the preceptor in England, written in 1244: "All those holy places where the name of God has not been invoked for fifty-six years have been restored and purified and, praise be to the Lord, the divine offices are celebrated there every day. These holy places are now accessible and safe for all visitors."[27] In that sense if no other, Frederick Hohenstaufen had laid the ground for a settlement more favorable to the Franks than anything since the battle of Hattin in 1187.

Weighed against all this was the perpetual infighting that Frederick had left behind. Plenty of land and castles had been restored, to be sure—but there was very little coherent leadership across the Latin states as a whole. The Hohenstaufen dynasty claimed the crown of Jerusalem, but neither Frederick nor his son Conrad had the slightest intention of being personally present to exercise office. Bitter feuding separated the supporters of the emperor and his policies of peace toward the Ayyubid sultans in Egypt from those who detested his overbearing influence and looked in turn to ally themselves with an anti-Egyptian sultan in Damascus. The military orders were divided along these lines, with the Hospitallers supporting the imperial party and the Templars on the other side.

This fractured state of affairs might in other times have presented a soft underbelly for the Ayyubids to attack. But during the 1230s and early 1240s they were themselves riven by squabbling and jostling for position. The Saracen empire was still grand in scope—stretching from Egypt on one side of the Red Sea to the holy cities of Mecca and Medina in the Hijaz on the other, north through the Jordan Valley through Palestine and Syria, all the way to the Jazira. In reality, however, rule was spread very thin across this vast expanse. Cairo and Damascus were often at odds, and preferred to seek Christian allies against one another, choosing to accommodate the Latins rather than unite to destroy them. No Ayyubid sultan after Saladin managed to project his personality or his presence forcibly enough to draw these disparate territories back into true union. The result was that, for a time at least, a form of messy equilibrium was achieved between two faith groups, each in as much disarray as the other.

For the Templars, Frederick's sojourn had been unpleasant and difficult. There was nothing new in their deciding to pursue their own policies against the wishes of a secular king, or taking sides in the often bitter disputes that flared up within the Latin nobility. After all, the Templars had openly defied Amalric in the 1160s and had been drawn into a dispute over the succession of Antioch in the early years of the thirteenth century. Never before, though, had they actually gone to war against a crowned Western king. They suffered accordingly. One of the drawbacks of being an international order was that offenses given on one side of Christendom might be punished on another. When the emperor returned to Sicily he took severe action against the Templars there, "seizing and despoiling their movable and immoveable property," as it was later described.[28] Frederick was not stupid. He knew exactly how to hurt the Templars best: by attacking their wealth.

Shortly after the emperor's departure, around 1231, Peter of Montaigu died. A new master was elected, Armand of Périgord, whose family was from the Dordogne region of France, but whose career in the order had taken him to the position of preceptor for Sicily and Calabria. A longstanding pattern was thus continued, by which the Templars reacted to a fractious period of rule under one master by electing (or accepting) a compromise candidate as his successor. In this instance reconciliation was not easy to achieve: in response to papal complaints that he would not relinquish confiscated Templar property, the emperor argued that it was entirely in his right to do so, and apparently refused to come to terms.

Outside the Hohenstaufen sphere the order continued to develop and even to thrive during the 1230s and early 1240s, not least in their commercial activities. Their fleet of ships, when not deployed in wartime, traveled back and forth across the Mediterranean, ferrying passengers to the holy sites. The Templars had a strong presence in Marseille, a popular port of departure for pilgrims heading for Acre and Jaffa, where from 1216 they had been allowed to run merchant and pilgrim ships in and out of the city's port without tariff. In 1233, perhaps in response to a boom in business that had accompanied the reopening of Jerusalem to Christian pilgrims, the municipal government of Marseille demanded a revision of terms, cutting down Templar and Hospitaller shipping runs to four a year, in order to protect private commercial activity. But out of Marseille and Barcelona, Pisa, Genoa and Venice, Templar goods, manpower and supplies continued to flow, drawing on the apparently limitless supply provided by their property empire in the West.

Templar banking operations were also maturing rapidly in this period. By the 1240s the order was providing diverse financial services to some of the richest and most powerful figures across Christendom. In England and France they provided safe storage for sensitive diplomatic documents, looked after charters and guarded official seals while high-ranking government officials were out of the country. They also protected particularly valuable pieces of royal treasure and, in the case of France, acted as an official deposit house for royal revenue.[29]

Templar houses provided numerous sensitive services: they were used to distribute pensions promised by monarchs to wartime allies, and were party to agreements in which they operated as a mutually respected third party between warring rivals.* They guaranteed debts, ransomed hostages and prisoners of war on credit, and could arrange very large loans— such as the one made in 1240 to Baldwin II, the emperor of Constantinople, secured by his very own fragment of the True Cross. They could be extremely effective in realms troubled by civil war: in England during the first decades of the thirteenth century senior Templar personnel had been very visible at the court of King John, who spent almost his entire reign either fighting or coming begrudgingly to terms with his own subjects. The Templars were one of the few groups whom John did not persecute, and in turn they stood by him while he was excommunicated by

---

* This was the case during the wars of the early thirteenth century between John, king of England, and Philip Augustus of France: John's allies around La Rochelle were not prepared to trust the king to pay them the fees he had promised them in return for wartime loyalty; the deal was brokered by depositing the monies in question in trust with the Templar house at La Rochelle for independent distribution. King John also borrowed large sums of money in coin from the Templars throughout his reign, secured on gold treasure equivalent to the loan. Effectively he pawned his crown jewels.

Pope Innocent III, protecting their position as both key creditors of the Crown and ample beneficiaries of John's largesse.[30] By the 1230s John's son Henry III had come of age, and the order made sure to maintain its cordial links with him, too.

Naturally, as kings and emperors turned to the Templars both to hold their valuables and to draw loans, the greater subjects began to mimic the practice. Like their royal overlords, noblemen, knights and rich townsmen saw the obvious advantage in storing their riches at Templar houses, which were not only physically secure but also protected by their status as religious institutions, which could not be raided without incurring the wrath of the Church, and eternal damnation in the afterlife. Some men left their entire fortunes in trust with the Templars before departing on pilgrimage or crusade, issuing the brothers with instructions for disposing of their possessions if they did not come home.

Others used the Templars' institutional wealth and massive geographical network to arrange money transfers, leaving sums of hundreds and even thousands of marks at a Templar house in one city and redeeming it in another hundreds or even thousands of miles away. In 1240 Pope Gregory IX employed a particularly complex version of this, enjoining the French Temple to help him settle his debts: papal revenue collected in Scotland, Ireland and England was routed through the Templar house in Paris; the pope's creditors could then present themselves before the Parisian brothers bearing letters of credit and redeem these for outstanding payments owed to them from Rome. Blanche of Castile, mother of the French king Louis IX, who came to the throne in 1226, employed the Templars to handle all of her private financial affairs, including controlling payments of thousands of livres connected to building work on the abbey she founded and funded at Maubuisson. Men like Louis IX's brother Alphonse, Count of Poitiers, used the Templars for his personal financial management, and from the 1240s it became fashionable and even common for noblemen and -women across Western Christendom to do the same.

As the middle of the thirteenth century approached, then, the Templars had reached extraordinary maturity as an organization. In the Holy Land they were an increasingly autonomous military entity, occupying large numbers of castles and pursuing policies best suited to themselves, even when these cut across the wishes and interests of the highest secular authorities. In the West, where outside the Spanish peninsula the day-to-day activity of Templar brothers involved no fighting and was very little different from that of the monastic orders, business was booming. The infrastructure the order had originally developed to fund its crusading mission was now exploited for many other purposes. The Order of the Temple was in reality far more than a fighting force: it was an international business network as useful to pilgrims seeking a safe passage to Jerusalem as it was to kings, queens and nobles looking for a comprehensive financial service to run their accounts, keep an eye on their valuables and raise loans when they got into trouble. For better or worse, the Poor Knights of the Temple of Solomon were no longer of the Temple, and no longer poor.

This is not to say that the Templars' crusading mission had been abandoned. Far from it. The one thing the Templars could never escape was their intimate connection with Christian fortunes in the Holy Land, and although the 1230s and early 1240s were a time of relative calm, one last burst of crusading activity would soon beckon. The enemy was evolving, but the root calling was the same: defend the kingdom of Jerusalem at any cost.

16

"Unfurl and Raise Our Banner!"

THE SYRIAN SCHOLAR and chronicler known as Ibn Wasil was on his way to Cairo in 1244 when he passed through Jerusalem. The city was still in Christian hands, and he was depressed by what he saw. Although Muslims were allowed into the city and on to the Haram al-Sharif, or Temple Mount, what greeted him there was a scene of sacrilege. Christian clerics conducted services within the Dome of the Rock, incanting the name of God the Father, Son and Holy Spirit—the Holy Trinity, which the Muslims saw as polytheistic. Worse than this, wine bottles rested on top of the rock from which Muhammad had ascended on the Night Journey. The al-Aqsa Mosque had also been desecrated and decorated with bells.[1]

Ibn Wasil had long been skeptical of the deal struck between al-Kamil and Frederick II in 1229. He had preached against it at the Great Mosque of Damascus as soon as it was announced, lamenting, "The road to Jerusalem is now closed to pious visitors!" and crying, "Shame on the Muslim rulers!" Now, seeing the effects fifteen years of Frankish occupation had taken, he was no less disheartened. The arrangement in Jerusalem clearly benefited the crusaders. But what had it done for Islam?

Al-Kamil was no longer available to contemplate such questions. The sultan had died in 1238 and his death had been followed by the customary period of jockeying for power. Within two years al-Kamil's son al-Salih Ayyub (or simply al-Salih) had emerged as his father's heir as sultan, with theoretical supremacy over his other ambitious relatives. But his rule was far from unchallenged. He was particularly troubled by the intrigues of his rebellious uncle, al-Salih Isma'il, the ruler of Damascus, who had made an alliance with the Franks of the kingdom of Jerusalem, guaranteeing their rights in the Holy City and handing over various castles, including Safad on the river Jordan, just above the Sea of Galilee, which the Templars were rebuilding in imposing fashion. To al-Salih Ayyub this was more than just political expediency. His uncle had crossed the line between accommodation and full-on alliance. As a new sultan, he could not stand by and let this happen.

His uncle might now count Franks as his allies, but al-Salih was turning to something bigger and much more dangerous. In Mesopotamia and northern Syria a new group was gathering strength: the Khwarizmian Turks, Sunni tribesmen originally from Persia and central Asia, who had been displaced when their homelands were conquered by Mongols and who were now moving to the west looking for territories in which to settle. They were tough warriors and expert horsemen—unpredictable and fiendishly difficult to work with but deadly in the field. Al-Salih forged a military partnership with them, and in 1244 he was ready to put it to use against his uncle of Damascus and the perfidious Christians of Jerusalem.

On July 11, just months after Ibn Wasil's visit, the Khwarizmians stormed the Holy City. Under the terms by which the Franks had been given Jerusalem its walls had not been rebuilt, so riding in was easy. Evicting the Christian rulers and occupants was even easier and the Khwarizmians ran amok: decapitating priests, disemboweling pilgrims seeking sanctuary in churches, smashing the marble decoration around the Lord's shrine at the Holy Sepulchre, destroying the tombs of Frankish kings and sending columns of refugees pouring out of the city, with nothing to cling to but their lives. The military orders tried to protect the fleeing citizens as they headed for Jaffa, but there were far too many to defend. Gerald of Newcastle, a Hospitaller, described the citizens' fate as they were set upon by bandits and Khwarizmian outriders. "The enemy . . . surrounding them on all sides, attacked them with swords, arrows, stones and other weapons, slew and cut [to] pieces . . . around seven thousand men and women and caused such a massacre that the blood of those of the faith . . . ran down the sides of the mountains like water." Inside Jerusalem, wrote Gerald, they had "cut the throats of nuns and aged and infirm men like sheep."[2] They smashed the city and spent a month plundering the surrounding area, then headed en masse for Gaza, to meet with al-Salih's army and prepare for the next assault.

With Jerusalem lost again and a new enemy riding at will through their territories, the Christians had no choice but to fight. They gathered an army with their allies from Damascus of around ten thousand men and prepared for battle.

On October 17, the Christian-Damascene army confronted the Khwarizmians-Egyptians at La Forbie (al-Harbiyya), a village not far from Gaza. The Christians fought bravely, "like athletes of God," according to one of the few survivors. They held off the much larger enemy army for an entire day, but when they rose the following morning to start again their Damascene allies had lost heart.[3] They fled the battlefield, and without them the Latin army, now cripplingly outnumbered, was obliterated.

The Templars threw every man they could into the battle at La For-bie, alongside hundreds of Hospitallers and Teutonic knights.[4] Of the nearly three hundred and fifty Templar knights in the field, only thirty-six survived. Their master, Armand of Périgord, disappeared and was never seen again. The master of the Hospitallers, William of Châteauneuf, was carried off to Cairo where he was held captive for six years. The arch-bishop of Tyre was mortally wounded, along with several other eminent churchmen. Count Walter of Brienne, a prominent figure among the noble leadership, was carried off to Jaffa where he was tortured (although not killed) by being crucified for a time on the city walls. The surviving rank and file of the Latin army were sold as slaves. The catapult operators and foot soldiers were victims of an "incalculable slaughter."[5] As a mili-tary disaster La Forbie was almost the equal of Hattin.

The patriarch of Jerusalem, Robert of Nantes, who was at the battle but managed to take refuge in Ascalon, was utterly depressed by what he had seen. "Having lost everything in the battle there is nothing to console us," the patriarch wailed in a letter to every leading churchman he could think of between England and the Holy Land. "If help is not forthcom-ing, the ruin and loss of the land will be quick."[6]

In Robert of Nantes's view, the defeat at La Forbie was a defeat for all of Christendom. Not everyone saw things that way. From his perch in Fog-gia, in Apulia, Frederick II, the Holy Roman Emperor and absentee king of Jerusalem, offered up a characteristically trenchant view of the battle's outcome. The emperor blamed a faction led by the Templars for ignoring orders to keep the peace with Egypt. Writing contemptuously of a battle he believed should never have been fought, he railed against "the effervescence of the religious pride of the Templars, nourished on the delicacies of the native barons of the land."[7]

It was easy for Frederick, from the safety of Foggia, to focus his ire on the Templars, all the more so as he had no intention of traveling back to Jerusalem to restore the kingdom himself. The man who would eventually come to the aid of the crusader states was a king of a rather different sensibility, far more amenable to the Order of the Temple.

✝

In mid-December 1244 Louis IX lay on his deathbed. Pale and thin, the thirty-year-old king of France was literally wasting away. He had dysentery, a wretched and painful ailment that could grip even the strongest soldiers by the gut and drag them rapidly to the grave. Louis had been suffering on and off for two years, ever since contracting the disease during a military campaign against the English, but the attack that overtook him now appeared fatal. His mother, Blanche of Castile, had come to his bedside in Pontoise to touch her son's fingertips with the holiest relics of the royal chapel. By royal decree the whole kingdom of France was praying for his recovery. Not even this had worked. It seemed that by Christmas the king would be dead and his infant son and namesake, not yet a year old, would succeed him.

As the hours passed and the king drifted deeper into his sickness, two ladies stood by his bedside, keeping a vigil over his motionless body. They were looking on when Louis appeared to stop breathing. The final moment seemed to have arrived, and one of the ladies reached for the king's sheet and began to pull it up to cover his eyes.

But was he really dead? Her colleague on the other side of the bed thought not. He was mute and unconscious and not visibly breathing, but she insisted that the king's soul was still in his body and prevented the sheet from being drawn up. The women began debating the issue in earnest, only to be interrupted when, beneath them, King Louis opened his eyes, then his mouth, and asked them to bring him a crusader's cross.[8]

Louis IX had been crowned king of France in 1226, at the age of twelve. He had spent much of his reign stamping his royal authority over areas of France that had been subject to English rule in the twelfth century, reforming the law and cultivating an image of royal magnificence that would seldom be equaled in the Middle Ages. Louis was a striking figure, with a thin, straight nose and high cheekbones, and he took care to project his majesty at all times, whether appareled in the colorful finery of his courtly dress or in the muted tones of dark silk trimmed with cheap squirrel fur he took to wearing as a crusader. He was a great builder, collector and patron of the arts, whose crowning achievement was the Sainte-Chapelle in Paris: a soaring Gothic masterpiece of vertical filigreed stonework and stained glass, which was nearing completion in 1244. It was being built to house Christ's crown of thorns, purchased from the Latin emperor of Constantinople in 1238.[9] Louis also owned a fragment of the True Cross, a piece of the holy sponge from which Jesus drank vinegar during his Crucifixion and the iron head of the lance that a Roman soldier had plunged into Christ's side. But architecture, splendor and relic accumulation alone was not the measure of a great Christian monarch. Louis's recovery was a personal miracle, and it convinced him that his mission as an adult king was to follow in the footsteps of his grandfather, Philip II Augustus, and great-grandfather, Louis VII. He would leave France to lead a crusade to the Holy Land.

The Parisian Templars were closely connected to the French Crown and the king's deathbed revival would directly and deeply affect the order. Their first task was to help the king pay for his adventure. For forty years French kings had outsourced treasury functions from the royal palace on Paris's Île de la Cité a mile or so north to where the Templars' lavish complex stood. The Paris Temple had been extensively refurbished since the land was first granted by Louis VII and was considered fit to house visiting royal courts, as it would when Henry III of England visited Paris in 1265.[10] At the time Louis IX decided to take up the cross, the treasurer was one Brother Gilles, and he was assigned to receive the receipts of a heavy crusading tax levied on the French Church at the rate of a tenth of movable possessions (doubled from the standard rate of a twentieth).*

The Templars were also responsible for ensuring that the French king would have ready money available when he arrived in the Holy Land.[11] When Louis commissioned ships to transport his armies out of his new custom-built port of Aigues-Mortes, just west of Marseille, he turned for help to Reginald of Vichiers, preceptor of France, who had invaluable experience in war provisioning, having served for a time as preceptor of the Templar house in Acre. In 1246 Reginald was sent with Prior Andrew Polin, the most senior French Hospitaller, to Genoa and Marseille, where the two men chartered ships for the royal army and reported directly back to the king.[12] When Louis finally set sail, landing at Limassol on Cyprus in mid-September 1248, one of the first Eastern dignitaries to greet him was the master of the Temple, William of Sonnac: a veteran crusader who had recently moved to Acre to take command of the order but had spent most of his career in Aquitaine, a region largely governed by the English, but under the ultimate lordship of the French Crown.

Cyprus became the forward base for Louis's crusade: a supply depot heaving with reserves of grain, wine and munitions. Soon after he landed there the destination of the new crusade was confirmed. The target was once again to be Damietta, the scene of the grinding amphibious battles, brief triumph and dismal retreat of the Fifth Crusade. It was an ignoble precedent to follow, but a quarter of a century's distance, the ascent of a new generation of crusade leaders and Louis's billowing confidence counted for more than the example of recent history. The sultan of Egypt presented a vulnerable target. Despite his crushing triumph at La Forbie, in 1246 he had broken with the Khwarizmian allies, driving them out of the city of Jerusalem the following year. His relatives continued to scheme against him and his power in Cairo was threatened by restive emirs, whom he had tried to counteract by building up a large private army of highly disciplined but increasingly uncontrollable Mamluks. On top of this,

---

* The concept of movable possessions, central to taxation in Europe in the Middle Ages, was very literal. It assessed the value of property that could physically be moved from one place to another, so included foodstuffs, furniture and fabrics, but not buildings or land.

al-Salih was seriously ill. He had consumption (now known as tuberculosis) and it severely reduced his physical stamina and grip on power.

Louis and his army set out for Egypt in excellent cheer on Thursday, May 13, 1249, with eighteen hundred vessels carrying them, "as if the whole sea, as far as the sight could reach, was covered with cloth, from the great quantity of sails that were spread to the wind."[13] A substantial Templar contingent sailed to Damietta with the fleet, led by William of Sonnac and Reginald of Vichiers, who had been appointed marshal. They did not have an easy crossing. The aristocratic French chronicler John of Joinville, whose biography of Louis was designed to gild the French king's reputation, described terrible weather during the journey south to the Egyptian coast, which blew nearly a third of the king's ships far off course. Yet this was not enough to discomfit Louis, who was spoiling for a fight. His plan to take retake Damietta was no secret, and when the crusader ships anchored off the coast on June 5, 1249, Joinville and his companions saw a shoreline heaving with al-Salih's soldiers blowing horns and trumpets. Among them was the sultan himself: dressed head to toe in burnished gold armor that shone like the sun.[14]

The crusaders were not intimidated. They had planned a mass beach assault, and followed through with their intention. Ignoring the cacophony on the shore, the king and his men leapt from shallow-bottomed boats, dragging whinnying horses into the sea and wading through chest-deep water toward the enemy. The veteran Walter of Brienne (who had been ransomed following his capture at La Forbie) arrived on a galley painted inside and out with a flared red cross on a golden background. Odo of Châteauroux, the cardinal bishop of Tusculum, held an obligatory fragment of the True Cross. The French banner known as the oriflamme was planted in the sand and the Templars, as they landed, would have rallied around their piebald standard. They, too, provided an intimidating sight.

For a few hours the beach was the scene of a fierce battle. The crusaders swarmed onto the sands in disciplined units, killing around five hundred Muslims, including four emirs.[15] Louis IX meant business. Preferring caution to confrontation, the sultan's field commander, Fakhr al-Din, pulled his men back and allowed the French king to complete his landing unopposed. Even more astonishingly, he ordered an evacuation of Damietta. During the Fifth Crusade the city had held out for over a year. In 1249 it was abandoned in a single day as the garrison handed it over to Christian occupation, burning what they could before fleeing up-river to defend Cairo. To the crusaders this seemed like divine providence. Yet there was military sense behind the withdrawal. History hung over both sides and the challenge to Louis was simple: did he dare to send his armies up the Nile?

While he thought this through, al-Salih's men mustered at al-Mansurah, where the Damietta branch of the Nile broke course with the Tanis: the exact spot where Cardinal Pelagius and John of Brienne had foundered on the Fifth Crusade. Meanwhile, units downriver launched raids on the Latin army billeted in and around Damietta. The sultan offered ten bezants for each Christian head that was cut off and brought back to him. The crusaders' camp was harried in this way for months, but to no conclusive effect. The summer passed and the Nile rose, and all the while Louis sat firm at Damietta, converting the mosques into churches and resisting the bait.

In November the stalemate broke. The Nile floods had receded and the summer's fierce heat had dimmed. If Louis was ever going to pursue his plan to conquer Egypt, now was the time. The only question was where to strike. A war council assembled and debated moving west along the coast and attacking Alexandria, but this plan was rejected on the advice of Louis's belligerent thirty-three-year-old brother Robert, Count of Artois. That could only mean one thing: risking the march up the Nile and storming Cairo. "Whoever wished to kill a snake should begin with the head," Robert argued, and he won the day.[16]

The decision to move out of Damietta had probably been taken when, on November 23, the sultan died. The news of his death was kept a secret for some time: long enough for Fakhr al-Din to seize control and begin organizing the Egyptian response to Louis's planned advance. A highly competent general, Fakhr al-Din had every reason to think that he could resist a march on Cairo, not least because he had at his disposal a large army including the late sultan's thousand-strong elite Mamluk slave-soldier regiment known as the Bahriyya. Like the Templars, the Bahriyya ("of the river") were named after their original base of operations: an island in the Nile in the middle of Cairo. Also like the Templars, they were uncompromising warriors who could bounce back repeatedly from major losses in battle. They were about to show just how effective those qualities made them.

The Templars rode in the vanguard as the Christians started a slow march south along the eastern bank of the Nile. Quite what the brothers thought of their mission is hard to say. William of Sonnac had been chastised early in the campaign for opening back-channel peace negotiations with the Egyptians: an episode that suggests the Templars were more inclined to caution than the enthusiastic French crusaders whom they accompanied. A letter William sent to the English high command reporting on the fall of Damietta referred only in the plainest terms to Louis's deliberations over which part of Egypt to attack, without passing comment on the merits of the plan.[17] If the master had doubts, he was keeping them to himself. But tensions were steadily building between the instinctively cautious William and the king's hawkish brother, the Count of Artois. As the campaign progressed, clashes between the two men would have fatal consequences.

The crusaders moved slowly up the Nile over the course of December and it was not until Christmas that Louis's army drew up before al-Mansurah, on the opposite bank of the river Tanis. At the time of the Fifth Crusade this had been a military encampment, but over the thirty intervening years it had become a town, which now stood directly between the crusading army and the approach to Cairo. It would have to be taken or destroyed.

With the full might of the Egyptian army gathered on the opposite side of the river, this was no easy task. A fierce battle for the Tanis began, which lasted until February. Louis's leading engineers worked on a pontoon bridge, while Fakhr al-Din's men responded with a massive catapult bombardment, sending stones and Greek fire in the Christians' direction, causing panic and terrible destruction. John of Joinville wrote in awe at the sight of the Muslims' nightly incendiary bombardments. "The noise was like thunder and it seemed like a great dragon of fire flying through the air," he wrote, "giving so great a light with its flame that we saw our camp as clearly as in broad daylight."[18] Each time Greek fire was discharged Louis would fall to the ground weeping profusely and calling on Jesus Christ to preserve his people. This was a splendidly pious spectacle— but the river remained uncrossed.

It was not until the start of Lent that the crusaders found a way to reach the far bank. In early February 1250 a Bedouin came to the Christian camp offering to show them a point where the Tanis could be forded on horseback, in exchange for a fat fee of five hundred bezants. He was suggesting an inherently dangerous operation, for knights wearing armor were especially vulnerable when wading through rivers. (Mamluk warriors trained specifically so that they could shed their mail coats by swimming upside down in case they were unhorsed in water—not an easy operation to pull off.) But there were few better options, save for retreat, which Louis would not countenance. So on February 8, Shrove Tuesday, Louis selected the best knights from his army—around a third of his total cavalry—and set out with them before dawn to the Bedouin's crossing point.

Fording the river in the semidarkness and emerging ready to attack an enemy camp required supreme horsemanship and bravery. Louis asked his brother to lead one group of knights through the water. He was not the first, though: for ahead of him, piebald banners aloft, went the Templars.

Just as the Egyptians had known about Louis's arrival at Damietta the previous summer, so they had also learned of his plan to ford the Tanis. As the crusaders emerged from the water, a reconnaissance party of around three hundred Muslim cavalry spotted them. This was a large enough band to have seriously disrupted the crossing if they had launched an immediate assault. But they did not. Instead they watched the crusaders wading across the river, then wheeled their horses around and galloped away toward al-Mansurah.

Once again, faced with Christian knights emerging from the water, an Egyptian defending force had scattered. The prudent thing for Louis's men to do was to wait, assemble and attack en masse. Unfortunately, the tension of the moment got the better of the Count of Artois. Instead of sticking to the plan, he called an immediate charge on the town. Abandoning discipline and caution, he sent his men flying off to lay into the retreating Muslim reconnaissance. All of a sudden, and much too soon, the battle of al-Mansurah was under way.

William of Sonnac and his Templar marshal, Reginald of Vichiers, were screaming for restraint. According to John of Joinville, their cries were ignored by the count and simply not heard by the man who held his bridle, Sir Foucquault of Melle, who was either stone-deaf or pretending to be so. Artois had given the order and Sir Foucquault's job was to relay the command. The Templars watched in horror as he "kept bawling out 'Forward, forward!'"[19] But forward they all went.

According to the English chronicler Matthew Paris, the count's purpose in advancing ahead of the rest of the army was pure vainglory. "His intention [was] to triumph alone, instead of allowing all to share it . . . for he was proud and arrogant."[20] Paris was biased, but he had a good source: his information came from frontline despatches sent directly to the English royal court. He heard that there was a lengthy exchange of views outside al-Mansurah between William of Sonnac and Robert of Artois, in which the Templar master did his best to impress some sanity on the count, who bullheadedly refused to listen. Describing William as "a prudent and circumspect man, well skilled and experienced in warlike matters," Paris gave the master a long speech in which he politely congratulated Robert of Artois on his superlative bravery, but warned that they had entirely lost the element of surprise. If they attacked al-Mansurah without waiting for the king and full reinforcements, William said, they would be charging headlong into "our destruction and ruin."[21]

In Paris's account, Robert responded to this entreaty with bald fury. He cursed "the ancient treachery" of the Templars, accused the military orders of deliberately sabotaging their fellow crusaders to profit from the continuation of war, and declared that "the ruin of all paganism is imminent, as well as the lasting exaltation of the Christian faith, all of which this Templar . . . endeavours to impede by his fictitious and fallacious arguments."[22] Most damningly of all, he invoked the Holy Roman Emperor Frederick Hohenstaufen's struggle with the Templars as a prime example of their mendacity.

How much of this bitter exchange happened as reported, and how much sprang from the fertile mind of Matthew Paris cannot be known.

What is certain is that Robert won the argument. Common to both Paris's and John of Joinville's accounts is the sense that Robert of Artois had goaded the Templars into following him on a suicidal raid. Harsh words gave way to action, as Artois's second division charged, and the Templars decided they had no honorable option but to spur on their horses behind them. "Unfurl and raise our banner!" shouted William of Sonnac, in Matthew Paris's version of events. "Let us proceed to battle, that we may this day all together try the fortune of war and the chances of death."[23]

The crusaders' descent on al-Mansurah, rashly conceived and hastily executed, was an entirely predictable bloodbath. Barreling into the narrow streets in pursuit of the fleeing Muslims, they ran into a trap and were soon outnumbered and surrounded. John of Joinville, who took part in the battle, witnessed the savage fighting at first hand, seeing one man with his nose sliced so badly it hung loose by his mouth; another with blood spouting from his shoulder like a freshly tapped barrel of wine. Nearly six hundred knights were lost in the street fighting, two hundred and eighty of whom were brothers of the Temple. William of Sonnac lived but lost an eye. His only consolation was that the Count of Artois was killed. He had urged his horse to swim across the river in a desperate bid to flee, but had slipped from his saddle and was dragged to his death under the weight of his iron armor. When his body washed up it was picked over for spoils. His surcoat was later used as a trophy to inspire the sultan's men before they ran into battle.[24]

The king crossed the river behind his brother and escaped the worst, but as soon as his men had established a camp on the southern bank of the river, they were forced to endure near-daily fighting to defend it. Hour by hour the death toll rose. Immediately after the battle, William of Sonnac had helped John of Joinville scatter a band of Muslims whom they caught trying to steal tents from the royal camp. Three days later, he was fighting again. On Friday, February 11, Fakhr's men advanced on the crusader positions, with the Mamluks launching their Greek fire. William of Sonnac commanded a company made up of the few Templars who had survived the battle on Shrove Tuesday, but he and his men were weakened by injury, desperately tired and poorly equipped to deal with the chaos raining all around them.

John of Joinville described the carnage that ensued. The master had built barricades for his men out of captured siege engines but these were as much of a handicap as a help. "The Saracens burned them with their Greek fire," wrote Joinville, "and seeing there were but few to oppose them, they did not wait until they were destroyed, but vigorously attacked the Templars, defeating them in a very short time." Behind the lines, Joinville saw "an acre of ground so covered with bolts, darts, arrows and other weapons that you could not see the earth beneath them." Having lost one eye on February 8, Master William now lost the other, and died of his wounds.[25]

The crusaders had come to al-Mansurah and been crushed, much as they had been thirty years earlier. Although Louis IX held his position for more than a month, by the beginning of April it had become obvious that to remain any longer would be a short road to total annihilation. A new sultan, Turanshah, had arrived in Cairo to succeed his father and although his court was riven by factional squabbles between various groups of Mamluks, Turanshah had no interest in negotiating an even-handed peace with the beleagured Christians.

The countryside around al-Mansurah told a story of desolation, starvation and disease. The Tanis was so full of bloated corpses that in places it was completely blocked. The Nile teemed with Muslim galleys, preventing resupply from, or escape to, Damietta. Malnutrition afflicted the living. As their scurvied gums rotted in their mouths barber-surgeons had to cut away the putrid flesh to allow the soldiers to eat. Louis himself had a recurrence of dysentery that was so bad he had to cut a hole in his undergarments. The only option was retreat.

The withdrawal down the Nile began in disorderly fashion at dawn on Tuesday, April 5, with men scrambling onto boats or wading through mud in their desperation to abandon the wretched camp. Those who managed to leave watched behind them as the flickering light from the night's fires illuminated Muslim soldiers swarming over the site, running through anyone who was too ill to crawl from his bed and flee.

The handful of surviving Templars made a pitiful attempt to shepherd what remained of Louis's army back to Damietta. It was a hopeless task. The straggling crusader army was picked off boat by boat and division by division, with no mercy shown to anyone who could not prove himself a captive of the highest worth. (John of Joinville only escaped murder when his boat ran aground on a mudbank in the Nile; he leapt overboard and claimed upon capture that he was King Louis's cousin.) By the time the last bands of fleeing crusaders were picked off, a dozen or so miles from Damietta, only three Templars remained alive.

The Arab poet Jamal ad-Din ibn Yahya ibn Matruh later wrote a celebratory ditty chiding the crusaders and their king. "You came to the East boasting of conquest, believing our martial drumroll to be a breath of wind," he wrote. "And your stupidity has brought you to a place where your eyes can no longer see any way of escape . . . of fifty thousand not one can be seen who is not dead or wounded and a prisoner."[26] As the news filtered back to Christendom, it was met with deep gloom. "The French," wrote Matthew Paris, "pined away more and more with internal grief, nor could their king console them."[27]

He could not console them because, like the cream of the French nobility who had accompanied him on his Egyptian adventure, Louis IX of France had been taken prisoner. He was now at the mercy of the men whom he had come to destroy. Turanshah demanded the return of Damietta and a ransom payment of 800,000 gold bezants—roughly equivalent to 400,000 livres tournois, or two years' royal revenue. This would also cover the thousands of other prisoners who had not yet had their throats slit.

A wobble in negotiations occurred on May 2, 1250, when Turanshah was murdered in a Mamluk coup: the sultan was attacked with a cutlass, trapped in a burning tower and thrown into the Nile. His corpse was then fished out and for good measure his heart removed. A major upheaval in the leadership of the Islamic world had begun, which would end with the Mamluks of the Bahriyya seizing outright control of Egypt, overturning nearly eighty years of Ayyubid rule. More pressingly for the crusaders, King Louis was still a prisoner, as was another of his brothers, Alphonse, Count of Poitiers. The ransom still had to be paid.

On Friday, May 6, Louis was sent to his camp to count out the first installment of his ransom: 400,000 bezants, or 200,000 livres tournois. Alphonse was held back as security, as were the large stockpiles of weapons and provisions the crusaders had been forced to leave in Damietta when they relinquished the city. Neither would be released, nor would the king be allowed to leave the Nile Delta until the money had been received.

A king's ransom was a vast sum, and weighing 200,000 livres out of the coin reserves Louis had brought to Egypt took nearly two days. By the evening of Sunday, May 8, 170,000 livres had been counted and the treasury was empty. The king was still 30,000 short of his target. An argument broke out about the best way to raise the outstanding sum.

John of Joinville, who was with the king, claimed that he recommended Louis borrow the thirty thousand from the few surviving Templars. Their highest-ranking survivors were Stephen of Ostricourt, the order's preceptor, and Louis's old ally and fixer Reginald of Vichiers, the marshal.

If anyone were suited to meeting this sort of urgent demand for money, it was the Templars. Yet as Joinville discovered, the brothers took their banking protocols seriously. Stephen of Ostricourt initially refused the request, arguing that the order's integrity depended on every depositor trusting in the safety of the money they placed in the brothers' hands. The Templars had received these deposits on oath, swearing that they would not release them except to the depositor. Even now they could not bend the rules.[28]

Stephen of Ostricourt was doing his diligent best to uphold Templar business practice under the most trying circumstances. But he was not being very helpful. Fortunately for Louis, Reginald of Vichiers was more resourceful. He had commissioned several ships in Marseille on the king's behalf in 1246, at the outset of the campaign; he had traveled from Cyprus to Egypt in the king's entourage; he had fought in the thick of the dreadful Shrove Tuesday battle, and so he may well have felt more personally invested in helping Louis limp out of Damietta with whatever shreds of dignity he could salvage.[29] The marshal countered that while it was true that the Templars could not release their clients' wealth "without acting contrary to our oaths and being perjured," if the king's men were to take the money by force, then the Templars would be forced to take reparations when the royal party returned to Acre.

Grasping exactly what the marshal meant, John of Joinville turned to the king and asked if he should board the Templars' galley in person, and take the thirty thousand livres by force. The king nodded his assent. John and Reginald went together to the Templar treasury and played out a charade that Joinville described in his chronicle. "Seeing a coffer of which they refused to give me the keys, I was about to break it open with a wedge in the king's name," he wrote. "But the marshal, observing I was in earnest, ordered the keys to be given me. I opened the coffer, took out the sum wanting and carried it to the king, who was much rejoiced by my return. Thus was the whole payment of the two hundred thousand livres completed."[30]

Louis was now free to leave Damietta, thanks to the man who had helped get him there in the first place. Neither, presumably, was very sorry to leave.

✛

On May 13, 1250, Louis IX arrived in Acre, chastened but not defeated. He had lost a brother, a battle and a certain degree of his royal dignity on the Nile. The cloak he was wearing when he was captured—a red woolen garment lined with ermine and fastened with a gold buckle—had found its way to Damascus, where an Ayyubid emir had taken to wearing it in public.[31] But the king still had his life, and his wish to fight for the kingdom of Jerusalem burned as brightly as it had on the day he had recovered from his near-fatal attack of dysentery six years earlier. Louis remained in Acre for nearly four years, working to free the prisoners he had lost in Damietta and overseeing the government of the kingdom of Jerusalem with the diligence and rigor that such a challenging task required.

Frederick II died of dysentery on December 13, 1250, and was buried in a bright red sarcophagus in Palermo Cathedral. He had spent most of his reign in a long and dizzyingly complex war with the pope and his enemies in Italy, and although he had succeeded where everyone since the First Crusade failed—he had taken back the city of Jerusalem for the Latin Christians—he died having offended the Church so consistently that he had been excommunicated four times and had led many churchmen to the conclusion that he was the devil incarnate. The sheer scale of Frederick's territories meant that he exported his many feuds and wars across them, so that factional conflicts beginning in Sicily and northern Italy were transferred to Cyprus and the Latin states. He also left his wars to his son and successor Conrad, who kept up the Hohenstaufen war against the papacy, and took even less interest in the Latin states of the East than his father. Between Conrad's accession as emperor in 1250 and his death in 1254 he never visited the Holy Land. Nor did his own son and heir, Conradin, who was beheaded at the age of sixteen in 1268 by his enemy Charles I of Naples, bringing the Hohenstaufen line to an end.

In 1250, therefore, Jerusalem was a vulnerable kingdom with an absentee king, and Louis IX's arrival from Damietta was welcome. The French king approved much-needed upgrades to the Holy Land's most important fortifications, and paid for improvements to the defenses of coastal strongholds at Sidon, Acre, Caesarea and Jaffa. He did not manage to negotiate the return of Jerusalem itself, but he gave the depleted crusader states leadership and resources at a moment when these were badly lacking.

One of Louis's first acts upon arriving in Acre was to support the election of Reginald of Vichiers to the position of master of the Templars, a promotion that was hard to gainsay in light of the services he had rendered, the battles he had fought and the sheer devastation wreaked on the order's membership by the dual blows of La Forbie and al-Mansurah.

Their relationship remained close thereafter and in an extraordinary display of fraternity between king and master, in 1251 Louis's fourth son, Peter, was born in the Templars' fortress of Château Pèlerin. Louis's intrepid wife, Margaret, had accompanied him throughout his crusade, staying at Damietta when he led the ill-starred march up the Nile, during which she had given birth to another boy, John Tristan. In terms of physical fortitude she was every bit as much a crusader as her husband. It showed considerable favor on the Templars' part to permit a woman—queen or not—to give birth in one of their most prestigious (and supposedly male-only) castles. To crown the irregularity of it all, Reginald stood as godfather to the little prince, directly disobeying the Templar Rule, which stated: "We forbid all brothers henceforth to dare to raise children over the font and none should be ashamed to refuse to be godfathers . . . this shame brings more glory than sin."[32]

Reginald of Vichiers was a pragmatist and not a disciplinarian, as his relationship in the service of Louis IX had shown. Despite occasional flashpoints when the master irritated the king by pursuing the order's interests contrary to royal policy, there were few more productive relationships between a Western crusader and a Templar master. John of Joinville, who stayed in Outremer with his king, recorded plentiful examples of cooperation between Crown and Temple, both on and off the battlefield. Certainly this was a marked improvement on the state of affairs under Frederick Hohenstaufen, when the order and the emperor fought one another more than their mutual enemy.

Yet Louis could not stay forever. His mother, Blanche of Castile, had been serving as regent during his absence, but in November 1252 she died, leaving a chasm in French politics that only the king himself could fill. After listening to the advice of the barons of the kingdom of Jerusalem and spending three full days weeping, he left Acre in April 1254 and sailed for home. Louis's life had been profoundly altered by his six years of crusading, and on his return to France he adopted an austere, pious way of life that would later earn him sainthood.

No one knew it at the time, but Louis was the last of the great crusader kings. His reign would be seen as a model for all future French kings: a shining example of Christian kingship, which beamed down the ages. It was also something of an apogee for relations between the French Crown and the Order of the Temple. After Louis departed, the defense of the Holy Land was conducted by the men of the East and the military orders, with precious little help from the monarchs of Western Christendom. And while the Order of the Temple continued to provide much-needed financial assistance to the wealthy and powerful, their fortunes and their reputation began slowly to wane as the Christian states in the Holy Land, which they had fought so valiantly to defend, were whittled steadily away. This was as much a mark of the times as the result of Louis's leaving. All the same, once the French king disappeared beyond the horizon in 1254, things were never quite the same. A shift in attitudes, in European politics and in Eastern empire building was about to sweep through the Mediterranean world.

The Templars would find themselves right at the heart of these changes, fighting a desperate rearguard action as the crusading movement collapsed around them, while finding themselves increasingly under suspicion in the West. During the later decades of the thirteenth century the brothers found they had two deadly enemies ranged against them, both seeking their destruction. The first was the Mamluks, who rose from the banks of the Nile to extend their power across the Muslim lands of the Levant, seeking to achieve what not even Saladin had managed before: the total obliteration of Christian presence in the East.

The second was Saint Louis's grandson, Philip IV, king of France.

PART IV

Heretics

1260–1314

Principium fini solet impar sepe uidere.
Often the end fails to equal the beginning.

—Medieval proverb[1]

17

"A Lump in the Throat"

AL-MALIK AL-ZAHIR RUKN al-Din Baybars al-Bunduqdari was tall and dark skinned with stunning blue eyes, one of which was flecked arrestingly with white. He was a terrible figure to behold. As fierce as Zengi, as calculating as Nur al-Din and as charismatic as Saladin, Baybars' personal secretary Ibn 'Abd al-Zahir wrote of his "bravery, the like of which was never seen before."[1]

His subjects called him "Father of Conquest" and "the Lion of Egypt." History knows him simply as Baybars.

Between 1260 and 1277 Baybars ruled over a resurgent Sunni empire in the eastern Mediterranean, which rose from the rubble of the collapsing Ayyubid empire in the decade following al-Salih's death. This was a Mamluk state with a pitiless and frighteningly effective war machine at its core. As sultan, Baybars could draw on a permanent army of forty thousand intensively drilled slave soldiers, light cavalry trained to shoot arrows soused in Greek fire from the saddles of their horses and the newest and most powerful siege artillery available. Presiding over this warrior caste allowed Baybars to propel himself and his successors to a position of absolute dominance in Syria and Egypt, with such success that even his own people were occasionally stunned. "They were shocked by the severity of the Bahriyya faction and their oppressive and tyrannical methods for dealing with others," wrote 'Abd al-Zahir.[2] He went on to explain that Baybars also appealed to the people of Egypt with tax cuts and a program of school building, and surrounded himself with scholars who "recited celebratory poems and were rewarded with robes of honor." Nevertheless, Baybars' success was founded on a philosophy of uncompromising force.

Born about 1220 on the steppe north of the Black Sea, Baybars was ethnically a Kipchak Turk, who had been sold into slavery at about the age of fourteen and taken to Egypt to train as a warrior. He joined the elite Bahriyya, the Mamluk corps that dominated Sultan al-Salih's court and fought Louis IX's army at the battle of al-Mansurah. A few months later he took part in the assassination of al-Salih's son and successor, Turanshah. Exiled from Egypt for his treachery, he traveled to Syria, working as a mercenary in the service of various hapless Ayyubid emirs squabbling over their splintering territories. In 1259 he returned to Egypt to join forces with a rival Mamluk, Qutuz, who had seized power in Cairo and was ruling as sultan. Qutuz was from a faction hostile to Baybars and the Bahriyya, but peace was convenient to both parties, as they braced to confront an even more dreadful menace looming in the east: the Mongols.

Ever since the earliest years of the thirteenth century, the whole world had trembled at the name of the Mongols. Their story began when an orphaned warlord by the name of Temüjin rallied together the nomadic tribes of the northeast Asian steppe and began to strike out at the ruling dynasties all around him. After a series of initial successes Temüjin took the name Genghis Khan (sometimes rendered as Chinggis Khan, loosely meaning Great Ruler). He and his descendants built the largest land empire in history, stretching from the East China Sea to Poland, uniting millions of people under a rule that was in many ways enlightened and tolerant, but was founded on the principles of total warfare. After Genghis's death, his sons and grandsons continued his conquests. In 1259 they split the empire into four enormous blocs known as khanates: the Yuan dynasty in the east, containing China and Mongolia; the Chagatai in central Asia around Transoxania; the Golden Horde in the northwest, stretching from Siberia to Eastern Europe; and the Ilkhanate, spilling out from Persia. What all the Mongol khans shared was their basic methods of conquest: massacres and the wholesale destruction of populations who defied them, with unconditional submission expected from all their enemies. Their warriors were expert horsemen and their military engineers highly skilled in reducing cities and fortifications to rubble. Yet for all this, the Mongols' greatest strength was their ability to spread panic and terror before them, as they deliberately targeted civilians and garnered a reputation for matchless brutality toward anyone foolish enough to resist them. In 1244 the patriarch of Jerusalem called the Mongols "an unknown people" who "persecuted all alike, making no distinction between Christians and infidels."[3]

It had been known for some time that the Mongols were bearing down on the Holy Land. In 1260 the Templar Master Thomas Bérard, who had taken over leadership of the order in 1256 after Reginald of Vichiers's death, sent dire letters from Acre to England and France warning of the Mongol advance. To Henry III of England and Brother Amadeus, the English Templar master, he wrote: "The Tartars [i.e., the Mongols], advancing with an innumerable force, [have] already occupied and devastated the Holy Land almost up to Acre . . . nor will Christendom be able to resist them unless supported by the powerful hand of God . . . unless help is brought quickly, God forbid, a horrible annihilation will swiftly be visited upon the world."[4]

These and other such baleful warnings met with an uneven response. Some in the West actively welcomed the Mongols, seeing them as their saviors from the threat posed by the Saracens. Popular Christian prophecies had long predicted the arrival of a great king from the east who would help restore the glory of Christ on earth. Many in Europe considered that the Mongols fitted the bill.* Prior to the Damietta campaign of 1249–1250, Louis IX entertained the idea of converting the pagan khans to Christianity and combining forces to squeeze the sultans of Egypt and Damascus into submission. This was not entirely fantastical. The Mongols were notably open-minded about religious conversions, often adopting the faith of the lands they conquered. Hülagü, the ruler of the Ilkhanate, which was expanding westward from Persia toward the Holy Land, had a Nestorian Christian woman as his chief wife, and in 1262 he was indeed considering a similar alliance, despatching his own letters to France to sound out Louis.[5] Hülagü described himself to Louis as an "avid destroyer of the perfidious Saracen people, friend and supporter of the Christian religion, energetic fighter of enemies and faithful friend of friends."[6] The dream alliance never fully came about, but it remained a tantalizing possibility in the minds of some Western princes and a vision of looming annihilation in those of the Ayyubids and their Mamluk successors.

The Mongols directly, if inadvertently, provided Baybars with his route to power, as he played a leading part (later exaggerated into a central role) in a massive battle between Mamluk and Mongol armies, which took

---

* The "Prester John" legend of the mid-thirteenth century told of an exotic king of Nestorian faith whose participation in the wars against the Saracens was imminent.

place in 1260. Hülagü had spent the late 1250s smashing his way through Persia. A Mongol army sacked Baghdad in 1258, murdering the Abbasid caliph by rolling him up in a carpet and riding their horses over him. They also destroyed the city's famous library: it was said that the Tigris ran black with the ink of the books thrown in its waters. This was greeted in Cairo and Damascus as a disaster of epic proportions that seemed to threaten the very existence of an Islamic Middle East.[7] Two years later the Mongol horde had moved across the Euphrates and Hülagü's armies were enjoying themselves in northern Syria, where they captured Aleppo and laid it waste. They seemed unstoppable. Desperate and seemingly staring at total eradication, Baybars and the Egyptian sultan, Qutuz, marched a huge army through Palestine to block their way. Such was the urgency of their mission that Latins of the kingdom of Jerusalem allowed them to pass unmolested through their lands. Bohemond VI, Prince of Antioch and Count of Tripoli, took a different tack and actively supported the Mongols, convincing himself that they were the lesser of two evils. He was joined by another northern Christian potentate, the Armenian King Hethum of Cilicia, who was his father-in-law.

The Mamluks made their stand against the Mongols at 'Ayn Jalut (also known as the Springs of Goliath) in Galilee on September 3, 1260, and won an almost miraculous victory, which saved Muslim Syria from subjugation. "The Mongols were routed, put to the sword and taken prisoner," wrote the Egyptian scholar Shihab al-Din al-Nuwayri.[8] Their feared general Kitbugha was among the dead. Buoyed by his role in this incredible feat and always alert to an opportunity, Baybars returned to Egypt, taking the liberty of murdering Qutuz in cold blood on the way home. It was the second time Baybars had helped to kill a sultan, and he was determined that there should not be a third. He claimed the title for himself, established a new Abbasid caliphate based in Cairo rather than in the ruins of Baghdad, made the caliph his puppet, then embarked on several grandiose building projects and started a major program of rearmament.

From that point on Baybars pursued two parallel goals. His first was to unite the Islamic peoples of Egypt and Syria to form a unified Mamluk state with a large, well-trained, ultradisciplined standing army capable of resisting the Mongols if and when they returned. The second was to rid Palestine and Syria of the Latin Christians.

Destroying the Franks was partly a matter of religious duty and partly of practical necessity. It was true that Western appetite for crusades appeared to have dimmed following a century and a half of more or less relentless and costly failure. Crusading enthusiasm was being turned toward heretics and unbelievers closer to home. The wars against the Almohads of southern Spain continued, but the European wars of religious conquest were also targeting Cathar heretics in southern France, pagans in the Balkans, northern European Slavs, Scandinavians, Livonians and Poles. It was also true that the Eastern Franks were an increasingly pitiful bunch. In 1260 the king of Jerusalem, Frederick Hohenstaufen's grandson Conradin, was eight years old and more than two thousand miles away in Bavaria. In his absence there was precious little political leadership and no serious armed capability, save for that of the Templars, the Hospitallers and the Teutonic Order, who between them garrisoned almost every important defensive outpost and controlled much of the dwindling territory still subject to Latin rule. Violent rivalries raged in Acre and Tyre between Genoan and Venetian merchants, and their warring factions were backed respectively by the Hospitallers and the Templars, putting a damaging tear in the fabric of the Frankish world.* But so long as the Christians possessed coastal cities such as Jaffa, Caesarea, Acre and Tyre they would be a potential hazard. And so long as there remained the possibility that they might be bolstered by the arrival of some new crusader king looking to glorify his own name through the holy war, the nightmare scenario of a crusader-Mongol compact was alive.[9]

At the beginning of his reign Baybars had engaged fairly moderately with the Franks, threatening them with his armies, but also showing himself open to truces and bargaining with individual lords for access to trading ports like Jaffa. This occasional accommodation was made more difficult by the attitudes of the Templars and Hospitallers, who,

---

* The so-called War of Saint Sabas gripped Acre and the surrounding land and seas for fourteen years between 1256 and 1270.

despite their differences, both objected to treating with Baybars, on the grounds that they would be forced to free large numbers of their Muslim slaves, who were skilled craftsmen and highly useful captives.[10] A sign of the sultan's growing intransigence came in 1263, when he ordered his men to burn to the ground the Church of Saint Mary in Nazareth. He also took direct action against the Templars, mining and destroying a fortified mill at Doc, part of the ring of defenses fanning out from Acre.

In February 1265 Baybars' real assault began. He marched into the kingdom of Jerusalem and attacked Caesarea, taking the inhabitants by surprise, seizing the town and smashing the citadel with a bombardment from five of his new trebuchets. Unable to defend themselves, the garrison abandoned Caesarea by sea on March 5, heading for the safety of Acre. Baybars sent in engineers to tear the city's defenses to the ground, rendering it useless for any Christian army that might in future wish to retake it.

Seeing the example of Caesarea—fortified by Louis IX in granite, which was supposed to make it unbreachable—the garrison in nearby Haifa surrendered and sailed away. Next in line stood Château Pèlerin. Baybars was not yet ready to besiege the Templar stronghold, but he leveled a few settlements in the area as a warning. Then he hammered Arsuf in an engagement that lasted several weeks. A lackluster attempt to relieve the siege was led by Hugh III of Cyprus, the nominal regent of the kingdom of Jerusalem. Hugh's mission, lukewarm and undermanned, came to nothing. On April 30 Arsuf fell and, like Caesarea and Haifa, it was destroyed.

Baybars returned to Cairo, but the following spring and summer he was back in Christian territory. This time he headed for the county of Tripoli, sweeping through a series of smaller castles and terrorizing the peasants and farmers who lived around Acre, Tyre and Sidon. He sent an army north to attack Hethum, king of Cilicia, severely punishing him for aiding the Mongols at 'Ayn Jalut: his cities were burned and forty thousand of his people taken prisoner.

From here Baybars turned his attention to the Templars in their castle at Safad. As one band of his men traveled north to mete out their vengeance on King Hethum, in June 1266 Baybars himself advanced to the Templar fortress.

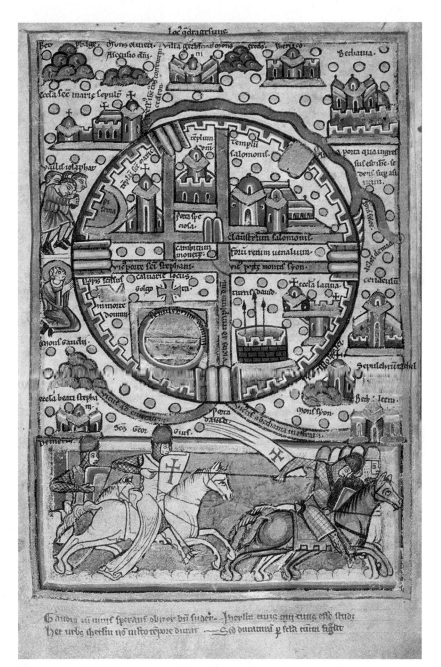

Jerusalem was the center of the world for Christian pilgrims, who risked their lives to pray at the Church of the Holy Sepulchre, built over Christ's tomb. This map, dating from ca. 1200, shows the Temple of Solomon—the Templars' headquarters—in the top right-hand section of the walled city.

A shrine in the Church of the Holy Sepulchre covers the cave in which Christ's body lay before the Resurrection. The structure we see today dates from the eighteenth century, but some medieval rituals are still observed.

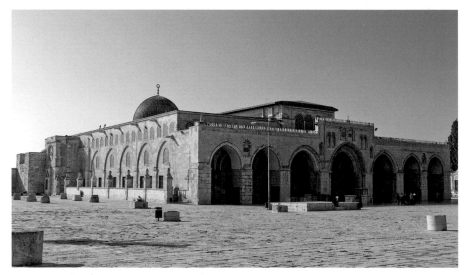

The al-Aqsa Mosque on the Temple Mount (Haram al-Sharif) was known as the Temple of Solomon by the Christians who ruled Jerusalem. It was given to the Templars by King Baldwin II and was the worldwide headquarters of the Order from 1119 until 1187.

The Cistercian abbot Bernard of Clairvaux was a tireless writer, friend of popes and kings, and passionate supporter of the Templars. He helped write their first Rule and championed their cause in Rome.

Saint Bernard thought Templar knights would be so devoted to their cause that they would avoid trivial pursuits such as hunting, dice, and chess. The Rule was more lenient, allowing brothers to gamble with wooden pegs. Here two Spanish Templars are seen playing chess. (Black appears to be in checkmate.)

This fresco, from a chapel built by the Templars at Cressac-sur-Charente, shows a crusader charging into battle.

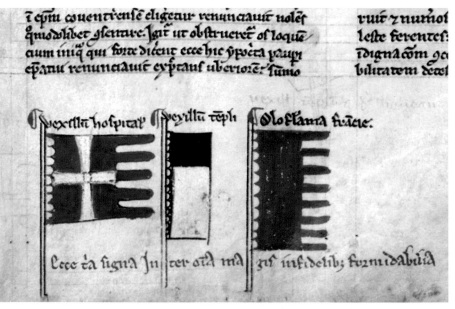

The battle flags of Hospitallers, Templars, and Kings of France. Every Templar swore to defend their black and white flag to the death.

The Castle of Monzón, in Aragón, served as a formidable base for the order as they fought Muslim armies in the wars of the Reconquista. The Aragónese Templars raised the child-king James I at Monzón before he took command of his kingdom.

This thirteenth-century fresco depicts a Syrian horseman in battle. His light armour reflects the fact that Syrian cavalry were quick and agile experts at lightning raids. The Templars recruited Syrian mercenaries, known as turcopoles, to fight alongside them.

Louis VII set out from Paris in 1147 on the Second Crusade, joined by a large number of Templar knights. When his forces were attacked in Asia Minor, the Templars helped restore discipline. When he ran out of money they made him a huge loan, which nearly bankrupted the order.

Saladin, Sultan of Egypt and Syria and founder of the Ayyubid dynasty, evicted the Christian kings from Jerusalem and turned the Templars' home back into the al-Aqsa mosque. This later portrait is a fanciful depiction, but it reflects his legendary status in both Christian and Islamic histories.

The battle of Hattin was a crushing military defeat for the armies of the Christian Holy Land and a blow felt right across the west. Saladin captured King Guy and confiscated the Franks' most treasured relic— a fragment of the True Cross. The battle was followed by an organized massacre of more than 200 Templars and Hospitallers in front of Saladin himself.

Richard the Lionheart revived the fortunes of the Templars when he led the Third Crusade to recover Acre and much of the rest of the Holy Land from Saladin.

The siege of Acre in 1191 was the first major triumph of the Third Crusade. The Templars recovered their fortress and supply depot near the city's docks. Richard the Lionheart and Philip II ("Philip Augustus") of France led military operations and are seen here receiving the keys to the city.

During the Fifth Crusade the Templars were pitched against Sultan al-Kamil, seen in this fresco with Saint Francis of Assisi. A poor preacher, Francis attempted unsuccessfully to convert al-Kamil to Christianity.

Although he was reviled by the Templars, the Holy Roman Emperor Frederick II Hohenstaufen used his sympathetic relationship with al-Kamil to reopen Jerusalem to Christian pilgrims.

The Templars built huge tunnels under the docks of Acre, linking their fortress with the city's main port and customs house. The tunnels were rediscovered in 1994 and can still be visited today.

Reginald of Vichiers, a leading French Templar and future master of the order, helped finance a fleet of ships to transport King Louis IX to Egypt, where he invaded Damietta in 1249. When Louis was captured, the Templars raised an emergency loan to pay his ransom.

From the 1260s on, the crusader kingdom of Jerusalem was under relentless assault by Mamluk armies from Egypt and by the Mongols. The Christians tried to forge an alliance with Hülagü Khan, who ruled the Ilkhanate of Persia. But the Mongols were unreliable allies, as the Templars discovered during a failed invasion of Tortosa in 1300.

Although the Christians briefly won back control of Jerusalem in 1229, they were driven out again in 1244 by a marauding army of Khwarizmian Turks, shown here in the margins of Matthew Paris's chronicle. The Templars were powerless to save the city.

This detail from a fourteenth-century brass basin shows a high-status Mamluk warrior (*far left*) who has sometimes been identified with the great Sultan Baybars. Baybars took the Templar fortress at Safad and beheaded all of its defenders.

Philip IV of France (*seated, center*) had a pronounced sense of his own royal magnificence, and a constant need for cash. Destroying the French Templars allowed him to present himself as a pious religious reformer and to confiscate much of the order's wealth.

The Templars' house in Paris was an urban fortress whose distinctive turrets soared over the city's skyline. It survived the order's fall and was used as a prison for the royal family during the French Revolution. This painting, from around that time, shows the tower in a state of advanced decay. It was demolished in 1808.

Bertrand of Got, archbishop of Bordeaux, became Pope Clement V in 1305. He never took up residence in Rome and was scorned as a puppet of the French king. He could not protect the Templars in 1307 and allowed a French witch hunt to develop into the total dissolution of the order.

CLEMENS V. Burdegalensis, creat. Sedit an.8.mens.io. Aprilis an.1314.Vac.

Bertrand. de Gotho, die s.Iunij an.1305, dies 16. Obijt die 20 Sed.an.2.men.3.d.17.

The French Templars were rounded up at dawn on Friday, October 13, 1307, in a raid carefully orchestrated by the government of Philip IV.

Several leading Templars, including James of Molay, were interrogated at Chinon castle by three cardinals and absolved of their sins. The records of this process, lost for centuries in the Vatican Secret Archives, were rediscovered in 2007 and published along with replicas of the cardinals' seals.

The burning of the Templars in Paris in 1314 is shown here as leading directly to Philip IV's death while hunting the same year. It was said that the last Templar master, James of Molay, called down God's curse on the men responsible for his demise.

• • • • •

Safad had been built by the Templars on the same scale as the coastal fortress of Château Pèlerin. In the words of one observer it was "inaccessible and impregnable," protected by towers over fifty yards high and controlled by eighty Templar knights and sergeants, fifty turcopoles and three hundred crossbowmen.[11] It had been commissioned in 1240 and its very existence told a story of shifting responsibility for the defense of the Holy Land. The site stood halfway between Christian Acre and Muslim Damascus and controlled a highly sensitive but lucrative stretch of border terrain that included numerous Christian pilgrim sites, such as the well where Joseph was sold by his brothers, the place where Jesus performed the miracle of the loaves and fishes and the birthplaces of several apostles and Mary Magdalene. A smaller castle there had been damaged by Saladin, and the initial plan to rebuild it was made by Theobald of Champagne, king of Navarre, during his crusade of 1239. Yet for all Theobald's talk, the seven thousand marks he had promised for the castle's reconstruction never materialized and it had been left to the Templars to see the project through. The order shouldered the massive cost of a twenty-year building project, and of garrisoning and manning an outpost "useful and necessary . . . to the whole of the Christian lands and . . . harmful . . . to the infidels."[12] Ibn al-Furat, an Egyptian chronicler who wrote an admiring biography of Baybars, called Safad "a lump in the throat of Syria and an obstacle to breathing in the chest of Islam."[13]

At once smartly situated and strongly built, Safad was staffed with "good soldiers, brethren and sergeants." On arrival Baybars sent gifts to the castle's garrison as a sign that he would treat them in good faith if they handed over the castle without resistance. On June 21 his gifts were returned with emphasis: flung from the battlements of the castle by defensive catapults. Baybars was insulted, and swore by Muhammad that he would put the defenders to the sword. Then, according to a chronicler known as the Templar of Tyre,* "he prepared his siege engines and they

---

* The so-called Templar of Tyre, whose chronicle is a valuable and favorable account of the last year of the order in the East, was not himself a professed brother, but a scribe in the service of the order.

attacked the castle."[14] His men dug mines and bombarded the walls with stones and Greek fire.

All this came to nothing, and by mid-July the sultan had grown frustrated, temporarily imprisoning several dozen of his emirs on the grounds that they were not trying hard enough to bring the castle down. On July 20, a resultant surge in activity secured Safad's barbican—the fortified gatehouse on the castle's outer perimeter—but even in the course of this small success the Mamluk army took very heavy casualties. "The sultan feared he would be unable to take [Safad] by force without losing [too many of] his men," wrote the Templar of Tyre. He called off the assault and came up with another plan.[15]

No Templar castle housed only members of the order, and in Safad the white-mantled knight-brothers and black-clad sergeants made up only a minority of the inhabitants. There were a large number of servants, mercenary crossbowmen, Syrian turcopole light cavalry and civilians who had fled from nearby towns and villages and sought refuge on Baybars' approach. This was a varied group, and the sultan decided to exploit their potential differences, adopting the timeless strategy of attacking morale rather than walls. Having first ensured that Safad was cut off from reinforcement or relief, he instructed public criers to stand within earshot of the castle compound and announce that he was prepared to offer safe conduct for all Syrians—an offer that was gratefully taken up by a large number of the turcopoles and mercenaries. The sultan wanted to sow discord inside the fortress, and he did. Soon many had deserted. Now, with the barbican still occupied, the Templars were "badly weakened" and in "considerable disunity."[16]

Inside the castle the brothers called a council. After some deliberation they decided to send out a sergeant named Leon Cazalier (known as Brother Leo), who spoke Baybars' native Turkish language, to demand the same rights for Frankish Christians as had been offered the Syrians. The sultan heard this request politely and gave a noncommittal response. Later he took Brother Leo aside for a private meeting in which he informed the sergeant that he was mortally offended by the Templars' rejection of his gifts, that he intended to have every member of the garrison put to death and that this would certainly include Brother Leo, who would suffer the most agonizing end of all if he did not return to the castle and deliver a specific message to his comrades.

Weak, scared and unwilling to sample the inventiveness of Baybars' cruelty, Brother Leo hurried back to his Templar brothers with a fresh mouthful of lies. "He returned to the castle and told them that the sultan had authorized a safe-conduct for everyone, and that the sultan himself would swear to it in their sight," wrote the Templar of Tyre.[17] He was sending them all to their doom.

The following morning Baybars appeared before Safad and announced that if the Templars would lay down their arms and hand over the castle he would escort them safely to Acre, which was fast becoming the only safe spot on the littoral for Frankish Christians. The deal was accepted and the brothers and their dependents made preparations to depart.

Unfortunately for the Templars, Baybars was not Baybars. The sultan had selected one of his emirs who most looked like him, dressed him in royal finery and sent him out to sell a phony deal. Anyone who knew the sultan by sight might have recognized the difference by looking for the white-flecked brilliant blue of his eyes, but from high up on the battlements of their castle, the Templars were fooled.

On July 24 fighting halted and the gates of Safad were opened. Out poured its inhabitants: Templar knights and sergeants together with more than one thousand others who had been sheltering behind the fortress walls for nearly two months. They set off with their escort in the direction of Acre, but had scarcely gone half a mile when they were stopped and corralled near a small hillock that the Templars had used as an execution spot. One by one they were all beheaded. This was justified on the grounds that several of the Templars had brought weapons out of the castle, and that there had been an attempt to bring Muslims out under the guise of Syrian Christians. This may or may not have been true. In any case, whatever safe conduct the Templars thought they had been promised was flimsy enough to be disregarded. Baybars had shown himself to be inventive and totally ruthless. He killed all but two of as many as fifteen hundred captives from Safad, piling up their bodies and building a small wall around them to preserve a well of bones and skulls for posterity.

Brother Leo was spared, taken to the sultan's tent and given a cup of mare's milk to drink, whereupon he apostatized and became a Muslim.

Another Christian, selected at random, was sent to Acre to tell his tale and give his fellow Christians a taste of what lay ahead. Unlike Caesarea, Arsuf and Haifa, Safad was not destroyed: Baybars installed a Muslim garrison and transformed the fortress into the hub of Mamluk power in Galilee. His work was far from finished.

✝

Losing Safad shook the Templars to their core. They still manned many castles in the steadily eroding crusader states, but very few were equal to Safad, which Baybars had managed to reduce in less than two months. It was hard to be optimistic. The Hospitallers sent a craven embassy to Baybars begging him to leave alone a pair of their most valuable castles, Margat and Crac des Chevaliers in the county of Tripoli. Baybars agreed to a ten-year nonaggression deal, but only on condition that the Hospitallers transferred to him the proceeds of tributes taken in from the surrounding districts.

Shortly after the fall of Safad a Templar knight called Ricaut Bonomel wrote a poem reflecting bitterly on the losses the order had suffered, spilling out his feelings with extraordinary candor. Bonomel cursed the pope for allowing Western Christians who had taken the cross to fight the Hohenstaufen in Sicily instead of insisting that they fulfill their vows in Acre resisting Baybars. Then he suggested that perhaps Christ no longer cared about the crusaders.

"Anger and grief are entrenched in my heart," he wrote. "So that I am almost ready to kill myself, or abandon the cross that I had taken in honor of the One who was put on the cross. For neither cross nor faith bring me succor or protection against those felon Turks, God curse them! On the contrary, from what one can see, God wants to support them to our detriment. . . . Since God who used to be vigilant is asleep, Muhammad is operating with all his might, and inciting [Baybars] to do the same."[18]

It was striking that Bonomel expressed his hatred for the Mamluks in terms that echoed those used by Muslims to describe the Franks. The phrase "God curse them!" had tumbled from the lips and pens of countless Islamic poets, chroniclers, administrators and scribes over the

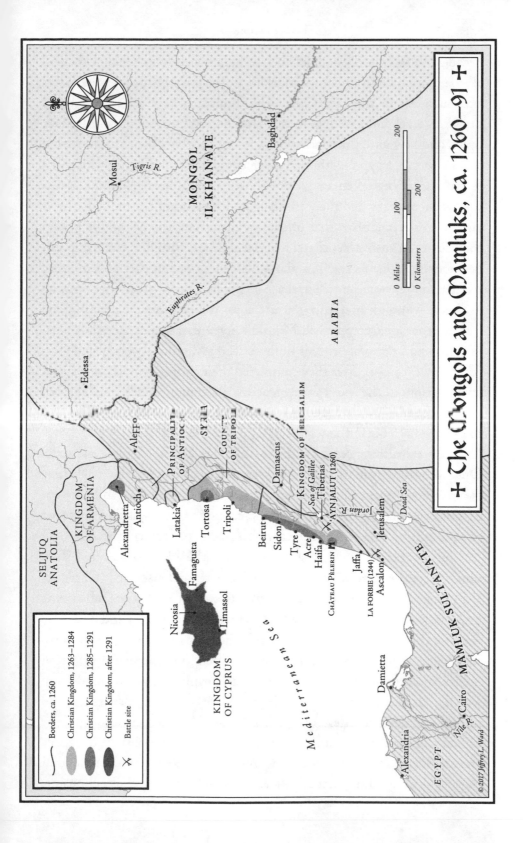

✠ The Mongols and Mamluks, ca. 1260–91 ✠

Borders, ca. 1260
Christian Kingdom, 1263–1284
Christian Kingdom, 1285–1291
Christian Kingdom, after 1291
Battle site

SELJUQ ANATOLIA

KINGDOM OF ARMENIA

MONGOL IL-KHANATE

Mosul

Tigris R.

Baghdad

Euphrates R.

Edessa

Aleppo

PRINCIPALITY OF ANTIOCH

SYRIA

COUNTY OF TRIPOLI

KINGDOM OF JERUSALEM

Damascus

Sea of Galilee

Tiberias

ʿAYN JALUT (1260)

Jordan R.

Dead Sea

Jerusalem

ARABIA

Alexandretta

Antioch

Latakia

Tortosa

Tripoli

Beirut

Sidon

Tyre

Acre

Haifa

Château Pèlerin

Jaffa

LA FORBIE (1244)

Ascalon

Famagusta

Nicosia

Limassol

KINGDOM OF CYPRUS

Mediterranean Sea

MAMLUK SULTANATE

Damietta

Alexandria

EGYPT

Nile R.

Cairo

0 Miles   100   200

0 Kilometers   200

© 2017 Jeffrey L. Ward

decades. In fact, the Mamluks and Templars were very much alike and all the more hateful to one another for it. Both were elite warrior castes and outsiders in the Near East. The Templars were self-selected and drawn by a religious calling, mostly traveling to Outremer from France, Spain and England; the Mamluks had been forcibly taken as slaves from the steppe to Egypt. Although they could have children—which the Templars, having taken an oath of chastity, could not—Mamluk status was nonhereditary and the well-being and survival of the individual was far less important than that of the organization. The Mamluks prided themselves on their exceptional martial abilities, with horsemanship valued above all. Just as the Templar Rule functioned in part as a military manual, preserving the essential aspects of field strategy, so there was an extensive Mamluk literature on *furusiyya*: the techniques, training and lifestyle that an accomplished Mamluk horseman was expected to master. Both had elaborate rituals of investiture: Mamluks were gifted with ceremonial trousers after they completed their training, much as respectable warriors in the West were girded with knighthood.[19] Finally, both groups placed a high value on martyrdom. The essence of the calling was to be willing to die in the service of God and the holy war.

The great difference was that the Templars had not *become* the state. Once a royal bodyguard, the Mamluks now commanded the machinery of government from Cairo to Damascus, directed their own military operations and made policy. The Abbasid caliph in Cairo was now a puppet of the Mamluk sultan. The military elite had taken full control.

The Templars, by contrast, shared with the Hospitallers and Teutonic Order the increasingly heavy burden of the defense of the Christian Latin states in Outremer: manning castles, fighting battles, absorbing heavy losses and financing the war effort from their estates and houses in the West. This was an ever harder task. Support for a new Western crusade had dried up, the absentee Hohenstaufen kingship had set Eastern nobles against one another and the ever-shrinking pool of land from which to draw tax revenue made the defense of castles and cities less and less affordable. The safety of the Latin states fell at their door, yet the military orders remained servants, answerable to a politicized papacy and shackled to the high politics of Western Christendom. Up to a point they could and did pursue policies and alliances of their choosing, whether or not these met with royal favor. Ultimately, though, they were vulnerable, as Pope Clement IV had pointed out to Master Thomas Bérard in a letter of 1265. A dispute concerning the behavior of the order's marshal, Stephen of Sissy, had led Clement to impress upon Thomas the natural order of things: "If the church removed for a short while the hand of its protection from you . . . you would not in any way subsist against the assaults of the prelates or the force of the princes."[20] The order was rich, independent and self-confident, but it was not truly autonomous. Far away in the Baltic region of northeast Europe, the Teutonic Order had begun carving out a state of their own stretching from Prussia to Estonia, thanks to the patronage of the Hohenstaufen princes. There was no such Templar state and never would be.

+

In 1268 Baybars made another thrust against the now heavily reduced Latin kingdom. In the spring he marched out of Egypt and attacked Jaffa, which fell in half a day, on March 17. The sultan marked his entry into Jerusalem's port by confiscating the citizens' treasured relic, the head of Saint George. His assault ended with the familiar sight of Christians leaping onto boats scattering from the harbor, heading for safer havens in the north. There were precious few of these left. Once Jaffa had fallen, nothing below Acre remained in Christian hands, other than the Templars' coastal castle of Château Pèlerin.

Deciding once again that Château Pèlerin could wait, Baybars set his sights on another Templar stronghold: the castle of Beaufort, east of Tyre in the county of Tripoli, built on a rocky outcrop behind a double ring of fortifications. The Templars had taken over Beaufort in 1260, adding to its defensive walls. In ordinary times they would have been able to hold it with ease. But in the spring of 1268 they were demoralized and massively outnumbered. Within a fortnight of Baybars' appearance the Templar garrison sued for peace, surrendering themselves into captivity on condition that the women and children from the nearby villages who had taken refuge there should be allowed to go freely and safely to Tyre. Baybars granted this, regarrisoned the castle with his own men, ripped down the Templars' new walls and continued north to Antioch, to attack

Bohemond VI in Antioch, who had been foolish enough to ally with the Mongols.

By this point, the sultan needed only to pass by a Christian town or castle to send its inhabitants scuttling out to beg for mercy. On hearing that Beaufort had fallen, the Templars of Tortosa and Château Blanc sent envoys asking the Mamluks not to destroy them, too. Baybars agreed on condition that he be given the coastal settlement and stronghold of Jabala, in the principality of Antioch, without a fight. The Templar responsible for negotiating with the sultan was the preceptor of Tortosa, Matthew Sauvage, who over the previous three years had struck up as cordial a relationship as was possible with the sultan, albeit one based on appeasement and acquiescence. Sauvage handed over the Templars' share of interests in Jabala, and the Hospitallers, with whom the order shared the town, soon followed suit.[21]

Resistance was melting. By early May Baybars had reached the great city of Antioch and laid it under siege. Its ruler Bohemond VI was in Tripoli, and without him the citizens of Antioch thought only of saving their lives. "[The citizens] put up scant defense," wrote the Templar of Tyre. Even so, they were shown no mercy. "When the city was taken, more than 17,000 people who were inside it were slain and more than 100,000 people, both religious and lay—men, women and children—were taken captive."[22] These figures were exaggerated, but the sense of grotesque cruelty was not. Antioch's gates were locked by the Mamluks, who went on a murderous rampage through the streets, enslaving those whom they did not kill and capturing so much booty that it took two full days to divide it up. A fire lit in the citadel swept through the surrounding buildings and one of the great cities of Eastern Christendom—the first in Syria to have been stormed by the original crusaders in 1098—was reduced to a backwater.

Since Bohemond VI was absent when Baybars attacked, he lost one of his titles from afar. Without the city of Antioch there could be no principality, and the castles controlling the region swiftly became redundant. Several of these were held by the Templars, who had no choice but to evacuate. Since the 1130s the order had guarded the Amanus Mountain passes joining Asia Minor with northwest Syria. Now, after more than a century, they quietly abandoned their positions, retreating from their castles of La

Roche de Roissol and Gaston (Baghras) with barely a whimper. Gaston had been memorably described by Imad al-Din as "towering on an impenetrable summit . . . shrouded in fog, inseparable from the clouds, suspended from the sun and moon . . . whoever coveted it had no means of getting there; whoever raised his eyes to it could not fix his gaze."[23] Not so for Baybars, who took it without a fight. He was handed the keys by a brother called Gins of Belin, who rode out on his own initiative to make peace with the sultan while the rest of his brothers were at dinner.

After this there was no hope. The brothers exited Gaston in such haste that they neglected to destroy all their equipment, a major breach of protocol for which the commander was later punished in Acre. Master Thomas Bérard took counsel with his senior officers and imposed on the deserters a severe sentence of a year and a day's penance, during which they were stripped of their habits and had to eat their meals on the floor with the dogs. Their case was written up and added to at least one edition of the Templars' official rule, on the grounds that their punishment was thought to be exceptionally lenient.[24]

✝

By 1268 Baybars had wiped out the principality of Antioch and the kingdom of Jerusalem's holdings in Palestine. Only the county of Tripoli remained, along with the Christian kingdom of Cyprus a short distance over the sea. The Latins of the East were wobbling on the brink of extermination. Without reinforcement from the West they would not survive another sustained Mamluk assault. Yet the appetite for crusading was barely flickering in the hearts of most princes of the West. The French poet known as Rutebeuf penned a work chastising his countrymen for their neglect of Jerusalem. This "Lament of the Holy Land" bewailed the lack of modern heroes fit to emulate the heroes of the First Crusade. "Instead they will allow the Bedouins to hold the Holy Land, which has been taken from us through our failings," he wrote. "The Tartars are coming . . . to destroy everything: there will not be anybody to defend it. . . . The world is coming to its end."[25]

That end was delayed by the arrival of two small missions from the West. Louis IX's promised second coming never arrived; instead the

French king chose to attack Tunis in North Africa, where dysentery finally claimed his life in 1270. The first mission to reach Outremer was led by two bastard sons of the king of Aragón. They landed in Acre in October 1269 hoping to coordinate with a Mongol assault on Baybars, but on their first attempt to engage a Mamluk army in the field they were unceremoniously wiped out. The second, led by the Lord Edward, as the English king Henry III's eldest son and heir was known, landed in 1271, made a few forays out toward Jerusalem accompanied by the military orders, but left the following year, having won little more than a few skirmishes. Edward's only lasting achievement was to broker a ten-year peace treaty designed to preserve Acre and the few coastal castles left until either a much larger crusading force could be sent, or the Latins of the East could somehow recover sufficiently to hold their own unaided. Neither seemed especially likely. Throughout this brief flurry, Baybars continued to make gains, taking the massive Hospitaller castle of Crac des Chevaliers in April 1270 and the Teutonic Order's proud fortress of Montfort in June 1271.

The peace brokered by Edward was ratified eleven months after the fall of Montfort, in April 1272, and this at long last brought Baybars' remorseless series of attacks on Frankish territories to an end. The sultan lived for another five years, dying a mysterious death, perhaps of poison, on June 1, 1277. His reign had transformed the entire complexion of the Holy Land. It had been a chastening, traumatizing time for all Franks, but particularly for the Templars, who had lost many men, some of their finest castles and much of their reputation for indomitability. They had been as helpless as their Hospitaller and Teutonic counterparts to resist the Mamluk surge—a failure with increasingly uncomfortable consequences as people began to search for reasons for Outremer's decay and annihilation.

In 1273 Thomas Bérard died and William of Beaujeu, the Templar preceptor of Sicily, was elected to lead the order in his place. William delayed his journey east to attend a large ecumenical council called by Pope Gregory X, known as the Second Council of Lyon, at which plans had been discussed for a Western response to Baybars' conquests. The council took place during the summer of 1274, after which William was free to travel to Acre, from where he reported on his first impressions.

On October 2, 1275, he wrote to Edward, who had now succeeded his father as King Edward I of England.

"We found the land and its inhabitants almost completely inconsolable," wrote William. "We have found the state of the house of the Temple weaker and more fragile than it ever was in the past; food is lacking, there are many expenses, revenues are almost nonexistent . . . all the brothers' goods . . . have been pillaged by the powerful sultan. And revenues from beyond the sea cannot suffice to keep us alive; we have countless costs in defending the Holy Land and strengthening the castles that have remained.

"All this, we fear, will cause us to fail in our duty and abandon the Holy Land in desolation. It is on this account in excuse for a failure of this sort that we ask your majesty to bring some suitable remedy, so that we cannot be blamed afterwards should something disastrous happen."[26]

Although he did not know it, Master William of Beaujeu was writing more than a letter of supplication to the king of England.

He was sending him a prophecy.

18

"The City Will Fall"

WHEN WILLIAM OF BEAUJEU heard the Saracen drums beating he leapt into action with such haste that he scarcely had time to buckle on his armor. The master was in the Templar house in Montmusard, a large northern suburb of Acre zoned off from the old town but still within its double ring of outer walls. The pounding came from near St. Anthony's Gate, on the east side, a section of the walls normally given over to the Hospitallers to defend.[1] It was loud and close enough for William to know that the worst had happened. After six weeks and one day of unyielding bombardment, on Friday, May 18, 1291, the Mamluk army had finally forced its way into Acre. If they could not be driven back immediately, a battle for the streets would begin and the imbalance in numbers alone would mean the Christians were done for. The Mamluk army was estimated to be hundreds of thousands strong. Acre's defenders were outnumbered by perhaps ten to one.

Already an evacuation of women and children was being attempted at the docks, though rough seas were making it difficult to get relief vessels out of the harbor. No one who remained inside the city could expect mercy. The besieging army was commanded by the new Mamluk sultan al-Ashraf Khalil, who succeeded to his office in 1290. He had recently written to William of Beaujeu, introducing himself immodestly but not altogether inaccurately as "The Sultan of Sultans, King of Kings, Lord of Lords . . . the powerful, the dreadful, the scourge of rebels, hunter of Franks and Tartars and Armenians, Snatcher of Castles from the Hands of Miscreants, Lord of the Two Seas, Guardian of the Two Pilgrim Sites."[2] This was a man who gave the catapults in his heavy artillery nicknames like "Furious" and "Victory." He did not deal in lenience or grace.

As William of Beaujeu scrambled into action he gathered with him as many able men as he could find. Most of Acre's Templars were based in the old city at the fortress by the docks, but William had ten or twelve brothers with him in Montmusard, along with his personal bodyguard of two knights, a sergeant, a turcopole, a squire and a pair of foot soldiers. It was not much, but it was the best he could do. The little squadron galloped through Montmusard's streets toward St. Anthony's Gate, gathering up on their way the master of the Hospitallers, John of Villiers, who had his own entourage of a similar size and composition.[3] They all reached the gate in time to see Mamluk soldiers piling through a breach in the walls, and threw themselves into the fray.

"It seemed," wrote the Templar of Tyre, "as if they hurled themselves at a stone wall. Those of the enemy who were hurling Greek fire hurled it so often and so thickly that there was so much smoke that one man could scarcely see another. Amongst the smoke, archers shot feathered arrows so densely that our men and mounts were terribly hurt."[4] One English squire, fighting on foot after his horse was killed under him, was hit directly with a burning missile which set alight his surcoat, the flames searing his face and then his whole body, "as if he had been a cauldron of pitch." The Mamluks held their ranks behind a wall of shields, fighting with spears, arrows and incendiaries and slowly pressing their way in. For several hours the Templars and Hospitallers launched cavalry charges at the shield wall, but on each occasion they were beaten back with a hail of projectiles. By midmorning morale was sinking. As the Mamluk troops inched forward behind their barricade, more invaders filled the gap behind them.

William of Beaujeu was fighting on horseback among his men, brandishing a lance in his right hand. As he raised his left arm, perhaps to signal another charge at the enemy line, a javelin hurled from the direction of the gate hit him directly under the left armpit, at a point where the plates of his light armor were unjoined. "The shaft sank into his body a palm's length," wrote the Templar of Tyre, who, as part of William's household staff, was watching the battle unfold.

William was not knocked from his saddle, but he knew his wound was fatal. He turned his horse and made as if to leave. Out of habit his personal retinue followed him, including the sergeant carrying his black-and-white standard. A band of Italian crusaders who had joined the battle saw him fold away and assumed that the Templars had lost heart. "For God's sake, sir, don't leave, or the city will fall at once!" they cried.

Alert to the danger of mass panic, William called back as loudly as he could, "My lords, I can do no more, for I am killed; see the wound here!" He pointed to where the javelin was still sticking out of his armpit, but as he raised his arm to display the damage, he was overcome. The master dropped his lance, his head slumped and he began to slip from his mount. Around him, his servants scampered to bring him down gently, and using a discarded shield as a stretcher, they carried him to a safe house and laid him down to assess his injuries. They managed to cut the straps of his breastplate but could not remove the armor at his shoulders, so they loaded him half undressed onto a blanket and carried him down to the beach to try and get him out of the city by boat. Behind them, the sultan's banners were being raised on Acre's walls.

Escape from the beach was impossible. Huge waves drove William's companions back, so they continued with their master, now prone and silent, to the Templar compound in the far southwest of the city, entering by a side gate and carrying him through a stable courtyard where horse dung stood in great piles. Once inside the main house, Master William lay unspeaking for the rest of the day. Toward the evening he heard a commotion outside and gestured to his attendants to tell him what was happening. "They told him that men were fighting," recalled the Templar of Tyre, "and he commanded them that they should leave him in peace."

✝

William of Beaujeu died that evening. The city of Acre fell. The Mamluks poured in at three points in the walls, tearing through the streets, killing as they pleased. The Templar of Tyre saw noblewomen and nuns bolting for the docks, some of the ladies pregnant or clutching babies to their breasts. Those who could not escape were separated from their children and either taken for slaves or trampled beneath the invaders' horses. Infants were disemboweled and crushed. Evacuations continued from the stormy beach, with Genoese galleys ferrying civilians to larger boats offshore, waiting to travel to Cyprus. The king of Cyprus, Hugh III, escaped to his kingdom, as did a number of Western grandees, but the patriarch of Jerusalem, Nicholas of Hanapes, drowned when he tried to board a crowded boat and slipped into the water. A group of Templars under the veteran preceptor Theobald Gaudin escaped to Sidon, where, holed up in the Templar castle, they elected Theobald as the order's new master. Those who could not find a berth on a ship headed for the only secure place left in the city, the Templar fortress, a defiant beacon on the seafront: its towers topped with golden lions each the size of a donkey.

With their master dead, the Templars of Acre fell under the command of Peter of Sevrey, the marshal, who herded as many civilians as he could into the Templar compound and barred the gates. After several days, al-Ashraf sent an envoy to the Templars, offering to escort noncombatants out of the city. Peter of Sevrey agreed, but when the safe-conduct was allowed into the compound, it was composed of four hundred ill-disciplined horsemen who began assaulting women and children before they were even out of the gates.[5]

The marshal refused to stand for this. He ordered the gates of the compound to be swung shut again, trapping the four hundred Muslims inside. A battle in the courtyard began. For once the Christians had the advantage, and they slew their prisoners almost to a man, cutting off their heads. The Templar of Tyre wrote that "none escaped alive." This was not quite true: one of al-Ashraf's men later wrote that he had fought for an hour before fleeing with nine others into one of the fortress's seaward towers, and jumping from there into the waves. "Some died, some were crippled, and some were spared for a time," he wrote.[6] The fighting was fierce and unrelenting for one simple reason: everyone knew that this was not just Acre's last stand. It was the endgame for the crusader states.

When the battle had ended, Peter of Sevrey received another message from the sultan. Al-Ashraf said that he understood that his men had brought about their own deaths and asked the marshal to come out and treat with him. For Peter this must have been an agonizing decision. If he left the fortress he would be putting himself and his men at the sultan's mercy. If he stayed, there was no hope of reinforcement or relief. Everyone who could leave Acre had now done so. Those who had been left were now on their own. Still hoping to save the lives of the civilians under his guard, Peter emerged with a delegation of Templar brothers behind him. As soon as they reached the enemy camp, they were beheaded. Mamluk engineers began digging tunnels to bring down one of the fortress's towers. Within three days, on Monday, May 28, the tower collapsed and troops rushed in.

The compound was overrun and Acre's capitulation was complete.

✝

James of Molay, a Burgundian knight of about forty-seven years old, was at Nicosia on Cyprus the year Acre fell. Like every other Templar of the Holy Land who was not sliced apart as the Mamluks swarmed through the streets, he would have heard firsthand of the terrible aftermath from a stream of horrified survivors.[7]

Most of the boats that had evacuated Acre unloaded their passengers in Cyprus. The exiles were soon joined by others fleeing the last settlements on the Levantine coast. Almost as soon as he was elected, the new Templar Master Theobald Gaudin abandoned his post and came to Cyprus, claiming that he was going to seek help. The rest of the brothers did not wait long to see if he would succeed, and left Sidon to its fate on July 14.

North of Acre, the Mamluks had found Tyre all but deserted when they rode in. Beirut was given up around the same time. By the beginning of August all that remained in Christian hands were two Templar castles, and these could not last long on their own. On August 3 Tortosa surrendered. Eleven days later, the garrison at Château Pèlerin also quit their resistance. "They perceived clearly that they no longer had the ability to defend the castle," wrote the Templar of Tyre, "so they abandoned it and went to the Isle of Cyprus and the Saracens completed their destruction of the land . . . Everything was lost, so that altogether the Christians held not so much as a palm's breadth of land in Syria."[8]

Observing all this must have been one of the most disheartening experiences in James of Molay's career as a Templar. James was a lifelong servant of the Temple, having joined in his early twenties in 1265, in a grand ceremony conducted by Aimery of La Roche, the most senior Templar in France, and attended by the master of the English Templars.[9] The usual pattern of recruitment was for the order to send its young and energetic entrants to the Holy Land, while old, less physically able members remained in the West. Youthful, ambitious, and ready to fight, James had landed in the East at some point during the late 1270s.[10]

By the time of his arrival Baybars had inflicted fatal damage on the Latin states, although this was the period of the ten-year truce brokered by Edward I. James would later recall that he had found this truce hard to bear, and had "murmured" against the master, resenting him for his willingness to observe a peace with an enemy of the Church. Only later did he come to understand that "the said master could not have acted otherwise."[11] Like any young soldier of his age, James had joined the Templars to fight, not to sit on his hands as the Christian Holy Land was wrenched apart. Yet that was exactly what he had been forced to do, as talk of a new crusade came to nothing, and al-Ashraf finished the job Baybars had begun.

In 1292 James of Molay's career was transformed with the demise of the short-lived master Theobald Gaudin.[12] The pool of candidates to succeed him must have been small. Within four days, through a fast, smart (and later much-criticized) campaign, James had managed to se-cure his own election over that of a rival candidate, Hugh of Pairaud. It was later said that he did this by claiming he had no desire for the posi-tion, and offering to oversee the election process as an impartial and temporary interim leader, only to then use that position to lobby for the full mastership. James knew how to game the order's procedures and protocols. Certainly he knew how to make enemies; the Templar of Tyre, whose direct association with the order ended on the death of his employer William of Beaujeu, called him greedy, and "miserly beyond reason."[13]

So much for elections. It was still an awful moment to take command. The order was broken, stripped of its castles and banished from the land it had been created to protect. Yet within the chaos, James of Molay spied an opportunity. He threw himself into the task of reconstructing the Templar membership in the East in preparation for what was to his mind an inevitable resurgence in the crusading movement.

He could hardly hope to spur this on from Cyprus, so, shortly after his election, he made the long journey west, to tour the royal courts with a view to firing up enthusiasm for a new mission to liberate the Holy Land.

✝

The terrible news of Acre's loss reached Paris in early August. One of the first news flashes came from the master of the Hospitallers, John of Villiers, who wrote a doleful note to a colleague in France reporting Acre's "unfortunate and pitiful fall."[14] Bad tidings from the Holy Land were hardly rare, but this was a serious blow. On hearing the "very harsh and bitter" news, Pope Nicholas IV ordered provincial church councils to assemble across Christendom and report back to Rome with their best suggestions for how to recover what had been lost.[15] In his letters mandating these meetings, Pope Nicholas demanded a clear plan of action, specific recommendations for how to pay for a new crusade and suggestions for the destination. He steered the councils toward an idea that had begun to circulate some years previously: a merger of the military orders into a single, unified institution capable of winning back Jerusalem and holding it for good.

The notion of merging the orders was not new. It had been first floated as early as 1274 at the Second Council of Lyon, a general synod convened to discuss resistance in the wake of Baybars' conquests. A proposal to merge the Templars, Hospitallers and Teutonic Order with the other, assorted bands that had sprung up in imitation had been vetoed by Spanish kings unwilling to let go of their own regional orders (such as the Castilian Order of Calatrava or the Leónese Order of Alcántara). In 1292 the idea was nonetheless revived. In Pope Nicholas's words, this was because "worthy men" and "the popular voice" both clamored for unification and reform.[16]

Whether or not this was true, the Templars and Hospitallers were vulnerable to criticism at a moment when the catastrophic losses to the Mamluks required a simple explanation. Ever since their clashes with the Holy Roman Emperor Frederick Hohenstaufen in the 1220s, they had been a partisan element in the politics of the Holy Land. They had taken sides in the ruinous struggle to dominate trade in Acre fought between Genoan and Venetian merchants from 1258 until 1272, throwing their weight behind the Venetians while the Hospitallers had backed the Genoans. Both orders had engaged in running battles around town and in the waters outside the harbor, leaving hundreds of men dead when the crusader states were already short of manpower. News of this dispute had spread and at least one chronicler attributed the "sorrowful misfortune" to "discord between the Hospitallers and the Templars."[17]

The Templars had also involved themselves in a bitter tussle in the county of Tripoli, siding with the Gibelet family in choosing to resist the peaceful accession of Bohemond VI's fourteen-year-old son, Bohemond VII, in 1275. Sieges and skirmishes had raged between Tripoli itself (where the Templar house was demolished by the angry count), Sidon and Tortosa. Even on Cyprus, where the Templars had military headquarters in Limassol and a second base in Nicosia, they had managed to upset their host.[18] In 1278 a dispute for the crown of Jerusalem had blown up between Hugh III of Cyprus and Charles of Anjou, brother of Louis IX. The Templars supported the Anjou claim, drawing the extreme displeasure of Hugh, who took revenge by destroying the Templar house in Limassol and harassing the brothers to the point of drawing admonition from the pope.[19] Although those who had died at Acre were routinely praised as martyrs, survivors were open to the accusation of cowardice, which was leveled at them by chroniclers such as Maurer Thaddeus of Naples.[20] All this meant that as James of Molay prepared to travel home he was returning to a world in which the desire for crusading remained high, but the Templars were now faced with open criticism.

Among those to answer Pope Nicholas's call for reform was the Franciscan friar Ramon Lull, who had spent much of the three decades leading up to the fall of Acre wandering far from his home in Mallorca in an effort to convert infidels, all the while considering the best way to reconfigure the Christian approach to the Near East. Unsurprisingly for an itinerant preacher, he concentrated his thought on education and conversion. He advised the pope to establish four world-class colleges to train fearless, multilingual missionaries who could inform Jews, Mongols, Greeks and Arabs about the iniquity of their beliefs and convince them to follow Christ in a fashion approved by Rome.

As Ramon was fond of pointing out, Christ himself had advocated a policy of two swords. As he developed his ideas over the following decade he became more militant, coming to the conclusion that "you should fight against the unbelievers both with preaching and with weapons."[21] Although he was not a fighter himself, Ramon Lull had no doubts as to the best way to organize a crusading army.

"The lord pope and the cardinals should select and establish a single noble order, to be called the order of knighthood," he wrote.

> The head of this order would be termed both master and warrior-king . . . if at all possible the kingdom of Jerusalem should be assigned to him. . . . It follows that this warrior should be a king's son, both because of the honor of the office which is given to him and in order that all the [religious] orders of knighthood should be the more willing to submit themselves to his order. . . . Further: the lord pope . . . should decree that this single order [of] knighthood should be created from the union of the order of the Temple and the knighthood of the Hospital, the Teutons . . . and all the other orders of knights without exception, whoever and wherever they are.

Ramon had no doubt of the efficacy of his plan—and he was willing to bet that God felt the same way. "And should anyone oppose it," he wrote, "he would be seen to be neither faithful nor devout, and he should consider the judgment on the Last Day, when the Lord Jesus Christ says, 'Depart into the everlasting fire, you accursed ones.'"[22]

✛

James of Molay was able to duck the issue of amalgamation for a time. In April 1292 Nicholas IV died and the College of Cardinals, which was required to elect his successor, fell into intractable rancor. It took them nearly two years to settle on the absurd candidacy of a seventy-nine-year-old hermit from Sicily called Peter of Morrone, who was crowned against his will as Pope Celestine V. (Celestine's election as pope was the last to take place without a conclave, in which the electors are summoned and forbidden to leave until they have come to a decision.) His papacy was a four-month farce, and by December 1294 Celestine had resigned and run away.* James of Molay was in Rome to see all this, and on Christmas Eve

---

*Celestine wished to return to his life as a hermit, but was prevented from doing so for fear that he would be raised up as an antipope by enemies of the new pontiff, Boniface VIII. He was instead imprisoned by his successor, in a cell not of his choosing, where he died in 1296.

he witnessed the election of the aggressive and lawyerly Italian cardinal Benedetto Caetani, who took the name Boniface VIII.

James's visit to Rome was the first step in his program to rebuild Templar strength in the East. He later said he found Boniface interested in but ultimately unconvinced by the idea of unification. "The Pope spoke of it several times," James would recall, "but all things considered he preferred to abandon the affair entirely."[23] This may well have been the result of direct lobbying by James himself. He stayed in Rome for the first six months of 1295 and his visit yielded tangible results in two areas. Drastic reorganization was avoided and he even secured tax relief on the exchange of goods between Templar estates in the East and West. In June Pope Boniface issued a papal bull that praised the Templars as "fearless warriors of Christ" and implored them to "constantly pay attention to the guardianship of the kingdom of Cyprus," to which end he granted them "the same liberties and immunities" that they had enjoyed in the Holy Land.[24]

Boniface further commanded the king of England, Edward I, to allow exports bound for Cyprus to pass freely through English ports and granted the Templars of Cyprus freedom from making gifts to the Church, on the grounds that their resources were bound to be badly stretched.[25] Charles II, the king of Naples, was a staunch advocate of merging the military orders as a means to win back Jerusalem—to which he laid claim as titular king. But he did not press his case and agreed to suspend export duties on goods traveling from the Templar estates in his lands to Cyprus.

During the second half of 1295 James of Molay went to England and France. His journey must have required tact. Church councils in Canterbury and Reims had both concluded that the military orders should bear the brunt of the cost of reconquering the Holy Land, with the clear implication that they had lost it and could clean up their own mess. Another English council favored merging the orders and giving them over to the command of Edward I, unique among the reigning kings of the day in having personally been on a crusade.[26] James's position in France, typically the center of Templar recruitment and support, was even more delicate, as he sought to court both the French king and his southern rival across the Pyrenees, James II, king of Aragón. There was history here: ten years earlier the French king had invaded Aragón and persuaded the

French-born Pope Martin IV to grant his war the status of a crusade. The Aragónese king at the time (Peter III) had called on the Templars to fight for him, asking them to join the royal army and deploy their galleys to defend his coastline from French shipping: a peculiar situation in which the Aragónese Templars found themselves taking up arms against Frenchmen and crusaders.[27]

By the end of the year James of Molay was ready to return to Cyprus. His tour had not been spectacular: he had not whipped up a storm of crusader fervor and he had certainly not killed off criticism of the military orders, who did nothing to help their cause by joining resurgent clashes between Genoa and Venice in the eastern Mediterranean, but he had tamped down the appetite for abolishing his order to the manageable level of churchmen tugging at their beards. In that sense the crisis of 1291 had been weathered and the regrouping process was under way. By the end of the decade confidence was sufficiently high for a new invasion of the lost lands in Syria and Palestine to be under consideration.

✛

For nearly two years at the start of the fourteenth century, the Templars reoccupied part of the Holy Land. It was a sliver—but for a time it was enough to suggest that more was possible. Under James of Molay they had been slowly expanding their naval capability, ordering new galleys from Venice in preparation for a war that would have to be fought as much at sea as on dusty land. On July 20, 1300, a fleet of sixteen of these galleys carried a high-profile raiding force out of Famagusta in Cyprus, heading for the enemy coastline. The master was on board, along with King Henry II of Cyprus, his brother Amalric of Tyre, and John of Villiers, master of the Hospital. This was not a fully-fledged crusade, but it was a fleet capable of causing serious damage as it cruised the shore raiding settlements around Acre.

There was good reason to think a resurgence in Christian fortunes lay ahead. Several hundred miles to the east, Ghazan, leader of the Il-Khan Mongols, was busily plotting against the Mamluks. Regular envoys continued to go back and forth between the Mongols and the Christians on Cyprus, with promises of mutual assistance. After the summer raids of

1300 a plan was concocted for a joint assault focusing on Tortosa, where the Templars' former castle had not yet been demolished. Later in the year around three hundred Templars and Hospitallers joined a royal party that sailed to the tiny island of Ru'ad, which lay a couple of miles off Tortosa. They disembarked, secured Ru'ad as a forward base and then set off again to take the fortress on the mainland and meet up with Ghazan's formidable troops.

Unfortunately, the Mongols did not turn up on time. The Christians fought their way into Tortosa but could not hold it, and within a month they had been forced back to Ru'ad, and most of their troops then returned to Cyprus. The Templars agreed to garrison the little island with a force of around one hundred and twenty knights, four hundred sergeants and five hundred archers, all commanded by their marshal, Bartholomew of Quincy. The thunderclap of the Lord's judgment had not quite sounded over the Mamluk kingdom. But it was at least a start.

By 1302 everything had been lost once more. Around one hundred and fifty miles of the eastern Mediterranean separated Ru'ad's garrison from Cyprus—presenting a supply line that was vulnerable to blockade or even bad weather. In the autumn of 1301 a Mamluk fleet appeared, commanded by a Muslim convert from Christian Georgia by the name of Sandamour. He and his men attacked the island and a siege began that lasted nearly a year, until in 1302 the garrison sued for peace, severely worn down by attritional fighting that had reduced them from nearly a thousand to just two hundred and eighty men. A deal was struck whereby the Templars agreed to surrender on condition of safe-conduct off the island. Had any of these men been veterans of Acre they would have known better. As the Templar of Tyre reported, "the Saracens had the heads of all the Syrian foot soldiers cut off, because they had put up such a stiff defense . . . and the brethren of the Temple were dishonorably conducted to Babylon." A life of slavery beckoned.

Once again the Templars had been wrenched out of a stronghold on the promise of safe passage and betrayed. Until a serious expedition could be mounted it would be desperately difficult for the order to extend much beyond Cyprus. James of Molay's tenure as master had been a struggle from the beginning—and despite regular talk of a new crusade it showed little sign of getting any better. He was now stuck on Cyprus, able neither to retreat nor advance.

Then, in 1306 James was summoned by a new pope. At first this seemed promising. It turned out to be anything but. In fact, this was the moment when darkness began to fall on the Templars.

19

"At the Devil's Prompting"

O N NOVEMBER 15, 1305, half of Christendom seemed to have descended on the city of Lyon. Princes and dukes, counts and cardinals, abbots and archbishops: the city heaved with dignitaries and townspeople eager to see a once-in-a-lifetime spectacle. Ambassadors in brightly colored bishops' robes had arrived from England and Aragón bearing gifts worth hundreds of pounds. The king of France and his two brothers had come, accompanied by their extensive household staffs. A babble of languages filled the air. All were gathering in the grand basilica of the Church of Saint-Just to witness the coronation of Bertrand of Got, archbishop of Bordeaux, as Pope Clement V.

Lyon was a patchwork of jurisdictions, long caught between allegiance to the Holy Roman Emperor and the king of France. By 1305 it was drifting decisively toward Frenchness. Certainly on the chilly morning of November 15 there was little doubt which of the city's masters had the greatest cause to celebrate. A pope born and raised in Gascony had come to be crowned in front of the gilded elite of the French nobility, under the approving eye of their king. This was quite a coup, and a firm indication of the expected Gallic flavor of Bertrand's papacy. The days when popes had scurried about in fear of the Hohenstaufen or bowed to the interests of influential Italian aristocratic dynasties were a memory; now God smiled most fondly on the realm of the fleur-de-lis and the oriflamme.

Bertrand was around forty years old: quite young to have reached such lofty office, and somewhat inexperienced, as he was not a cardinal. He was certainly an adept and malleable politician, having negotiated a successful career in Bordeaux without major upset. This was no small feat. Gascony was ruled by the English, but under a treaty of 1259 it was considered to be ultimately subject to the authority of the French king. This relationship was the cause of dispute, tension and occasional warfare between the two realms. As archbishop, Bertrand was accustomed to balancing the competing wishes of great powers, while remaining on good terms with all. It helped that he was basically an amenable man. Gascons suffered from a terrible reputation outside their native country and were generally thought greedy and nepotistic, but Bertrand put the lie to this easy stereotype. Although troubled by a painful bowel complaint that frequently laid him low and sapped his strength, he remained by nature a pleasant character who lavished praise on great men without seeming sycophantic, and who had a notably good sense of humor.[1]

Nevertheless, the jump from archbishop to the Throne of Saint Peter was significant, and it had taken a poisonously deadlocked College of Cardinals a full eleven months to settle on Bertrand. Part of the reason for the delay was the widespread perception that the French cardinals were trying to force the election of a pope who would be pliant to the demands of their own king, as indeed they were. A long time after the election, one of the senior pro-French cardinals present in the conclave admitted that he had seen in Bertrand a man who could be molded into a bagman for King Philip IV.[2] Certainly Bertrand's choice of papal name left little doubt as to his allegiance. In choosing to be known as Clement V, he was taking his name from Clement IV, a close friend and ally of Philip's grandfather Louis IX. Even the choice of venue for the coronation had been run by the French court.[3] And as it turned out, Bertrand would spend his entire papacy north of the Alps. Daunted by the murderous factional politics of Rome, he calculated that his chances of launching a new crusade were best served by close attendance on the French king. Unsurprisingly, his name in Italy was mud. The Florentine banker and chronicler Giovanni Villani characterized the relationship between Philip and Clement as it was seen by Italians: "You command and I will obey, and it will always be settled this way."[4]

The coronation ceremony in Lyon was suitably magnificent. Tapers, censers and Latin chants filled the church, where proceedings were overseen by the esteemed cardinal Napoleone Orsini, who presented the new pope with the Ring of the Fisherman (a signet ring bearing an image of Saint Peter fishing) and crowned him with the great silver tiara studded with emeralds and sapphires, a mark of his status as Christ's representative on earth. After the formalities were complete, the parade of great men left the church and made their way through Lyon's streets, to show off Clement to the faithful.

In pride of place as the procession emerged was King Philip, tall, blond and straight backed, with a naturally regal bearing and ruddy cheeks he owed to the many hours he spent hunting—a conventional hobby for kings that bordered in him on an obsession. Philip's good looks had earned him the nickname *Le Bel* (the Fair). The Templar of Tyre claimed he was a clear hand taller than most other men, his hips so wide and legs so long that his feet seemed to trail the ground when he sat in his saddle. Philip's personal physician called him "handsome and pious."[5] Cold and distant, Philip shimmered with an unapproachable majesty deliberately cultivated to remind his subjects of the sacred aspect of his kingship.

Lyon was not a large city at the time and it was not in the habit of hosting coronations. As the procession passed through the streets on its way to the bishop's palace, there was a great crush to catch a glimpse of the new pope, the French king and the luminaries surrounding them. An old section of wall holding back spectators, strained by the press of bodies, gave way with a groan, collapsing forward onto the papal parade and taking down many onlookers.

Clement was riding in full papal regalia, and when the wall came down he was thrown headlong from his horse. His tiara flew off, hitting the ground with such force that it lost a number of its jewels, including a massive ruby, which rolled into the rubble and disappeared.[6] The two princes holding the pope's bridle, the king's brother Charles of Valois and the sixty-six-year-old John, Duke of Brittany, were thrown off their feet. Charles was seriously hurt, and the Duke of Brittany, who was closest to the wall, died a few days later from his wounds. Also injured was one of Clement's brothers. The king suffered superficial injuries and the papal party hurried to the bishop's palace much shaken. Nine days later there was a further disturbance when the pope's Gascon supporters fought through the town against Italians who resented his appointment.

These disturbances were seen by many as a bad omen. The new pope, who remained in Lyon with King Philip and Charles of Valois until Christmas, hoped to use the momentum of his election to push for a new crusade. Clement lobbied hard to make the most of a pause in hostilities between France and their long-standing enemies in Flanders and England

to turn their attentions to the East. He found both men broadly recep-
tive: their only point of disagreement was where to attack. Was it better
to target Constantinople, where the Latin emperor had been deposed by
resurgent Byzantines in 1261—or to help shore up the Christian kingdom
of Lesser Armenia, which was menaced by Mamluk forces from the south?
Without settling on a final answer, on December 29, 1305, Philip IV
promised Clement that he would take the cross and lead a new crusade.

One of his conditions was that he should decide where and when to
make his formal crusading vows. Another was that his crusade should
involve major reform of the military orders. The king later said he told
the pope he had heard rumors of irregularities taking place in Templar
houses. The old plans for reform would be revived: the Templars and
Hospitallers would be united into a single army of God. At the head
would be a prince of the royal house of France.[7]

+

In the late summer of 1306 letters from the pope arrived on Cyprus, addressed to Fulk of Villaret, master of the Hospitallers, and James of Molay.[8] They had been sent from Bordeaux on June 6, and their instructions
must have filled both masters with a combination of excitement and ap-
prehension. Plans were afoot, the pope said, for a new crusade to "exterminate the perfidious pagans" and take back the Holy Land. To that end,
both masters were summoned to appear in the papal court in Poitiers by
the festival of All Saints (November 1) or a fortnight thereafter. They
were also asked to prepare two reports: their best plans for taking back
the Holy Land, and a response to the idea that their orders should be
merged.

James of Molay had not been idle on Cyprus. He had lost many men
on the foray to Tortosa and Ru'ad in 1300–1302, but in the aftermath of
that operation he had made more substantial changes to the Templar
personnel under his direct command. Absorbing a regular influx of new
recruits was a normal part of the job for a Templar master in the East,
but turnover had been high. Of the one hundred eighteen Templar
knights and sergeants on Cyprus—French, English, German, Aragónese,

Portuguese, Italian, Cypriote, Romanian and Armenian—most were young and almost all were new to the order. Almost 80 percent had taken their vows since the fall of Acre in 1291.[9]

The Templars had managed to save their treasure and their valuable archive of documents when Acre and Château Pèlerin had fallen—and were cash rich enough to pay a ransom of forty thousand bezants when the prominent baron Guy of Ibelin and his family were kidnapped by pirates in May 1302. But money was always needed, and when Templar preceptors from the West traveled to meet with the master they were nagged to remember their *responsiones*—a third share of the profits of their estates was to pour into the central coffers.

There was plenty of other business besides warfare. The Templars imported goods and matériel from the West, including horses and pack animals, cloth to make robes, cured meets and cheeses. They owned ships such as the *Faucon*, a galley used to evacuate Acre in 1291, which they deployed to transport goods, patrol the waters around Cyprus and effect a blockade of ships hoping to trade with Mamluk Egypt. Boats were also loaned out to Italian trading companies, who used them to transport cotton, spices and sugar to ports such as Marseille and Barcelona.[10] Finally, there was the oldest task of all: pilgrim duty. Despite the obvious dangers of travel and a papal ban imposed to stop the Mamluks from taxing pilgrim routes, there was still an appetite for travel to the holy sites, and pilgrims appeared steadily on Cyprus. They needed to be greeted, guarded and sent on their way. Some had come to visit the tomb of the apostle Barnabus, on Cyprus itself, but many brave souls had to be discouraged from attempting a crossing to Jerusalem.

Despite all this activity, James of Molay must have felt a certain thrill at receiving the pope's letter. Renting boats and greeting new recruits was all well and good, but this was not the Templars' purpose. Clement's summons made it plain that the political will had at last been mustered to launch another crusade. His request for a written plan suggested that the floor was open for an ambitious expedition.

Of course, Clement's invitation had come with a barb. If there was to be a crusade, the price might be the long-threatened merger of the orders. So, as he prepared to make his second journey west as master, James of

Molay began to compose two letters: a plan for saving the Holy Land and a plan for saving the Templars.

"In the name of the Lord, Amen," began his first letter. "This is the advice of the Master of the Temple concerning the matter of the Holy Land. Holy Father, you have asked me what is the best course of action, a large or small expedition."[11] He went on to make one very blunt point: the only way to do any serious damage to the Saracen armies was to deploy a massive army he called a "general passage": "a large, all-embracing expedition to destroy the infidels and restore the blood-spattered land of Christ," with an army consisting of "twelve to fifteen thousand armed horsemen and five thousand foot soldiers . . . note that two thousand of the said armed horsemen should be crossbowmen." These were to be transported and backed by a fleet of transporter ships. The whole army should decamp at Cyprus, recover and recuperate and then proceed to a location he declined to name "since this will give advance warning to the Saracens."

Overwhelming force was the key, argued James. "If you are willing to accept some advice on the numbers of people, I repeat what [Baybars], more famous, powerful and wiser in military matters than anyone of his sect has ever been said on many occasions, that he would confront thirty thousand of the Tartars with his army, but that he would leave them in the field if their numbers were larger.

"Similarly he said that if fifteen thousand Frankish knights came to his land he would meet and join battle with them, but if a larger number arrived he would retreat and leave them the field."

Elsewhere the master affected modesty. "I offer no opinion about where the expedition should gather, since this is in the purview of the lord kings." Plainly James knew he was preparing a document that needed to appeal to Philip IV as well as to Clement, and he carefully hinted at the extent of his knowledge. "If it pleases you and the lord king of France, I will give you in secret so much useful information that I am sure you will follow my advice, because I will indicate so clearly which are the good and the bad places for [a point of invasion]." Indeed, he urged Clement not to wait until his arrival in Poitiers to start preparing for the work ahead, and asked for a fleet of ten galleys to be fitted out for the winter, under the captaincy of Rogeron of Lauria, son of a famous Italian admiral,

Roger of Lauria, a hero of the Sicilian wars. These would enforce the trade embargo on Egpyt, which would be strengthened by a papal ban on Genoese and Venetians trading arms with Muslims. James concluded the letter politely and hopefully. "I ask almighty God to grant you grace in deciding what will be best in these matters, and the ability to recover in your lifetime the holy places in which our Lord Jesus Christ deigned to be born and die for the salvation of the human race."

A comparison between James of Molay's letter and Fulk of Villaret's reveals one major disagreement. Whereas the Templar master advocated a single, massive seaborne landing along the model of the Damietta crusades, putting his faith in overwhelming force, the Hospitaller suggested a two-step invasion: a "special passage" in which an elite force carried in galleys would spend a year softening up the coast with lightning raids, backed by a naval blockade, followed by a subsequent "general passage," or mass invasion.[12] This represented the broad split in crusade thinking among the leaders of the day. Both plans had their merits. James of Molay's was less complicated but required a great deal more commitment and expense up front. The differences between the two plans would mean nothing, though, if his second missive did not have its desired effect.

The Templar master approached the defense of his order with relish. He sought first to write off the idea as a scheme that had been examined many times in the past and dismissed so many times that it was not worth exhuming. Three popes had contemplated uniting the orders, he said, and all had seen their error, with Pope Boniface declaring the matter "closed completely."[13]

This was true, but James knew it was not clinching. Five years earlier Ramon Lull had visited Cyprus, and the famous preacher and reform theorist was now even more set on union than before, as was the inflammatory French pamphleteer Pierre Dubois, who had close links to the French court and had followed Lull in writing a tract called "The Recovery of the Holy Land." Dubois insisted that this unification of the military orders was overdue, writing that "in times of most urgent need these orders have been divided amongst themselves . . . if they are to be of any benefit to the Holy Land it is desirable and advisable to combine them into one order as regards appearance, rank, habit and property."[14] It was not enough to write the merger down as yesterday's scheme and trust that Clement would let it go. So the master ran through, point by point, the arguments for and against the idea.

For a start, he said, things were fine as they were. The separation of the military orders had produced "positive results," and to meddle with the formula would simply be bad in itself, "as innovation seldom or never fails to produce grave dangers." This was a rather bold line of reasoning to pursue: the loss of the entire Holy Land was hard to spin as a positive development. Nevertheless, James of Molay ploughed on. It would be dishonorable, he said, to ask men who had sworn to obey the rule of one order suddenly to switch and adopt a new identity. Then he warmed to his main theme. The Templars and Hospitallers were successful because they were rivals. Throwing them together would cause disputes, perhaps even violence, as "at the devil's prompting quarrels might arise between them, such as 'we were worthier than you and did more good.' . . . If rumors of that sort spread among them they could easily be the cause of serious scandal." Furthermore any attempt to throw together parallel hierarchies and networks of property would be confusing for the men involved; it would also be hard to combine the orders' separate charitable functions, with the likely result that there would be a fall in assistance for the poor and needy.

The rivalry between Templars and Hospitallers, wrote James, was not just a reason to avoid placing their members under the same banner; it was a reason for the orders' success. Competition pushed both to excel: "If the Templars transported to Outremer a large number of brothers, horses and other animals, the Hospitallers did not rest until they had done as much or more. . . . If one religious order had good knights, reputed for their fighting and other good actions, the other order always strove with all its might to have better ones. . . . If the two orders had already been united, I do not believe they would have made such great efforts." Finally, grasping somewhat, James argued that the Templars and Hospitallers had always formed the vanguard and rear guard of royal armies on the crusades, and this would no longer be possible if there were only one order, while the standard of hospitality offered to "pilgrims of the Lord, of high or low estate" could not be guaranteed.

This last point was vague and tendentious, but it led James of Molay on to the last section of his memo, in which he admitted, as faintly as he could, some advantages to union. People no longer respected monasticism very much, he wrote; perhaps a single order might change that. There was a clear financial case for slimming down the number of houses and castles maintained by the two orders: "The savings would be enormous." Beyond that, his letter contained only respectful pleading for the idea to be junked as it had in the past and the promise that he could tell the pope much more in person. To that end, in October 1306 the master readied himself for the long journey west. He left behind as his deputy Aimo of Oiselay, a veteran of thirty years' who had served as marshal since 1300. Then James of Molay left Cyprus for the court of Clement V and the kingdom of Philip IV, hoping to return with the future of his order secure and some clarity on the direction of the next crusade.

He would never see Cyprus again.

✝

The crossing was slow and the Templar master missed the date of his appointment with the pope by several weeks, but it did not matter much. Clement had been struck down during the autumn by a crippling bout of intestinal troubles and was too ill to see anyone until the new year. James could therefore proceed in a leisurely fashion after his arrival in France— probably through the port of Marseille, where the Templars had a strong naval presence and a house that managed the shipping between Cyprus and the West. His ultimate destination was the papal court in Poitiers, an elegant French town on the river Clain with a glorious palace, including a vast receiving chamber built for Louis VII's queen Eleanor of Aquitaine, known as the Hall of Lost Footsteps. As he made his way there he had plenty of time to familiarize himself with the state of the French kingdom.

Philip IV's dynasty, the Capetians, had ruled France for more than four centuries. During the thirteenth century they had massively expanded the direct reach of the Crown throughout the realm, asserting direct authority over Normandy, Anjou, Brittany and Toulouse, which had earlier been ruled by virtually independent magnates or foreign kings. From a small pocket of royal demesne (directly controlled land) around Paris, the Capetians had mastered most of the western seaboard of the kingdom, and stamped their mark south to the Pyrenees and east to the river Rhone.

The dynasty claimed ultimate descent from Charlemagne. Their long history and recent sharp expansion had bred in successive generations of kings a pronounced sacerdotal self-importance. In 1297 Philip had secured sainthood for his illustrious grandfather Louis IX, and just as he idolized Louis, so he considered himself a superlatively Christian king of a genuinely special kingdom. He was keen that everyone else should acknowledge this as well.

Philip's religiosity was not far from pomposity, and inevitably some of his subjects sniggered, although they found in short order that this was a bad idea. In 1301 Bernard Saisset, bishop of Pamiers, called Philip a useless owl, "the handsomest of birds which is worth absolutely nothing . . . such is our king of France, who can do nothing except to stare at men." This was both unwise and inaccurate and it landed the bishop on trial for sorcery, blasphemy, fornication, heresy and treason. Philip was a man of little warmth and no great intellectual curiosity, but he was a calculating zealot, committed to his own self-serving form of piety, able to convince himself of the worst intentions in others and quite unafraid of destroying anyone who stood in his way.

The most notorious example of Philip's righteous anger was his vicious and highly personal vendetta against Pope Boniface VIII between 1296 and 1301. This had begun over Philip's attempts to grab tax revenue raised from the French Church to spend on his military projects, but it rapidly spiraled into an ill-tempered contest for absolute authority. (A furious dispute over Bishop Saisset's arrest was one battle in this fiercely fought war.) Boniface tried to browbeat Philip with a series of papal edicts, culminating with a bull known as *Unam Sanctam*, which aggressively set out the spiritual supremacy of the Church and argued that obedience to Rome was expected from all men, including kings. It stated with little ambiguity that "it is altogether necessary for salvation for every human creature to be subject to the Roman pontiff."[15]

The king's response to this was simple and brutal. In September 1303 Philip's trusted minister William of Nogaret took several thousand mercenaries to Anagni, near Rome, surrounded Boniface in the papal residence there, barged in and roughed him up. Legend later had it that William of Nogaret slapped Boniface; whether or not this was true, the pope was held hostage for several days and his house ransacked. He was so badly shaken that he died within a month of returning to Rome, raging and delirious with fever. (When Boniface's corpse was exhumed and examined in 1605 the legend that he had died after gnawing off his own hands was finally put to rest.) Boniface's successor, Benedict XI, died after only nine months, and the French had their way in the end with the election of Clement.

✢

Churchmen were not the only group to have been ill treated during Philip's reign. The king's pressing need for money, the catalyst for his first clashes with Boniface, arose from France's continual involvement in wars against her neighbors. When Philip took the crown as a seventeen-year-old in 1285 he inherited a bitter and fruitless struggle against Aragón. The French had lost the war, which was technically a crusade, although really nothing more than a southern turf war absurdly sanctified by a partisan pope, and incurred large debts in the process.

War with Aragón was followed in the late 1290s by a sapping series of military campaigns against England's aging warrior king Edward I over his refusal to play the role of a French subject in respect to his lands in Gascony. By 1305 this had been settled with a peace treaty that betrothed Philip's daughter to Edward's son, but the end of hostilities had been complicated by a major series of campaigns against Flanders. On top of this, Philip's wife of twenty years, Jeanne of Navarre, died at the end of March 1305, and Philip, given over to superstition as well as suspicion, came to believe she had been murdered by the sorcery of Guichard, bishop of Troyes, whom he hounded from the kingdom.[16]

By the time of James's arrival in France in 1306, France's greatest problems were neither Philip's bereavement nor the threat of foreign kings. They were financial: the kingdom was in the throes of a full-blown monetary crisis. The cost of the campaigns against England and Flanders had been enormous, and the government had resorted to a number of precarious financial tactics to cope with the strain on its treasury. The most damaging of these was currency manipulation. Louis IX had undertaken a major review of the coinage, issuing in 1266 a new coin of almost pure silver known as the *gros tournois*. These were worth twelve *derniers*, the common physical currency of the realm. The official monetary value of the *gros* was at first stable and the coin was trusted. But this changed in 1295, when Philip and his ministers began to devalue the currency in order to meet the needs of the king's war policy.[17] To raise money for the straining royal treasury, the *gros* was revalued at fifteen *derniers*, and the amount of silver in each coin was reduced. Eight years later, in 1303, the *gros* was revalued again to twenty-six and a quarter *derniers*. By 1306 there were forty-one and a half *derniers* to a *gros*, and the government had been forced to ban its subjects from taking coin out of the country to preserve what scarce supply of silver they had left in circulation. This ruinous policy had crashed the French currency, causing rapid and damaging inflation and reducing the real value of money more than threefold.

In the summer of 1306 Philip's ministers had attempted to reverse the policy by taking a large amount of money out of circulation. This new initiative was sold with a pious twist as a return to the "good money" of Saint Louis, but a sharp deflationary policy was even more unpopular than the drift to devaluation, since it meant people had to return their coins to the royal mints, where they were paid out a much smaller amount than they put in. Meanwhile, debts and food prices were still accounted in the old, "bad" money—which remained in circulation.

The cost of living doubled at a stroke and in Paris on December 30 there was such serious rioting—exacerbated by dreadful weather and flooding—that the king was forced to take refuge behind the gates of the Temple, which he decided was a safer stronghold than the royal palace on the Île de la Cité.

The first victim of Philip's financial policies was France's Jewish population. Jews in the West had traditionally been protected by their Christian monarchs, who permitted them to engage in moneylending at interest—which was in theory prohibited to followers of the Roman Church. Through a combination of heavy one-off taxes and loans extorted with menaces, many secular rulers had found the Jews to be a valuable source of revenue. The rise of Italian banking in the late thirteenth century had diminished the importance of Jews to royal finance, just as poisonously anti-Semitic attitudes arose across Europe, making mistreatment of Jewish communities a tool of easy populist policy. Jews were lampooned in public plays, attacked by mobs, and became the subjects of absurd myths that portrayed them as child murderers and sexual monsters. Philip IV believed and encouraged a popular prejudice that held that French Jews would obtain Communion wafers and attack them with water, fire and knives, thus recrucifying Christ, whose presence was held to be contained within.[18]

Driven by financial opportunism and naked bigotry, kings and nobles had begun to expel Jews from their lands, taking or auctioning their property. Philip Augustus had ordered Jews to leave the royal lands around Paris in 1182. Jews had been thrown out of Brittany in 1240 and Philip's cousin Charles II of Anjou had ejected the Jews from his lands in 1289. Edward I, who had his own cripplingly expensive wars to fund, expelled the Jews of Gascony and England by royal edict in 1288 and 1290 respectively, helping himself to a windfall seizure of Jewish wealth, estates, shops and houses.

Desperate for a supply of silver with which to stock the royal mints, Philip issued orders on June 21, 1306, for his officials to carry out a coordinated roundup one month and one day later. On July 22 around one hundred thousand* Jewish men, women and children were arrested and imprisoned while their wealth and property were inventoried. They were told to leave the kingdom within a month on pain of death. The persecution of the Jews was not limited to land directly ruled by the king: it was carried out, pointedly, in parts of France where another lord technically held sovereignty over the Jewish population. "Every Jew must leave my land, taking none of his possessions with him; or let him choose a new God for himself, and we will be One People." This was the sentence of exodus later attributed by a Jewish writer to Philip IV as columns of hungry, broken refugees traipsed toward the Pyrenees, the Netherlands and the Holy Roman Empire.

The expulsion of the Jews, closely supervised by William of Nogaret,

---

* The large number of Jews in France (estimated as being between forty and one hundred forty thousand) was in part a result of expulsions elsewhere. The Jews of Europe had fled to French royal lands seeking safety as refugees. See William Chester Jordan, *The French Monarchy and the Jews: From Philip Augustus to the Last Capetians* (Philadelphia: University of Pennsylvania Press, 1989), 203–4.

had been completed just weeks before James of Molay's arrival in France, and the master must have heard about it at first hand. In itself the policy did not concern the Templars, or bear any relevance to the policies he had come to discuss. But its outcome would. The physical expulsion of the Jews was completed successfully, but it did not bring in anything like the amount of silver that the king needed to restore the currency to its former value. This left Philip's government critically short of options, and casting about for other rich groups to raid.

The Templars were hardly inconspicuous in this regard. Their treasuries in Aragón, England and Cyprus held hundreds of pounds of silver, as did the vaults in the Paris Temple.[19] In 1306 the Temple was still providing essential accounting services to the king under its treasurer John of Tour, who advanced the Crown credit to make routine payments. These services made the Temple valuable. They would also make it vulnerable.

+

Philip was in a particularly zealous mood that summer, more determined than at any other point in his reign to demonstrate his special credentials as the "most Christian king." Expelling the Jews was both expedient and a demonstration of the king's muscular hatred of all false faith. His "good money" financial policy explicitly cast him as a true heir to his grandfather Saint Louis. To emphasize his link Philip had also rearranged the royal tombs in the abbey of Saint-Denis, so that his own projected resting place would be close to his grandfather's.

In May 1307 Philip IV was at the papal court in Poitiers, hectoring a reluctant Clement V to give him permission to put Pope Boniface VIII on posthumous trial for a familiar cocktail of ridiculous charges including heresy, sodomy, sorcery and murder.* Blackening Boniface's reputation served a dual purpose: it satisfied Philip's grudge against the pope, and it pounded home the notion of the god-sponsored wondrousness of French kingship.

---

* The small matter of Boniface having been dead for over three years was no impediment. A papal corpse had been tried at least once before, when in A.D. 897 the late pope Formosus was exhumed and held to account for perjury, for which he was found guilty. His papacy was duly struck from the records.

The pope was deeply uneasy, and tried to make a bargain: he would formally forgive all of those involved in the Anagni incident (chief among them William of Nogaret) if the king would withdraw his unprecented persecution of Boniface's memory. No deal was forthcoming and Philip took his leave of Clement around May 15, not long before James of Molay reached the papal court. It is likely that William of Nogaret and his colleague William of Plaisians, another leading minister of Philip IV, remained with the pope long enough to encounter the Templar master. The mood can only have been tense. It was well known that the French king had raised with the pope the issue of uniting the Templars and the Hospitallers. One ambassador at the papal court wrote to his master in Aragón saying, "According to insistent rumor the pope must deal with the merging of the orders, and intends to do so with them."[20]

By the time James crossed paths with William of Nogaret in Poitiers, the minister had begun to compile a dossier on the Templars: quietly interviewing disgruntled members of the order who had been expelled or had otherwise left under a cloud. The purpose of the dossier was not yet clear—but at best it was a ledger of skeletons in the closets, to be stored away for future use as ammunition against the Templars and, by proxy, the pope. Whatever the initial intention, its contents were already lurid.

The first contributor to William of Nogaret's files was a dissolute townsman by the name of Esquin of Floyran, from Béziers in the Languedoc. Around 1305 he had been in prison with a Templar who had run away from the order, and he claimed that while they were locked up together his cell mate had confided tales of immorality, particularly involving the ceremonies by which new knights and sergeants were received.

Esquin had talked up these salacious stories to his jailers, and on release he had attempted to sell his story to the highest bidder. He began with the king of Aragón, James II, securing an audience with the king's confessor and offering to give up his story in return for one thousand livres in annual income and three thousand in ready cash if what he said was found to be true. James had brushed him off, but Esquin was not discouraged: he took the story to the king of France. On arriving at court he was pushed toward William of Nogaret, who saw the value in keeping track of whatever gossip he could that might be detrimental to the order at a sensitive time. Esquin was questioned, his story was taken down, and further evidence was sought out. Moles were planted in Templar houses in France. So it was that a pool of accusation, hearsay, rumor and gossip began to be assembled at the French royal court. By the time James of Molay reached the papal court at Poitiers, surveillance had been under way for as long as two years. William was not quite ready to act on the evidence he was compiling. But he could and he would.

+

In the early summer of 1307 James traveled north from Poitiers to Paris, where, on June 24, a general chapter of the order was held: a conference of leading officials at which the foremost topics of discussion must have been the threat of merger. The master was often in the company of Hugh of Pairaud, who had held many senior offices, including the posts of master of France, acting master of Provence and visitor (a senior supervisory post) of England and France. It must have given James a degree of confidence to know that Hugh had backed Philip decisively during the conflict with Boniface, and that the Temple in Paris had retained many of its financial duties to the kingdom on his watch, working in tandem with royal accountants in the Louvre, and paying troops and royal wages on behalf of the Crown under the supervision of John of Tour.

James returned to the papal court toward the end of July, and on August 4 the master struck out from Poitiers to visit Montgauguier in Angoulême. Here he wrote a few letters addressing the election of a new provincial master in Aragón and Catalonia, including one to King James II. By September 8 he had returned to Poitiers and was still focused on the Aragónese mastership, now settled on Simon of Lenda.[21] Micromanaging Simon's accession to his new job occupied the next few days, as James dictated several long letters, exhorting him to do his duty to God, the Temple and himself, and telling him what to do with the effects and servants of his predecessor. Another letter was dashed off to Blanche, queen of Aragón, recommending with all his heart the "provident and trustworthy" new master.[22]

All this was business as usual. Yet as he went about his work, the master was filled with a growing sense that something was awry.* It was later claimed that on a visit to Philip's court that summer he had appeared in front of the king and some of his ministers and "explained several statutes of his order."

The first stories of Templar impropriety to reach the royal court, by way of Esquin of Floyran, concerned reception ceremonies. New recruits would be lectured about the onerous duties and tough existence of a brother, questioned about their willingness to devote themselves to the harsh existence of knighthood in the East, and promised that they would receive "the bread and water and poor clothing of the house and much pain and suffering."[23] Then they would be given their white or black mantle, and would receive a prayer from the Temple chaplain, before the person leading the induction (usually a senior official of the order) "should raise him up and kiss him on the mouth and it is customary for the chaplain brother to kiss him also."[24]

Exchanging kisses was an accepted part of feudal relationships and a common way of expressing Christian peace. If it shocked the king or his ministers, they made no mention of it in their first meeting with James. Neither did they take the master to task on any other issues of sexualized contact between brothers in the order, although the rule certainly mentioned them. Several clauses denounced the "filthy, stinking sin" of sodomy. An entry in the case studies on penance related the story of three brothers who had been caught having sex with one another, who were sentenced to perpetual imprisonment in Château Pèlerin.[25]

The king chose to take issue with another, seemingly more innocuous practice: that of irregular confession. James admitted that as master he had sometimes heard the confessions of fellow knights who were

---

*There is a peculiar and problematic story in the chronicle of the Templar of Tyre, suggesting the source of discord between king and Temple was a huge loan made to the king by the Templar treasurer John of Tour, which was supposedly unauthorized by James of Molay. By this account, James of Molay sacked the treasurer and then refused to reinstate him on the king's request, throwing a letter sent via the pope in the fire. Few historians give any credit to this story, which appears to be an ill-informed and garbled piece of anti-James prejudice, and stands in sharp contrast to the excellent eyewitness testimony in the Templar of Tyre's account of the fall of Acre in 1291. Paul F. Crawford, ed., The "Templar of Tyre." Part III of the Deeds of the Cypriots (Aldershot, UK: Ashgate, 2003), 179–80.

unwilling to speak of their sins to a chaplain for fear of the harsh penalties they would impose for even small misdemeanors. He explained that he often heard the brothers confess and gave them absolution privately, overlooking the fact that since he was not ordained as a priest he had no spiritual authority to do so.[26]

How or why he volunteered this information is not clear. The most plausible explanation is that he was simply trapped. Having admitted the order's established practices of kissing new inductees the master may well have sought to offset it with a defense of the Templars' uncompromising code of discipline. He had after all boasted of the order's extreme rigor in his memo arguing against union of the orders. Now, perhaps, he tried to demonstrate to the king just how tough sanctions against wayward brothers were by means of a purely self-deprecating anecdote, meant to illustrate the severity of Templar penance—so harsh that at times he took pity on his brothers and absolved them himself. James of Molay may have been offering up a minor fault as a virtue. If so, he had badly misread his audience. For when it came to the Templars, Philip IV and his ministers were not looking to be persuaded. They were looking for evidence.

The meeting with Philip did not kill off rumors of Templar misconduct. By late August these were worrying enough for James of Molay to decide he needed to act. The man he turned to for help was the pope. On August 24 Clement wrote to the king of France, explaining that the master of the Templars had come to him in person asking for an inquiry to be opened into "slanders of which Your Majesty has been informed." He went on to say that James had implored him "to inquire into the deeds with which they have been unjustly charged, so that they may be given penance if they are found guilty, or be discharged from this accusation if they are innocent."[27] The pope concurred that there were indeed "many strange and unheard of things" being spoken about the order. Therefore, Clement said, he would be inspecting the Templar Rule for himself. As soon as he returned from a bout of treatment for his gut trouble, due to run from September 1 until October 15, he would open an official inquiry to settle the matter once and for all. This sounded like a chance for a fair hearing and for the Templars to subject themselves to minor, voluntary reform.

With the pope on medical leave, William of Nogaret and the French party seized their moment. On September 14, sealed letters composed at the royal abbey of Saint Mary, near Pontoise, were distributed to government officials. These were to be acted upon one month from their receipt, when coordinated action was to be taken against the brothers of the Temple, carried out with the same efficiency as the expulsion of the Jews.

Eight days later another set of letters were sent by the king's personal confessor, William of Paris, an energetic Dominican friar who also served as the chief papal inquisitor in France. He was officially a servant of the Church: the man with with overall responsibility for rooting out heresy and wayward belief. His ultimate master was Clement V, but his position in the royal household, where he had direct access to Philip, made him a creature of the king. On September 22 he wrote to his teams of inquisitors all over the realm, telling them to prepare for a burst of activity against the Templars.

The letters were kept secret. On September 30 one brother fled the order, but three days later, brothers were still being initiated, plainly suspecting nothing.

In early October James of Molay traveled to Paris, where he joined Philip at the funeral of the king's sister-in-law Catherine, the titular Latin empress of Constantinople. The Templar master was appointed a pallbearer, hardly suggesting he was out of favor.

At dawn on the morning after the funeral all across France the king's bailiffs and seneschals moved into action. At every Templar house in the realm, from Normandy to Toulouse, men wearing the royal livery and carrying warrants bearing the royal seal appeared before the gates, demanding that the brothers inside surrender. They were to leave their houses and come into royal custody. The charges against them were utterly heinous and scandalous almost beyond description.

"The brothers of the Order of the Knights of the Temple, wolves in sheep's clothing, in the habit of a religious order vilely insulting our religious faith, are again crucifying our Lord Jesus Christ," read the royal letters. The bailiffs were ordered to "hold them captive to appear before an ecclesiastical court; you will seize their movable and immovable goods . . . until you receive further instructions from us on this matter."[28]

So the roundups began. There was little resistance and only a handful of brothers tried to flee. Instead, the Templars, long renowned for their valor on the battlefield, trooped out blinking into the autumn dawn to be led away meekly to their fate.

It was Friday, October 13, 1307.

20

"Heretical Depravity"

T HERE HAS RECENTLY echoed in our ears, to our not inconsiderable astonishment and vehement horror, vouched for by many people worthy to be believed, a bitter thing, a lamentable thing, a thing horrible to contemplate, terrible to hear, a heinous crime, an execrable evil, an abominable deed, a hateful disgrace, a completely inhuman thing, indeed remote from all humanity. Having weighed up its seriousness we felt the immensity of our grief increase in us the more bitterly as it became evident that crimes of this nature and importance were so great as to constitute an offence against the divine majesty, a loss for the orthodox faith and for all Christianity, a disgrace for humanity, a pernicious example of evil and a universal scandal."

The letters, written in the king's voice, burned with a righteous fury kindled by the Templars' despicable crimes. They were addressed to bailiffs and seneschals—men of knightly rank who had the power to make arrests in the name of the Crown, and spoke of dark deeds and strange rituals performed as new brothers were received into the order. The inspiration for the charges was the kiss of peace given to each new brother, but fed through the royal propaganda machine directed by William of Nogaret, this had become a ceremony of orgiastic depravity calculated to shock all faithful Christians.

According to "very reliable people," brothers were forced on entering the order to deny Christ three times, spit on his image, remove their clothes and stand naked before their receiver, who celebrated their entry to the order by kissing them "first on the lower part of the dorsal spine, secondly on the navel and finally on the mouth, in accordance with the profane rite of their order but to the disgrace of the dignity of the human race." Having thus entered the Temple, brothers were obliged by their vows to have sex with one another, "and this is why the wrath of God has fallen on these sons of infidelity." Sodomy, heresy, attacks on the image of Jesus Christ and a dash of black magic: familiar charges to anyone who had fallen foul of Philip IV of France to date. A reference was made to the Templars having "made offerings to idols," which would come to have great importance as investigations proceeded. The government had heard that the cord binding the brothers' habits had been "blessed" by touching it to "an idol in the form of a man's head with a large beard, which head they kiss and worship in their provincial chapters."

For all their scandalized verbiage, the letters authorizing the arrests were mostly hot air and familiar assertions of Philip's personal righteousness. (The king described himself as "We who have been placed by the Lord on the watchtower of regal eminence to defend the liberty of the faith of the Church.") The king claimed that "the deeper and fuller" his investigation had gone, "the greater are the abominations that are uncovered, as when one knocks down a wall." Just what these further abominations were was never specified. So although the king gave notice of the Crown's intention to try every Templar in France, announcing the engagement of his confessor William of Paris, "inquisitor of heretical depravity," to lead the effort and promising to freeze Templar assets until the truth was determined, a close reading of the arrest warrant revealed nothing beyond a hysterically exaggerated account of the Templars' idiosyncratic induction ceremony, puffed up with insults and titillating hearsay.

A second note, sent out on September 22, was more revealing. It gave specific instructions for the bailiffs and seneschals who would be making the arrests.[1] By royal order they were to impound, inventory and guard the order's properties and make provision to continue any farming work necessary on vineyards and in the fields. Meanwhile, they were to take the brothers themselves into solitary confinement, where they should "determine the truth carefully, with the aid of torture if necessary."

✛

James of Molay was among hundreds of brothers arrested and processed between October and November 1307 under the instruction of William of Nogaret and William of Paris. The king's men questioned Raimbaud of Caron, preceptor of Cyprus; Hugh of Pairaud, visitor of France; Geoffrey of Charney, preceptor of Normandy; and John of Tour, trusted financial adviser to the Crown and treasurer of the Paris Temple. Beyond this circle of high-ranking officers most of the men arrested were middle-aged and distinctly unwarlike. Most Templars in France were not warriors. They were agricultural managers, shepherds and pig farmers, carpenters or wine merchants.[2] Only a tiny minority were knights, since by the early fourteenth century some preceptories were staffed entirely by sergeants: this was true in areas of Champagne, Picardy, Auvergne, Poitou and Limousin.[3] Forty percent of those questioned were over fifty years old. A third were veterans of the order, having served in this apparent hotbed of sodomy and irreligion for more than twenty years without complaint.[4]

All the same, the king's orders called for torture and there is no reason to think they were disobeyed. The methods of the day were not inventive but they were well tested: starvation, sleep deprivation, solitary imprisonment, relentless questioning, shackling, racking, foot burning and the strappado, a device that yanked the victim's tethered arms behind him until he was raised from the ground and his shoulders dislocated. One Templar, Ponsard of Gisy, later described having his arms tied so tightly behind his back that blood flowed from under his nails, and being kept in a pit so small he could only take a single step in any direction—an experience to which he said death by decapitation, burning or scalding with boiling water would be greatly preferable.[5]

Rooting out heretics had been an obsession of Church leaders and pious secular rulers in Western Europe ever since a fear of heresy first gripped the Roman Church in the 1160s. From the 1230s the Inquisition had become a fully fledged institution, organized by the Church but operated in tandem with earthly authorities who had the power to inflict corporal punishment on heretics who would not reform their ways. The goal of the Inquisition was to bring heretics back to the correct teachings of the Church, and to stop them from infecting others. In practice that meant persecuting people who had either strayed from official doctrine or were objectionable in some other way that could be framed in heretical terms.[6] Those who admitted to heresy and agreed to reform could be given penance and accepted back into the Church. Those who refused were often tormented until they changed their mind. Pope Innocent IV had explicitly sanctioned the use of torture against heretics in a papal ruling of 1252. Those who confessed and later relapsed were the worst category of all: they could be handed over from the Inquisition to the secular authorities for capital punishment, which often meant being burned alive. The papal Inquisition largely employed the mendicant preaching orders— the Dominicans and Franciscans—as inquisitors. These men tended to combine a solid knowledge of approved Church teachings with a self-selecting interest in sufferings of the flesh and, occasionally, an outright taste for violence. In 1307 they knew what they were doing, and they knew what they were looking for.

The inquisitors' job was to extract confessions that would match the accusations leveled at the order in Philip IV's letters. This was not a task of open-minded inquiry but of confirmation: to supply the evidence to prove that irreligion ran through the order like a cancer. Heresy was the essential charge to prove, since it was a crime that was rooted out by the Church but punished by the secular authorities. Proving it was rife among the Templars would allow the king to take over from the pope the task of winding up the order and redirecting its resources.

✝

James of Molay was staying in Paris on the night of the arrests, following his attendance at the empress of Constantinople's funeral. He was still there eleven days later, for on October 24, 1307, he made a confession before the inquisitors at the Paris Temple, one of one hundred and thirty-eight brothers to appear at the same session over the course of a fortnight. Brought before William of Paris and his staff of notaries and witnesses, the Templar master placed his hand on the Gospels and testified that he was telling "the full, whole and complete truth about himself and others in a case pertaining to the faith."[7]

He had been a Templar for forty-two years, James said, having been received in the Temple house at Beaune (between Dijon and Lyon) by Brother Humbert of Pairaud and several other brothers, most of whose names he could not remember. According to the inquisitors' report, James then said "that after many promises made by him concerning the observances and statutes of the said order, they placed a mantle on his neck. The said receiver caused a bronze cross bearing the image of the Crucified to be brought into his presence, and told and ordered him to deny Christ whose image was there. Against his will he did this. Then the said receiver ordered him to spit on it, but he spat on the ground. Asked how many times, he said on oath that he spat only once, and he remembered this clearly." The master denied having ever had carnal relations with his brothers, but he said other brothers' receptions resembled his and as master he had ordered this to be so.

The other senior Templars interrogated around the same time gave much the same answers; so similar indeed that the inquisitors' records suggest they were simply being induced to admit a specific list of misdeeds, offered with face-saving caveats. Geoffrey of Charney, the preceptor of Normandy, described denying an image of Jesus once and said he could not remember if he spat on the image because it was "thirty-seven or thirty-eight years previously" and they had been acting in haste. He admitted he had "kissed the receiving master on the navel," and had once heard it said in a chapter meeting that it would be better for brothers to have sex with one another than "to assuage their lust with women." He confessed to receiving one brother in the same fashion as himself, before realizing that "the manner in which he had been received was wicked, profane and contrary to the Catholic faith."[10]

When Hugh of Pairaud, visitor of France, was interrogated on November 9, he was given special attention by the inquisitors—considerably more so than James of Molay. While the master had spent almost his entire adult career in the East, Hugh was a veteran of forty-four years' service, the greater part of which had been spent in the West. He had held the highest rank in England, France and Provence, and was a prominent figure in French politics, having been close enough to the king to support him in his clash with Pope Boniface. His confession carried the maximum possible value, as his admission could be said to characterize Templar activity throughout France. The king's inquisitors were more invested in Hugh's testimony than in that of any other Templar.

Hugh began by describing his induction in 1263. He told his interviewers he had denied Christ once, but had disobeyed the command to spit on the cross and only kissed his receiver on the mouth in a conventional kiss of peace. He then said that when performing reception ceremonies for others, he took his new recruits "to some secret place" and forced them to go through with the whole foul rigmarole: kissing his spine and navel, denying Christ three times and spitting on the cross.

Apparently this information had been wrung out of Hugh with the promise that it could be forgiven if he admitted to the deed but claimed he regretted it. Added to his description of those perverted inductions was the statement: "Although this is what he ordered them to do, he did not do it with his heart." A similar disclaimer accompanied his admission that he had allowed some brothers to relieve the "heat of nature with other brothers." He maintained he only did so "because it was the usage according to the statutes of the order."⁹ This odd claim ought to have been easily disproven—no surviving editions of the Templar Rule permitted any such thing. But the Templar Rule was plainly not well known, guarded as a secret of the order since it contained detailed accounts of Templars' military strategy. A code of careful silence had protected the Templars' tactical advantage in the field throughout their existence—now that secrecy turned against them.

From his inquisitors point of view, of course, Hugh was providing model answers: he had overseen depravity of precisely the sort described in the king's letters, painting a picture of sodomy and blasphemy rotting the order in France from the top down. Halfway through his deposition, however, Hugh seemed to lose his way. First he equivocated: asked whether other senior members of the order had carried out the same induction process as he did, he said "he did not know, since what took place in chapters could not in any way be revealed to people who were not present." Then, "asked whether he thought that all the brothers of the said order were received in that manner, he replied that that was not his opinion."

This was enough for his inquisitor. The Dominican brother Nicholas of Ennezat, who was deputizing for William of Paris, had the hearing adjourned until later in the day, and Hugh was taken from the room. Something was done to change his mind, and when the hearing resumed Hugh said, "On the contrary, he thought that all brothers were received in that manner rather than in another; and he was saying this to correct his words." He went on to add some detail to another line of inquiry that had been opened up during the depositions: the matter of idol worship, which James of Molay and Geoffrey Charney had not touched upon. By now he was prepared to say more or less anything. Hugh described a "head that had four feet, two under the face and two behind," that existed in Montpellier, which he had worshipped "with his lips and not his heart, and then only in pretence." This "idol" sounded rather like a reliquary—one of those bejeweled caskets, often given human forms, in which scraps of saints' remains were kept for the purpose of perfectly orthodox Catholic adoration. This was of no consequence. Having satisfied his inquisitors and sworn that he had not "included any lie or omitted any fact . . . because of threats or fear of torture or imprisonment," Hugh was taken away.

The interrogations continued through the autumn of 1307 and into the new year, both at the Paris Temple and in provincial hearings across France. A uniform pattern of activity was established. Templars were imprisoned in miserable conditions, chained and fed bread and water. They were periodically tortured, and since this was accepted practice in the pursuit of heresy, the inquisitors did not bother to conceal it, speaking frankly in their communications with the royal court.

When Templars were called before the inquiry, the same instructions stated:

> They will be told that the king and the pope have been informed by several very trustworthy witnesses in the order of the errors and the buggery they commit particularly on their entry and their profession. They will be promised a pardon if they confess the truth and return to the faith of the holy Church; otherwise they will be condemned to death.[10]

One of the few men who tried to resist the pressure placed on him was sixty-year-old Raimbaud of Caron, who as preceptor of Cyprus evidently considered himself tougher than the aging accountant-farmers in France.[11] Raimbaud was questioned in Paris on the day after Hugh of Pairaud. He initially refused to admit any wrongdoing, saying that he had taken oaths of poverty, chastity and obedience and "he had never known or heard of anything evil or dishonorable in the reception of brothers or in the order." The laconic notes of his deposition record him making this highly unsatisfactory statement in the presence of Brother Nicholas of Ennezat. "But later the same day," he made a full confession.[12] Evidently there were methods of persuasion available to the inquisitors that could break even a hardened crusader. This left little hope for the rest, and the admissions freely flowed. From teenagers to wizened old men, from the highest-ranking officers to the meanest laborers, Templar brothers were lined up before their black-clad interrogators and confessed one by one to the same heretical actions: illicit kisses in secret ceremonies, spitting on the cross, denying Christ, sex between brothers, worshipping idols. Almost to a man they told them exactly what they wanted to hear.[13]

+

The speed with which the Templars were rounded up and persuaded to start their confessions was a key element in French strategy. But rounding up the Templars was harder than rounding up the French Jews: popular prejudice was not so easy to manipulate in the case of an order tightly associated with the crusading movement and deeply embedded into Christian society across the realm. The government had to work fast. It had to be unsubtle. It had to push the Templars beyond redemption before any serious resistance could be organized.

On October 25 and 26, 1307, following James of Molay's confession, the master and a parade of other senior brothers were forced to repeat their misdeeds in front of a specially invited audience of scholars and students from the University of Paris: a group whose opinion, writings and connections in other realms could be used to broadcast the king's side of the story and entrench it in the popular consciousness. This was an educated audience, and it could have been an opportunity for James of Molay and his senior officials to make a stand. Unfortunately at this stage the master of the Templars was a broken man, who had decided that the only way out of trouble was to comply as fully as possible with royal demands. He repeated his confession to the scholars, and described the king of France as an all-seeing "bringer of light." Then he acquiesced as letters were sent in his name calling on other Templars to follow his lead in making their confessions. In short, he abdicated any responsibility for defending the order's good name, in the hope that by giving his rabid persecutors what they wanted, they would tire and move on to the next victim.

Had James had more political sense he might have realized that Philip's desire to ruin the reputation of the Templars was not shared by other rulers. As well as courting intellectual support in Paris, the French king had written to James II of Aragón and the new English king Edward II (who succeeded his father Edward I when the old warrior king died in the summer of 1307) explaining his discoveries and urging them to begin rounding up Templars in their own jurisdictions. He was met with blank bafflement from both. A worldly view of the arrests was expressed by another of James II's correspondents, who wrote to the king of Aragón from Genoa and explained that "the pope and the king did this in order to have [the Templars'] money and because they wished to make one single house of the Hospital and the Temple . . . of which house the king intended and desired to make one of his sons the ruler."[14]

The pope was affronted by Philip IV's drastic actions. Clement V was in poor health and undergoing medical treament, but he could hardly ignore the assault Philip had made on the Order of the Temple and the authority of the papacy. It was one thing for a pope to be an ally of the French Crown; quite another to appear to be led around by the nose. Three days after James of Molay's confession, Clement wrote politely but indignantly to the king from Poitiers. Treading lightly at first, he praised the unparalleled holiness of the Capetian kings, who were "like shining stars," but pointed out to Philip that the reason for their godliness was their "wisdom and obedience," and above all their understanding that in matters "where ecclesiastical and religious persons could be harmed they would . . . leave everything to the ecclesiastical courts."[15]

Perhaps, thought the pope, this had slipped Philip's mind. "You have laid hands on the persons and goods of the Templars, and not just anyhow but going as far as imprisoning them as though we were privy to events." The pope made it clear he knew the brothers were being tortured: "add[ing] a greater affliction to those who are already considerably afflicted by their imprisonment."

He was disappointed, he told Philip, since he had been "better disposed toward you than all the bishops of Rome . . . in your lifetime." He had told Philip that he intended to investigate the Templars; Philip had completely ignored him and arrested "the said persons and their goods which are under the direct jurisdiction of ourselves and the Church of Rome." The pope now wished to take custody of all the Templar prisoners and their possessions, and to be allowed to take command of the investigation himself. "We desire ardently with all our strength radically to cleanse this garden of the Church . . . so that there shall remain no spark of this type of infection . . . if there is an infection, which God forbid!"

The pope may have been ill, and he may have been compromised by his residence in France and not Rome, but he was not about to be turned into a lapdog for a king of France who had decided to dismember the Church militant because he felt like it.

✝

On November 22, 1307, Clement sent a papal bull known as *Pastoralis Praeeminentiae* to all the leading Christian kings of the West, including Edward II of England, James II of Aragón and the rulers of Castile, Portugal, Italy and Cyprus. The Church, it argued, took precedence over the throne. It was a familiar theme to anyone who had followed relationships between popes and the king of France, but coming from Clement V it had special resonance. He would not and could not allow the House of Capet to destroy the Templars. *Pastoralis Praeeminentiae* gave notice of his intentions.

Clement's problem was that he was fighting a rearguard action. Too much evidence had been presented, and however incredible it seemed, he could not simply sweep it all away. The king of France was an enthusiastic hunter, who would never give up the chase. The fact that Boniface was still being hounded four years after he was cold in his tomb served as a warning to Clement not to attack Philip directly.

The pope hit on a different approach. The case of the Templars would fall under papal supervision, but it would be widened to take in all of Christendom. All of the rulers who received the bull were invited to begin their own arrests, using the model followed in France. Clement rehearsed the order's supposed misdeeds, but carefully noted that he retained an open mind, that the allegations could be untrue and that if so, everything would be settled accordingly.[16] With a stroke of his pen, Clement had inserted himself into the heart of the process against the Templars. The price was that he had implicitly hitched himself to Philip's policy, and the pursuit of the Templars had now to be carried out everywhere, from Dublin to Famagusta, until whatever end it should reach.

For the French king and his ministers this was frustrating, but they cannot possibly have been shocked. They had pressed the Templars fast and hard and publicly, knowing the window for winding up the order would be short. Clement's intervention now meant they would lose overall control of the proceedings. It was true that pressure on the order remained intense: on January 7, 1308, every Templar in England was arrested, and on January 10 royal officers also picked up the brothers of Scotland, Ireland and Wales. Three days later Charles II, king of Naples, executed the pope's orders.[17] Suddenly the case had ballooned, and the chances of a swift resolution all but vanished.

Less than two months into the new year the pope abruptly halted the Templar inquiry in France. In December 1307 cardinals had been allowed access to the highest-ranking Templar prisoners in Paris. Faced with friendlier interviewers, the order's leaders began to backtrack on their statements. Around Christmas James of Molay had withdrawn his confession, risking being branded as a relapsed heretic but heaping doubt on every other Templar statement extracted so far. By February 1308 the pope had grown concerned that the evidence gathered by the French authorities was tainted beyond usefulness. Although his previous orders for the arrests of Templars outside France were still being enacted, he ordered the inquisitors to stop their work. The charges remained outstanding, and brothers remained imprisoned, but there was now some time for the order to recover, and perhaps to resist.

Philip grew restless and his ministers shifted tactics. The king could not restart proceedings against the Templars, but he could certainly try to rally the rest of France around him. He began with the University of Paris, whose members had been already treated to a privileged early viewing of the Templars' confessions. In February a series of questions was sent to the university's finest scholars concerning the king's legal right to take action against heresy in his own realm. Philip and his ministers hoped a favorable legal opinion might bounce the pope into reopening hearings.

The consultation was not so much a resounding victory as an apologetic whimper. The academics squirmed, and on March 25 the king was sent a groveling advisory note explaining that while he was certainly to be commended in his "zeal for the faith," he was perhaps overstepping the mark. "If there is doubt concerning [the Templars'] profession," they argued, "it belongs to the Church which instituted their religious order to decide this case." They also argued that the proceeds of all confiscations from the order should be put to the use for which they were originally intended: saving the Holy Land.[18]

This was inconvenient, but the king did not give up. Between May 5 and May 15 he summoned an assembly of the estates of the realm—representatives from the towns and countryside all over the kingdom—to Tours to advise the king. In reality, this meant that they were forced to listen to him and his ministers rant about the Templars. The estates went along with the royal opinion that the Templars were evil, corrupt and heretical and deserved to be put to death. Buoyed by this agreeable display of subservience, Philip now set out for the papal court for a personal meeting with Clement. He took with him an enormous entourage, including his sons, his brother Charles of Valois, bishops, noblemen and as many important-looking dignitaries from across France as could be brought along from Tours. This great deputation arrived in Poitiers at the end of May.

The French came to Poitiers with smiles, but soon made it clear what they wanted. In a series of conferences with the pope and his advisers, royal ministers and supporters gave long speeches denouncing the Templars in ever more hysterical terms. Much of this was done by William of Plaisians, a lawyer who had been active with William of Nogaret in the attacks on Boniface in 1303. According to letters sent to the king of Aragón, on May 30 William of Plaisians stood on a stool and hectored the pope and his audience on the familiar theme of Philip IV's inherent grace: "The providence of God chose as minister in this affair the king of France who is the vicar of God in his kingdom in temporal matters, and to be sure nobody more suitable could be found. For he is a most devout and Christian prince, the richest and the most powerful. So all those slanderers should be silent." The king was not motivated by avarice or a desire for the Templars' wealth, said William, but by the noble Christian aim of cleansing the Church in his realm. He would do the same if his own brother or sons (both of whom were in attendance) were themselves Templars. All he was asking of the pope was to declare the order condemned, so that he could carry on with the business of judging and punishing the brothers themselves.[19]

William was a skilled advocate and a subtle rhetorician. (He was also an able mouthpiece for William of Nogaret, who was not welcome in the pope's presence.) Yet his adversary was resolute. Clement offered some placatory remarks, praising the king's godliness and denying that he would ever suspect him to be motivated by greed in his pursuit of the Templars. Beyond this he would not be moved. On June 14 William of Plaisians tried again, this time more emphatically. He concluded this speech by making a series of thinly veiled threats against Clement himself. If the pope continued to delay, the king might act alone. Philip had every right to take hold of heresy in his own realm, and by continuing to obstruct him, the pope was abetting the heretics. There was a whiff here of deposition. Yet still the pope held firm. He and he alone was qualified to judge the Templars, he argued, and he would not respond to threats. He seemed unmovable. Little by little, though, he was weakening.

+

On May 6, 1308, the papal bull *Pastoralis Praeeminentiae* finally arrived on the island of Cyprus. It had taken nearly six months, thanks to the slowdown in communication over the stormy winter months in the Mediterranean. In the meantime, news of the fate of the Templars in France had made its way to the islanders. Lightning arrests, false confessions and claims of bizarre rituals were more than enough to suggest their fate hung in the balance. Their acting leader, Marshal Aimo of Oiselay, had begun making preparations for the likely opening of proceedings against them. Treasure and other valuable goods had been moved from inland Nicosia to Limassol, on the south coast, where Templar galleys began surreptitiously to spirit brothers off the island. Perhaps a third of the membership had disappeared when, on May 12, six days after the arrival of the papal bull, the command was given to arrest all the order's members and confiscate their goods.

The man who issued the order was Amalric of Lusignan, King Henry II of Cyprus's brother, who in 1306 had led an uprising against royal rule and had himself appointed regent of Cyprus for life, a position he had secured in part with Templar help. Amalric should in theory have been an ally, but he could hardly protect an organization whose master had confessed to blasphemy and whose entire membership was under arrest.

Amalric was confronting a much livelier group of men than those who had been herded like sheep by the bailiffs and seneschals of France. They were armed. They had boats. They were among the best fighting men on the island and capable of manning castles against a full siege. In short, they would only be taken in peacefully if they wanted to. Rather than resorting to brute force, Amalric would have to ask politely, and it was only after several days of negotiation, during which Marshal Aimo of Oiselay suggested that the order retire to one of their estates and await resolution of the case back in France, that they agreed to cooperate by making a limited collective statement. On Monday, May 27, one hundred and eighteen brothers appeared in Nicosia and gave a public address in which they proclaimed their innocence. They outlined their good service in the East, enumerated some of their most famous battles against the Mamluks and stated their absolute dedication to the Christian cause. Then they left for their house at Limassol.

If they thought they had put the matter to rest they were soon disabused. The following night Amalric held his own conference of leading knights and churchmen, read them various documents illustrating the progress of the case against the Templars, and commanded his troops to muster, so as to capture the Templars and bring them to justice. On June 1 they were ambushed at Limassol, taken prisoner and incarcerated until they could be tried. It would be a long and miserable wait. It took nearly two years for proceedings on Cyprus to begin.

✝

In Poitiers at the end of June Philip's ministers changed the tone of their negotiations. Seeing that Clement would not respond to outright threats and harassment, they decided instead to present him with a carefully curated gallery of the accused, inviting him to come to his own conclusions. This was a sharp strategy. As things were, Clement could go neither forward nor back; he could not rescind his orders for arrests, nor could he proceed to a full trial if it appeared he was doing so as a puppet of the French king. On June 29 the first of a handpicked group of seventy-two Templars were brought to the papal court, and over the next four days they once again recounted their sins in the hope of winning a swift pardon and penance. In many cases these had become rather more color-ful since thir first confession: some gave the impression of having been delib-erately inflated to provide the pope with a legitimate sense of horror. Circumstantial details were added: some spoke of being physically manhan-dled or threatened with swords at the time of reception; others gave shape and life to the strange idols they claimed to have worshipped. One brother, Stephen of Troyes (an informer to William of Nogaret from the beginning), spoke of being forced to adore a jewel-encrusted head that represented Hugh of Payns.[20]

By July 2, Clement V had seen enough to convince him either of the Templars' guilt, or (more likely) that he could accede to the French de-mands without seeming simply to be rolling over. To the Templars who had confessed before him he granted personal absolution. Then he turned to the order at large. On August 12 he issued a bull known as *Faciens Misericordiam*, setting up two parallel investigations: a series of diocesan hearings, where individual Templars would be investigated by panels of bishops, cathedral canons and Dominican or Franciscan friars; and a central, papal commission to examine the fabric of the Order of the Tem-ple itself. In France this was to be conducted in the province of Sens (which effectively meant Paris, the biggest city in that area), and parallel hearings would be set up in England, Cyprus, Aragón and every other state where the Templars had a significant presence. Each of these would investigate one hundred and twenty-seven articles, to establish the credi-bility and purity of the order at large and whether it could be saved. After this work was complete, an assembly would gather in Vienne, near Lyon on the borders of France and the Holy Roman Empire, for a general council of the Church, scheduled for October 1, 1310. Here, on the basis of all the assembled evidence, a final decision on the order's future would be taken.

The pope prepared to leave Poitiers and struck out toward the Alps. He aimed to get as far away as practical from Paris, Philip IV, William of Nogaret and the men who had made his first thirty months in office so disagreeable. He could not go back to Rome, for Philip had made it known that the condition of their coexistence was Clement's continued residence in France. He chose, therefore, to go to Avignon—as close as possible to the fringe of the French king's territories, and close enough to communicate quickly with Rome. In early August the papal court at Poitiers began to disperse, preparing to reassemble in its new home by the beginning of December. Thus was the "Avignon papacy" established, where popes would continue to be based for nearly seventy years, a time that they came to speak of bitterly as a Babylonian captivity.

21

"God Will Avenge Our Death"

WHILE THE POPE was heading to one form of captivity in Avignon, Master James of Molay, Hugh of Pairaud, Raimbaud of Caron, Geoffrey of Charney, preceptor of Normandy, and Geoffrey of Gonneville, preceptor of Poitou and Aquitaine, were enduring another, more literal one, locked in Chinon castle, a large, round-towered stone fortress above a bend in the river Vienne, about sixty miles north of Poitiers. All had been damaged by their experiences at the hands of the Inquisition. (When retracting his initial confession James of Molay had reportedly shown a cardinal the scars across his upper body left by the inquisitors.) All the same, no chances were taken with such high-profile captives. In February 1308 a prominent Templar accountant, Oliver of Penne, preceptor of Lombardy, had fled from house arrest, causing significant embarrassment to his jailors. Another escapee would not do.

None of the Templar leaders had been taken to testify before the pope in Poitiers, despite the city's relatively close proximity to Chinon. The official explanation was that they were not fit to travel—and that may have been so, although it was also the case that the brothers who had been presented to the pope in late June had been carefully vetted to convince him of their guilt. Naturally there was a risk that the order's senior officials might have disrupted this carefully staged performance.

On August 14, the day before the pope's departure, a deputation of cardinals and royal ministers was sent to Chinon. The party included two French cardinals, Bérengar Frédol and Stephen of Suisy, and one Italian, Landolf Brancacci. They reached the gates of the castle on the August 17, and one by one the five Templars went through their stories, while notaries busied themselves scribbling down the new statements. These were later written up onto a large piece of parchment* that was sent to Clement to be stored in the papal archives.

---

* This is the famous "Chinon Parchment," lost for many years in the Vatican Archives and discovered in 2001 by Dr. Barbara Frale. In 2007 eight hundred facsimiles of the document

The first to be questioned was Raimbaud of Caron, the tough preceptor of Cyprus. He admitted to denying Christ once following his reception
into the order, but otherwise said he had no knowledge of any wrongdoing. The only sodomy he knew of in the order's entire history, he said, was
that of the three brothers in the East who had been caught and sentenced
to perpetual imprisonment in Château Pèlerin: a case so unusual and ab-
horrent it had been preserved in the rule as an example of extreme way-
wardness.

When he was finished, Raimbaud knelt before the cardinals and
begged for forgiveness, which he was granted. He was absolved from his
sins and reinstated "in the communion of the faithful and the sacraments
of the Church."

This same process followed for his four colleagues. Geoffrey of Charney, the preceptor of Normandy, who had also seen service on Cyprus as
the order's draper, admitted to denouncing a crucifix at his initiation and
kissing his receiver on the mouth and "on the chest, through garments, to
show respect," a new piece of information he had not revealed at the time
of his first confession. He asked forgiveness and was absolved. Geoffrey
of Gonneville—who had traveled between Cyprus and the papal court as
messenger for Master James of Molay—said he had refused to deny
Christ but had promised to pretend to do, as to keep his receivers from
getting into trouble. Hugh of Pairaud admitted to scorning a crucifix,
but said that this was only after being threatened. He said he had forced
others to kiss him on the back and belly and had condoned sodomy in
preference to sex with women, although he insisted he had never indulged
in it himself. He also repeated his former assertion about the strange
head in Montpellier. Both men were forgiven and welcomed back into
the communion of the Church.

On August 20 James of Molay finally appeared. In December he had
gone back on his confession, but now he changed his mind again, hoping
to secure papal absolution. The only charge he admitted was that of denying Christ, but that was enough to satisfy his interviewers. The notary
recorded for posterity that the master "had denounced in our presence

---

were produced; some are in private hands and others in public libraries across the world.
See *Processus contra Templarios* (Vatican City: Scrinium, 2007).

the aforementioned and other heresy" and had been dealt with in the same merciful fashion as his colleagues. Later that day, the account of each man's confession was read aloud to him in his native tongue, and he swore that it was true. All five remained imprisoned after their absolution, for the papal investigators looking into the corruption of the order as an institution were due to start in Paris later in the year, and would want to hear their evidence, too. But with regard to their personal confession, the process was completed. The cardinals packed up and left Chinon.

✦

The wide-scale inquiry set up by the pope now swung slowly into motion. Across France and throughout the Catholic world, bishops began to establish commissions to examine the conduct of the Templars in their dioceses, with the aim of inducing confessions, which could then be followed by absolutions and penance.

In France, the transfer of responsibility for the Inquisition from king to pope had done nothing to improve conditions for the brothers lined up to admit their misdeeds, as most of the bishops overseeing the regional inquiries had close links to the Crown. Recalcitrant Templars faced long imprisonment without warm clothing, and with a paltry diet of bread and water, shackling, repeated interrogation, violent threats and, finally, torture. A number of brothers went mad or died as a result of harsh treatment, some turning up with their brains so addled by months of isolation and beatings that they were unable to respond to questioning at all.[1] Those who could speak were taken through a set list of questions designed to tick off however many misdeeds as could be levered out of them. Eighty-seven or eighty-eight articles were presented to each brother, who either admitted or denied each in turn. Any interesting features of the confession would be noted down, but otherwise this was an exercise in bureaucratic terror. The questions were repetitive, formulaic and numbing:

Did the brother deny Christ at his reception? Was this done with the whole community? Was it repeated afterward? Were they taught that Jesus was not the true God or a false prophet? Did they spit on a cross? Did they trample on a cross? Did they do it regularly? Did they urinate on the cross? Did they trample on the cross *and* urinate on it? Was this done at Easter? Did they deny the sacraments of the Church? Did they confess to the master instead of to an ordained priest? Did they ever kiss another brother improperly? Where did they kiss him? On his back? His belly? His penis? Were they told they could have sex with their brothers? Did they do it? Did they penetrate or were they penetrated? Did anyone tell them this was not a sin? Did they worship idols? Did the idols look like heads? Did the idols look like heads with three faces? How did they worship them? Did they call them "God"? Did they call them "Savior"? Did some of their brothers do this? Did most of their brothers do this? Did anyone tell them the idol would save them? Make them rich? Make the soil fertile? Make the trees flower? And so on, and so on.[2] Eventually, most brothers confessed, defeated both by their physical sufferings and the sheer relentlessness of the process—although sometimes it took many months to break them. The Council of Vienne had been set for October 1310, and would eventually be postponed until October 1311. Time was on the interrogators' side, and they made full use of it. After a year or more of being locked up in the cold on thin rations, most Templars either gave up or died. In one area one third of the brothers who had been arrested in 1307 were dead five years later.[3]

✝

By the spring of 1310, from Ireland to Cyprus investigators had gathered their evidence, interviewing Templar brothers and nonaligned witnesses. In most places this revealed that the charges concocted by Philip IV's ministers and circulated by the pope were unproven and largely fantastical. Yet in France, the order's heartland, the picture that emerged from almost every one of the brutal Inquisitions was of a diabolically corrupt order. From Easter 1309 the French Crown had begun leasing out confiscated Templar property for profit, working on the assumption that it would never be returned, preempting not only the individual investigations but the central inquiry into the corruption of the order as a whole. The injustice was palpable.

The Templars' central leadership was in poor shape to resist. James of Molay had been personally absolved in Chinon, but his long and violent incarceration had taken its toll. Having endured grueling interrogation in Paris and Chinon, he was now taken back to the French capital to appear before the papal commission, whose aim was to take evidence about the order as a whole.

On Wednesday, November 26, and Friday, November 28, 1309, the broken Templar master was brought to the ancient abbey of Sainte-Geneviève to appear before a panel of justices made up largely of French bishops and cardinals. The president of the panel, Gilles Aycelin, archbishop of Narbonne, was a member of the king's council. James gave muddled, erratic answers. At first he said he was neither wise nor learned enough to defend the order, and could only remark that he thought it "very surprising" that the Church wanted to destroy the Templars when they had threatened for thirty-two years to depose Frederick II Hohenstaufen without ever getting around to it.[4] When his previous self-incriminating statements were read to him he became irate, made the sign of the cross and said that "may it please God that what was practiced by Saracens and Tartars might be practiced against evildoers in this case, for those Saracens and Tartars either chop off the heads of evildoers they find or else cleaved them in two." At this point William of Plaisians, listening from outside the room, walked in and put his arm around the master, telling him "to take care not to demean or destroy himself unnecessarily." The master asked for time to think over what he had said and his deposition was postponed until later in the week.

When James returned on Friday, November 28, he seemed in no fitter state of mind to answer questions. Asked if he wished to defend the order he told them he was an "impoverished knight who knew no Latin," but he understood there was a letter in existence by which the pope reserved the right to deal with his case in person. Informed that his own deeds were not the business of the Paris commission, which was looking into the order as a whole, James said that he had only three things to contribute: the order had better churches than any of their rivals; they distributed more alms; and "he knew of no other order . . . more prepared to expose their bodies to death in defense of the Christian faith against its enemies." Then, once again, he started to rant about the war, launching into an animated but irrelevant story about Louis IX's brother Robert of Artois leading Templars to their deaths in Damietta in 1250.

This time, as the master was speaking, William of Nogaret entered the room. Where William of Plaisians had been avuncular, he was sinister and unpleasant. Upon hearing history being rehearsed he announced that he himself had read chronicles at the royal abbey of Saint-Denis, claiming that the Templars had treacherously paid homage to Saladin, but that the sultan had despised them, believing they had lost the battle of Hattin in 1187 because "they were laboring under the vice of sodomy."[5]

As informed historical debate this had very little to recommend it. The only point it illustrated was that James of Molay was now a rambling old man whose ability to save his order from destruction was somewhere near nil, and that although the commission was fronted by bishops, the king's ministers were directing it from behind the scenes. Called back to give evidence for a third time on March 2, 1310, James of Molay was now beyond even anecdotes, and merely asked to be sent to the pope for judgment.

As the master bumbled his way through his inadequate depositions, a sense of defiance began to grow among the Templars' ordinary membership. Across France literally hundreds of brothers were arriving in Paris to give evidence to the commission. They were kept under curfew in venues across the city, ranging from the Paris Temple to bishops' houses equipped with secure rooms. However, some were allowed limited freedom to travel and communicate with one another, and collectively the brothers began to organize a serious and spirited defense. In February more than five hundred Templars presented themselves at the abbey, volunteering to give testimony in praise of the order. Some of their evidence was heard by the commissioners, but soon so many brothers had been brought to the capital that a form of official representation had to be arranged.

In late March an open-air meeting was held in the abbey grounds at which hundreds of the assembled Templars angrily declared the accusations against them to be baseless. The commissioners asked them to put forward "procurators" who might advocate for the brothers en bloc. Four men were chosen: two chaplains and two knights. The chaplains were Peter of Bologna, a forty-four-year-old who had represented the order as an ambassador to the pope, and Reginald of Provins, the preceptor of Orléans, and the knights were William of Chambonnet and Bertrand of Sartiges, both long-standing veterans. In a series of presentations they complained about the conditions in which brothers were kept, questioned the legal grounds for the trial and challenged the activities of the king's ministers, who were interfering in what ought to be strictly a Church matter.

On April 7, Peter of Bologna led his delegation into the hearing chamber and put forward the Templars' case for survival. His presentation was a fierce and fearless demolition of everything that had been done by the king and his men since Friday, October 13, 1307.

Every single piece of evidence gathered by the commissioners, he argued, should be tossed out, as the Templars who had incriminated themselves "will have spoken . . . under compulsion, force or corruption, persuasion, bribery or from fear." In the future, he asked that no layperson—and here the names of William of Nogaret and William of Plaisians hung unspoken in the air—should be present at any Templar interrogation "nor any person whom they might rightly fear . . . since all brothers in general are so struck by fear and terror that it is not surprising how some tell lies." Nowhere but in France, said Peter, could any Templar brother be found "who tells or has told these lies." Those who tried to tell the truth "have suffered and are suffering daily in prisons so many tortures, punishments, tribulations, hardships, insults, calamities and miseries, with only their conscience to drive them on."[6]

Peter then recounted the Templars' foundation story: they were an order "developed in the charity and love of true brotherhood . . . without the filth or dirt of any vice. There is and always has been a strong monastic discipline [and] a strong observance for our salvation." Reception to the order was no perverted rite of sexualized blasphemy: "Whoever enters this order promises four essentials, namely obedience, chastity, poverty and the deployment of all his strength in the service of the Holy Land . . . He is received with the pure kiss of peace, takes his habit with the cross which he wears permanently on his breast . . . and is taught to observe the rule and ancient customs handed down to them by the Roman Church and the holy fathers."

The allegations against them were "as impossible as they are obscene . . . false and mendacious." Those who told them "are motivated by zealous cupidity and the ardour of jealousy." They had been proposed by "liars and corruptors," and only confirmed through brothers' testimony because the brothers "were forced by death threats to make confessions that went against their consciences."

Peter declared the commission illegal, and complained that his brothers remained in fear for their lives, unable to retract their false confessions since they were told daily that this would make them relapsed heretics, good for nothing but the agonies of the stake and a public bonfire. "Retraction, they say, inevitably means being burnt." He had promised at the start of his speech that the Templars intended to appear before the Council of Vienne (the meeting scheduled for October 1310 where Clement V would make final judgment on the case) to put the case for their survival before the pope. Were they to do so, given the limp results from Inquisitions in other realms, they would have a very good case.

Neither the influx of Templars to Paris nor their solid legal representation before the commission was at all pleasing to Philip IV. More vexing still was the fact that on April 4 Pope Clement had postponed the Council of Vienne, pushing it back a year to October 1311, owing to the time it had taken to fully gather evidence. The trial of the Templars had been initiated with a lightning raid at dawn; over the years their ordeal had turned into an endless twilight. Decisive intervention was required.

The government began to cherry-pick who would be allowed to give evidence in Paris. Soft witnesses were brought before the commission to repeat the usual slanders, amplifying the grotesque wherever they could: obscene kisses now shifted from navels to anuses. The king also sought a second round of legal opinion from the University of Paris, to confirm his right to cleanse the Church in his realm.[7] Then he shifted to the tactic that had always served him best: intimidation.

While the papal commission wrestled with the Templars' spirited defense, many of the brothers who had come to testify were still under personal investigation for heresies and blasphemy. With this in mind the king turned to the ecclesiastical investigation covering the city of Paris, which lay in the diocese of Sens and was overseen by Archbishop Philip of Marigny, the brother of one of Philip's closest councillors.

In the second week of May, the archbishop proceeded suddenly to a final judgment of fifty-four Templars who had been investigated before his local inquiry, but were now in Paris backing the Templars' defense of their order as a whole. His intention was to point to the discrepancies between the confessions they had given to the episcopal inquiry and the evidence the same brothers had given before the papal commission, to demonstrate that the witnesses were effectively relapsed heretics.

Gilles Aycelin immediately absented himself from his own hearings in disgust. His commission continued to sit without him, but on the morning of Tuesday, May 12, 1310, they were interrupted by a messenger who informed them that the fifty-four Templars of Sens who had given evidence to them had indeed been found to be relapsed heretics and were to be burned at the stake without delay. Despite frantic efforts by Peter of Bologna and his fellow procurators to launch a legal challenge, the royal will now trampled over due process. The Templars of Sens were all gathered together by the king's officers, strapped to wagons and taken through the streets of Paris to a field on the outskirts where dozens of stakes and pyres had been set up. Every one of them was burned alive.

In a single furious act, the king had crushed the Templars' resistance. Reginald of Provins was from Sens, and although he was not one of the fifty-four who were reduced to ashes on May 12, the implication was that he still might be. To continue his resistance would be a death sentence.

Peter of Bologna had complained bitterly to the commissioners of witness intimidation; now the king showed what intimidation really looked like: Peter of Bologna simply disappeared. The commission was told flatly that he had escaped from the cell where he was being held at night. He was never seen again. The Templars' legal defense dissolved and rank-and-file resistance broke down. Within weeks, volunteers had stopped coming forward to defend the order, while a stream of witnesses appeared to repeat the well-worn confessions with which the whole sorry episode had begun. Hearings continued for months as the commissioners continued to probe for evidence that the order was institutionally heretical. Little was added to the evidence previously compiled beyond the exotic fantasies of terrified men hoping to escape a fiery death. But the weight of confession quickly became damning. On July 5, 1311, the commissioners were called to Pointoise for an audience with Philip IV. He told them to stop work. They had quite enough material. The paperwork was forwarded to Clement V, to be considered at the Council of Vienne in October.

✝

Outside France, the prosecution of the Templars varied sharply, according to the preoccupations and character of the ruler in question. Nowhere was this more apparent than in England, where Edward II had come to the throne in July 1307, just three months before the mass arrests in France. His first reaction to the accusations leveled at the order was ridicule. This was rather in keeping with his character: occasionally clear-sighted but often politically quite stupid. Twenty-three at the time of his accession, Edward was betrothed to Philip IV's daughter Isabella. Some might have counseled discretion, but on receiving the news of the Templars' arrests Edward wrote immediately to the kings of Aragón, Navarre, Castile, Portugal and Naples, telling them the allegations were absurd and that they should be careful what they believed. He had complied with *Pastoralis Praeeminentiae* only reluctantly, and when one hundred and forty-four English Templars (only fifteen of whom were knights) were arrested in January 1308, the sheriffs who made the arrests were warned not to put the brothers into "hard and vile" prisons.[8] The English master William de la More was allowed good rooms in Canterbury, a daily spending allowance and several servants, and he could wander the town as he pleased. Later in the same month Edward traveled to France to marry Philip's daughter, but even when he returned he showed no great interest in carrying out the persecutions his new father-in-law wished to see.

What eventually changed Edward's attitude toward the Templars was shallow self-interest. Although he married Isabella of France in Boulogne in January 1308, he did not much care for her. He was far more interested in an older friend from his youth by the name of Piers Gaveston. The king and Gaveston formed a very obnoxious couple in the eyes of the

English political class, and in May a coalition of English bishops and nobles forced the king to exile his favorite to Ireland, on pain of excommunication if he returned. From this point everything in Edward's life became secondary to bringing Gaveston safely home. The backing of Clement V, who had the power to lift Gaveston's suspended excommunication, became suddenly important—and Edward's Templar policy changed accordingly. In November Edward ordered the rearrest of all the Templars in England who had been allowed to live in relative freedom. This had exactly the desired effect. By spring 1309 Gaveston's excommunication had been canceled and by June he was home, much to the displeasure of Edward's barons. In September Edward allowed two papal inquisitors into his realm to begin investigating Templar malpractice.

The order in England was still not battered as roughly it had been in France. In part this was because the whole concept of Inquisition was foreign to the English, whose legal system was built around the testimony of juries, not on confessions wheedled out of agonized suspects. Torture was not widely practiced and on the few occasions when it was suggested during the inquiry into the Templars, it mostly failed. Three centers of investigation were set up, in London, Lincoln and York, and almost every brother who came before the papal delegates denied every charge on the long list put before them. The worst that could be wrung out of most was a mistaken belief that when a brother was flogged for breaking one of the order's rules, the master's subsequent grant of forgiveness was a holy absolution and not an internal declaration of a disciplinary case being closed. This was small beer indeed.

Proceedings continued against the Templars until the summer of 1311, during which time the French inquisitors wrote letters expressing their frustration and wondering whether they could carry out extraordinary rendition: taking all their prisoners to the French county of Ponthieu (held by Edward II but owing its ultimate feudal loyalty to Philip IV), where they could be properly interrogated. In the end all these efforts amounted to nothing. There was a brief flurry of excitement when a pair of runaways were caught and attempted to buy their way out of trouble by admitting they had denied Christ at their receptions, but in the end this came to very little. The inquiry broke up with most brothers sent off to monasteries, some to do penance for minor sins and others simply to be adopted into different religious orders. Only the two highest-ranking suspects faced any serious punishment, more for their status than their deeds. William de la More, the master in England, was sent to the Tower of London, and died in 1312 still awaiting absolution from the pope. Imbert Blanke, preceptor for Auvergne, who had managed to flee arrest in France by skipping across the channel in 1307, was also jailed. He probably died in custody some time after 1314. Neither had admitted to any wrongdoing. Edward II took control of Templar lands for more than ten years, adding the revenues of their estates, once catalogued so diligently by Master Geoffrey Fitz Stephen, to the royal coffers, until in 1324 they were taken over by the Hospitallers. It was a quiet and unspectacular death.

Elsewhere the pattern of proceedings varied according to the local conditions. In Ireland the inquisitors proceeded in lackadaisical fashion, performing only perfunctory interviews and pensioning off the brothers in 1312 without even requiring them to join another order. On the Spanish peninsula the Templars were more of a fighting force than in France or England, and this was a major consideration in their arrest. King James II was as doubtful as Edward, and like Edward he initially resisted acting against them. In the five years preceding the arrests in France James had actually been helping the order to build up its landholdings in his other kingdom of Valencia.[9] However, their military capability in Aragón soon became a reason for their effective destruction. Once the arrests began in France, the Aragónese Templars began to prepare for an attack: stockpiling goods, converting their wealth into gold for easy transportation and reinforcing their numerous castles. James was not naturally hostile to the order, but the prospect of fortresses being held against the Crown was unacceptable. Over the new year of 1308 he arrested the local master and started besieging Templar bases. One angry brother cursed James II for his ingratitude, recounting the number of times that the Templars had given their lives in service to the kingdom of Aragón. James took no notice. A small civil war ensued as royal forces surrounded Templar strongholds in Miravet, Monzón, Asco and several other fortresses originally built for holy war against the Moors. It took the king months to starve the last of the defenders from their boltholes: the huge castles at Monzón (where James's grandfather had been raised under Templar guardianship) and Chalamera only surrendered in July 1309.

Prisoners were taken and some were tortured, although the practice was found to be as ineffective in Aragón as it was in England. No Aragónese Templars admitted to any serious wrongdoing, and in 1312, proceedings against the order were abandoned without a single confession having been extracted.[10] The brothers were sent off with pensions to live as men of religion in monastic houses and their property was divided up between the king, the Hospitallers and a new military order based at Montesa in Valencia, who modeled themselves on the Order of Calatrava. The Order of the Temple was soon nothing more than a memory.

In Castile-León the Templars were examined and found innocent in 1310. No serious scandal was unearthed in Mallorca. In the various Italian states there was only passing interest in proceeding against the Templars. While some brothers admitted to the usual gamut of indiscretions, from walking on crucifixes to sodomy and idol worship, the convulsions caused were relatively small, and in regions such as the northwest of Italy the investigators forbade torture and actively tried to prove the innocence of their captives.[11] In Sicily the authorities were largely uninterested in persecuting the brothers, and although there were arrests and trials, these produced unsalacious findings and appear to have involved only a small number of brothers, none of whom lost his life.[12]

Likewise in Germany, individual rulers took limited action against the order's members, but without great enthusiasm. The farther northeast one traveled through Christendom, the fewer Templars there were to be found. The German principalities were far more heavily populated by the Teutonic Order. There was one novelty to the movement against the Templars in Germany, which concerned the nuns of a house in Mühlen. Since 1272 their nunnery had been officially owned and governed by the order, an arrangement brokered by the Bishop of Worms, who was likely influenced by the fact that the Teutonic Order admitted women as full sisters away from the front line. When the Templars were wound up, the nuns of Mühlen were forcibly transferred to membership of the Hospitallers, although they were not happy about it and complained about their treatment.[13]

In Cyprus as in Aragón the Templars presented a real military force as well as an alleged spiritual menace. Since the early summer of 1307 they had been imprisoned in various locations on the island. Nearly three years passed before hearings began on May 5, 1310.[14] Of the one hundred and eighteen Templars originally arrested, only seventy-six were by then alive and fit to answer questions. More than half of these were knights— a far greater ratio than in the West, where only one in ten were of knightly rank. Every Templar to a man flatly denied the whole list of allegations. All they would say was that there had been an entirely proper kiss of peace to welcome each new member. They affirmed that normal Templar procedure meant that chapter meetings were secret affairs closed to outsiders.

To widen the inquiry, evidence was also heard from fifty-six non-Templar witnesses, including some of the island's loftiest figures: Philip of Ibelin, the royal seneschal; Rupen of Montfort, the titular lord of Beirut; the bishop of Beirut and two abbots. These men crossed the sharp political divide between Henry II and his brother Amalric, who had deposed the king and exiled him to Armenia. All of them swore to the probity and upstanding character of the Templars. Many noted that they had seen the Templars take Communion, and distribute large amounts of alms to the poor: "bread, meats and sometimes money, and this every week."[15] The character witnesses could not have been more glowing. The testimony was shot through with a deep-rooted pride in and affection for the order, which for all its faults was held in high esteem on the front line of the war against Islam. One witness, John of Norris, treasurer of Limassol and canon of Paphos, recounted that there was a common saying among Cypriots that went, "I will defend you in the manner of the Templars, whether you are right or wrong."[16]

✝

The Council of Vienne opened in October 1311 and issued its judgment on March 22, 1312. Many of the senior clerics who attended from all across Christendom—including four patriarchs, twenty cardinals and scores of archbishops and bishops—were skeptical of the accusations leveled against the Templars, and demanded to hear their defense. This was not in itself unreasonable, but weighed against their outrage was the nearby presence of the king of France, who kept an army twenty miles away in Lyon, and wrote letters to the pope demanding the Templars' suppression and the creation of a new order that could resume the fight against the infidel. The message was clear: Clement V had to make his choice. He could either suffer the fate of Boniface VIII or accept the truth that had burdened him ever since the papal tiara had landed on his head in 1305: he was a French pope, and in the end he would do the bidding of the French king.

The decision regarding the Templars was summed up in a papal bull known as *Vox in Excelso* ("A Voice on High"). Framing his words in biblical quotations drawn from the Old Testament, Clement summarized the Templar affair from the beginning. He described how the Church had honored and respected the Temple, but "against the Lord Jesus Christ himself . . . they fell into the sin of impious apostasy, the abominable vice of idolatry, the deadly crime of the Sodomites and various heresies." The pope fawned to Philip IV, "our dear son in Christ," who "had no intention of claiming or appropriating for himself anything from the Templars' property . . . he was on fire with zeal for the orthodox faith, following in the well-marked footsteps of his ancestors." The list of misdeeds and blasphemies was repeated and summed up with the allegation that "the master, preceptors, and other brothers of the order as well as the order itself had been involved in these and other crimes," all of which were proved by the many confessions the inquisitors had compiled. Clement mentioned specifically the confessions made at Chinon by James of Molay, Hugh of Pairaud, Raimbaud of Caron and their colleagues and noted that they had been granted absolution. Then he announced his final decision.

"These confessions render the order very suspect," he wrote. "The infamy and suspicion render it detestable to the holy Church of God, to her prelates, to kings and other rulers and to Catholics in general. It is also believed that in all probability from now on there will be no good person who wishes to enter the order, and so it will be made useless to the Church of God and the carrying on of the undertaking to the Holy Land."

The Templars were not given the chance to defend themselves at Vienne, and although fanciful rumors circulated that two thousand of them were on the outskirts of the city waiting to barge their way into the conference hall, nothing of the sort occurred. They had gone undefended and largely unseen at the very gathering that decided their fate. In *Vox in Excelso* the pope worked his way deftly around this blatant injustice, arguing that to delay his decision for enough time to hear counterarguments would have caused Templar possessions to fall into ruin and their usefulness to the crusading mission to be impaired. No good would come from more procrastination. "Therefore with a sad heart . . . we suppress, with the approval of the sacred council, the Order of the Templars, and its rule, habit and name, by an inviolable and perpetual decree, and we entirely forbid that anyone from now on enter the order, or receive or wear its habit, or presume to behave as a Templar. If anyone acts otherwise he incurs automatic excommunication."[17]

With the stroke of a scribe's pen, and the application of the papal seal, the Order of the Temple, which had existed for one hundred and ninety-two years, was abolished. The only small victory, if it could be seen as such, was that its property was not given to Philip IV, but reserved by the pope "for our disposition and that of the apostolic see." Neither was there any mention of merging the military orders. In May 1312 it was decided that Templar property would be granted to the Hospitallers, to support their mission in the East. This was only partially good news for the Hospitallers. While in theory they gained huge tranches of property across two thousand miles, the legal wrangling required to secure their claims to their new bounty tied them up for more than a decade.

In the Spanish peninsula the Templars' lands were to be carved up between the secular rulers, the Hospitallers and the new military order based at Montesa in Aragón. In all likelihood the silver in the Templar treasury in Paris disappeared into the king's mints, but Philip was never able to perpetrate a full land grab, nor to assume for himself or his sons the role of crusader king in charge of a unified military order. His victory was strictly personal: he had triumphed over an organization that he had convinced himself was riddled with secrecy, heresy, filth, fornication, blasphemy, carnality and evil.

With Templar properties parceled up, hundreds of prisoners needed to be rehabilitated or rehomed. The unrepentant were given a life sentence in prison, but many had voiced their supposed crimes and been granted forgiveness. These men were sent to live in other monastic institutions, supported by pensions paid by the papal court at Avignon. For the most part their lives would not have been so different from their existence in a Templar house. In areas where the Templars had been on active military duty, they were sometimes able to continue their work in a new guise. In Portugal in 1319 a new order was founded: the Order of Christ, which subsumed Templar properties and in some cases re-dressed Templar soldiers in new uniforms and allowed them to continue manning former Templar castles and participating in the holy war against the Moors.

A few stray Templars were untouched by the dissolution of the order altogether. The German chronicler Ludolph of Sudheim came across two old men wandering in Palestine in 1340, claiming to be Templars who had fallen into Mamluk hands with the fall of Acre in 1291.[18]

In the Muslim world the disappearance of the Templars was far from the cause for celebration that it would have been had Saladin managed to wipe out the order with his parade of beheadings in the aftermath of Hattin. Templars had not been seen in the Holy Land for a generation. In effect, they had been wiped out long ago.

For all of their martial renown, the Templars put up remarkably little fight. But some could not simply be paid to wear a new habit and forgotten. In 1310 James of Molay, Hugh of Pairaud, Geoffrey of Charney and Geoffrey of Gonneville had been moved from Chinon to Gisors, a huge castle north of the Seine, halfway between Paris and Rouen. (Raimbaud of Caron seems to have died in prison in Chinon.) At his final appearances before the commissioners investigating his order, James had thrown himself pathetically on the mercy of the pope—a tactic he had clung to throughout the ordeal, which had ultimately paid no dividend whatever. Neither would it after the order was dissolved.

In December 1313 Clement turned his attention to the master and his three surviving colleagues. They had hoped to appeal to him in person, but Clement had evidently seen quite enough of the Templars. He appointed in his place a panel of cardinals to examine the four brothers. Arnaud Novelli, Arnaud d'Auch and Nicholas of Fréauville would bear the responsibility of hearing one last round of evidence and deciding their sentence.

On March 18, 1314, a crowd gathered around a raised platform set up outside the Cathedral of Notre Dame in Paris, to see these elderly men, who had once commanded the most famous military order in the world, sentenced for their role in its collapse. Among the crowd was Philip of Marigny, the archbishop of Sens whose episocopal inquiry had sent fifty-four Templars to their deaths. The three cardinals in their wide-brimmed hats inspected the accused and announced what penalty they were to suffer.

The continuator of a chronicle by the monk of Saint-Denis known as William of Nangis recorded that he had seen James of Molay and his colleagues examined that day. They were briefly questioned and all four stood by their confessions. They had been absolved of their sins, but their penances were to be exemplary and severe. "They were adjudged to be taken into hard, perpetual imprisonment," wrote the chronicler.[19]

For James of Molay, who had been in prison for six and a half years, this was too much. At one of his examinations before papal commissioners he had recalled his experience as a young man, when he had been sent to the Holy Land to fight the Saracens, and found himself chafing against the then master William of Beaujeu, whose only wish was to hold the peace. He had been frustrated then, and the frustration had continued ever since. In fact, James's entire career had been a succession of disappointments, culminating in a trial in which he had been forced to confess to deeds that disgraced his name, imperiled his soul and destroyed the order to which he had given himself. Now he was told he would live out his days in stony solitude, and die a perjured failure.

To the shock of the audience before him, he decided to speak out. As one of the cardinals was lecturing the crowd, James interrupted him and began to argue again for his innocence. Geoffrey of Charney joined him, decrying the injustice both men had suffered. They berated the cardinal and the archbishop of Sens, "and without any respect began to deny everything they had confessed."[20]

Behind James and Geoffrey of Charney, Hugh of Pairaud and Geoffrey of Gonneville kept quiet. Each man understood what was happening. To stay silent was to accept the sentence of imprisonment. To speak was to condemn oneself to the flames as a relapsed heretic. The crowd stood stunned. A stage-managed spectacle had taken an unexpected and unwanted turn. James of Molay continued to rave about his innocence until a sergeant standing by stepped forward, "and struck [the master] across the mouth so that he might speak no further, and he was dragged by his hair into a chapel."[21]

Whatever due process ought to have taken place was jettisoned. Geoffrey of Charney was hauled off with James of Molay. The intention was for both to be held "until they could deliberate more fully over them the next day." But word soon spread through the city of the scenes at Notre Dame, and within hours the news had reached Philip IV. His patience was exhausted. "He consulted with his own advisers," wrote the chronicler, "and without speaking of it to the clergy, made a prudent decision to have the two Templars consigned to the flames."[22]

As evening fell on March 18, the master of the Temple and the preceptor of Normandy were taken in a little boat to an island in the river Seine known as the Île-des-Javiaux, not far from the gardens of the royal palace. Two pyres stood waiting, the wood already smoldering.

The Templar of Tyre heard an eyewitness account from a merchant who was in Paris that March and who saw what happened on the island. "The master begged them to suffer him to say his prayers, which he did say to God," he wrote. "Then his body was bound over to the working of their will."[23]

Another French chronicler recorded in verse the last minutes of the two Templars, and described a calm scene in which James of Molay stripped to his underclothes without shivering or showing any signs of being afraid. As he was tied to the stake he asked to be allowed a prayer. He added: "God knows who is in the wrong and has sinned. Soon misfortune will come to those who have wrongly condemned us: God will avenge our death." Then he said he was ready to die. The flames were stoked, the wood crackled, and before long James of Molay was gone. "So gently did death take him," wrote the poet, "that everyone marveled."[24] All that was left of the last master of the Order of the Poor Knights of the Temple was the curse that had spilled from his lips in the moments before he died.

✠

Hugh of Pairaud and Geoffrey of Gonneville died in prison many years after the violent events in Paris. Geoffrey of Charney was also burned on March 18, and it was alternately reported that his bones and James of

Molay's were either saved for relics or burned and the ashes scattered. The Templar master's hope that God would avenge his death could have meant anything, but it appeared to have some effect. The two men who had done most to destroy the Templars—Philip IV of France and Pope Clement V—were dead within the year. Clement's health had never been good and in April he died of his long-standing intestinal complaint. Philip, who was only forty-six, suffered a fatal stroke while hunting in 1314 and was buried near his saintly predecessor Louis IX in Saint-Denis.

Had either of them gained anything from the destruction of the order of the Temple? It was probably true that in 1306 the Templars and the Hospitallers were ripe for reform and amalgamation. Robbed of their purpose after the fall of Acre, they had been sustained for two decades by the ambition of a new crusade, refusing like many others to accept the reality of the drastically changed situation in the East following the arrival of the Mongols and the Mamluk conquests. In that sense Clement had contributed, albeit in a ham-fisted and unnecessarily destructive fashion, to the redirection of Christian resources. Beyond that there was little to recommend in his conduct. When Dante Alighieri completed the *Divine Comedy* in 1320, his readers found Clement in hell, being roasted feetfirst upside down. Dante described Clement as a "lawless shepherd from the west" who had bought his position and been dealt with "softly" by the king of France.[25]

Philip, meanwhile, had proven himself repeatedly throughout his reign to be cold, cruel and willfully antagonistic toward any individual or group from whom he perceived the smallest slight toward his royal majesty or his self-image as the "most Christian king." Shortly before his death he turned his moralizing paranoia on his own family. Needled by rumors that the wives of two of his sons were having adulterous affairs with a pair of Norman knights in a riverside watchtower known as the Tour de Nesle, he had all of them arrested, as well as his third son's wife, who was believed to have some knowledge of the case. The knights were tortured, interrogated relentlessly and brutally executed in public; his daughters-in-law were imprisoned for life.

The Tour de Nesle scandal brought Philip nothing but misery. It was nearly identical in its methods to the persecution of Pope Boniface, the

French Jews and the Templars, all of which bound together the Crown's need for new sources of revenue with the king's desire to stamp the authority of the Crown over new parts of his kingdom and his extraordinary ability to convince himself of the foulest moral deviance in anyone who crossed his path. Even by the standards of his day he was a violent prig, and the best that can be said of his conduct is that the Templars were only one group of victims among many.

Between October 13, 1307, and March 18, 1314, the Templars were comprehensively crushed. Their property was impounded. Their wealth was taken. Their reputation was shredded. Their members were imprisoned, tortured, killed, ejected from their homes and humiliated. Those who survived this process either died in prison, were uprooted and sent to new homes or in a few rare cases redeployed to new military orders. Despite colorful myths of their survival as a secret society, by the third decade of the fourteenth century the order had ceased to exist in any meaningful sense. The Templar central archive, their most valuable possession in the East after their treasury, was preserved on Cyprus and taken over by the Hospitallers, but it was subsequently lost, most likely in the sixteenth century when Cyprus was conquered by the Ottomans. So in the end, the Templars' bodies were taken by the French monarchy that had done so much to help establish the order and their memories were swallowed up by an Islamic enemy they had first been banded together to resist. "They were the fiercest fighters of all the Franks," wrote Ibn al-Athir, who knew the order in its prime. In the end they could simply fight no more.

+

The crusades in which the Templars had played a leading role did not end with the order's disappearance. The idea of sanctified war was deeply ingrained in the minds of Europe's faithful, and even if it had become practically impossible to raise the sorts of armies that had marched on Jerusalem, Damascus and Damietta between 1096 and 1250, the dream of reconquering the Holy Land lived on. So did the willingness of the Roman Church to curry favor with secular rulers by allowing them to beg crusade status for their border wars and assaults on various "pagans" on the fringes of Europe.

In Spain the Reconquista continued throughout the fourteenth and fifteenth centuries, during which a significant Muslim presence remained in the emirate of Granada—technically a vassal state of the kingdom of Castile but in practice a proudly independent Muslim realm. Moments of Castilian weakness or war with the neighboring kingdoms of Aragón and Portugal generally caused flare-ups of violence emanating from Granada. These kept the military orders of Calatrava and Santiago engaged in garrisoning castles and guarding the mountain passes in the borderlands between Christian and Muslim territory. The emirate of Granada was only destroyed after King Ferdinand V of Aragón married Queen Isabella of Castile in 1479, joining their two great kingdoms and presenting a united front against the Nasrid ruler Muhammad XII. Piece by piece the two "Catholic monarchs" began to dismantle the emirate and in January 1492 Muhammad was driven out of his Alhambra palace in the capital city of Granada, never to return.

Beyond Spain, plans abounded to regain a Christian footing in the Holy Land, but few ever came to anything more than excited plans written by men who had more ideas than experience and had never seen a Mamluk in their lives. In 1318 Philip IV's son and successor, Philip V, envisaged a noble-led mission to Outremer under his cousin Louis of Clermont, whom he appointed "captain, leader and governor-general of all the men at arms whom we dispatch before the general passage by land or by sea for the assistance of the Holy Land."[26] A few years later the Venetian geographer Marino Sanudo Torsello presented Pope John XXII with a massive book, complete with detailed maps and charts of the Syrian and Egyptian coast, all illustrating his complex idea for a mass blockade, sea invasion and land march on the Nile Delta, with participants coming from Genoa, Venice, Crete, Rhodes, Cyprus and Armenia, which required five thousand knights merely to hold a sea blockade during the first military phase of operations.[27] Needless to say, the crusade never took place.

As the Middle Ages advanced, the crusading spirit found new targets. During the 1330s and 1340s naval leagues were formed between Venetians, Cypriots and the Hospitallers to attack various Turkish Mediterranean ports. Between 1362 and 1369 King Peter I of Cyprus organized recruiting tours of Europe to raise crusader armies, piled them onto ships, then used them to sack and in some cases briefly conquer Muslim towns including Adalia and Corycus on the Turkish coast, Alexandria and Rosetta on the Nile Delta, and Sidon, Beirut, Tripoli, Tortosa and Latakia in the Mamluk empire. When the Western Church fell into schism in 1378, with rival popes elected in Avignon and Rome, each side recruited kings and nobles and declared their war on the opposite faction to be a crusade. Military campaigns in Bohemia against followers of the Czech spiritual leader Jan Hus were granted crusade status between 1420 and 1431.

Northeast Europe had become another thriving theater of Christian warfare, and much of the work here was done by the Teutonic Order. In 1309 they established their official headquarters in Marienburg, in the middle of a huge, all but autonomous Prussian state, their territories stretching hundreds of miles through northern Poland into Livonia. Their ostensible purpose was to aid the conversion of pagans, and the chronicle of their official historian-knight, Wigand of Marburg, abounds with stories of *Reisen*—minicrusades against localized enemies. A typical entry from 1344 explains that the then master Ludolf König allied with William, Count of Holland, and "entered Lithuania, which he devastated for two days, inflicting a great deal of damage there, for the land was fertile. But because of the flooding caused by the snow melting and the ice breaking up he was forced to leave."[28] This was the story of much of the fourteenth century. Soon after, the order's fortunes began to wane. Rather too successful in conversion and conquest, they ran short of pagan enemies to attack and instead fell to bickering with their Christian neighbors. Prussia developed into one of the great states of modern Europe, but it was by that stage out of Teutonic hands. By the beginning of the sixteenth century they held only a rump of territories in the Holy Roman Empire. They were formally dissolved as a military order by Napoleon Bonaparte in 1809 and today exist only as a small religious order of Catholic priests and nuns who offer care to expatriate Germans in various countries—a decline almost to their origins at the first siege of Acre of 1191.

Enriched with Templar possessions, albeit weighed down by the complexity of laying claim to all of them, the Hospitallers survived as the

Templars had not. Crucial to their successful transition was their conquest of Rhodes, a large island at the far south of the Dodecanese, with shipping links to Constantinople, Cyprus, Beirut and Alexandria. They governed the island from a fortified harbor town and acquired a small chain of nearby islands including Kos and Leros. The order remained there for more than two centuries, involved in the busy trade of the Aegean Sea and occasionally joining Italian adventurers in military raids on Turkish ports like Smyrna on the west coast of Asia Minor. But by the fifteenth century Rhodes itself had become a valuable prize, and the Hospitallers were forced to repel seaborne invasions, first by Mamluk forces in the 1440s and then by a new Islamic superpower, the Ottoman Empire, which rose like so many empires before it from Turkish tribal lands south of the Black Sea, sweeping away the Mamluks and eventually conquering Asia Minor, Greece, Serbia, Macedonia, Bosnia, Hungary, Syria, Palestine and Egypt. The Hospitallers' time on Rhodes came to an end when the Ottoman sultan Suleiman the Magnificent pushed northwest toward Greece and Constantinople in 1522 and blasted the Hospitallers of Rhodes into submission with an armada said to have comprised more than four hundred ships carrying one hundred thousand men.

Remarkably, the Hospitallers were still not wiped out, and in 1530 Charles II of Spain awarded them a new base on the island of Malta, from where they were ejected by Napoleon in 1798–99. Today the Hospitallers still exist. The Sovereign Military Hospitaller Order of Saint John of Jerusalem of Rhodes and of Malta (or simply the Knights of Malta) is a Catholic order based in Rome, where it is recognized by international law as a sovereign body with its own anthem, flag, passports and army. Other versions of the order survive in countries including Finland, France, Germany, Hungary, the Netherlands, Sweden and Switzerland. The Hospitaller movement in Britain was reorganized during the nineteenth century in 1888 as the Order of Saint John of Jerusalem and granted a royal charter by Queen Victoria. Today it is a Christian order, predominantly Protestant and subject to the authority of the Crown. Its members are invited to join by merit and are sworn to uphold the charitable works that the order carries out. Its dependent organizations include St. John Ambulance, which provides voluntary first aid.

• • • • •

In 1530 the Dutch scholar Erasmus prepared a Latin tract called the *Consultatio de Bello Turcis Infirendo* ("On the Question of Waging War on the Turks"). As he wrote, Suleiman the Magnificent's armies occupied large swaths of the Balkans, Hungary, Bulgaria and Romania. The previous year they had besieged Vienna, and a new Islamic empire appeared to be heading relentlessly westward.

As an enlightened, humanist thinker this presented Erasmus with several problems. He despised populist bigotry, warning that "when the ignorant masses hear the Turks mentioned, they immediately become incensed and bloodthirsty, labeling them as dogs and enemies of the Christian name. . . . They do not consider whether the war's cause is just and whether it is expedient to take up arms, which will exasperate the enemy and make him more vicious."[29] He also noted the violence of the early Reformation, which suggested that "what Christians do to Christians is crueler" than many of the worst evils perpetrated by Muslims.

Yet Erasmus was by no means a pacifist, and he reserved equal scorn for "folk [who] consider the right to wage war to be totally forbidden to Christians . . . this opinion is so absurd it does not need to be rebutted. . . . What I teach is that war should never be undertaken except as a last resort, all else having failed." Of course the Ottomans were a danger, he wrote, and he went on to consider at length the philosophical justifications for war, the corruption that had bedeviled crusading in centuries gone by and his ultimate belief that the best route to peace between Islam and the West was through converting unbelievers to the path of Jesus Christ.

In the middle of his essay Erasmus mentioned, almost as an aside, the lost ideal of the Christian warrior, who was sorely missed in such a time of trouble and confusion. This was the ultimate crusader-type whose example men of the sixteenth century could only dream of matching.

He called them "those soldiers whom Saint Bernard describes, whom he doesn't know whether to call monks or knights, so great was their moral probity and their warrior courage."[30]

The Templars were long gone. But so long as crusading continued, they would have a place in men's imaginations.

Epilogue: The Holy Grail

B ETWEEN 1200 AND 1210 the German writer Wolfram von Eschenbach composed a romantic poem called *Parzival*. Tens of thousands of lines long, it drew on the legends of King Arthur, which had been wildly popular across Europe for decades. These stories delighted aristocratic audiences with tales of love, chivalry, questing, betrayal, magic and combat. Eschenbach's patron was one Hermann, landgrave of Thurangia, but the readership his work eventually found was enormous and its influence immense. More than eighty medieval manuscripts of the poem still survive.

In *Parzival*, the eponymous young hero appears at Arthur's court and straightaway becomes embroiled in a dispute with a "red knight," whom he kills in a fight. After going away to learn to be more chivalrous, Parzival embarks on a search for the Holy Grail: both a literal hunt for a mysterious, life-giving stone and a spiritual journey toward enlightenment in God. The Grail is initially guarded in a magical castle by a character called the Fisher King, who is in constant pain from a wound to his leg, divine punishment for his failure to remain chaste.

Parzival meets the Fisher King, then becomes sidetracked by other escapades. Eventually, after fighting a knight who turns out to be his own brother, he learns that he himself has become the new king destined to guard the Grail, and the story eventually draws to a close.

Much of *Parzival*, as written by Eschenbach, was unoriginal. Earlier writers such as Geoffrey of Monmouth and Chrétien de Troyes had already established the world he described and provided many of the plots. Eschenbach was essentially updating, expanding the characters' adventures and giving the tales a flavor which he thought his own readers (and listeners, for many would have heard the poems read aloud in their lords' halls) would enjoy. One of the ingredients he added was the appearance of a military order called the *Templeise*, warriors sworn to chastity who help the Fisher King keep watch in their "temple" over the Holy Grail.

These men were not identical to Templars: their symbol was a turtledove rather than the crusaders' cross, and they did not appear to have a developed rule. All the same, the resemblance was striking and the story proved to be enduring. The Templars had been transformed for the first time from a crusader militia into the guardians of the mythical Holy Grail.*

That writers were beginning to fictionalize the Templars even in their own times was not surprising. By the first decade of the thirteenth century the order was well known. Although it did not have much of a presence in Germany, where Eschenbach lived, anyone with a passing interest in the Holy Land could not fail to have heard of the Templars' deeds. They had clashed with Saladin, starred in Richard the Lionheart's crusade, manned dozens of castles in the Holy Land, become bound up in the Reconquista, put down a presence at most of the royal courts in Europe, acquired estates all over Christendom and made powerful enemies. It was not much of a jump to become a literary trope as well.

In a sense, the order had always existed in two spheres, the real and the imaginary. The idea of the Templars was otherwordly right from the start. When Bernard of Clairvaux wrote *De Laude*, exalting the first generation of knights in the 1130s, he was not composing a factual account of Hugh of Payns and his men. Through his soaring language, the idealized moral character of the knights and the biblical literalism of the Holy Land he described, Bernard was overlaying the reality of the Templars with his own dreams for an order of men who swung swords like warriors but lived like Cistercians.

Chroniclers who described the Templars before their fall also had their own agendas. On the Muslim side there were those who admired the Templars' military skill, and painted the brothers as the least depraved of the accursed Franks. Usama ibn Munqidh portrayed the order as open-minded, worldly and chivalrous, noting that they had allowed him to use one of their churches in Jerusalem for his daily prayers. But less than a decade later, when Saladin ordered the execution of every

---

* The Holy Grail, although often assumed to have been a real physical object dating to the Last Supper or Christ's Crucifixion is in fact the invention of late medieval Arthurian romances following Chrétien of Troyes's *Perceval: The Story of the Grail*, which was written in the 1180s.

Templar and Hospitaller captured at Hattin, Imad al-Din described them as "two unclean orders, whose practices are useless, who never give up their hostility and who have no use as slaves. The one and the other are the worst of the infidels." Ibn Munqidh's aim in his storytelling was to place honor and chivalry above the squalor of war, whereas Imad al-Din sought to portray Saladin as the glorious sultan who had defeated the enemies of Islam. The Templars were merely a vehicle for their contrasting preoccupations.

Christian writers of the twelfth and thirteenth centuries were no less divided, and for every Bernard of Clairvaux there was a William of Tyre, whose influential account of the kingdom of Jerusalem under Amalric I and his family imposed a clear shape on the Templar story. William thought the Templars had sprung from a legitimate and noble concept but had been corrupted by wealth, and he selected his material accordingly, overemphasizing the poverty of the order's beginnings to magnify its later missteps, such as the disastrous charge into Ascalon in 1153 or the murder of the Assassin envoy twenty years later.

The author of the *Itinerarium Peregrinorum* (who may have been a Templar) depicted an order of martyrs, embellishing stories of heroic defiance such as that of James of Maillé, killed at the Springs of Cresson, who was given a conventional but inspiring literary afterlife as a miracle worker. The so-called Templar of Tyre (who almost certainly was not a Templar) occupied a middle ground. He had great personal affection for William of Beaujeu, whose death at the fall of Acre was rendered in epic and heroic terms, but thought James of Molay an arrogant fool and recorded his appalling death in Paris in 1314 with disinterest bordering on disdain.

For better or worse the Templars had been adopted by writers and storytellers long before they were crushed by Philip IV, in depictions that ranged from the realistic to the outlandish. A cartoon of knights on the charge survives in a fresco at the twelfth-century Templar chapel in Cressac-sur-Charente in southwest France: here brothers are shown at their most militant and heroic, doing battle with a Muslim army. Matthew Paris's *Chronica Majora*, written some decades later, contains a more peaceful sketch of two brothers on horseback beside their famous black-and-white flag. Templars appeared in works like *Raoul de Cambrai;*

in the multiauthored *Roman de la Rose*, a dream vision poem completed around 1275 on the theme of courtly love; and in *Sone de Nansai*, a romance from the late thirteenth century, in which a Templar in Ireland acts as a matchmaker between a Norwegian warrior and a lovelorn queen. Only rarely—as in *Parzival* and *Sone*—did the Templars play unconventional roles: ordinarily they were typecast warriors of a fairly rigid probity, or else a destination for heroes and villains who could be removed from the action of the plot by joining the order in the Holy Land.

Even in their own day the Templars were of vastly more interest to writers of fiction than the Hospitallers and Teutonic Order. The Templars' rivals long outlasted them in both their martial and pastoral roles, but they have left nothing like the same impression in the popular imagination. No one, either in the Middle Ages or today, has seemed very interested in epic poetry (still less Hollywood movies) about the Teutonic Order or the Sword Brothers of Livonia. Only the Templars can really be said to have passed from the realm of reality into mythology and staked a place in the popular imagination.

To be fair, the Templars *were* different from the other major international military orders. Uniquely, from the beginning they were knights who took up a religious calling, rather than servants of a hospital that added a paramilitary wing. This gave them a certain quality that was useful for medieval romance: they corresponded exactly to the archetype of the truly chivalrous men—violent but chaste, tough but pure of heart, merciless but godly. They were the ideal that all knights in Arthurian legend strove toward.

But this is only part of the story, and much of the Templars' enduring popularity must also be attributed to the manner of their fall. Half a century after James of Molay's death, the Florentine poet and storyteller Giovanni Boccaccio composed a book known as *De Casibus Vivorum Illustrium*, a compilation of great men's lives, selected to illustrate the turning of fortune's wheel. This was a literary commonplace in the Middle Ages, a metaphor suggesting that life moved in perpetual flux, with moments of triumph followed by despair (and vice versa). The subjects of Boccaccio's potted biographies range from Xerxes I and Alexander the Great to King Arthur, and his book was hugely successful, circulating throughout Europe and much more famous in its day than the *Decameron*, which is his best-known work today.

De Casibus was so successful that it was copied, expanded and translated by the French writer Laurence of Premierfait and the Englishman John Lydgate, who embellished and added further edifying examples to the text. A beautiful illuminated French edition, presented in 1409 to the Duke of Berry, contains a vivid (if historically questionable) image of James of Molay being burned at the stake along with three colleagues, in front of a satisfied Philip IV.[1] It also contains a detailed account of James's life. In this telling, his death and the order's downfall were the result of divine vengeance. The order's wealth and status grew in inverse proportion to its religiosity until its members received the ultimate punishment for their sins. That was quite a glossing of the story, but it had poetic shape and a healthy dose of natural justice. It was an appealingly simple narrative, in which the Templars' collective fate pivoted on the same moral flaws that William of Tyre had perceived in them: greed and pride.

In the popular consciousness the Templar story has tended toward this trajectory ever since. From Boccaccio to Sir Walter Scott, who created the thuggish, lascivious and power-crazed Templar villain Sir Brian de Bois-Guilbert in his 1820 novel *Ivanhoe*, to Ridley Scott, who depicted Gerard of Ridefort as a brutalized villain in his 2005 film *Kingdom of Heaven*, generations of writers have found rich material in the gap between the Templar ideal and real life. In the recent *Assassin's Creed* video game and movie franchise the Templars are also debased, crude enemies of a more elegant and noble time-traveling organization of Assassins. The spirit of the one-eyed Walter of Mesnil lives on.

Over the past two hundred years the Templars have also provided rich material for cranks, conspiracy theorists and fantasists. There is a thriving industry in what-if history about the Templars, much of it resting on the false supposition that an order so wealthy and powerful could not simply have been rolled up and dissolved. Alternative histories have been concocted suggesting an outlandish posthistory. Did a small group of Templars escape persecution in France? Could they have sailed from La Rochelle with a stash of treasure? If so, did that include the Turin Shroud or the Ark of the Covenant? Did the Templars set themselves up as a secret organization elsewhere? Are they still out there, running the world from the shadows?

One needs no more than an Internet connection and an imagination to find the theories that have been piled onto this platform of speculation, including the notion that the Templars were the keepers of a real-life Holy Grail—be that an actual cup or a metaphor for some ancient truth—that they had inherited their role of guardians of the truth from the Cathars (the collective name for heretics in southern France persecuted to obliteration in the early thirteenth century) and that this was what lay behind their downfall.

The popular pseudohistory *Holy Blood, Holy Grail*, first published in 1983, suggested and popularized the idea that the Templars were linked to a corporation known as the Priory of Sion, established to guard a secret bloodline of kings descended from Jesus Christ and Mary Magdalene. Dan Brown's bestselling *The Da Vinci Code*, published in 2003 and subsequently made into a successful movie, presented broadly similar ideas faux-seriously, adding greatly to the novel's success but leaving readers to work out for themselves whether or not the author's hypotheses had some basis in fact. (Many concluded that they did.) In Umberto Eco's novel *Foucault's Pendulum*, published in 1988 to a similarly misplaced credulity, three writers concoct a method for knitting together all of world history in one giant conspiracy, which they call the Plan. This features secret cells of Templars waiting to be revenged for their destruction by the king of France. Although archly postmodern, obviously satirical and directly mocking of those who place the Templars at the heart of a grand scheme for world domination, Eco's novel has added to the popular mystique about the order. What if just 10 percent of it were true?

Sadly, none of it is. Although fragments of supposed evidence are often stitched together with convenient lacunae in the historical record to provide "proof" for Templar-related fake history, it must be stressed that almost every plank of Templar survival theory is borrowed from fiction or simply made up. This sort of thing is unique to the history of the military orders, although it is very common in the history of the world. One of the supposed Templar survivalist bolt-holes, Oak Island in Nova Scotia, has been put forward as a possible location for the order's lost treasure. It has also been linked with evidence proving the true authorship of

Shakespeare manuscripts, the location of Marie Antoinette's jewelry and the hidden archives of a secret society of Rosicrucians led by Sir Francis Bacon. Needless to say, no Templar treasure has yet been discovered.

More interesting than conspiracy theory is the phenomenon of Templar revivalism, which began in earnest with the emergence of Freemasonry in England and France. As secret societies devoted to mutual assistance, characterized by their use of covert symbols, rituals and handshakes, masonic lodges in the early eighteenth century self-consciously sought to emphasize their ancient roots. Prominent masons in Scotland, France and Germany deliberately linked the movement with the history of the Templars, claiming a connection with the twelfth-century crusaders who lived in the "Temple of Solomon" and implying a continuum of nobility, wisdom and religious inside knowledge that was alluring even if bogus.

Today many people are still members of masonic societies, while others belong to legitimate orders of nobility including the various incarnations of the Hospitallers, including the Knights of Malta, whose indirect relation to the historical Templars has already been described. Others claim to be members of the revived Order of the Temple itself. These range from peaceful networks of Christian-minded human rights activists connected on social media to much less pleasant organizations who equate the historical Templars' mission in the Holy Land with a modern clash between Christianity and Islam in Europe and America. The Norwegian fascist and terrorist Anders Behring Breivik, who murdered seventy-seven people and injured more than three hundred in a bombing and shooting attack in Oslo and Utøya in 2011, claimed to be part of a revived international Templar cell founded by nine men in London but with a growing worldwide membership of several dozen "knights" and many more lay followers.

The fellowship that Breivik claimed with the Templars shows that their legacy today is not always benign. On April 2, 2014, the *New York Times* reported the death of a Mexican drug lord, Enrique Plancarte, who had been hiding out in a rented house in the state of Querétaro.[2] Plancarte was shot dead by marines as he walked down the street. His death was announced in Mexico and the United States with some satisfaction, for Plancarte was one of the highest-ranking members of a notorious cartel called Los Caballeros Templarios: The Knights Templar.

·····

Los Caballeros Templarios was founded in Michoacán in western Mexico in March 2011. Its members have been held responsible for a range of violent crime associated with the drug business, including murder, trafficking and extortion, but they have attempted to attach a higher purpose to their activities, blending a stern Christian zealotry with populist left-wing politics: a strategy successfully modeled in the 1980s by Pablo Escobar's infamous Medellín Cartel. In this case, Los Caballeros Templarios modeled themselves on the original Templars. Shortly after their founding the cartel produced a twenty-two-page booklet called "The Code of the Knights Templar," inspired by the medieval rule. "[Our] principal mission is to protect the inhabitants and the sacred territory . . . of Michoacán," it begins. The code mandates an admission process overseen by committee, a sworn oath of obedience enforceable by death and an obligation on every member to struggle against evils including materialism, injustice, tyranny, "the disintegration of moral values and the destructive elements that prevail today in human society."

"The Templar should be a model of gentlemanliness," it reads, exhorting its followers to avoid "brutality, drunkenness in an offensive manner, immorality, cowardice, lying and having malicious intentions," as well as "kidnapping for money" and using drugs "or any mind-altering substance." The only hints that the code might not be establishing a genuine revival of some rigorous twelfth-century monastic order are instructions that "to use lethal force, authorization is required," and frequent reminders that errors and disrespect toward the organization and fellow members will invite summary execution.

At the time of writing, authorities in Mexico are claiming fresh victories in their attempt to destroy the leadership of Los Caballeros Templarios, and people have openly begun to speak of the group's final demise. So one day soon, Los Caballeros Templarios may be gone: dissolved by the strong arm of an unsympathetic state. It would be a fitting historical parallel, if nothing else. But whatever their fate, they will not be the last people to pay tribute to the organization begun in Jerusalem by Hugh of Payns in 1119. The legend of the Templars will live on, inspiring, entertaining and intriguing generations to come.

That, perhaps, is the real legacy.

APPENDIX I:
CAST OF MAJOR CHARACTERS

Al-Adid: Last Fatimid caliph of Egypt, who agreed to a peace deal with the Christian kingdom of Jerusalem, brokered by the Templars. Died in 1171, after which Egypt under Saladin switched allegiance to the Abbasid caliph in Baghdad.

Al-Adil: Saladin's brother and eventual successor, who ruled Egypt and Syria from 1201 to 1218. Sometimes known as Saphadin.

Al-Afdal: Son of Saladin and general. Commanded troops at the Springs of Cresson and briefly ruled Damascus after his father's death.

Al-Ashraf Khalil: Mamluk sultan who completed the destruction of the crusader states, successfully besieging Acre in 1291.

Al-Kamil: Sultan of Egypt and son of Al-Adil. Ruled from 1218 to 1238, overseeing the defeat of the Fifth Crusade, but subsequently ceding Jerusalem to Christian rule in a 1229 treaty with Frederick II Hohenstaufen.

Al-Salih: Ayyubid sultan who ruled from 1240 to 1249 and died during the course of Louis IX's crusade to Damietta. Responsible for building up the strength of the Bahriyya Mamluks, who eventually produced Baybars.

Alfonso I, king of Aragón: Also known as "the Battler," the Christian hero of the Reconquista—the wars against the Muslims in Spain—died in 1134, leaving a third of his kingdom to the Templars.

Amalric I, king of Jerusalem: Brother of Baldwin III, he ruled from 1163 to 1174. He attempted to secure Christian interests south of Jerusalem by invading Egypt, and had a frosty relationship with the Templars, who undermined his policies.

Baldwin II, king of Jerusalem: Crusader king of Jerusalem who ruled from 1118 until 1131. Granted the Templars their home at the al-Aqsa Mosque on the Temple Mount.

Baldwin III, king of Jerusalem: King of Jerusalem from 1143 until 1163. Aided in his struggle against Imad al-Din Zengi and Nur al-Din by the arrival of the Second Crusade.

Baldwin IV, king of Jerusalem: Boy king who suffered from leprosy; his rule between 1174 and 1185 saw a series of setbacks as the Latin states were attacked by Saladin.

Baybars: Ruthless and brilliant Mamluk sultan who destroyed many crusader possessions between 1260 and 1277 and massacred the Templars of Safad castle in 1263.

Bernard, patriarch of Antioch: First Latin patriarch of Antioch, he was installed in 1100 after the First Crusade. A warrior churchman, who organized the military defense of the city against Il-ghazi in 1119.

Bernard of Clairvaux (Saint Bernard): Influential abbot, writer and Church reformer who founded a Cistercian abbey at Clairvaux and greatly influenced the first Latin Rule of the Templars. Died in 1153.

Bernard of Tremelay: Fourth master of the Templars, killed leading a suicidal charge into Ascalon in 1153.

Bertrand of Blancfort: Sixth master of the Templars, who led the order between 1156 and 1169. A veteran of wars against Nur al-Din, he spent three years as a prisoner of war and clashed with Amalric I over Egyptian policy in 1168.

Conrad III, king of the Germans: Leader of the German contingent of the Second Crusade, Conrad stayed with the Templars in Jerusalem and led the failed assault on Damascus in 1148.

Edward I, king of England: Visited Acre in 1272 and brokered a ten-year peace deal with Baybars. Then known as the Lord Edward, he succeeded to the English throne on his return and ruled until 1307.

Edward II, king of England: Son of Edward I and son-in-law of Philip IV of France, he suppressed the English Templars in exchange for papal support against his enemies. Ruled from 1307 to 1327.

Eleanor of Aquitaine: The wife of Louis VII, who traveled to the Holy Land on the Second Crusade.

Everard of Barres: Master of the Templars from 1149 to 1152 and a key ally of Louis VII of France, he helped finance the Second Crusade and eventually resigned to become a Cistercian monk.

Francis of Assisi (Saint Francis): Italian missionary and preacher who founded the Friars Minor, or the Franciscan Order. Visited Egypt during the Fifth Crusade and attempted to convert Sultan al-Kamil to Christianity.

Frederick II Hohenstaufen: Holy Roman Emperor, king of Sicily and king of the Germans, he extended his rule to include the crown of Jerusalem from 1225 to 1228. Fiercely intelligent, cosmopolitan but belligerent. Fell into dispute with the papacy many times in his long career and was excommunicated four times. Clashed with the Templars during a visit to the Holy Land from 1228 to 1229, but secured a treaty with al-Kamil restoring Jerusalem to crusader rule. Died in 1250.

Fulk I, king of Jerusalem: Count Fulk V of Anjou, persuaded by Hugh of Payns and others to leave his French lands and become king of Jerusalem, ruled from 1131 to 1143 alongside his wife, Melisende. An early Templar patron.

Geoffrey of Charney: Templar preceptor of Normandy and associate of James of Molay, he was burned as a recusant heretic in 1314.

Geoffrey Fitz Stephen: Master of the Templars in England, he produced a detailed inventory of all property belonging to the order there in 1185.

Gerard of Ridefort: Tenth master of the Templars. Highly political, rash and aggressive. Led the Templars to disastrous defeats at Cresson, Hattin and the siege of Acre in 1189, where he was finally captured and killed.

Guy of Lusignan: Controversially chosen husband of Sibylla, queen of Jerusalem. Captured after leading the Christian army into the battle of Hattin in 1187. Lost the crown of Jerusalem by election in 1192 but was compensated with the kingdom of Cyprus, which he ruled from 1192 to 1194.

Hugh of Pairaud: Senior Templar in the West, and variously master of the order in England and France. One of the senior leaders of the order imprisoned and absolved at Chinon castle.

Hugh of Payns: The founder and first master of the Order of the Temple.

Hülagü: Mongol ruler of the Persian Ilkhanate, in power between 1256 and 1265. Corresponded with Christian kings, including Louis IX of France, seeking an alliance against Baybars and the Mamluks.

Ibn al-Athir: Muslim chronicler born in 1160 to a family from Mosul. Kept a detailed chronicle of relations between Franks and Muslims until his death in 1233.

Il-ghazi: Artuqid ruler in northern Syria who routed a Christian army at the Field of Blood in 1119, preempting the establishment of the Templars.

Imad al-Din Zengi: Turkish governor of Aleppo, he expanded his rule between 1127 and 1146 and conquered the crusader town of Edessa, sparking the Second Crusade.

James I, king of Aragón: He succeeded to the crown of Aragón as a child in 1213 and was raised by the Templars of Monzón castle. A hero of the Reconquista, conquering Mallorca and Valencia with Templar assistance. Died in 1276.

James II, king of Aragón: Ruled from 1291 to 1327, and oversaw the winding up of the Aragónese Templars.

James of Maillé: Templar knight killed at Cresson in 1187. Miracles were associated with his corpse and stories preserved of his heroic death.

James of Molay: Last master of the Templars, elected in 1292. Defended the order against calls for merger with the Hospitallers. Targeted by Philip IV of France and Pope Clement V from 1307, he was imprisoned, tortured and burned at the stake in Paris in 1314.

John of Brienne: Ruler of Jerusalem from 1210 to 1225 by right of his wife, Maria, and subsequently his daughter, Isabella. Replaced when his daughter married Frederick II Hohenstaufen, and was awarded the position of Latin emperor of Constantinople. Died in 1237.

Louis VII, king of France: King of France from 1137 until 1180, and leader of the French contingent of the Second Crusade. An important patron of the early Templars.

Louis IX, king of France: Grandson of Philip Augustus, he ruled France from 1226 until 1270 and led two crusades: a huge assault on Damietta in 1248 and a failed attack on Tunis. Famous for his piety and ambitious religious building works, he died in 1270 and was awarded sainthood in 1297.

Matthew Paris: Thirteenth-century monk from St. Alban's whose vivid chronicle included information about the Templars gleaned from sources at the court of the English king Henry III.

Melisende, queen of Jerusalem: Daughter of King Baldwin II of Jerusalem. Coruler with her husband, Fulk I, from 1131 to 1143, and then with her son, Baldwin III, until he reached adulthood in 1153.

Nasr al-Din: Son of the Egyptian vizier Abbas, he fled Cairo after murdering the Fatimid caliph in 1154. Captured by the Templars of Gaza.

Nur al-Din: Son of Imad al-Din Zengi and ruler of Aleppo, he extended his rule to include most of Syria between 1146 and 1174. Highly religious, he was described by William of Tyre as a "mighty persecutor of the Christian name and faith."

Old Man of the Mountain, The: Mysterious leader of the Assassin sect based in the mountains around Masyaf; his real name was Rashid al-Din Sinan. Attempted a pact with the Christian kingdom of Jerusalem, which was sabotaged by the Templars.

Oliver of Paderborn: German churchman, eventually a cardinal, he traveled to Damietta on the Fifth Crusade, helped design siege machinery and kept a detailed chronicle of the campaign. Died in 1227.

Pelagius: Bishop of Albano and papal legate sent to the Fifth Crusade in 1219. Partly responsible for the disastrous decision to reject peace with al-Kamil and march up the Nile to attack al-Mansurah.

Peter of Montaigu: Master of the Templars from 1219 to 1231 and staunch opponent of Frederick II Hohenstaufen.

Philip II Augustus, king of France: Son of Louis VII. Ruled France from 1180 until his death in 1223. Leader of the French contingent of the Third Crusade, he quarreled with Richard the Lionheart and left the Holy Land following the fall of Acre in 1191.

Philip IV, king of France: Grandson of Louis IX, who became king of France in 1285. Pious, cold and aggressive, he attacked Pope Boniface VIII, persecuted France's Jews and ordered the mass arrests and trial of French Templars. Died in 1314.

Pope Clement V: Gascon archbishop Bertrand of Got, who was crowned pope in Lyon in 1305. Ruled the Church from France and established the Avignon papacy. Unable to resist the French crown's attack on James of Molay and the Templars. Died in 1314.

Pope Honorius III: Successor to Innocent III, who saw through the plans for the Fifth Crusade. Used the military orders, including the Templars, to help channel money raised from faithful Christians to the front line of the war against Islam.

Pope Innocent II: Pope from 1130 to 1143. Granted the Templars the bull *Omne Datum Optimum*, giving the order official papal recognition and the right to all spoils they took in war.

Pope Innocent III: A towering figure in the medieval Church, whose papacy lasted from 1198 until 1216. Launched the Fourth Crusade, which sacked Constantinople, and set in motion the Fifth Crusade, but died before it began.

Raimbaud of Caron: Templar preceptor of Cyprus, arrested in France in 1307 and imprisoned at Chinon with James of Molay and others.

Reginald of Vichiers: Templar master who worked closely with Louis IX of France to help organize his first crusade, and helped pay the ransom demanded after his defeat. Led the order from 1250 to 1256.

Richard I the Lionheart: King of England between 1189 and 1199. Led a large crusading army to relieve Acre in 1191 and restore Christian possessions taken by Saladin, but was captured on his way back to England and held prisoner in Germany from 1192 to 1194.

Robert of Sablé: Eleventh master of the Temple. A close supporter of Richard I, appointed to strengthen ties between the order and the English crusader king.

Saewulf: Christian pilgrim, probably English, who traveled to Jerusalem on pilgrimage ca. 1101–3, after the First Crusade.

Saladin: Sultan of Egypt and Syria from 1175 until his death in 1193 and founder of the Ayyubid dynasty. Victorious at the battle of Hattin in 1187 and restored Jerusalem to Islamic rule later that year.

Shawar: Fatimid vizier of Egypt, who served Caliph al-Adid until he was murdered in 1169 during a coup.

Shirkuh: Kurdish general who served Nur al-Din in Egypt. An adversary of Amalric I, king of Jerusalem, and uncle of Saladin, who assumed command in Egypt after his death in 1169.

Sibylla, queen of Jerusalem: Daughter of Amalric I; her marriage to Guy of Lusignan disastrously split the Christian nobles of Jerusalem. Ruled from 1186 until her death in 1190.

Terricus: Preceptor of the Temple from 1187 to 1188, who escaped from the battlefield at Hattin and helped rebuild the order in the immediate aftermath.

William of Beaujeu: Twenty-first master of the Templars, killed at the siege of Acre in 1291 during the evacuation of the city.

William of Chartres: Master of the Templars from 1210 to 1219, he was killed in Egypt during the Fifth Crusade.

William of Nogaret: Leading adviser to Philip IV of France and the intellectual architect of attacks on the French Templars from 1307.

William of Paris: Dominican friar and personal confessor to Philip IV of France, he led the Inquisition into Templar heresies from 1307 to 1308.

William of Plaisians: A lawyer in the service of the French Crown, who argued for the Templars' destruction and oversaw judicial inquiries into the order's alleged misdeeds.

William of Tyre: Chronicler, scholar and friend of kings, his *History of Deeds Done Beyond the Sea* was one of the most important chronicles of the kingdom of Jerusalem in the twelfth century. Naturally suspicious of the Templars.

APPENDIX II:
POPES
Antipopes have been excluded from this table.

Paschal II
1099–1118

Gelasius II
1118–1119

Calixtus II
1119–1124

Honorius II
1124–1130

Innocent II
1130–1143

Celestine II
1143–1144

Lucius II
1144–1145

Eugene III
1145–1153

Anastasius IV
1153–1154

Adrian IV
1154–1159

Alexander III
1159–1181

Lucius III
1181–1185

Urban III
1185–1187

Gregory VIII
1187

Clement III
1187–1191

Celestine III
1191–1198

Innocent III
1198–1216

Honorius III
1216–1227

Gregory IX
1227–1241

Celestine IV
1241

Innocent IV
1243–1254

Alexander IV
1254–1261

Urban IV
1261–1264

Clement IV
1265–1268

Gregory X
1271–1276

Innocent V
1276

Adrian V
1276

John XXI
1276–1277

Nicholas III
1277–1280

Martin IV
1281–1285

Honorius IV
1285–1287

Nicholas IV
1288–1292

Celestine V
1294

Boniface VIII
1294–1303

Benedict XI
1303–1304

Clement V
1305–1314

John XXII
1316–1334

APPENDIX III:
KINGS AND QUEENS OF JERUSALEM

Godfrey of Bouillon*
1099–1100

Baldwin I
1100–1118

Baldwin II
1118–1131

Fulk I and Melisende
1131–1143

Baldwin III†
1143–1163

Amalric I
1163–1174

Baldwin IV
1174–1183

Baldwin IV and Baldwin V
1183–1185

Baldwin V
1185–1186

Sibylla and Guy of Lusignan
1186–1190

Guy of Lusignan
1190–1192

Isabella I and Conrad of Montferrat
1192

Isabella I and Henry of Champagne
1192–1197

Isabella I and Amalric II
1197–1205

Maria I
1205–1210

Maria I and John of Brienne
1210–1212

Isabella II and John of Brienne
1212–1225

Isabella II and Frederick II
Hohenstaufen
1225–1228

Conrad II‡
1228–1254

Conrad III (aka Conradin)
1252–1268

Hugh I
1268–1284

John II
1284–1285

Henry II§
1285–1324

---

* Never crowned; used the title "Prince and Defender of the Holy Sepulchre."

† With Melisende, 1143–1153.

‡ Power exercised by Frederick II Hohenstaufen until 1243 and later by other regents.

§ Titular only from 1291.

APPENDIX IV:
MASTERS OF THE ORDER OF THE TEMPLE

Hugh of Payns
1119–1136

Robert of Craon*
1136–1149

Everard of Barres
1149–1152

Bernard of Tremelay
1152–1153

Andrew of Montbard
1154–1156

Bertrand of Blancfort
1156–1169

Philip of Nablus
1169–1171

Odo of Saint-Amand
1171–1180

Arnold of Torrolla
1180–1184

Gerard of Ridefort
1184–1189

Robert of Sablé
1191–1193

Girbert Eral
1193–1200

Philip of Plessis
1201–1210

William of Chartres
1210–1218

Peter of Montaigu
1219–1231

Armand of Périgord
1232–1244

Richard of Bure
1245–1247

William of Sonnac
1247–1250

Reginald of Vichiers
1250–1256

Thomas Bérard
1256–1273

William of Beaujeu
1273–1291

Theobald Gaudin
1291–1292

James of Molay
1292–1314 [†]

---

* Or Robert Burgundio.

† Date of death. The Order of the Temple was dissolved at the Council of Vienne in 1311.

NOTES

Introduction

1. The term "grand master," often used today to describe the overall master of the Templars (as opposed to regional masters), was in fact neither a commonly used nor a formal title in the East. See Jochen Burgtorf, *The Central Convent of Hospitallers and Templars: History, Organization and Personnel* (1099/1120–1310) (Leiden and Boston: Brill, 2008), 182.
2. Helen Nicholson, *The Knights Templar: A New History* (Stroud, Gloucestershire, UK: Sutton Publishing, 2004), 1.
3. Summarized judiciously in Malcolm Barber, *The New Knighthood: A History of the Order of the Temple* (Cambridge: Cambridge University Press, 1994), 315–18.

1: "A Golden Basin Filled with Scorpions"

1. Rev. Canon Brownlow, M.A., trans., *Saewulf, 1102, 1103* A.D. (London: Palestine Pilgrims' Text Society, 1892), 7. For an alternative English translation of Saewulf's pilgrimage memoir, see John Wilkinson with Joyce Hill and W. F. Ryan, eds., *Jerusalem Pilgrimage 1099–1185* (London: Hakluyt Society, 1988), 94–116.
2. Brownlow, *Saewulf*, 7.
3. Ibid., 31, and introduction, vi.
4. Ibid., 31.
5. Ezek. 5:5.
6. Wilkinson et al., *Jerusalem Pilgrimage*, 101.
7. Ibid., 102.
8. According to the account of Daniel the Abbot, a Russian pilgrim who wrote a detailed account of his own trip to Jerusalem a couple of years after Saewulf. Ibid., 128.
9. Qur'an 17:1. "Exalted is He who took His Servant by night from al-Masjid al-Haram [i.e., Mecca] to al-Masjid al-Aqsa [i.e., Jerusalem], whose surroundings We have blessed, to show him of Our signs. Indeed, He is the Hearing, the Seeing."
10. This was the term used, for example, by the Damascus scholar Ali ibn Tahir al-Sulami in his *Kitab al-Jihad* (*Book of Jihad*). See Carole Hillenbrand, *The Crusades: Islamic Perspectives* (Edinburgh: Edinburgh University Press, 1999), 71. Extracts from the *Kitab al-Jihad* can be found in French translation in Emmanuel Sivan, "La Genèse de la Contre-Croisade: Un Traité Damasquin du Début du XIIe Siècle," *Journal Asiatic* 254 (1966), and in English at www.arts.cornell.edu/prh3/447/texts/sulami.html.
11. D. S. Richards, trans., *The Chronicle of Ibn al-Athir for the Crusading Period from al Kamil fi'l Ta'rikh*, vol. 1 (Aldershot, Hampshire, UK: Routledge, 2006), 22.
12. According to Fulcher of Chartres. Edward Peters, ed., *The First Crusade: The Chronicle of Fulcher of Chartres and Other Source Materials* (Philadelphia: University of Pennsylvania Press, 1971), 77.
13. Letter of Godfrey of Bouillon and others to the pope, September 1099, in Peters, *The First Crusade*, 234; Hillenbrand, *The Crusades: Islamic Perspectives*; Jirkimish, the Seljuq lord of Mosul, quoted in Paul M. Cobb, *The Race for Paradise: An Islamic History of the Crusades* (Oxford: Oxford University Press, 2014), 107.

14. Wilkinson et al., *Jerusalem Pilgrimage*, 104.

15. Ibid., 105.

16. Ibid., 100. The traveler known as Daniel the Abbot agreed, calling the road from Jaffa to Jerusalem "hard and fearsome" (ibid., 126).

17. Ibid., 100–101.

18. Ibid., 109.

19. Ibid., 110.

20. Ibid., 112.

21. Ibid., 110.

22. Ibid., 109.

23. Ibid., 112–13.

24. Harold S. Fink, ed., and Frances R. Ryan, trans., *Fulcher of Chartres: A History of the Expedition to Jerusalem 1095–1127* (Knoxville: University of Tennessee Press, 1969), 149.

25. Wilkinson et al., *Jerusalem Pilgrimage*, 126, 134, 156, 162–63.

26. Ibn al-Khayyat, H. Mardam Bek, ed., *Diwan* (Damascus: n.p., 1958), quoted in Hillenbrand, *The Crusades: Islamic Perspectives*, 70–71.

27. Niall Christie, trans., *A Translation of Extracts from the Kitab al-Jihad of Ali ibn Tahir Al-Sulam*, [f. 189 b], www.arts.cornell.edu/prh3/447/texts/Sulami.html.

28. Al-Muqaddasi, *The Best Divisions for the Knowledge of the Regions*, ed. Basil Collins and rev. M. H. Alta'I (Reading, UK: Garnet Publishing, 2001), 141.

2: "The Defense of Jerusalem"

1. This dating is proposed and discussed in Anthony Luttrell, "The Earliest Templars," in M. Balard, ed., *Autour de la Première Croisade* (Paris: Publications de la Sorbonne, 1996), 195–96; see also Malcolm Barber, *The New Knighthood: A History of the Order of the Temple* (Cambridge: Cambridge University Press, 1994), 8–9.

2. The four writers on whom we rely for anecdote and evidence of the Templars' first roots are William of Tyre (who wrote in the early 1180s), Michael the Syrian (1190s), Walter Map (between 1181 and 1193) and an account contained in the history of Ernoul Bernard the Treasurer (1232). Paradoxically, the latest of these accounts may in fact be the closest to events, drawing in the view of one scholar on a source dating from before 1129: see Luttrell, "The Earliest Templars," in Balard, *Autour de la Première Croisade*, 194. None, however, is contemporaneous with the founding of the order itself, and in the case of William of Tyre, the Templars' humble origins may well have been exaggerated to emphasize their later acquisitiveness and wealth, of which William strongly disapproved.

3. Harold S. Fink, ed., and Frances R. Ryan, trans., *Fulcher of Chartres: A History of the Expedition to Jerusalem 1095–1127* (Knoxville: University of Tennessee Press, 1969), 208, 210, 218, 220–21.

4. Ibid., 150.

5. Albert of Aachen, *Historia Ierosolimitana: History of the Journey to Jerusalem*, ed. Susan B. Edgington (Oxford: Clarendon Press, 2007), 881. Albert of Aachen was not an eyewitness to events in the kingdom of Jerusalem, but rather compiled his long and very detailed account from oral testimony he collected from crusading veterans in Germany.

6. Susan B. Edgington and Thomas S. Asbridge, eds. and trans., *Walter the Chancellor's The Antiochene Wars: A Translation and Commentary* (Aldershot, UK: Routledge, 2006), 88; Thomas Asbridge, *The Crusades: The War for the Holy Land* (London: Simon & Schuster, 2010), 164–67.

7. Francesco Gabrieli, ed., and E. J. Costello, trans., *Arab Historians of the Crusades* (London: Routledge, 1969), 37–38.

8. Edgington and Asbridge, *Walter the Chancellor's The Antiochene Wars*, 132–35.

9. Fink and Ryan, *Fulcher of Chartres*, 227.

10. For this and more on Bernard's character and career, see Edgington and Asbridge, *Walter the Chancellor's The Antiochene Wars*, 34–42.

11. Ibid., 138.

12. Ibid., 139.

13. Ibid., 140.

14. The literature on Christian ideas of holy war is very voluminous—but considered concisely in Katherine Allen Smith, *War and the Making of Medieval Monastic Culture* (Woodbridge, Suffolk, UK: Boydell Press, 2011), especially 71–111.

15. Matt. 26:52.

16. Eph. 6:14, 17.

17. Jonathan Sneddon, "Warrior Bishops in the Middle Ages," *Medieval Warfare* 3, no. 2 (2013): 7.

18. G. T. Dennis, "Defenders of the Christian People: Holy War in Byzantium," in *The Crusades from the Perspective of Byzantium and the Muslim World*, ed. Angeliki E. Laiou (Washington, DC: Dumbarton Oaks, 2001), 31–33. See for example Anna Komnene, *The Alexiad*, trans. E. R. A. Sewter and rev. Peter Frankopan (London: Penguin, 2009), 39, 279.

19. Ivo, bishop of Chartres, described Hugh, Count of Champagne, thus in 1114. Jacques Paul Migne, ed., *Patrologia Latina: Patrologiae Cursus Completus. Series Latina*, vol. 162 (Paris: n.p., 1844–1864), 251–53. See for context Helen J. Nicholson, *The Knights Templar: A New History* (Stroud, Gloucester, UK: History Press, 2004), 22.

20. For a contemporary description of Nablus (Nabalus) written by an Arab Muslim from Jerusalem see Al-Muqaddasi, *The Best Divisions for the Knowledge of the Regions*, ed. Basil Collins and rev. M. H. Alta'I (Reading, UK: Garnet Publishing, 2001), 146.

21. These appear in Latin in Benjamin Z. Kedar, "On the Origins of the Earliest Laws of Frankish Jerusalem: The Canons of the Council of Nablus, 1120," *Speculum* 74 (1999). On the political context of the Council of Nablus see Hans Eberhard Mayer, "The Concordat of Nablus," *Journal of Ecclesiastical History* 33, no. 4 (1982): 531–43.

22. The most convenient source in which to find the four main accounts of the Templars' origins, including this extract from Michael the Syrian's chronicle, is Malcolm Barber and Keith Bate, eds. and trans., *The Templars: Selected Sources* (Manchester, UK: Manchester University Press, 2002), 25–31.

23. According to Michael the Syrian. Ibid., 27.

24. Alan Forey, "The Emergence of the Military Order in the Twelfth Century," *Journal of Ecclesiastical History* 36, no. 2 (1985): 175–95.

25. Nine is the number given by William of Tyre, thirty by Michael the Syrian.

26. Louis, comte de Mas Latrie, ed., *Chronique d'Ernoul et de Bernard le Trésorier* (Paris: Renouard, 1871), 7–9.

27. Marquis d'Albon, ed., *Cartulaire Général de l'Ordre du Temple, 1119?–1150. Recueil des Chartes et des Bulles Relatives à l'Ordre du Temple* (Paris: H. Champion, 1913), 99.

28. I Kings 6–8.

29. Al-Muqaddasi, *The Best Divisions*, 143. The Dome of the Rock had been built by the Umayyad caliph 'Abd al-Malik, completed in A.D. 691. It covered the Foundation Stone, thought to be the site of the Holy of Holies in the First Temple.

30. Guy Le Strange, ed. and trans., *Diary of a Journey through Syria and Palestine. By Nâsir-i-Khusrau, in 1047 A.D.* (London: Palestine Pilgrims' Text Society, 1893), 30.

31. D. S. Richards, trans., *The Chronicle of Ibn al-Athir for the Crusading Period from al Kamil fi'l Ta'rikh*, vol. 1 (Aldershot, Hampshire, UK: Routledge, 2006), 21.

32. Barber and Bate, *The Templars*, 31.

33. Ibid., 26.

34. Luttrell, "The Earliest Templars," 198, 202.

35. Walter Map, *De Nugis Curialium, Courtiers' Trifles*, ed. and trans. M. R. James and rev. C. N. L. Brooke and R. A. B. Mynors. Oxford Medieval Texts. (Oxford: Oxford University Press, 1983), 54–55.

36. Barber and Bate, *The Templars*, 26.

37. Fink and Ryan, *Fulcher of Chartres*, 118.

38. The so-called "Work on Geography," written between 1128 and 1137. John Wilkinson with Joyce Hill and W. F. Ryan, eds., *Jerusalem Pilgrimage 1099–1185* (London: Hakluyt Society, 1988), 200.

3: "A New Knighthood"

1. For a clear summary of Bernard's life see G. R. Evans, *Bernard of Clairvaux* (New York and Oxford: Oxford University Press, 2000), 5–21.

2. Pauline M. Matarasso, trans., *The Cistercian World: Monastic Writings of the Twelfth Century* (London: Penguin, 1993), 287–92.

3. Peter the Venerable, who wrote this, was a Benedictine abbot who, like Bernard of Clairvaux, counted kings and princes among his friends and thought deeply about the changing nature of monasticism in the twelfth century. This translation is from Giles Constable, *The Reformation of the Twelfth Century* (Cambridge: Cambridge University Press, 1996), 45.

4. Ibid., 47.

5. The letter is in Marquis d'Albon, ed., *Cartulaire Général de l'Ordre du Temple, 1119?–1150. Recueil des Chartes et des Bulles Relatives à l'Ordre du Temple* (Paris: H. Champion, 1913), I; I follow here the dating and attribution suggested in Malcolm Barber, *The New Knighthood: A History of the Order of the Temple* (Cambridge: Cambridge University Press, 1994), 337n29.

6. d'Albon, *Cartulaire Général*, I.

7. Ibid. The two men Baldwin said he was sending were named as Andrew and Godemar.

8. B. S. James, trans., *The Letters of St. Bernard of Clairvaux* (London: Burns Oates, 1953), 357.

9. Ibid., 175–76.

10. For dating see Barber, *The New Knighthood*, 12.

11. Marjorie Chibnall, ed. and trans., *The Ecclesiastical History of Orderic Vitalis*, vol. 6 (Oxford: Oxford University Press, 1978), 310–11.

12. Jonathan Phillips, *Defenders of the Holy Land: Relations between the Latin East and the West, 1119–1187* (Oxford: Oxford University Press, 1996), 26. The Cathedral of St. Julian is the burial place of Fulk's famous son, Geoffrey Plantagenet.

13. Ibid., 23.

14. E. A. Babcock and A. C. Krey, trans., *A History of Deeds Done Beyond the Sea: By William, Archbishop of Tyre*, vol. 2 (New York: Columbia University Press, 1943), 27.

15. Babcock and Krey, *A History of Deeds Done Beyond the Sea*, vol. 1 (New York: Columbia University Press, 1943), 524.

16. These five men were named as Hugh's companions at the Council of Troyes in 1129. See Phillips, *Defenders of the Holy Land*, 36.

17. G. N. Garmonsway, ed. and trans., *The Anglo-Saxon Chronicle* (London: J. M. Dent, 1972), 259.

18. Ibid. William of Tyre agreed: "led by [his] persuasive words, many companies of noblemen" made the journey. Babcock and Krey, *A History of Deeds Done Beyond the Sea*, vol. 2, 40.

19. On this perspective see Jonathan Phillips, "Hugh of Payns and the 1129 Damascus Crusade," in Malcolm Barber, ed., *The Military Orders I: Fighting for the Faith and Caring for the Sick* (Aldershot, UK: Variorum, 1994), 141–47.

20. H. A. R. Gibb, *The Damascus Chronicle of the Crusades: Extracted and Translated from the Chronicle of Ibn Al-Qalanisi* (London: Luzac, 1932; repr., New York: Dover, 2000), 195.

21. M. J. Peixoto, "Templar Communities in Medieval Champagne: Local Perspectives on a Global Organization" (PhD diss., New York University, 2013), 137.

22. James, *The Letters of St. Bernard of Clairvaux*, 65.
23. The only clerics not connected directly with the region were the legate Matthew and the bishops of Beauvais, Orléans and Laon. Peixoto, "Templar Communities in Medieval Champagne," 140. Theobald of Blois, Count of Champagne, was the aforementioned count Hugh's nephew and successor.
24. Judith M. Upton-Ward, trans. and ed., *The Rule of the Templars: The French Text of the Rule of the Order of the Knights Templar* (Woodbridge, Suffolk, UK: Boydell Press, 1992), 19.
25. Ibid., 19–38.
26. Ibid., 24; on previous dress see Babcock and Krey, *A History of Deeds Done Beyond the Sea*, vol. 1, 524–27.
27. Translated in Malcolm Barber and Keith Bate, eds. and trans., *The Templars: Selected Sources* (Manchester, UK: Manchester University Press, 2002), 54–59.
28. Conrad Greenia, trans., Malcolm Barber, introduction, *Bernard of Clairvaux: In Praise of the New Knighthood*. Revised edition. (Collegeville, MN: Cistercian Publications, 2000), 31.
29. Ibid., 33.
30. Ibid., 37–38, 46.
31. Ibid., 40.
32. Evans, *Bernard of Clairvaux*, 30.
33. Greenia, *Bernard of Clairvaux*, 53.
34. Ibid., 55.
35. Ibid., 31.

4: "Every Good Gift"

1. The relics of Alfonso el Battalador are described in the *Chronica Adefonsi*, which can be found in English translation in Glenn Edward Lipskey, trans., *The Chronicle of Alfonso the Emperor: A Translation of the Chronica Adefonsi Imperatoris, with Study and Notes* (Evanston, IL: n.p., 1972), also available online at libro.uca.edu/lipskey/chronicle.htm. Alfonso had stolen his fragment of the True Cross from the monastery of Saint Facundus and Saint Primitivus, near Sahagún.
2. See Patrick J. O'Banion, "What Has Iberia to Do with Jerusalem? Crusade and the Spanish Route to the Holy Land in the Twelfth Century," *Journal of Medieval History* 34, no. 4 (2008): 383–84.
3. Ibid., 387.
4. Lipskey, *The Chronicle of Alfonso the Emperor*, vol. 1, 81.
5. D. S. Richards, trans., *The Chronicle of Ibn al-Athir for the Crusading Period from al Kamil fi'l Ta'rikh*, vol. 1 (Aldershot, Hampshire, UK: Routledge, 2006), 323.
6. Marjorie Chibnall, ed. and trans., *The Ecclesiastical History of Orderic Vitalis*, vol. 6 (Oxford: Oxford University Press, 1978), 411.
7. Lipskey, *The Chronicle of Alfonso the Emperor*, vol. 1., 81–82.
8. Richards, *The Chronicle of Ibn al-Athir*, vol. 1, 323.
9. Lipskey, *The Chronicle of Alfonso the Emperor*, vol. 1, 82.
10. Richards, *The Chronicle of Ibn al-Athir*, vol. 1, 323.
11. Alfonso's will is in Marquis d'Albon, ed., *Cartulaire Général de l'Ordre du Temple, 1119?–1150. Recueil des Chartes et des Bulles Relatives à l'Ordre du Temple* (Paris: H. Champion, 1913), 30. It can be found in English translation in Malcolm Barber and Keith Bate, eds. and trans., *The Templars: Selected Sources* (Manchester, UK: Manchester University Press, 2002), 161–63.
12. E. A. Babcock and A. C. Krey, trans., *A History of Deeds Done Beyond the Sea: By William, Archbishop of Tyre*, vol. 2 (New York: Columbia University Press, 1943), 40–41.
13. G. N. Garmonsway, ed. and trans., *The Anglo-Saxon Chronicle* (London: J. M. Dent, 1972), 259.
14. Babcock and Krey, *A History of Deeds Done Beyond the Sea*, vol. 2, 103–5.

15. Ibid., 104.

16. Jochen Burgtorf, *The Central Convent of Hospitallers and Templars: History, Organization and Personnel (1099/1120–1310)* (Leiden and Boston: Brill, 2008), 644–45.

17. An English translation of *Omne Datum Optimum* can be found in Barber and Bate, *The Templars: Selected Sources*, 59–64.

18. J. K. Elliott, ed. and trans., *The Apocryphal New Testament: A Collection of Apocryphal Christian Literature in an English Translation* (Oxford: Oxford University Press, 1993), passim.

19. *Milites Templi* and *Militia Dei* are both translated into English in Barber and Bate, *The Templars: Selected Sources*, 64–66.

20. Pierre Gérard and Elizabeth Magnou-Nortier, eds., "Le Cartulaire des Templiers de Douzens," in *Collection des Documents Inédits sur l'Histoire de France*, Book III (Paris: Imprimerie Royal, 1835), 50–51. A translation appears in Philippe Joserand, "The Templars in France: Between History, Heritage, and Memory," *Mirabilia: Electronic Journal of Antiquity and Middle Ages* 21 (2015): 452.

21. Translation appears in Barber and Bate, *The Templars: Selected Sources*, 134–60.

22. Helen J. Nicholson, *The Knights Templar: A New History* (Stroud, Gloucestershire, UK: History Press, 2004), 132–34.

23. Malcolm Barber, *The New Knighthood: A History of the Order of the Temple* (Cambridge: Cambridge University Press, 1994), 20.

24. Beatrice A. Lees, ed., *Records of the Templars in England in the Twelfth Century: The Inquest of 1185 with Illustrative Charters and Documents* (Oxford: Published for the British Academy by Humphrey Milford, Oxford University Press, 1935), xxxviii–xxxix.

25. Ibid., 1. Also see Simon Brighton, *In Search of the Knights Templar: A Guide to the Sites of Britain* (London: Weidenfeld & Nicolson, 2006), 86–89.

26. See the introduction to Charles Wendell David, trans., and Jonathan Phillips, ed., *The Conquest of Lisbon: De Expugnatione Lyxbonensi* (New York: Columbia University Press, 2001), xiv–xv.

27. Translation appears in Barber and Bate, *The Templars: Selected Sources*, 132.

28. Elena Lourie, "The Confraternity of Belchite, the Ribat, and the Templars," *Viator* 13 (1982): 159–76.

29. Alan Forey, *The Military Orders: From the Twelfth to the Fourteenth Centuries* (Basingstoke, UK: Macmillan, 1992), 23–24; A. J. Forey, *The Templars in the Corona de Aragón* (Oxford: Oxford University Press, 1973), 20–25.

30. Translation appears in Barber and Bate, *The Templars: Selected Sources*, 95–97.

31. Forey, *The Templars in the Corona de Aragón*, 23.

5: "A Tournament Between Heaven and Hell"

1. H. A. R. Gibb, *The Damascus Chronicle of the Crusades: Extracted and Translated from the Chronicle of Ibn Al-Qalanisi* (London: Luzac, 1932; repr., New York: Dover, 2000), 267.

2. Ibid., 266; E. A. Babcock and A. C. Krey, trans., *A History of Deeds Done Beyond the Sea: By William, Archbishop of Tyre*, vol. 2 (New York: Columbia University Press, 1943), 142.

3. D. S. Richards, trans., *The Chronicle of Ibn al-Athir for the Crusading Period from al Kamil fi'l Ta'rikh*, vol. 1 (Aldershot, Hampshire, UK: Routledge, 2006), 382–83; Paul M. Cobb, trans., *Usama ibn Munqidh: The Book of Contemplation: Islam and the Crusades* (London: Penguin, 2008), 202–3.

4. Carole Hillenbrand, "Abominable Acts: The Career of Zengi," in *The Second Crusade: Scope and Consequences*, ed. Jonathan Phillips and Martin Hoch (Manchester, UK: Manchester University Press, 2001), 120–25.

5. Babcock and Krey, *A History of Deeds Done Beyond the Sea*, vol. 2, 85, 407.

6. Ibid. On Edessa's varied Christian population, see J. B. Segal, *Edessa: "The Blessed City"* (Oxford: Oxford University Press, 1970), 238–42.

7. Carole Hillenbrand, *The Crusades: Islamic Perspectives* (Edinburgh: Edinburgh University Press, 1999), 531–32.

8. Segal, *Edessa*, 243–44.

9. Babcock and Krey, *A History of Deeds Done Beyond the Sea*, vol. 2, 143.

10. Gibb, *The Damascus Chronicle of the Crusades*, 268.

11. Segal, *Edessa*, 246.

12. Philippe Joserand, "The Templars in France: Between History, Heritage, and Memory," *Mirabilia: Electronic Journal of Antiquity and Middle Ages* 21 (2015): 452.

13. Marquis d'Albon, ed., *Cartulaire Général de l'Ordre du Temple, 1119?–1150. Recueil des Chartes et des Bulles Relatives à l'Ordre du Temple* (Paris: H. Champion, 1913), 280.

14. On this occasion see Jonathan Phillips, *The Second Crusade: Extending the Frontiers of Christendom* (New Haven, CT, and London: Yale University Press, 2007), 122–23.

15. For an English translation of *Quantum Praedecessores* see Louise and Jonathan Riley-Smith, *The Crusades: Idea and Reality, 1095–1274* (London: Edward Arnold, 1981), 57–59.

16. Estimates by contemporaries varied from nearly one million men to a more believable total of fifty thousand, comprising both combatants and nonfighting pilgrims. The figures are discussed in Phillips, *The Second Crusade*, 168–69.

17. Babcock and Krey, *A History of Deeds Done Beyond the Sea*, vol. 2, 171.

18. V. G. Berry, ed. and trans., *Odo of Deuil: De Profectione Ludovici VII in Orientem* (New York: W. W. Norton, 1948), 58–59.

19. Ibid., 58–59, 87.

20. On this point, see John France, "Logistics and the Second Crusade," in *Logistics of Warfare in the Age of the Crusades: Proceedings of a Workshop Held at the Centre for Medieval Studies, University of Sydney*, ed. John H. Pryor (Aldershot, UK: Ashgate, 2006), 83.

21. Berry, *Odo of Deuil*, 66–67.

22. The disaster at Mount Cadmus is described in terrible detail by Odo of Deuil, ibid., 102–23; also see Phillips, *The Second Crusade*, 199–201.

23. Babcock and Krey, *A History of Deeds Done Beyond the Sea*, vol. 2, 177.

24. Gibb, *The Damascus Chronicle of the Crusades*, 281.

25. Berry, *Odo of Deuil*, 124–25.

26. Judith M. Upton-Ward, trans. and ed., *The Rule of the Templars: The French Text of the Rule of the Order of the Knights Templar* (Woodbridge, Suffolk, UK: Boydell Press, 1992), 29.

27. On Turkish tactics see Hillenbrand, *The Crusades: Islamic Perspectives*, 512–15. William of Tyre describes the same in Babcock and Krey, *A History of Deeds Done Beyond the Sea*, vol. 2, 171.

28. For a summary of the mounted archer's training, tack and horsemanship, see Ann Hyland, *The Medieval War Horse: From Byzantium to the Crusades* (London: Grange, 1994), 118–19.

29. Berry, *Odo of Deuil*, 124–25.

30. A point made by Berry, ibid., 124n6: "The elementary nature of these commands makes the former disorder of the army very apparent."

31. In French in Joseph Bedier and Pierre Aubry, eds., *Les Chansons de Croisade avec Leurs Melodies* (Paris: H. Champion, 1909), 8–11.

32. Berry, *Odo of Deuil*, 127.

33. Ibid.

6: "The Mill of War"

1. Otto of Freising gives St. Symeon as Louis's docking point; this is now Samandag, in Turkey. Charles Christopher Mierow, trans., and Richard Emery, *The Deeds of Frederick*

Barbarossa by Otto of Freising and His Continuator, Rahewin (New York: Columbia University Press, 2004), 101.

2. Malcolm Barber, *The New Knighthood: A History of the Order of the Temple* (Cambridge: Cambridge University Press, 1994), 67–68.

3. Achille Luchaire, *Études sur les Actes de Louis VII* (Paris: A. Picard, 1885), 174.

4. Louis, comte de Mas Latrie, ed., *Chronique d'Ernoul et de Bernard le Trésorier* (Paris: Renouard, 1871), 9.

5. A study of the architecture of the Temple Mount during the Templars' tenure there is given in Adrian J. Boas, *Archaeology of the Military Orders: A Survey of the Urban Centres, Rural Settlement and Castles of the Military Orders in the Latin East (c. 1120–1291)* (Abingdon, UK: Routledge, 2006), 19–28.

6. Paul M. Cobb, trans., *Usama ibn Munqidh: The Book of Contemplation: Islam and the Crusades* (London: Penguin, 2008), 147; for a slightly extended version of the same passage see Francesco Gabrieli, ed., and E. J. Costello, trans., *Arab Historians of the Crusades* (London: Routledge, 1969), 79–80.

7. Mierow and Emery, *The Deeds of Frederick Barbarossa*, 102.

8. Ibid.

9. Al-Muqaddasi, *The Best Divisions for the Knowledge of the Regions*, ed. Basil Collins and rev. M. H. Alta'I (Reading, UK: Garnet Publishing, 2001), 133–36; R. J. C. Broadhurst, trans., *The Travels of Ibn Jubayr: Being the Chronicles of a Mediaeval Spanish Moor Concerning His Journey to the Egypt of Saladin, the Holy Cities of Arabia, Baghdad the City of the Caliphs, the Latin Kingdom of Jerusalem, and the Norman Kingdom of Sicily* (London: Jonathan Cape, 1952), 272.

10. Ibn al-Athir describes his own father being present as Zengi died: he begged to be granted a swifter end. D. S. Richards, trans., *The Chronicle of Ibn al-Athir for the Crusading Period from al Kamil fi'l Ta'rikh*, vol. 2 (Aldershot, Hampshire, UK: Routledge, 2007), 382.

11. Ibid., 222.

12. For a full and sympathetic reassessment of the crusaders' objectives in attacking Damascus, see Martin Hoch, "The Choice of Damascus as the Objective of the Second Crusade: A Re-evaluation," in *Autour de la Première Croisade: Actes du Colloque de la "Society for the Study of the Crusades and the Latin East."* Clermont-Ferrand, France, June 22–25 1995, ed. M. Balard (Paris: Publications de la Sorbonne, 1996), 359–69.

13. E. A. Babcock and A. C. Krey, trans., *A History of Deeds Done Beyond the Sea: By William, Archbishop of Tyre*, vol. 2 (New York: Columbia University Press, 1943), 186.

14. Mierow and Emery, *The Deeds of Frederick Barbarossa*, 102.

15. Broadhurst, *The Travels of Ibn Jubayr*, 271–72.

16. Babcock and Krey, *A History of Deeds Done Beyond the Sea*, vol. 2, 188.

17. H. A. R. Gibb, *The Damascus Chronicle of the Crusades: Extracted and Translated from the Chronicle of Ibn Al-Qalanisi* (London: Luzac, 1932; repr., New York: Dover, 2000), 284.

18. Ibid., 285.

19. On the debate about Frankish strategy at the siege of Damascus, see Jonathan Phillips, *The Second Crusade: Extending the Frontiers of Christendom* (New Haven, CT, and London: Yale University Press, 2007), 221–27.

20. Babcock and Krey, *A History of Deeds Done Beyond the Sea*, vol. 2, 192.

21. Ibid., 195.

7: "The Godforsaken Tower"

1. Gaza is mentioned approvingly by Al-Muqaddasi as "a large town on the main road into Egypt . . . there is here a beautiful mosque. . . ." Al-Muqaddasi, *The Best Divisions for the Knowledge of the Regions*, ed. Basil Collins and rev. M. H. Alta'I (Reading, UK: Garnet Publishing, 2001), 146.

2. E. A. Babcock and A. C. Krey, trans., *A History of Deeds Done Beyond the Sea: By William, Archbishop of Tyre*, vol. 2 (New York: Columbia University Press, 1943), 202.

3. Al-Ghazzi died in 1129–30, and fragments of his poetry were preserved by the chronicler Ibn al-Athir. D. S. Richards, trans., *The Chronicle of Ibn al-Athir for the Crusading Period from al Kamil fi'l Ta'rikh*, vol. 1 (Aldershot, Hampshire, UK: Routledge, 2006), 285.

4. Jochen Burgtorf, *The Central Convent of Hospitallers and Templars: History, Organization and Personnel (1099/1120–1310)* (Leiden and Boston: Brill, 2008), 481–82.

5. For Andrew's analogy with the ant, see Bernard of Clairvaux's reply to him in B. S. James, trans., *The Letters of St. Bernard of Clairvaux* (London: Burns Oates, 1953), 479.

6. This letter appears in modern English translation in Malcolm Barber and Keith Bate, trans., *Letters from the East: Crusaders, Pilgrims and Settlers in the 12th–13th Centuries* (Farnham, UK: Ashgate, 2013), 47–48; the original French can be found in M. Bouquet et al., eds., *Recueil des Historiens des Gaules et de la France,* vol. XV (Paris: Victor Palme, 1878), 540–41.

7. Babcock and Krey, *A History of Deeds Done Beyond the Sea*, vol. 2, 203.

8. Ibid., 219.

9. On Bethgibelin and other castles in the region see Hugh Kennedy, *Crusader Castles* (Cambridge: Cambridge University Press, 1994), 30–32; also see R. C. Smail, "Crusaders' Castles of the Twelfth Century," *Cambridge Historical Journal* 10 (1952): 140.

10. The only detailed account of the siege of Ascalon is by William of Tyre. Babcock and Krey, *A History of Deeds Done Beyond the Sea*, vol. 2, 217–34.

11. James, *The Letters of St. Bernard of Clairvaux*, 519, 521.

12. Babcock and Krey, *A History of Deeds Done Beyond the Sea*, vol. 2, 221.

13. H. A. R. Gibb, *The Damascus Chronicle of the Crusades: Extracted and Translated from the Chronicle of Ibn Al Qalanisi* (London: Luzac, 1932; repr., New York: Dover, 2000), 315.

14. As seems evident from their position when Ascalon's wall was breached and the tower fell. Ibid., 227.

15. Paul M. Cobb, trans., *Usama ibn Munqidh: The Book of Contemplation: Islam and the Crusades* (London: Penguin, 2008), 25.

16. Gibb, *The Damascus Chronicle of the Crusades*, 227.

17. Babcock and Krey, *A History of Deeds Done Beyond the Sea*, vol. 2, 227.

18. For the strategic implications for the secular rulers of Jerusalem see R. C. Smail, *Crusading Warfare, 1097–1193*, second edition (Cambridge: Cambridge University Press, 1995), 103–4.

8: "Power and Riches"

1. A detailed eyewitness report of Nasr al-Din's flight from Cairo and the extraordinary circumstances that prompted it is contained in Paul M. Cobb, trans., *Usama ibn Munqidh: The Book of Contemplation: Islam and the Crusades* (London: Penguin, 2008), 26–36. Also see D. S. Richards, trans., *The Chronicle of Ibn al-Athir for the Crusading Period from al Kamil fi'l Ta'rikh*, vol. 2 (Aldershot, Hampshire, UK: Routledge, 2007), 67–68.

2. This allegation is made by Richards, *The Chronicle of Ibn al-Athir*, vol. 2, 67.

3. E. A. Babcock and A. C. Krey, trans., *A History of Deeds Done Beyond the Sea: By William, Archbishop of Tyre*, vol. 2 (New York: Columbia University Press, 1943), 251.

4. Cobb, *Usama ibn Munqidh*, 37–38. Usama took a particular interest in this saddle since it actually belonged to him.

5. Richards, *The Chronicle of Ibn al-Athir*, vol. 2, 68.

6. Walter Map, *De Nugis Curialium, Courtiers' Trifles*, ed. and trans. M. R. James and rev. C. N. L. Brooke and R. A. B. Mynors. Oxford Medieval Texts. (Oxford: Oxford University Press, 1983), 62–67.

7. Babcock and Krey, *A History of Deeds Done Beyond the Sea*, vol. 2, 253.

8. Judith M. Upton-Ward, trans. and ed., *The Rule of the Templars: The French Text of the Rule of the Order of the Knights Templar* (Woodbridge, Suffolk, UK: Boydell Press, 1992), 147–48.

9. Babcock and Krey, *A History of Deeds Done Beyond the Sea*, vol. 2, 253.

10. Richards, *The Chronicle of Ibn al-Athir*, vol. 2, 69.

11. Babcock and Krey, *A History of Deeds Done Beyond the Sea*, vol. 2, 253.

12. Léopold Delisle, *Memoire sur Les Operations Financières des Templiers* (Paris: n.p., 1889), 681–82.

13. John Wilkinson with Joyce Hill and W. F. Ryan, eds., *Jerusalem Pilgrimage, 1099–1185* (London: Hakluyt Society, 1988), 293–94.

14. Ibid., 303.

15. Adrian J. Boas, *Archaeology of the Military Orders: A Survey of the Urban Centres, Rural Settlement and Castles of the Military Orders in the Latin East (c. 1120–1291)* (Abingdon, UK: Routledge, 2006), 106, 111, 112; Hugh Kennedy, *Crusader Castles* (Cambridge: Cambridge University Press, 1994), 31, 55.

16. Boas, *Archaeology of the Military Orders*, 111–12.

17. Ibid., 188.

18. Wilkinson et al., *Jerusalem Pilgrimage*, 310.

19. Ibid., 312.

20. Kennedy, *Crusader Castles*, 56.

21. Ibid., 57.

9: "Troubles in the Two Lands"

1. E. A. Babcock and A. C. Krey, trans., *A History of Deeds Done Beyond the Sea: By William, Archbishop of Tyre*, vol. 2 (New York: Columbia University Press, 1943), 300.

2. D. S. Richards, trans., *The Chronicle of Ibn al-Athir for the Crusading Period from al Kamil fi'l Ta'rikh*, vol. 2 (Aldershot, Hampshire, UK: Routledge, 2007), 172.

3. William of Tyre recorded that "the death of Baldwin was the occasion of much discord among the barons of the realm, who were variously affected by the change of monarchs. In fact it came near causing a serious quarrel involving the danger of schism." Babcock and Krey, *A History of Deeds Done Beyond the Sea*, vol. 2, 295.

4. Malcolm Barber and Keith Bate, trans., *Letters from the East: Crusaders, Pilgrims and Settlers in the 12th–13th Centuries* (Farnham, UK: Ashgate, 2013), 53.

5. Babcock and Krey, *A History of Deeds Done Beyond the Sea*, vol. 2, 300.

6. H. A. R. Gibb, *The Damascus Chronicle of the Crusades: Extracted and Translated from the Chronicle of Ibn Al-Qalanisi* (London: Luzac, 1932; repr., New York: Dover, 2000), 336–37.

7. Richard Clarke Sewell, *Gesta Stephani, Regis Anglorum et Ducis Normannorum* (London: Sumptibus Societatis, 1846), 38.

8. Babcock and Krey, *A History of Deeds Done Beyond the Sea*, vol. 2, 306.

9. Malcolm Barber, *The Crusader States* (New Haven, CT, and London: Yale University Press, 2012), 241.

10. Barber and Bate, *Letters from the East*, 61.

11. Babcock and Krey, *A History of Deeds Done Beyond the Sea*, vol. 2, 317.

12. Ibid., 312.

13. Ibid.

14. Ibid., 330.

15. Helen J. Nicholson, *The Chronicle of the Third Crusade: The Itinerarium Peregrinorum et Gesta Regis Ricardi* (Farnham, UK: Ashgate, 1997), 28.

16. This quote and the description of the palace that follows appear in Babcock and Krey, *A History of Deeds Done Beyond the Sea*, vol. 2, 319–21.

17. Ibid., 351.

18. D. S. Richards, trans., *The Rare and Excellent History of Saladin by Baha al-Din Ibn Shaddad* (Farnham, UK: Ashgate, 2002), 26.

19. Nicholson, *The Chronicle of the Third Crusade*, 23.

10: "Tears of Fire"

1. Francesco Gabrieli, ed., and E. J. Costello, trans., *Arab Historians of the Crusades* (London: Routledge, 1969), 146–47.

2. D. S. Richards, trans., *The Rare and Excellent History of Saladin by Baha al-Din Ibn Shaddad* (Farnham, UK: Ashgate, 2002), 45.

3. Ibid., 28.

4. E. A. Babcock and A. C. Krey, trans., *A History of Deeds Done Beyond the Sea: By William, Archbishop of Tyre*, vol. 2 (New York: Columbia University Press, 1943), 391.

5. J. Bird, E. Peters, and J. M. Powell, eds., *Crusade and Christendom: Annotated Documents in Translation from Innocent III to the Fall of Acre, 1187–1291* (Philadelphia: University of Pennsylvania Press, 2013), 189.

6. Babcock and Krey, *A History of Deeds Done Beyond the Sea*, vol. 2, 392.

7. Malcolm Barber, *The New Knighthood: A History of the Order of the Temple* (Cambridge: Cambridge University Press, 1994), 103.

8. Babcock and Krey, *A History of Deeds Done Beyond the Sea*, vol. 2, 392–93.

9. Ibid., 393.

10. Ibid., 394.

11. On the physical site of the Hospital in Jerusalem, see Denys Pringle, "The Layout of the Jerusalem Hospital in the Twelfth Century: Further Thoughts and Suggestions," in Judith M. Upton-Ward, ed., *The Military Orders, Volume 4: On Land and by Sea* (Aldershot, UK: Ashgate, 2008), 91–110.

12. Malcolm Barber and Keith Bate, trans., *Letters from the East: Crusaders, Pilgrims and Settlers in the 12th–13th Centuries* (Farnham, UK: Ashgate, 2013), 72.

13. See Benjamin Z. Kedar, "The Tractatus de Locis et Statu Sancte Terre Ierosolimitane" in John France and W. G. Zajac, *The Crusades and Their Sources: Essays Presented to Bernard Hamilton* (Aldershot, UK: Ashgate, 1998).

14. Abu Shama, "The Book of the Two Gardens," in *Recueil des Historiens des Croisades: Historiens Orientaux*, vol. IV (Paris: Imprimerie Nationale, 1898), 185.

15. Ibid.

16. Richards, *The Rare and Excellent History of Saladin*, 54.

17. Abu Shama, "The Book of the Two Gardens," 185.

18. Babcock and Krey, *A History of Deeds Done Beyond the Sea*, vol. 2, 431.

19. Ibid.

20. Richards, *The Rare and Excellent History of Saladin*, 54.

21. Barber and Bate, *Letters from the East*, 73.

22. D. S. Richards, trans., *The Chronicle of Ibn al-Athir for the Crusading Period from al Kamil fi'l Ta'rikh*, vol. 2 (Aldershot, Hampshire, UK: Routledge, 2007), 253.

23. Babcock and Krey, *A History of Deeds Done Beyond the Sea*, vol. 2, 437.

24. Gen. 32:10–32.

25. Ronnie Ellenblum, *Crusader Castles and Modern Histories* (Cambridge: Cambridge University Press, 2007), 264.

26. Ibid., 273; Abu Shama, "The Book of the Two Gardens," 208.

27. Babcock and Krey, *A History of Deeds Done Beyond the Sea*, vol. 2, 444.

28. Richards, *The Chronicle of Ibn al-Athir*, 264.

29. Ibid., 266.

30. Babcock and Krey, *A History of Deeds Done Beyond the Sea*, vol. 2, 440.

31. Ibid., 443, quoting Job 27:3–4, KJV: "All the while my breath *is* in me, and the spirit of God *is* in my nostrils; My lips shall not speak wickedness, nor my tongue utter deceit."

32. Ibid.

33. *Recueil des Historiens des Croisades*, vol. IV, 200.

34. Ibid., 194.

35. Richards, *The Chronicle of Ibn al-Athir*, 265.

36. Ibid.

37. *Recueil des Historiens des Croisades*, vol. IV, 205; Richards, *The Chronicle of Ibn al-Athir*, 266.

38. *Recueil des Historiens des Croisades*, vol. IV, 205.

39. Ibid., 206–7.

40. The historian and archaeologist Ronnie Ellenblum excavated the site in the early twenty-first century and discovered "the body of at least one of the defenders . . . in situ, opposite the breach in the wall." Ellenblum, *Crusader Castles and Modern Histories*, 273.

41. Richards, *The Chronicle of Ibn al-Athir*, 266.

42. *Recueil des Historiens des Croisades*, vol. IV, 203.

43. Richards, *The Chronicle of Ibn al-Athir*, 266.

44. Babcock and Krey, *A History of Deeds Done Beyond the Sea*, vol. 2, 444.

11: "Woe to You, Jerusalem!"

1. The canons of the Third Lateran Council can be consulted in English translation most conveniently at www.papalencyclicals.net/Councils/ecum11.htm.

2. Jonathan Phillips, *Defenders of the Holy Land: Relations between the Latin East and the West, 1119–1187* (Oxford: Oxford University Press, 1996), 246–47.

3. Jochen Burgtorf, *The Central Convent of Hospitallers and Templars: History, Organization and Personnel (1099/1120–1310)* (Leiden and Boston: Brill, 2008), 279.

4. See, for example, Antonio Gargallo Moya, Maria Teresa Iranzo Muñío, and Maria José Sánchez Usón, eds., *Cartulario Del Temple De Huesca* (Zaragoza, Spain: Anubar, 1985), 44, 58.

5. Burgtorf, *The Central Convent of Hospitallers and Templars*, 543.

6. E. A. Babcock and A. C. Krey, trans., *A History of Deeds Done Beyond the Sea: By William, Archbishop of Tyre*, vol. 2 (New York: Columbia University Press, 1943), 455–56.

7. During his career to 1186 the sultan spent a combined total of just eleven months actively fighting Frankish armies, compared to nearly three years engaged in campaigns against Muslims. Thomas Asbridge, *The Crusades: The War for the Holy Land* (London: Simon & Schuster, 2010), 335.

8. Babcock and Krey, *A History of Deeds Done Beyond the Sea*, vol. 2, 502.

9. Burgtorf, *The Central Convent of Hospitallers and Templars*, 539–40. Also see Malcolm Barber, "The Reputation of Gerard of Ridefort," in Judith M. Upton-Ward, ed., *The Military Orders, Volume 4: On Land and by Sea* (Aldershot, UK: Ashgate, 2008), 116–17.

10. Helen J. Nicholson, *The Chronicle of the Third Crusade: The Itinerarium Peregrinorum et Gesta Regis Ricardi* (Farnham, UK: Ashgate, 1997), 79.

11. Louis, comte de Mas Latrie, ed., *Chronique d'Ernoul et de Bernard le Trésorier* (Paris: Renouard, 1871), 161–62.

12. Zehava Jacoby, "The Tomb of Baldwin V, King of Jerusalem (1185–1186), and the Workshop of the Temple Area," *Gesta* 18, no. 2 (1979): 3–14, discusses the tomb, now lost except for fragments of carved stone.

13. D. S. Richards, trans., *The Rare and Excellent History of Saladin by Baha al-Din Ibn Shaddad* (Farnham, UK: Ashgate, 2002), 68.

14. For this interpretation of Gerard of Ridefort's actions at Cresson see Christopher Tyerman, *God's War: A New History of the Crusades* (London: Penguin, 2006), 367.

15. Louis, comte de Mas Latrie, *Chronique d'Ernoul*, 446.

16. Now identified as 'Ain Gozeh. See P. F. Abel, *Géographie de la Palestine I* (Paris: Gabalda, 1938), 445.

17. Letter to Frederick I of Germany, in Malcolm Barber and Keith Bate, trans., *Letters from the East: Crusaders, Pilgrims and Settlers in the 12th–13th Centuries* (Farnham, UK: Ashgate, 2013), 76–77.

18. H. Hoogeweg, ed., *Die Schriften des kölner Domscholasters, späteren Bischofs von Paderborn und Kardinal-Bischofs von S. Sabina Oliverus* (Tübingen: Bibliothek des Litterarischen Vereins in Stuttgart 202, 1894), 142.

19. Barber and Bate, *Letters from the East*, 76.

20. Account of the continuator of William of Tyre, in Peter Edbury, ed. and trans., *The Conquest of Jerusalem and the Third Crusade: Sources in Translation* (Farnham, UK: Ashgate, 1998), 32.

21. Joseph Stevenson, ed., *Ralph of Coggeshall: Chronicon Anglicanum* (London: Longman, 1875), 212.

22. Rules 659, 675 and 676. Judith M. Upton-Ward, trans. and ed., *The Rule of the Templars: The French Text of the Rule of the Order of the Knights Templar* (Woodbridge, Suffolk, UK: Boydell Press, 1992), 170–71.

23. For the Templars' response to Gerard's order, see the letter to Frederick I of Germany, in Barber and Bate, *Letters from the East*, 76. This broadly agrees with Ralph of Coggeshall's rendering of the Templars' response: "Whether we live or die we will always be victorious in Christ's name," in Stevenson, *Ralph of Coggeshall*, 212.

24. Bernard was here invoking Rom. 24:8. Conrad Greenia, trans., Malcolm Barber, introduction, *Bernard of Clairvaux: In Praise of the New Knighthood*. Revised edition. (Collegeville, MN: Cistercian Publications, 2000), 34. On Templar approaches to martyrdom see Joachim Rother, "Embracing Death, Celebrating Life: Reflections on the Concept of Martyrdom in the Order of the Knights Templar," *Ordines Militares* 19 (2014).

25. Urs's fate at Cresson is slightly uncertain, but it seems very likely that he was killed. For a summary of the prospographical evidence see Burgtorf, *The Central Convent of Hospitallers and Templars*, 666. For the fate of Roger of Moulins, the continuator of William of Tyre names decapitation, in Edbury, *The Conquest of Jerusalem and the Third Crusade*, 32.

26. D. S. Richards, trans., *The Chronicle of Ibn al-Athir for the Crusading Period from al Kamil fi'l Ta'rikh*, vol. 2 (Aldershot, Hampshire, UK: Routledge, 2007), 319.

27. Stevenson, *Ralph of Coggeshall*, 212.

28. Nicholson, *The Chronicle of the Third Crusade*, 25–26.

29. Ibid., 26.

30. The pope's précis of Gerard's letter is in English translation in Edbury, *The Conquest of Jerusalem and the Third Crusade*, 33.

31. Stevenson, *Ralph of Coggeshall*, 218.

32. Louis, comte de Mas Latrie, *Chronique d'Ernoul*, 457.

33. Abu Shama, "The Book of the Two Gardens," in *Recueil des Historiens des Croisades: Historiens Orientaux*, vol. IV (Paris: Imprimerie Nationale, 1898), 264.

34. Ibid., 263.

35. Nicholson, *The Chronicle of the Third Crusade*, 31.

36. Letter to Frederick I of Germany, in Barber and Bate, *Letters from the East*, 77; Louis, comte de Mas Latrie, *Chronique d'Ernoul*, 460–61.

37. Louis, comte de Mas Latrie, *Chronique d'Ernoul*, 461.

38. C. P. Melville and M. C. Lyons, "Saladin's Hattin Letter," in Benjamin Z. Kedar, ed., *The Horns of Hattin* (Jerusalem and London: Yad Izhak Ben-Zvi/Israel Exploration Society & Variorum, 1992), 210–11.

39. Richards, *The Chronicle of Ibn al-Athir*, 321.

40. Nicholson, *The Chronicle of the Third Crusade*, 32.

41. C. P. Melville and M. C. Lyons, "Saladin's Hattin Letter," 211.

42. The "Eracles"; this translation is given in Edbury, *The Conquest of Jerusalem and the Third Crusade*, 159.

43. Barber and Bate, *Letters from the East*, 82.

44. Ibid., 78.

45. Richards, *The Chronicle of Ibn al-Athir*, 322.

46. C. P. Melville and M. C. Lyons, "Saladin's Hattin Letter," 211.

47. Richards, *The Rare and Excellent History of Saladin*, 74.

48. Richards, *The Chronicle of Ibn al-Athir*, 323.

49. Ibid.

50. C. P. Melville and M. C. Lyons, "Saladin's Hattin Letter," 212.

51. Richards, *The Rare and Excellent History of Saladin*, 74.

52. Letter to the master of the Hospitallers in Italy, translated in Edbury, *The Conquest of Jerusalem and the Third Crusade*, 161.

53. Richards, *The Rare and Excellent History of Saladin*, 75.

54. Richards, *The Chronicle of Ibn al-Athir*, 324.

55. Quoted by Abu Shama, "The Book of the Two Gardens," 277.

56. Ibid., 278.

57. The continuator of William of Tyre relates this story, in Edbury, *The Conquest of Jerusalem and the Third Crusade*, 47.

58. Quoted by Abu Shama, "The Book of the Two Gardens," 333.

59. The continuator of William of Tyre, in Edbury, *The Conquest of Jerusalem and the Third Crusade*, 64–65.

Part III: Bankers

1. Francesco Gabrieli, ed., and E. J. Costello, trans., *Arab Historians of the Crusades* (London: Routledge, 1969), 288.

12: "The Pursuit of Fortune"

1. Jochen Burgtorf, *The Central Convent of Hospitallers and Templars: History, Organization and Personnel (1099/1120–1310)* (Leiden and Boston: Brill, 2008), 81.

2. Judith M. Upton-Ward, trans. and ed., *The Rule of the Templars: The French Text of the Rule of the Order of the Knights Templar* (Woodbridge, Suffolk, UK: Boydell Press, 1992), 169.

3. R. J. C. Broadhurst, trans., *The Travels of Ibn Jubayr: Being the Chronicles of a Mediaeval Spanish Moor Concerning His Journey to the Egypt of Saladin, the Holy Cities of Arabia, Baghdad the City of the Caliphs, the Latin Kingdom of Jerusalem, and the Norman Kingdom of Sicily* (London: Jonathan Cape, 1952), 318. Ibn Jubayr is citing Qur'an, Ar-Rahman 55:24.

4. Theoderic in John Wilkinson with Joyce Hill and W. F. Ryan, eds., *Jerusalem Pilgrimage, 1099–1185* (London: Hakluyt Society, 1988), 310; also see a sketch of the ruined Templar house, made in 1752 by Ladislaus Mayr, which is reproduced in Adrian J. Boas, *Archaeology of the Military Orders: A Survey of the Urban Centres, Rural Settlement and Castles of the Military Orders in the Latin East (c. 1120–1291)* (Abingdon, UK: Routledge, 2006), 30.

5. Upton-Ward, *The Rule of the Templars*, 49.

6. Broadhurst, *The Travels of Ibn Jubayr*, 317.

7. Boas, *Archaeology of the Military Orders*, 29.

8. *Recueil des Historiens des Croisades: Historiens Orientaux*, vol. IV (Paris: Imprimerie Nationale, 1898), 296.

9. The continuator of William of Tyre, in Peter Edbury, ed. and trans., *The Conquest of Jerusalem and the Third Crusade: Sources in Translation* (Farnham, UK: Ashgate, 1998), 80.

10. Helen J. Nicholson, *The Chronicle of the Third Crusade: The Itinerarium Peregrinorum et Gesta Regis Ricardi* (Farnham, UK: Ashgate, 1997), 78.

11. According to a contemporary poem transcribed in Hans Prutz, "Ein Zeitgenössisches Gedicht über die Belagerung Accons," *Forschungen zur Deutschen Geschichte* 21 (1881): 478.

12. For Geoffrey Morin's biographical summary see Burgtorf, *The Central Convent of Hospitallers and Templars*, 534–35.

13. Upton-Ward, *The Rule of the Templars*, 59–60.

14. D. S. Richards, trans., *The Chronicle of Ibn al-Athir for the Crusading Period from al Kamil fi'l Ta'rikh*, vol. 2 (Aldershot, Hampshire, UK: Routledge, 2007), 367; D. S. Richards, trans., *The Rare and Excellent History of Saladin by Baha al-Din Ibn Shaddad* (Farnham, UK: Ashgate, 2002), 102.

15. This interpretation would seem to reconcile Nicholson, *The Chronicle of the Third Crusade*, 79, and Richards, *The Chronicle of Ibn al-Athir*, 367.

16. Nicholson, *The Chronicle of the Third Crusade*, 78–79.

17. Ibid., 79.

18. Richards, *The Chronicle of Ibn al-Athir*, 368.

19. Nicholson, *The Chronicle of the Third Crusade*, 79.

20. Ibid., 80.

21. This would seem to explain the gap in the dates between the attack on the Great Ship, dated by most sources as June 7, and details of the attack reaching Saladin, which Ibn Shaddad and the author of the *Itinerarium Peregrinorum* agree took place on June 11. Richards, *The Rare and Excellent History of Saladin*, 151. Nicholson, *The Chronicle of the Third Crusade*, 199. Ibn Shaddad is surely mistaken in placing the naval engagement on June 11.

22. Richards, *The Rare and Excellent History of Saladin*, 150.

23. Ibid., 145.

24. Ibid., 146.

25. Burgtorf, *The Central Convent of Hospitallers and Templars*, 79–80.

26. Malcolm Barber, *The New Knighthood: A History of the Order of the Temple* (Cambridge: Cambridge University Press, 1994), 119.

27. Burgtorf, *The Central Convent of Hospitallers and Templars*, 523–27.

28. Richards, *The Rare and Excellent History of Saladin*, 158.

29. Nicholson, *The Chronicle of the Third Crusade*, 209.

30. Richards, *The Rare and Excellent History of Saladin*, 162.

31. Nicholson, *The Chronicle of the Third Crusade*, 237; see also Thomas Asbridge, *The Crusades: The War for the Holy Land* (London: Simon & Schuster, 2010), 461.

32. Nicholson, *The Chronicle of the Third Crusade*, 245.

33. Ibid.

34. Ibn Shaddad was an eyewitness and participant in the battle of Arsuf and gives a markedly less rhetorical and standardized account of events than the author of the *Itinerarium Peregrinorum*. Richards, *The Rare and Excellent History of Saladin*, 174–76.

35. Nicholson, *The Chronicle of the Third Crusade*, 258.

36. Richards, *The Rare and Excellent History of Saladin*, 178.

37. Ibid., 186–88.

38. Nicholson, *The Chronicle of the Third Crusade*, 278.

39. Louis, comte de Mas Latrie, ed., *Chronique d'Ernoul et de Bernard le Trésorier* (Paris: Ren-
    ouard, 1871), 296–97.

40. According to John of Joinville. J. A. Giles, ed., *Chronicles of the Crusades: Being Contempo-
    rary Narratives of the Crusade of Richard Coeur de Lion, by Richard of Devizes and Geoffery
    de Vinsauf; and of the Crusade of Saint Louis, by Lord John de Joinville* (London: Henry G.
    Bohn, 1892), 495.

41. For a succinct overview of the Templars' brief tenure in Cyprus see George Francis Hill, *A
    History of Cyprus, Volume II: The Frankish Period, 1192–1432* (Cambridge: Cambridge Uni-
    versity Press, 1948), 34–38; a more in-depth and recent study is Peter Edbury, "The Tem-
    plars in Cyprus," in Malcolm Barber, ed., *The Military Orders I: Fighting for the Faith and
    Caring for the Sick* (Aldershot, UK: Variorum, 1994), 189–95.

13: "Nowhere in Poverty"

1. This book is today in the UK National Archives at Kew, E.164/16, and its Latin text has
   been usefully transcribed with an informative introduction in English in Beatrice A. Lees,
   ed., *Records of the Templars in England in the Twelfth Century: The Inquest of 1185 with Illustrative Charters and Documents* (Oxford: Published for the British Academy by Humphrey Milford, Oxford University Press, 1935), 139–41.

2. A. J. Holden, S. Gregory, and D. Crouch, *History of William Marshal*, vol. 2 (London:
   Anglo-Norman Text Society, 2002–2006), 419–21.

3. Michael Gervers, "Pro Defensione Terre Sancte: The Development and Exploitation of the
   Hospitallers' Landed Estate in Essex," in Malcolm Barber, ed., *The Military Orders I: Fighting for the Faith and Caring for the Sick* (Aldershot, UK: Variorum, 1994), 5.

4. Lees, *Records of the Templars in England in the Twelfth Century*, 139–40.

5. The most up-to-date edition and translation of Magna Carta 1215 is online at magnacarta
   .cmp.uea.ac.uk/.

6. M. R. James, ed. and trans., C. N. L. Brooke and R. A. B. Mynors, rev., Walter Map, *De
   Nugis Curialium, Courtiers' Trifles*, ed. and trans. M. R. James and rev. C. N. L. Brooke and
   R. A. B. Mynors. Oxford Medieval Texts. (Oxford: Oxford University Press, 1983), 54–55.

7. Ibid., 60–61.

8. Karl Borchardt, "The Military-Religious Orders in the Crusader West," in Adrian J. Boas,
   ed., *The Crusader World* (Abingdon, UK, and New York: Routledge, 2016), 111–28.

9. For Richard I's confirmation of the Templars' rights at Garway, see Lees, *Records of the
   Templars in England in the Twelfth Century*, 142.

10. Map, *De Nugis Curialium*, 60–61.

11. For a discussion of John of Salisbury's attitude to the Templars, including this translation
    of his *Polycraticus*, see Malcolm Barber, *The New Knighthood: A History of the Order of the
    Temple* (Cambridge: Cambridge University Press, 1994), 59–61.

12. Ibid., 61.

13. Elena Bellomo, *The Templar Order in North-West Italy (1142–c. 1330)* (Leiden and Boston:
    Brill, 2008), 34–35. The pope also made use of the other major military orders, the Hospi-
    tallers and the Teutonic Order.

14. Ignacio de la Torre, "The London and Paris Temples: A Comparative Analysis of Their Fi-
    nancial Services for the Kings During the Thirteenth Century," in Judith M. Upton-Ward,
    ed., *The Military Orders, Volume 4: On Land and by Sea* (Aldershot, UK: Ashgate, 2008), 122.

15. Barber, *The New Knighthood*, 262–63.

16. Antonio Gargallo Moya, Maria Teresa Iranzo Muñío, and Maria José Sánchez Usón, eds.,
    Cartulario Del Temple De Huesca (Zaragoza, Spain: Anubar, 1985), 85, 87, 94.

17. Damian J. Smith and Helena Buffery, eds., *The Book of Deeds of James I of Aragón: A Trans-
    lation of the Medieval Catalan Llibre dels Fets* (Farnham, UK: Ashgate, 2003), 26–28.

18. A. J. Forey, *The Templars in the Corona de Aragón* (Oxford: Oxford University Press, 1973), 34–35.

19. D. S. Richards, trans., *The Rare and Excellent History of Saladin by Baha al-Din Ibn Shaddad* (Farnham, UK: Ashgate, 2002), 240–45.

20. See the papal bull *Post Miserabile* in English translation in J. Bird, E. Peters, and J. M. Powell, eds., *Crusade and Christendom: Annotated Documents in Translation from Innocent III to the Fall of Acre, 1187–1291* (Philadelphia: University of Pennsylvania Press, 2013), 28–37.

14: "Damietta!"

1. Château Pèlerin is often now known as 'Atlit. For details of modern studies on its remains see Hugh Kennedy, *Crusader Castles* (Cambridge: Cambridge University Press, 1994), 124–27; Adrian J. Boas, *Archaeology of the Military Orders: A Survey of the Urban Centres, Rural Settlement and Castles of the Military Orders in the Latin East (c. 1120–1291)* (Abingdon, UK: Routledge, 2006), 32–38.

2. Judith M. Upton-Ward, trans. and ed., *The Rule of the Templars: The French Text of the Rule of the Order of the Knights Templar* (Woodbridge, Suffolk, UK: Boydell Press, 1992), 155–56, 153–54, 148.

3. Letter traditionally, probably wrongly, attributed to James of Vitry, bishop of Acre; translation appears in Malcolm Barber and Keith Bate, trans., *Letters from the East: Crusaders, Pilgrims and Settlers in the 12th–13th Centuries* (Farnham, UK: Ashgate, 2013), 110.

4. James of Vitry identifies the ships as cogs. Ibid., 112.

5. Sam Zeno Conedera, *Ecclesiastical Knights: The Military Orders in Castile, 1150–1330* (New York: Fordham University Press, 2015), 87.

6. Joseph F. O'Callaghan, *A History of Medieval Spain* (Ithaca, NY: Cornell University Press, 1975), 243–49.

7. On the siege of Alcácer do Sal, see Joseph F. O'Callaghan, *Reconquest and Crusade in Medieval Spain* (Philadelphia: University of Pennsylvania Press, 2002), 78–80.

8. I have given page references here to the most widely available edition of J. J. Gavigan's 1948 English translation of Oliver of Paderborn's chronicle, "The Capture of Damietta," to be found in J. Bird, E. Peters, and J. M. Powell, eds., *Crusade and Christendom: Annotated Documents in Translation from Innocent III to the Fall of Acre, 1187–1291* (Philadelphia: University of Pennsylvania Press, 2013), 158–225. This quote is ibid., 165–66.

9. Ibid., 187.

10. Ibid., 194.

11. Alan V. Murray, "The Place of Egypt in the Military Strategy of the Crusades, 1099–1221," in E. J. Mylod, Guy Perry, Thomas W. Smith, and Jan Vandeburie, *The Fifth Crusade in Context: The Crusading Movement in the Early Thirteenth Century* (London and New York: Routledge, 2017), 130–31.

12. On Honorius's role in crusading, particularly as distinct from Innocent III's, see T. W. Smith, "The Role of Pope Honorius III in the Fifth Crusade," in Mylod et al., *The Fifth Crusade in Context*, 15–26.

13. Letter quoted by Pierre-Vincent Claverie, "'Totius Populi Christiani Negotium': The Crusading Conception of Pope Honorius III, 1216–21," in Mylod et al., *The Fifth Crusade in Context*, 34.

14. Léopold Delisle, ed., *Recueils des Historiens des Gaules et de la France*, vol. 19 (Paris: Imprimerie Nationale, 1880), 640.

15. Letter from John of Brienne to Frederick II Hohenstaufen, in Mylod et al., *The Fifth Crusade in Context*, 43–45.

16. Described by various chroniclers, including Ibn al-Athir, who wrote: "Had it not been for this tower and these chains nobody would have been able to keep the enemy's ships out of

any part of Egypt, near or far." D. S. Richards, trans., *The Chronicle of Ibn al-Athir for the Crusading Period from al Kamil fi'l Ta'rikh*, vol. 2 (Aldershot, Hampshire, UK: Routledge, 2007), 176.

17. Bird et al., *Crusade and Christendom*, 168–69.

18. Ibid.

19. The provenence of the relic is given by James of Vitry, in Barber and Bate, *Letters from the East*, 112.

20. Ibid., 114.

21. Bird et al., *Crusade and Christendom*, 173.

22. Ibid.

23. Ibid., 175.

24. For an introduction to the history of the order, see Udo Arnold, "Eight Hundred Years of the Teutonic Order," in Malcolm Barber, ed., *The Military Orders I: Fighting for the Faith and Caring for the Sick* (Aldershot, UK: Variorum, 1994), 223–35.

25. Bird et al., *Crusade and Christendom*, 182.

26. Matt. 10:8–11, NIV.

27. Upton-Ward, *The Rule of the Templars*, 40–41.

28. The letter is translated in Barber and Bate, *Letters from the East*, 123. The meeting between Francis of Assisi and al-Kamil inspired centuries of Christian devotional art, described in John V. Tolan, *Saint Francis and the Sultan: The Curious History of a Christian-Muslim Encounter* (Oxford: Oxford University Press, 2009).

29. Bird et al., *Crusade and Christendom*, 184.

30. Ibid., 185.

31. Ibid., 187.

32. Barber and Bate, *Letters from the East*, 120.

33. Bird et al., *Crusade and Christendom*, 200.

34. James M. Powell, *Anatomy of a Crusade, 1213–1221* (Philadelphia: University of Pennsylvania Press, 1986), 92–93.

35. The letter can be read in C. Rodenburg, ed., *Monumenta Germaniae Historica, Epistolae I* (Berlin: Weidemanns, 1883), 89–91, or in a more readily available English translation in Malcolm Barber and Keith Bate, eds. and trans., *The Templars: Selected Sources* (Manchester, UK: Manchester University Press, 2002), 203–7.

36. Letter from Honorius to the prelates of Sicily, dated November 24, 1218, translated ibid., 230–32.

37. Malcolm Barber, *The New Knighthood: A History of the Order of the Temple* (Cambridge: Cambridge University Press, 1994), 129.

38. The letter was preserved by the English chronicler Roger of Wendover. J. A. Giles, ed. and trans., *Roger of Wendover's Flowers of History*, vol. 2 (London: H. G. Bohn, 1849), 433–35.

39. Ibid.

40. Ibid., 436–39; also translated in Barber and Bate, *Letters from the East*, 123–25.

41. Richards, *The Chronicle of Ibn al-Athir*, 180.

42. Barber and Bate, *Letters from the East*, 124.

15: "Animosity and Hatred"

1. J. A. Giles, ed. and trans., *Roger of Wendover's Flowers of History*, vol. 2 (London: H. G. Bohn, 1849), 511; John L. La Monte and Merton Jerome Hubert, eds. and trans., *The Wars of Frederick II Against the Ibelins in Syria and Cyprus by Philip De Novare* (New York: Columbia University Press, 1936), 88.

2. J. L. Baird, G. Baglivi, and J. R. Kane, eds. and trans., *The Chronicle of Salimbene de Adam* (Binghamton, NY: Medieval and Renaissance Texts and Studies, 1986).

3. Daniel P. Franke, "Crusade, Empire and the Process of War in Staufen Germany, 1180–1220," in Adrian J. Boas, ed., *The Crusader World* (Abingdon, UK, and New York: Routledge, 2016), 132.

4. Louis, comte de Mas Latrie, ed., *Chronique d'Ernoul et de Bernard le Trésorier* (Paris: Renouard, 1871), 437.

5. Udo Arnold, "Eight Hundred Years of the Teutonic Order," in Malcolm Barber, ed., *The Military Orders I: Fighting for the Faith and Caring for the Sick* (Aldershot, UK: Variorum, 1994), 225.

6. Giles, *Roger of Wendover's Flowers of History*, vol. 2, 502.

7. D. S. Richards, trans., *The Chronicle of Ibn al-Athir for the Crusading Period from al Kamil fi'l Ta'rikh*, vol. 2 (Aldershot, Hampshire, UK: Routledge, 2007), 285.

8. On Frederick's preference for the fleshly culture of the East, see the letter of Patriarch Gerold of Lausanne to Gregory IX, in English translation in Malcolm Barber and Keith Bate, trans., *Letters from the East: Crusaders, Pilgrims and Settlers in the 12th–13th Centuries* (Farnham, UK: Ashgate, 2013), 127–33.

9. For its status as a "castiel del Temple," and for an account of the episode described here, see Louis, comte de Mas Latrie, *Chronique d'Ernoul*, 462.

10. Ibid.

11. Barber and Bate, *Letters from the East*, 129.

12. Giles, *Roger of Wendover's Flowers of History*, vol. 2, 522–24; more recently reprinted in S. J. Allen and Emilie Amt, *The Crusades: A Reader* (Toronto: University of Toronto Press, 2010), 287–90.

13. Quoted in Thomas Curtis Van Cleve, *The Emperor Frederick II of Hohenstaufen, Immutator Mundi* (Oxford: Clarendon Press, 1972), 220.

14. Richards, *The Chronicle of Ibn al-Athir*, 293.

15. Ibid., 334.

16. Barber and Bate, *Letters from the East*, 129.

17. Jean-Louis-Alphonse Huillard-Bréholles, *Historia Diplomatica Friderici Secundi*, vol. 3 (Paris: Plon Brothers, 1852), 89.

18. Peter Jackson, "The Crusades of 1239–41 and Their Aftermath," *Bulletin of the School of Oriental and African Studies, University of London* 50, no. 1 (1987).

19. Barber and Bate, *Letters from the East*, 126–27.

20. La Monte and Hubert, *The Wars of Frederick II*, 89.

21. Huillard-Bréholles, *Historia Diplomatica Friderici Secundi*, vol. 3, 135–40, and in English translation (quoted here), Edward Peters, ed., *Christian Society and the Crusades 1198–1229: Sources in Translation Including "The Capture of Damietta" by Oliver of Paderborn* (Philadelphia: University of Pennsylvania Press, 1948), 165–70.

22. La Monte and Hubert, *The Wars of Frederick II*, 91.

23. Peters, *Christian Society and the Crusades 1198–1229*, 168.

24. Ibid., 169.

25. La Monte and Hubert, *The Wars of Frederick II*, 91.

26. The most recent study of these arrivals is Michael Lower, *The Barons' Crusade: A Call to Arms and Its Consequences* (Philadelphia: University of Pennsylvania Press, 2005).

27. Letter preserved by Matthew Paris; see Henry Richards Luard, ed., *Matthæi Parisiensis: Monachi Santi Albani, Chronica Majora*, vol. 4 (London: Longman, 1876), 288–91, or in English translation in Barber and Bate, *Letters from the East*, 140–42.

28. Luard, *Matthæi*, 535, or in English translation in J. A. Giles, *Matthew Paris's English History: From the Year 1235 to 1273*, vol. 1 (London: H. G. Bohn, 1852), 168–69.

29. A detailed and anecdote-rich source for all of this is still Léopold Delisle, *Memoire sur Les Operations Financières des Templiers* (Paris: n.p., 1889), on which much of the below draws. See also Jules Piquet, *Des Banquiers au Moyen Âge. Les Templiers; Étude de Leurs Opérations*

Financières (Paris: Hachette, 1939). For an easily accessible digest (in French), see www .templiers.net/leopold-delisle.

30. See Paul Webster, "The Military Orders at the Court of King John," in Peter W. Edbury, ed., *The Military Orders, Volume 5: Politics and Power* (Farnham, UK: Ashgate, 2012), 209–19.

16: "Unfurl and Raise Our Banner!"

1. Ursula Lyons and M. C. Lyons, eds., J. S. C. Riley-Smith, introduction, *Ayyubids, Mamlukes and Crusaders: Selections from the Tārīkh al-duwal wa'l-Mulūk*, vol. 2 (Cambridge: Heffer, 1971), 1–2.

2. J. A. Giles, *Matthew Paris's English History: From the Year 1235 to 1273*, vol. 1 (London: H. G. Bohn, 1852), 497–500.

3. Patriarch of Jerusalem, in Malcolm Barber and Keith Bate, trans., *Letters from the East: Crusaders, Pilgrims and Settlers in the 12th–13th Centuries* (Farnham, UK: Ashgate, 2013), 140–42.

4. The various estimates include 312 killed. M. R. Morgan, *La Continuation de Guillaume de Tyr (1184–1197)* (Paris: P. Geuthner, 1982), 564; 296 killed according to Frederick Hohenstaufen in Giles, *Matthew Paris's English History*, 491–92; 296 killed according to the patriarch of Jerusalem, also preserved by Matthew Paris and recently in Barber and Bate, *Letters from the East*, 140–42.

5. Patriarch of Jerusalem, Barber and Bate, *Letters from the East*, 140–42.

6. Ibid.

7. Letter of Frederick II Hohenstaufen to Richard, Earl of Cornwall, this translation from Giles, *Matthew Paris's English History*, 491–92.

8. The most vivid account of Louis IX's crusade (which includes this anecdote) is John of Joinville's Life of Saint Louis. Various English translations are available; I have used J. A. Giles, ed., *Chronicles of the Crusades: Being Contemporary Narratives of the Crusade of Richard Coeur de Lion, by Richard of Devizes and Geoffery de Vinsauf; and of the Crusade of Saint Louis, by Lord John de Joinville* (London: Henry G. Bohn, 1892), 351–531.

9. Jacques Le Goff, *Saint Louis* (Notre Dame, IN: University of Notre Dame Press, 2009), 94–101.

10. Malcolm Barber, *The New Knighthood: A History of the Order of the Temple* (Cambridge: Cambridge University Press, 1994), 267.

11. Andre-E. Sayous, "Les Mandats de Saint Louis Sur Son Trésor et le Mouvement International des Capitaux Pendant la Septième Croisade (1248–1254)," *Revue Historique* 167 (1931): 255.

12. Jochen Burgtorf, *The Central Convent of Hospitallers and Templars: History, Organization and Personnel (1099/1120–1310)* (Leiden and Boston: Brill, 2008), 126.

13. Giles, *Chronicles of the Crusades*, 388.

14. Ibid., 389.

15. Letter of John Sarrasin, chamberlain of France, from Damietta on June 23, in J. M. A. Beer, "The Letter of John Sarrasin, Crusader," in Barbara Nelson Sargent-Baur, ed., *Journeys Towards God: Pilgrimage and Crusade* (Kalamazoo, MI: Medieval Institute Publications, Western Michigan University, 1992), 136–45.

16. Giles, *Chronicles of the Crusades*, 400.

17. For this letter (in Latin) see Henry Richards Luard, ed., *Matthæi Parisiensis: Monachi Santi Albani, Chronica Majora*, vol. 4 (London: Longman, 1876), 162.

18. Giles, *Chronicles of the Crusades*, 407.

19. Ibid., 410.

20. Giles, *Matthew Paris's English History*, 367.

21. Ibid., 368.

22. Ibid., 369.

23. Ibid.

24. Giles, *Chronicles of the Crusades*, 423.

25. Ibid., 425–26.

26. Recorded by Ibn Wasil in his book *The Dissipator of Anxieties Concerning the History of the Ayyubids*. A short excerpt, including the verse quoted here, can be found in J. Bird, E. Peters, and J. M. Powell, eds., *Crusade and Christendom: Annotated Documents in Translation from Innocent III to the Fall of Acre, 1187–1291* (Philadelphia: University of Pennsylvania Press, 2013), 361.

27. Giles, *Matthew Paris's English History*, 374.

28. Giles, *Chronicles of the Crusades*, 455.

29. For references attesting Reginald's career see Burgtorf, *The Central Convent of Hospitallers and Templars*, 636–40.

30. Giles, *Chronicles of the Crusades*, 455–56.

31. According to Abu Shama, who saw the cloak worn in Damascus. Translation from P. M. Holt, *The Age of the Crusades: The Near East from the Eleventh Century to 1517* (London and New York: Longman, 1986), 83.

32. Judith M. Upton-Ward, trans. and ed., *The Rule of the Templars: The French Text of the Rule of the Order of the Knights Templar* (Woodbridge, Suffolk, UK: Boydell Press, 1992), 36.

Part IV: Heretics

1. Marjorie Chibnall, ed. and trans., *The Ecclesiastical History of Orderic Vitalis*, vol. 6 (Oxford: Oxford University Press, 1978), 314–15. See also "Sir Gawain and the Green Knight," line 499, "The forme to the finishment foldez ful selden." Casey Finch, trans., *The Complete Works of the Pearl Poet* (Berkeley: University of California Press, 1993), 232–33.

17: "A Lump in the Throat"

1. S. F. Sadeque, *Baybars I of Egypt* (Karachi: Oxford University Press, 1956), 92–94.

2. Quoted here by al-Zahir's fellow scholar Shihab al-Din al-Nuwayri in *The Ultimate Ambition in the Arts of Erudition*, ed. and trans. E. Muhanna (New York: Penguin, 2016), 253–54.

3. J. A. Giles, *Matthew Paris's English History: From the Year 1235 to 1273*, vol. 1 (London: H. G. Bohn, 1852), 523.

4. Preserved in the annals of Burton Abbey. Henry Richards Luard, *Annales Monastici*, vol. 1 (London: Longman, Green, 1864), 491–95.

5. See Reuven Amitai-Preiss, "Mamluk Perceptions of the Mongol-Frankish Rapprochement," *Mediterranean History Review* 7 (1992): 50–65.

6. In Paul Meyvaert, "An Unknown Letter of Hulagu, Il-Khan of Persia, to King Louis IX of France," *Viator* 11 (1980): 252–59.

7. For context on the scale of the disaster see Peter Jackson, "The Crisis in the Holy Land in 1260," *English Historical Review* 95 (1980): 481–513.

8. Shihab al-Din al-Nuwayri, *The Ultimate Ambition in the Arts of Erudition*, 251.

9. On this point see Reuven Amitai-Preiss, "The Early Mamluks and the End of the Crusader Presence in Syria (1250–1291)," in Adrian J. Boas, ed., *The Crusader World* (Abingdon, UK, and New York: Routledge, 2016), 337.

10. See Peter Thorau and P. M. Holt, trans., *The Lion of Egypt: Sultan Baybars I and the Near East in the Thirteenth Century* (London: Longman, 1992), 144.

11. The famous Latin description of the building of Safad, known as *De Constructione Castri Saphet*, is now in English translation in Hugh Kennedy, *Crusader Castles* (Cambridge: Cambridge University Press, 1994), 190–98.

12. Ibid., 197.

13. Ursula Lyons and M. C. Lyons, eds., J. S. C. Riley-Smith, introduction, *Ayyubids, Mamlukes and Crusaders: Selections from the Tārīkh al-duwal waāl-Mulūk*, vol. 2 (Cambridge: Heffer, 1971), 89.

14. Paul F. Crawford, ed., *The "Templar of Tyre." Part III of the Deeds of the Cypriots* (Aldershot, UK: Ashgate, 2003), 50.

15. Ibid.

16. Ibid.

17. Ibid. Although scholars dispute this account, which is uncorroborated by other sources; it is possible that Brother Leo himself was duped. See Thorau and Holt, *The Lion of Egypt*, 170.

18. Malcolm Barber and Keith Bate, eds. and trans., *The Templars: Selected Sources* (Manchester, UK: Manchester University Press, 2002), 232–34.

19. Carole Hillenbrand, *The Crusades: Islamic Perspectives* (Edinburgh: Edinburgh University Press, 1999), 437. See for comparison Matthew Bennett, "La Règle du Temple as a Military Manual or How to Deliver a Cavalry Charge," in Judith M. Upton-Ward, trans. and ed., *The Rule of the Templars: The French Text of the Rule of the Order of the Knights Templar* (Woodbridge, Suffolk, UK: Boydell Press, 1992), 175–88.

20. The letter is in E. Jordan, ed., *Les Registres de Clément IV (1265–1268): Recueil des Bulles de ce Pape* (Paris: Thorin & Fils, 1845), 326–27. This translation is by Malcolm Barber, *The Trial of the Templars* (Cambridge: Cambridge University Press, 1978), 17.

21. Jochen Burgtorf, *The Central Convent of Hospitallers and Templars: History, Organization and Personnel (1099/1120–1310)* (Leiden and Boston: Brill, 2008), 593–94.

22. Crawford, *The "Templar of Tyre,"* 59.

23. This translation is from Judith M. Upton-Ward, "The Surrender of Gaston and the Rule of the Templars," in Malcolm Barber, ed., *The Military Orders I: Fighting for the Faith and Caring for the Sick* (Aldershot, UK: Variorum, 1994), 181.

24. See Judith M. Upton-Ward, trans., *The Catalan Rule of the Templars* (Woodbridge, Suffolk, UK: Boydell Press, 2003), 81–87.

25. J. Bird, E. Peters, and J. M. Powell, eds., *Crusade and Christendom: Annotated Documents in Translation from Innocent III to the Fall of Acre, 1187–1291* (Philadelphia: University of Pennsylvania Press, 2013), 361.

26. Malcolm Barber and Keith Bate, trans., *Letters from the East: Crusaders, Pilgrims and Settlers in the 12th–13th Centuries* (Farnham, UK: Ashgate, 2013), 163.

18: "The City Will Fall"

1. There is a useful map of Acre and Montmusard in Adrian J. Boas, *Archaeology of the Military Orders: A Survey of the Urban Centres, Rural Settlement and Castles of the Military Orders in the Latin East (c. 1120–1291)* (Abingdon, UK: Routledge, 2006), 30.

2. The "Templar of Tyre" had personally seen this letter and translated it from Arabic to French for William of Beaujeu. Paul F. Crawford, ed., *The "Templar of Tyre." Part III of the Deeds of the Cypriots* (Aldershot, UK: Ashgate, 2003), 104. The "Two Seas" are the Mediterranean and Red Sea; the "Two Pilgrim Sites," Mecca and Medina.

3. It is difficult to reconstruct the exact placement of the gates in Acre's system of walls, but from the eyewitness account by the "Templar of Tyre," it seems that St. Anthony's Gate was part of the inner wall that connected Acre's old town to Montmusard, rather than being part of the double walls surrounding the whole city.

4. The "Templar of Tyre" had personally seen this letter and translated it from Arabic to French for William of Beaujeu. Crawford, The "Templar of Tyre," 111.

5. D. P. Little, "The Fall of Akka in 1291: The Muslim Version," in M. Sharon, ed., Studies in Islamic History and Civilization in Honour of Professor David Ayalon (Jerusalem: Cana, 1986), 175.

6. Ibid., 176.

7. The basic outline of James of Molay's career is excellently summarized in Malcolm Barber, "James of Molay, the Last Grand Master of the Order of the Temple," in Studia Monastica 14 (1972): 91–124, which is also collected in Barber, Crusaders and Heretics: 12th–14th Centuries (Aldershot, UK: Ashgate, 1995).

8. Crawford, The "Templar of Tyre," 119.

9. According to James of Molay's testimony at his trial in the autumn of 1307. See G. Lizerand, ed., Dossier de l'Affaire des Templiers (Paris: Champion, 1923), 35.

10. On the ages of Templars in the East see A. J. Forey, "Towards a Profile of the Templars in the Early Fourteenth Century," in Malcolm Barber, ed., The Military Orders I: Fighting for the Faith and Caring for the Sick (Aldershot, UK: Variorum, 1994), 196–204 and esp. 198.

11. Lizerand, Dossier de l'Affaire des Templiers, 169–71.

12. Jochen Burgtorf, The Central Convent of Hospitallers and Templars: History, Organization and Personnel (1099/1120–1310) (Leiden and Boston: Brill, 2008), 665. Alan Forey, "Letters of the Last Two Templar Masters," Nottingham Medieval Studies 45 (2001): 155.

13. Crawford, The "Templar of Tyre," 179.

14. Malcolm Barber and Keith Bate, trans., Letters from the East: Crusaders, Pilgrims and Settlers in the 12th–13th Centuries (Farnham, UK: Ashgate, 2013), 165.

15. Ernest Langlois, ed., Registres de Nicholas IV: Recueil des Bulles de ce Pape, vol. 2 (Paris: E. Thorin, 1891), 903. See also Sylvia Schein, Fideles Crucis: The Papacy, the West, and the Recovery of the Holy Land, 1274–1314 (Oxford: Oxford University Press, 1991), 74–76.

16. Langlois, Registres de Nicholas IV, 904.

17. Henry Richards Luard, ed., Annales Monastici, vol. 3 (London: Longman, Green, 1866), 366.

18. On Limassol and Nicosia, see Burgtorf, The Central Convent of Hospitallers and Templars, 133–36.

19. August Potthast, ed., Regesta Pontificum Romanorum, vol. 2 (Berlin: Rudolf de Decker, 1875), 1791. It should be pointed out that Pope Martin IV, who issued this slap on the wrist, was a Frenchman who also favored Charles's claim to the crown of Jerusalem over Hugh's.

20. Helen Nicholson, Templars, Hospitallers, and Teutonic Knights: Images of the Military Orders, 1128–1291 (Leicester, UK: Leicester University Press, 1993), 126.

21. N. Housley, ed., Documents on the Later Crusades (Basingstoke, UK: Macmillan, 1996), 36.

22. Ibid., 37.

23. Lizerand, Dossier de l'Affaire des Templiers, 4–5.

24. Georges Digard, Maurice Faucon, Antoine Thomas, and Robert Fawtier, eds., Les Registres de Boniface VIII; Recueil des Bulles de ce Pape (Paris: E. Thorin, 1881), 169–70.

25. Barber, "James of Molay," 94–95.

26. Schein, Fideles Crucis, 135–38.

27. A. J. Forey, The Templars in the Corona de Aragón (Oxford: Oxford University Press, 1973), 137.

19: "At the Devil's Prompting"

1. Sophia Menache, Clement V (Cambridge: Cambridge University Press, 1998), 32–33.

2. Ibid., 18, quoting Napoleone Orsini in a letter of 1314.

3. Ibid., 17.

4. Ibid., 19.

5. Paul F. Crawford, ed., The "Templar of Tyre." Part III of the Deeds of the Cypriots (Aldershot, UK: Ashgate, 2003), 164.

6. On Clement's coronation see Monique Dollin du Fresnel, *Clément V (1264–1314): Le Pape Gascon et les Templiers* (Bordeaux: Editions Sud-Ouest, 2009), 13–14.

7. Sylvia Schein, *Fideles Crucis: The Papacy, the West, and the Recovery of the Holy Land, 1274–1314* (Oxford: Oxford University Press, 1991), 182, 197–98.

8. The extant copy of the letters is to Fulk of Villaret, but there is no reason to think that the content of the letter to James of Molay differed significantly. *Regestum Clementis Papae V* (Rome: Typographia Vaticana, 1885), 190–91.

9. A. J. Forey, "Towards a Profile of the Templars in the Early Fourteenth Century," in Malcolm Barber, ed., *The Military Orders I: Fighting for the Faith and Caring for the Sick* (Aldershot, UK: Variorum, 1994), 198.

10. Alain Demurger, *The Last Templar: The Tragedy of Jacques de Molay, Last Grand Master of the Temple* (London: Profile Books, 2004), 117–18.

11. The original letter is transcribed in Etienne Baluze and Guillaume Mollat, eds., *Vitae Paparum Avenionensium*, vol. 3 (Paris: Letouzey, 1921), 145–49, and in English translation in Malcolm Barber, and Keith Bate, eds. and trans., *The Templars: Selected Sources* (Manchester, UK: Manchester University Press, 2002), 105–9.

12. In English translation in N. Housley, ed., *Documents on the Later Crusades* (Basingstoke, UK: Macmillan, 1996), 40–47.

13. James of Molay's case for resisting the union of the orders is in G. Lizerand, ed., *Dossier de l'Affaire des Templiers* (Paris: Champion, 1923), 2–15, and in English translation, Barber and Bate, *The Templars: Selected Sources*, 234–38.

14. Pierre Dubois, *The Recovery of the Holy Land*, ed. and trans. W. I. Brandt (New York: Columbia University Press, 1956), 81.

15. Henry Bettenson, ed., *Documents of the Christian Church*, second edition (Oxford: Oxford University Press, 1963), 159–61.

16. Elena Woodacre, *Queens Regnant of Navarre: Succession, Politics and Partnership, 1274–1512* (New York: Palgrave Macmillan, 2013), 37–38.

17. The political drive to devalue the *gros* was exacerbated by a severe shortage of silver with which to mint new coins. Stéphane Mechoulan, "The Expulsion of the Jews from France in 1306: A Modern Fiscal Analysis," *Journal of European Economic History* 33, no. 3 (2006): 555–84; Ignacio de la Torre, "The Monetary Fluctuations in Philip IV's Kingdom of France and Their Relevance to the Arrests of the Templars," in Jochen Burgtorf, Paul F. Crawford, and Helen J. Nicholson, eds., *The Debate on the Trial of the Templars (1307–1314)* (Farnham, UK: Ashgate, 2010), 57–68.

18. On the background to Jewish expulsion in 1306 see William Chester Jordan, *The French Monarchy and the Jews: From Philip Augustus to the Last Capetians* (Philadelphia: University of Pennsylvania Press, 1989), 178–99.

19. De la Torre, "The Monetary Fluctuations in Philip IV's Kingdom," 66.

20. Translation in Demurger, *The Last Templar*, 163.

21. Alan Forey, "Letters of the Last Two Templar Masters," *Nottingham Medieval Studies* 45 (2001): 166–67.

22. Ibid., 170.

23. Judith M. Upton-Ward, trans. and ed., *The Rule of the Templars: The French Text of the Rule of the Order of the Knights Templar* (Woodbridge, Suffolk, UK: Boydell Press, 1992), 172.

24. Ibid.

25. Ibid., 112, 148.

26. The letter of William of Plaisians containing this allegation is in H. Finke, ed., *Papsttum und Untergang des Templerordens*, vol. 2 (Berlin: Munster, 1907), 143.

27. Demurger, *The Last Templar*, 171.

28. Original text transcribed in Lizerand, *Dossier de l'Affaire des Templiers*, 16–25, and in English translation, Barber and Bate, *The Templars: Selected Sources*, 244–47.

20: "Heretical Depravity"

1. G. Lizerand, ed., *Dossier de l'Affaire des Templiers* (Paris: Champion, 1923), and in English translation in Malcolm Barber and Keith Bate, eds. and trans., *The Templars: Selected Sources* (Manchester, UK: Manchester University Press, 2002), 247–48.
2. Malcolm Barber, *The Trial of the Templars* (Cambridge: Cambridge University Press, 1978), 69.
3. Jochen Schenk, "Aspects of Non-Noble Family Involvement in the Order of the Temple," in Judith M. Upton-Ward, ed., *The Military Orders, Volume 4: On Land and by Sea* (Aldershot, UK: Ashgate, 2008), 157.
4. A. J. Forey, "Towards a Profile of the Templars in the Early Fourteenth Century," in Malcolm Barber, ed., *The Military Orders I: Fighting for the Faith and Caring for the Sick* (Aldershot, UK: Variorum, 1994), 197–98.
5. According to a deposition made in 1309. Jules Michelet, *Procès des Templiers*, vol. 1 (Paris: Imprimerie Royale, 1841), 36–39, translated in Barber and Bate, *The Templars: Selected Sources*, 289–92.
6. R. I. Moore, *The War on Heresy: Faith and Power in Medieval Europe* (London: Profile, 2012), 6.
7. Transcribed in Michelet, *Procès des Templiers*, 305–6, translated in Barber and Bate, *The Templars: Selected Sources*, 252–53.
8. Michelet, *Procès des Templiers*, 295–96, translated in Barber and Bate, *The Templars: Selected Sources*, 251–52.
9. Michelet, *Procès des Templiers*, 361–63, translated in Barber and Bate, *The Templars: Selected Sources*, 247–48.
10. See Lizerand, *Dossier de l'Affaire des Templiers*, 24–29; translated in Barber and Bate, *The Templars: Selected Sources*, 251–52.
11. For key points in his biography see Jochen Burgtorf, *The Central Convent of Hospitallers and Templars: History, Organization and Personnel (1099/1120–1310)* (Leiden and Boston: Brill, 2008), 625–28.
12. Michelet, *Procès des Templiers*, 374–75.
13. On the ages and occupations of those interrogated in 1307–8 see Barber, *The Trial of the Templars*, 73.
14. H. Finke, ed., *Papsttum und Untergang des Templerordens*, vol. 2 (Berlin: Munster, 1907), 51; this translation in Barber, *The Trial of the Templars*, 85.
15. English translation in Barber and Bate, *The Templars: Selected Sources*, 249–50.
16. The text of the bull addressed to Edward II of England is in Thoma Rymer, *Foedera, Conventiones, Litterae et Cujuscunque Generis Acta Publica inter Reges Angliae*, vol. 1 (The Hague: Joannem Neaulme, 1744), part 4, 99–100.
17. K. Schottmüller, *Der Untergang des Templer-Ordens* (Berlin: n.p., 1887), 656.
18. Lizerand, *Dossier de l'Affaire des Templiers*, 62–71, and in English in Barber and Bate, *The Templars: Selected Sources*, 260–63.
19. Verbatim report in a letter to the king of Aragón, Finke, *Papsttum und Untergang des Templerordens*, translated in Barber and Bate, *The Templars: Selected Sources*, 263–72.
20. Barber, *The Trial of the Templars*, drawing on Finke, *Papsttum und Untergang des Templerordens*, 334–37. Barber makes the suggestion that the Hugh of Payns head was in fact a reliquary containing the head itself, although given the wild nature of Stephen of Troyes's confession, reading any sense into it seems generous.

21: "God Will Avenge Our Death"

1. Malcolm Barber, *The Trial of the Templars* (Cambridge: Cambridge University Press, 1978), 135.
2. Records from most of the local inquiries have disappeared, but one place that preserved its records was at Clermont in the Auvergne, where sixty-nine Templars were interrogated

during a single week in the summer of 1309. See Roger Sève and Anne-Marie Chagny-Sève, eds., *Le Procès du Templiers d'Auvergne (1309–1311): Edition de l'Interrogatoire de Juin 1309* (Paris: Editions du Comité des Travaux Historique et Scientifiques, 1987).

3. Thomas Krämer, "Terror, Torture and the Truth: The Testimonies of the Templars Revisited," in Jochen Burgtorf, Paul F. Crawford, and Helen J. Nicholson, eds., *The Debate on the Trial of the Templars (1307–1314)* (Farnham, UK: Ashgate, 2010), 83.

4. Jules Michelet, *Procès des Templiers*, vol. 1 (Paris: Imprimerie Royale, 1841), 32–35, translated in Malcolm Barber and Keith Bate, eds. and trans., *The Templars: Selected Sources* (Manchester, UK: Manchester University Press, 2002), 286–89.

5. Michelet, *Procès des Templiers*, 42–45, translated in Barber and Bate, *The Templars: Selected Sources*, 292–95.

6. Michelet, *Procès des Templiers*, 87–88, translated in Barber and Bate, *The Templars: Selected Sources*, 296–301.

7. Barber, *The Trial of the Templars*, 172.

8. Jeffrey S. Hamilton, "King Edward II of England and the Templars," in Burgtorf et al., *The Debate on the Trial of the Templars*, 217.

9. Luis Garcia-Guijarra Ramos, "The Extinction of the Order of the Temple in the Kingdom of Valencia and Early Montesa 1307–30: A Case of Transition from Universalist to Territorialized Military Orders," in ibid., 203–5.

10. Barber, *The Trial of the Templars*, 229–37; also see A. J. Forey, *The Templars in the Corona de Aragón* (Oxford: Oxford University Press, 1973), 356–64.

11. Elena Bellomo, "The Templar Order in North-Western Italy: A General Picture," in Victor Mallia-Milanes, ed., *The Military Orders, Volume 3: History and Heritage* (Aldershot, UK: Ashgate, 2008), 105; Anne Gilmour-Bryson, "A Look Through the Keyhole: Templars in Italy from the Trial Testimony," in ibid., 123–30.

12. Kristjan Toomaspoeg, "The Templars and Their Trial in Sicily," in Burgtorf et al., *The Debate on the Trial of the Templars*, 281.

13. Helen J. Nicholson, *The Knights Templar: A New History* (Stroud, Gloucestershire, UK: History Press, 2004), 130–31.

14. On dating and the unsettled question of whether there were two trials on Cyprus see Anne Gilmour-Bryson, *The Trial of the Templars in Cyprus: A Complete English Edition* (Leiden: Brill, 1998), 24–30.

15. Ibid., 428.

16. Ibid., 407.

17. The bull is translated into English in Barber and Bate, *The Templars: Selected Sources*, 309–18.

18. Malcolm Barber, *The New Knighthood: A History of the Order of the Temple* (Cambridge: Cambridge University Press, 1994), 1.

19. "Adjudicati sunt muro et carceri perpetuo retrudendi," H. Géraud, ed., *Chronique Latine de Guillame de Nangis de 1113 a 1300* (Paris: Chez Jules Renouard, 1843), 402.

20. Ibid., 403.

21. Paul F. Crawford, ed., *The "Templar of Tyre." Part III of the Deeds of the Cypriots* (Aldershot, UK: Ashgate, 2003), 180.

22. Géraud, *Chronique Latine de Guillame de Nangis*, 403.

23. Crawford, *The "Templar of Tyre,"* 180.

24. "Seingnors, dit il, sachiez, sans tère. / Que tous celz qui nous sont contrère, / Por nous en aront à souffrir / En ceste foy veil-je mourir," J.-A. Buchon, *Chronique Métrique de Godefroy de Paris* (Paris: Verdière, 1827), 220.

25. Dante, *Inferno* XIX, 83–87.

26. N. Housley, ed., *Documents on the Later Crusades* (Basingstoke, UK: Macmillan, 1996), 51.

27. The full plan is now available in translation: Peter Lock, ed. and trans., *Marino Sanudo Torsello: The Book of the Secrets of the Faithful of the Cross* (Farnham, UK: Ashgate, 2011).

28. Housley, *Documents on the Later Crusades*, 55.
29. Ibid., 178.
30. Ibid., 180.

Epilogue: The Holy Grail

1. The original is in the British Library in London, BL Royal 14 E V f.492v.
2. Paulina Villegas, "Mexico: Police Kill a Gang Leader," *New York Times*, April 2, 2014.

BIBLIOGRAPHY

Primary Sources

Al-Muqaddasi. *The Best Divisions for the Knowledge of the Regions.* Edited by Basil Collins and reviewed by M. H. Alta'I. Reading, UK: Garnet Publishing, 2001.

Al-Nuwayri, Shihab al-Din. *The Ultimate Ambition in the Arts of Erudition.* Edited and translated by E. Muhanna. New York: Penguin, 2016.

Ailes, Marianne, trans. *The History of the Holy War. Ambroise's Estoire de la Guerre Sainte.* Woodbridge, Suffolk, UK: Boydell Press, 2003.

Albert of Aachen. *Historia Ierosolimitana: History of the Journey to Jerusalem.* Edited by Susan B. Edgington. Oxford: Clarendon Press, 2007.

Babcock, E. A., and A. C. Krey, trans. *A History of Deeds Done Beyond the Sea: By William, Archbishop of Tyre.* Vols. 1 and 2. New York: Columbia University Press, 1943.

Baird, J. L., G. Baglivi, and J. R. Kane, eds. and trans. *The Chronicle of Salimbene de Adam.* Binghamton, NY: Medieval and Renaissance Texts and Studies, 1986.

Barber, Malcolm, and Keith Bate, trans. *Letters from the East: Crusaders, Pilgrims and Settlers in the 12th–13th Centuries.* Farnham, UK: Ashgate, 2013.

———, eds. and trans. *The Templars: Selected Sources.* Manchester, UK: Manchester University Press, 2002.

Bedier, Joseph, and Pierre Aubry, eds. *Les Chansons de Croisade avec Leurs Melodies.* Paris: H. Champion, 1909.

Berry, V. G., ed. and trans. *Odo of Deuil: De Profectione Ludovici VII in Orientem.* New York: W. W. Norton, 1948.

Bettenson, Henry, ed. *Documents of the Christian Church.* Second edition. Oxford: Oxford University Press, 1963.

Bird, J., E. Peters, and J. M. Powell, eds. *Crusade and Christendom: Annotated Documents in Translation from Innocent III to the Fall of Acre, 1187–1291.* Philadelphia: University of Pennsylvania Press, 2013.

Bouquet, M., et al., eds. *Recueil des Historiens des Gaules et de la France.* Vol. XV. Paris: Victor Palme, 1878.

Broadhurst, R. J. C., trans. *The Travels of Ibn Jubayr: Being the Chronicles of a Mediaeval Spanish Moor Concerning His Journey to the Egypt of Saladin, the Holy Cities of Arabia, Baghdad the City of the Caliphs, the Latin Kingdom of Jerusalem, and the Norman Kingdom of Sicily.* London: Jonathan Cape, 1952.

Brownlow, Rev. Canon, M. A., trans. *Saewulf, 1102, 1103 A.D.* London: Palestine Pilgrims' Text Society, 1892.

Carrière, Victor, ed. *Histoire et Cartulaire des Templiers de Provins, avec une Introduction sur les Débuts du Temple en France.* Paris: E. Champion, 1919.

Chibnall, Marjorie, ed. and trans. *The Ecclesiastical History of Orderic Vitalis.* Vols. 1–6. Oxford Medieval Texts. Oxford: Oxford University Press, 1969–1978.

———. *The Historia Pontificalis of John of Salisbury.* Oxford Medieval Texts. Oxford: Oxford University Press, 1986.

Cobb, Paul M., trans. *Usama ibn Munqidh: The Book of Contemplation: Islam and the Crusades.* London: Penguin, 2008.

Collection des Documents Inédits sur l'Histoire de France. Book III. Paris: Imprimerie Royal, 1835.

Crawford, Paul F., ed. *The "Templar of Tyre." Part III of the Deeds of the Cypriots.* Aldershot, UK: Ashgate, 2003.

d'Albon, Marquis, ed. *Cartulaire Général de l'Ordre du Temple, 1119?–1150. Recueil des Chartes et des Bulles Relatives à l'Ordre du Temple.* Paris: H. Champion, 1913.

David, Charles Wendell, trans., and Jonathan Phillips, ed. *The Conquest of Lisbon: De Expugnatione Lyxbonensi.* New York: Columbia University Press, 2001.

Delisle, Léopold, ed. *Recueils des Historiens des Gaules et de la France.* Vols. 1–24. Paris: Imprimerie Nationale, 1878–1904.

Digard, Georges, Maurice Faucon, Antoine Thomas, and Robert Fawtier, eds. *Les Registres de Boniface VIII; Recueil des Bulles de ce Pape.* Paris: E. Thorin, 1881.

Dostourian, A. E., trans. *Armenia and the Crusades: Tenth to Twelfth Centuries: The Chronicle of Matthew of Edessa.* Lanham, MD: London: University Press of America.

Dubois, Pierre. *The Recovery of the Holy Land.* Edited and translated by W. I. Brandt. New York: Columbia University Press, 1956.

Edbury, Peter, ed. and trans. *The Conquest of Jerusalem and the Third Crusade: Sources in Translation.* Farnham, UK: Ashgate, 1998.

Edgington, Susan B., and Thomas S. Asbridge, eds. and trans. *Walter the Chancellor's The Antiochene Wars: A Translation and Commentary.* Aldershot, UK: Routledge, 2006.

Elliott, J. K., ed. and trans. *The Apocryphal New Testament: A Collection of Apocryphal Christian Literature in an English Translation.* Oxford: Oxford University Press, 1993.

Fink, Harold S., ed., and Frances R. Ryan, trans. *Fulcher of Chartres: A History of the Expedition to Jerusalem 1095–1127.* Knoxville: University of Tennessee Press, 1969.

Finke, H., ed. *Papsttum und Untergang des Templerordens.* Vols. 1 and 2. Berlin: Munster, 1907.

Gabrieli, Francesco, ed., and E. J. Costello, trans. *Arab Historians of the Crusades.* London: Routledge, 1969.

Gargallo Moya, Antonio, Maria Teresa Iranzo Muñío, and Maria José Sánchez Usón, eds. *Cartulario Del Temple De Huesca.* Zaragoza, Spain: Anubar, 1985.

Garmonsway, G. N., ed. and trans. *The Anglo-Saxon Chronicle.* London: J. M. Dent, 1972.

Gavigan, J. J., trans. *The Capture of Damietta by Oliver of Paderborn.* Philadelphia: University of Pennsylvania Press, 1948.

Géraud, H., ed. *Chronique Latine de Guillame de Nangis de 1113 a 1300.* Paris: Chez Jules Renouard, 1843.

Gibb, H. A. R. *The Damascus Chronicle of the Crusades: Extracted and Translated from the Chronicle of Ibn Al-Qalanisi.* London: Luzac, 1932; repr., New York: Dover, 2000.

Giles, J. A., ed. *Chronicles of the Crusades: Being Contemporary Narratives of the Crusade of Richard Coeur de Lion, by Richard of Devizes and Geoffery de Vinsauf; and of the Crusade of Saint Louis, by Lord John de Joinville.* London: Henry G. Bohn, 1892.

———, ed. and trans. *Roger of Wendover's Flowers of History.* Vols. 1 and 2. London: H. G. Bohn, 1849.

Greenia, Conrad, trans. Malcolm Barber, introduction. *Bernard of Clairvaux: In Praise of the New Knighthood.* Revised edition. Collegeville, MN: Cistercian Publications, 2000.

Hagenmeyer, Heinrich, ed. *Fulcher of Chartres: Historia Hierosolymitana 1095–1127.* Heidelberg: Carl Winters, 1913.

Hill, Rosalind, ed. *Gesta Francorum: The Deeds of the Franks and the Other Pilgrims to Jerusalem.* Oxford Medieval Texts. Oxford: Oxford University Press, 1979.

Holden, A. J., S. Gregory, and D. Crouch. *History of William Marshal.* Vols. 1–3. London: Anglo-Norman Text Society, 2002–2006.

Hoogeweg, H., ed. *Die Schriften des kölner Domscholasters, späteren Bischofs von Paderborn und Kardinal-Bischofs von S. Sabina Oliverus.* Tübingen: Bibliothek des Litterarischen Vereins in Stuttgart 202, 1894.

Housley, N., ed. *Documents on the Later Crusades*. Basingstoke, UK: Macmillan, 1996.

Huillard-Bréholles, Jean-Louis-Alphonse. *Historia Diplomatica Friderici Secundi*. Vol 3. Paris: Plon Brothers, 1852.

Ibn al-Khayyat. *Diwan*. Edited by H. Mardam Bek. Damascus: n.p., 1958.

James, B. S., trans. *The Letters of St. Bernard of Clairvaux*. London: Burns Oates, 1953.

Jordan, E., ed. *Les Registres de Clément IV (1265–1268): Recueil des Bulles de ce Pape*. Paris: Thorin & Fils, 1845.

Komnene, Anna. *The Alexiad*. Translated by E. R. A. Sewter and revised by Peter Frankopan. London: Penguin, 2009.

La Monte, John L., and Merton Jerome Hubert, eds. and trans. *The Wars of Frederick II Against the Ibelins in Syria and Cyprus by Philip De Novare*. New York: Columbia University Press, 1936.

Langlois, Ernest, ed. *Registres de Nicholas IV: Recueil des Bulles de ce Pape*. Paris: E. Thorin, 1886–91.

Le Strange, Guy, ed. and trans. *Diary of a Journey through Syria and Palestine. By Nâsir-i-Khusrau, in 1047 A.D*. London: Palestine Pilgrims' Text Society, 1893.

Lees, Beatrice A., ed. *Records of the Templars in England in the Twelfth Century: The Inquest of 1185 with Illustrative Charters and Documents*. Oxford: Published for the British Academy by Humphrey Milford, Oxford University Press, 1935.

Lipskey, Glenn Edward, trans. *The Chronicle of Alfonso the Emperor: A Translation of the Chronica Adefonsi Imperatoris, with Study and Notes*. Evanston, IL: n.p., 1972.

Lizerand, G., ed. *Dossier de l'Affaire des Templiers*. Paris: Champion, 1923.

Lock, Peter, ed. and trans. *Marino Sanudo Torsello: The Book of the Secrets of the Faithful of the Cross*. Farnham, UK: Ashgate, 2011.

Luard, Henry Richards, ed. *Annales Monastici*. Vols. 1–5. London: Longman, Green, 1864–1869.
———. *Matthæi Parisiensis: Monachi Sancti Albani, Chronica Majora*. Vols. 1–6. London: Longman, 1872–1883.

Luchaire, Achille. *Études sur les Actes de Louis VII*. Paris: A. Picard, 1885.

Lyons, Ursula, and M. C. Lyons, eds. J. S. C. Riley-Smith, introduction. *Ayyubids, Mamlukes and Crusaders: Selections from the Tārīkh al-duwal waâl-Mulūk*. Vols. 1 and 2. Cambridge: Heffer, 1971.

Map, Walter. *De Nugis Curialium, Courtiers' Trifles*. Edited and translated by M. R. James. Revised by C. N. L. Brooke and R. A. B. Mynors. Oxford Medieval Texts. Oxford: Oxford University Press, 1983.

Mas Latrie, Louis, comte de, ed. *Chronique d'Ernoul et de Bernard le Trésorier*. Paris: Renouard, 1871.

Matarasso, Pauline M., trans. *The Cistercian World: Monastic Writings of the Twelfth Century*. London: Penguin, 1993.

Mierow, Charles Christopher, trans., and Richard Emery. *The Deeds of Frederick Barbarossa by Otto of Freising and His Continuator, Rahewin*. New York: Columbia University Press, 2004.

Migne, Jacques Paul, ed. *Patrologia Latina: Patrologiae Cursus Completus. Series Latina*. Vols. 1–221. Paris: n.p., 1844–1864.

Morgan, M. R. *La Continuation de Guillaume de Tyr (1184–1197)*. Paris: P. Geuthner, 1982.

Nicholson, Helen J. *The Chronicle of the Third Crusade: The Itinerarium Peregrinorum et Gesta Regis Ricardi*. Farnham, UK: Ashgate, 1997.

O'Callaghan, Joseph F. *A History of Medieval Spain*. Ithaca, NY: Cornell University Press, 1975.

Peters, Edward, ed. *Christian Society and the Crusades 1198–1229: Sources in Translation Including "The Capture of Damietta" by Oliver of Paderborn*. Philadelphia: University of Pennsylvania Press, 1948.

———. *The First Crusade: The Chronicle of Fulcher of Chartres and Other Source Materials*. Philadelphia: University of Pennsylvania Press, 1971.

Potthast, August, ed. *Regesta Pontificum Romanorum*. Vols. 1 and 2. Berlin: Rudolf de Decker, 1873–
    1875.
Recueil des Historiens des Croisades. Paris: Imprimerie Nationale, 1841–1906.
Regestum Clementis Papae V. Rome: Typographia Vaticana, 1885.
Richards, D. S., trans. *The Chronicle of Ibn al-Athir for the Crusading Period from al Kamil fi'l
    Ta'rikh*. Vols. 1–3. Aldershot, Hampshire, UK: Routledge, 2006–2008.
———. *The Rare and Excellent History of Saladin by Baha al-Din Ibn Shaddad*. Farnham, UK:
    Ashgate, 2002.
Rodenburg, C., ed. *Monumenta Germaniae Historica, Epistolae I*. Berlin: Weidemanns, 1883.
Roehricht, Reinhold, ed. *Regesta Regni Hierosolymitani, 1097–1291*. Oeniponti: Libraria Academ-
    ica Wagneriana, 1893.
Rymer, Thoma. *Foedera, Conventiones, Litterae et Cujuscunque Generis Acta Publica inter Reges
    Angliae*. Vol. 1. The Hague: Joannem Neaulme, 1744.
Schottmüller K. *Der Untergang des Templer-Ordens*. Berlin: n.p., 1887.
Sepet, Marius Cyrille Alphonse. *John of Joinville: The Life of St. Louis, King of France*. New York:
    P. J. Kennedy, 1902.
Sève, Roger, and Anne-Marie Chagny-Sève, eds. *Le Procès du Templiers d'Auvergne (1309–1311):
    Edition de l'Interrogatoire de Juin 1309*. Paris: Editions du Comité des Travaux Historique et
    Scientifiques, 1987.
Sewell, Richard Clarke. *Gesta Stephani, Regis Anglorum et Ducis Normannorum*. London: Sump-
    tibus Societatis, 1846.
Smith, Damian J., and Helena Buffery, eds. *The Book of Deeds of James I of Aragón: A Translation
    of the Medieval Catalan Llibre dels Fets*. Farnham, UK: Ashgate, 2003.
Stevenson, Joseph, ed. *Ralph of Coggeshall: Chronicon Anglicanum*. London: Longman, 1875.
Tanner, Norman P., ed. and trans. *Decrees of the Ecumenical Councils*. Vols. 1 and 2. London: 1990.
Tyerman, Christopher. *Chronicles of the First Crusade*. London: Penguin, 2012.
Upton-Ward, Judith M., trans. *The Catalan Rule of the Templars*. Woodbridge, Suffolk, UK:
    Boydell Press, 2003.
———, ed. and trans. *The Rule of the Templars: The French Text of the Rule of the Order of the
    Knights Templar*. Woodbridge, Suffolk, UK: Boydell Press, 1992.
Wilkinson, John, with Joyce Hill and W. F. Ryan, eds. *Jerusalem Pilgrimage, 1099–1185*. London:
    Hakluyt Society, 1988.

Secondary Sources

Abel, P. F. *Géographie de la Palestine*. Paris: Gabalda, 1938.
Addison, Charles G. *History of the Knights Templar*. New York: AMS Press, 1978.
Allen, S. J., and Emilie Amt. *The Crusades: A Reader*. Toronto: University of Toronto Press,
    2010.
Asbridge, Thomas. *The Crusades: The War for the Holy Land*. London: Simon & Schuster, 2010.
Balard, M., ed. *Autour de la Première Croisade: Actes du Colloque de la "Society for the Study of the
    Crusades and the Latin East."* Clermont-Ferrand, France, June 22–25, 1995. Paris: Publica-
    tions de la Sorbonne, 1996.
Barber, Malcolm. *Crusaders and Heretics: 12th–14th Centuries*. Aldershot, UK: Ashgate, 1995.
———. *The Crusader States*. New Haven, CT, and London: Yale University Press, 2012.
———, ed. *The Military Orders I: Fighting for the Faith and Caring for the Sick*. Aldershot, UK:
    Variorum, 1994.
———. *The New Knighthood: A History of the Order of the Temple*. Cambridge: Cambridge Uni-
    versity Press, 1994.
———. *The Trial of the Templars*. Cambridge: Cambridge University Press, 1978.

Bartlett, Robert. *England Under the Norman and Angevin Kings: 1075–1225*. Oxford: Oxford University Press, 2000.

Baudin, Arnaud, Ghislain Brunel, and Nicolas Dohrmann. *The Knights Templar: From the Days of Jerusalem to the Commanderies of Champagne*. Paris: n.p., 2012.

Bellomo, Elena. *The Templar Order in North-West Italy (1142–c. 1330)*. Leiden and Boston: Brill, 2008.

Best, Nicholas. *The Knights Templar*. London: Weidenfeld & Nicolson, 1997.

Boas, Adrian J. *Archaeology of the Military Orders: A Survey of the Urban Centres, Rural Settlement and Castles of the Military Orders in the Latin East (c. 1120–1291)*. Abingdon, UK: Routledge, 2006.

———, ed. *The Crusader World*. Abingdon, UK, and New York: Routledge, 2016.

Bom, Myra Miranda. *Women in the Military Orders of the Crusades*. New York: Palgrave Macmillan, 2012.

Brighton, Simon. *In Search of the Knights Templar: A Guide to the Sites of Britain*. London: Weidenfeld & Nicolson, 2006.

Buc, Philippe. *Holy War, Martyrdom, and Terror: Christianity, Violence and the West*. Philadelphia: University of Pennsylvania Press, 2015.

Bulst-Thiele, Marie Louise. *Sacrae Domus Militiae Templi Hierosolymitani Magistri: Untersuchungen zur Geschichte des Templerordens 1118/19–1314*. Gottingen: Vandenhoeck & Ruprecht, 1974.

Burgtorf, Jochen. *The Central Convent of Hospitallers and Templars: History, Organization and Personnel (1099/1120–1310)*. Leiden and Boston: Brill, 2008.

Burgtorf, Jochen, Paul F. Crawford, and Helen J. Nicholson, eds. *The Debate on the Trial of the Templars (1307–1314)*. Farnham, UK: Ashgate, 2010.

Burtrigieg, Emanuel, and Simon Phillips, eds. *Islands and Military Orders, c. 1291–c. 1798*. Farnham, UK: Ashgate, 2013.

Catlos, Brian A. *Muslims of Medieval Latin Christendom, c. 1050–1614*. Cambridge: Cambridge University Press, 2014.

Cobb, Paul M. *The Race for Paradise: An Islamic History of the Crusades*. Oxford: Oxford University Press, 2014.

Conedera, Sam Zeno. *Ecclesiastical Knights: The Military Orders in Castile, 1150–1330*. New York: Fordham University Press, 2015.

Constable, Giles. *The Reformation of the Twelfth Century*. Cambridge: Cambridge University Press, 1996.

Delisle, Léopold. *Memoire sur Les Operations Financières des Templiers*. Paris: n.p., 1889.

Demurger, Alain. *The Last Templar: The Tragedy of Jacques de Molay, Last Grand Master of the Temple*. London: Profile Books, 2004.

Dollin du Fresnel, Monique. *Clément V (1264–1314): Le Pape Gascon et les Templiers*. Bordeaux: Editions Sud-Ouest, 2009.

Duby, Georges. *The Three Orders: Feudal Society Imagined*. Translated by Arthur Goldhammer. Chicago: University of Chicago Press, 1980.

Edbury, Peter W., ed. *The Military Orders, Volume 5: Politics and Power*. Farnham, UK: Ashgate, 2012.

Ellenblum, Ronnie. *Crusader Castles and Modern Histories*. Cambridge: Cambridge University Press, 2007.

Evans, G. R. *Bernard of Clairvaux*. New York and Oxford: Oxford University Press, 2000.

Faith, Juliet. *The Knights Templar in Somerset*. Stroud, Gloucestershire, UK: History Press, 2009.

Ferguson, Robert. *The Knights Templar and Scotland*. Stroud, Gloucestershire, UK: History Press, 2010.

Forey, Alan. *Military Orders and Crusades*. Aldershot, UK: Variorum, 1994.

———. *The Military Orders: From the Twelfth to the Fourteenth Centuries*. Basingstoke, UK: Macmillan, 1992.

———. *The Templars in the Corona de Aragón*. Oxford: Oxford University Press, 1973.

France, John, and W. G. Zajac. *The Crusades and Their Sources: Essays Presented to Bernard Hamilton*. Aldershot, UK: Ashgate, 1998.

Frankopan, Peter. *The First Crusade: The Call from the East*. Cambridge, MA: Belknap Press of Harvard University Press, 2012.

———. *The Silk Roads: A New History of the World*. London: Bloomsbury, 2015.

Gervers, Michael, ed. *The Second Crusade and the Cistercians*. New York: St. Martin's Press, 1992.

Giles, J. A. *Matthew Paris's English History: From the Year 1235 to 1273*. Vol. 1. London: H. G. Bohn, 1852.

Gilmour-Bryson, Anne. *The Trial of the Templars in Cyprus: A Complete English Edition*. Leiden: Brill, 1998.

Glasse, Cyril. *The New Encyclopedia of Islam*. Fourth edition. London: Rowman & Littlefield, 2013.

Griffith-Jones, Robin. *The Knights Templar*. Stroud, Gloucestershire, UK: History Press, 2014.

Grishin, A. A. *The Knights Templar Absolution: The Chinon Parchment and the History of the Poor Knights of Christ*. London: Knights Templar Vault, 2013.

Haag, Michael. *The Templars: History & Myth*. London: Profile Books, 2008.

Hill, George Francis. *A History of Cyprus, Volume II: The Frankish Period, 1192–1432*. Cambridge: Cambridge University Press, 1948.

Hillenbrand, Carole. *The Crusades: Islamic Perspectives*. Edinburgh: Edinburgh University Press, 1999.

Holloway, Diane. *The Knights Templar in Yorkshire*. Stroud, Gloucestershire, UK: History Press, 2008.

Holt, P. M. *The Age of the Crusades: The Near East from the Eleventh Century to 1517*. London and New York: Longman, 1986.

Hopper, Vincent Foster. *Medieval Number Symbolism. Its Sources, Meaning and Influence on Thought and Expression*. New York: Columbia University Press, 1938.

Housley, N., ed. *Knighthoods of Christ: Essays on the History of the Crusades and the Knights Templar, Presented to Malcolm Barber*. Aldershot, UK: Ashgate, 2007.

Howarth, Stephen. *Knights Templar*. New York: Marboro Books, 1982.

Hunyadi, Z., and J. Laszlovszky, eds. *The Crusades and the Military Orders: Expanding the Frontiers of Medieval Latin Christianity*. Budapest: Central European University Press, 2001.

Hyland, Ann. *The Medieval War Horse: From Byzantium to the Crusades*. London: Grange, 1994.

Irwin, R. *The Middle East in the Middle Ages: The Early Mamluk Sultanate, 1250–1382*. Carbondale: Southern Illinois University Press, 1986.

Jordan, William Chester. *The French Monarchy and the Jews: From Philip Augustus to the Last Capetians*. Philadelphia: University of Pennsylvania Press, 1989.

———. *Louis IX and the Challenge of the Crusade*. Princeton, NJ: Princeton University Press, 1979.

Kedar, Benjamin Z., ed. *The Franks in the Levant, 11th to 14th Centuries*. Aldershot, UK: Variorum, 1993.

———. *The Horns of Hattin*. Jerusalem and London: Yad Izhak Ben-Zvi/Israel Exploration Society & Variorum, 1992.

Kennedy, Hugh. *Crusader Castles*. Cambridge: Cambridge University Press, 1994.

Khowaiter, Abdul-Aziz. *Baibars the First: His Endeavours and Achievements*. London: Green Mountain Press, 1978.

Labarge, Margaret Wade. *Saint Louis: The Life of Louis IX of France*. London: Eyre & Spottiswoode, 1968.

Laiou, Angeliki E., ed. *The Crusades from the Perspective of Byzantium and the Muslim World*. Washington, DC: Dumbarton Oaks, 2001.

Le Goff, Jacques. *Saint Louis*. Notre Dame, IN: University of Notre Dame Press, 2009.

Lord, Evelyn. *The Knights Templar in Britain*. Abingdon, UK: Routledge, 2004.

Lower, Michael. *The Barons' Crusade: A Call to Arms and Its Consequences*. Philadelphia: University of Pennsylvania Press, 2005.

Mallia-Milanes, Victor, ed. *The Military Orders, Volume 3: History and Heritage*. Aldershot, UK: Ashgate, 2008.

Mayer, L. A. *Saracenic Heraldry*. Oxford: Oxford University Press, 1933.

Menache, Sophia. *Clement V*. Cambridge: Cambridge University Press, 1998.

Moore, R. I. *The War on Heresy: Faith and Power in Medieval Europe*. London: Profile, 2012.

Mylod, E. J., Guy Perry, Thomas W. Smith, and Jan Vandeburie. *The Fifth Crusade in Context: The Crusading Movement in the Early Thirteenth Century*. London and New York: Routledge, 2017.

Nicholson, Helen. *Templars, Hospitallers, and Teutonic Knights: Images of the Military Orders, 1128–1291*. Leicester, UK: Leicester University Press, 1993.

Nicholson, Helen, ed. *The Military Orders: Welfare and Warfare*. Aldershot, UK: Ashgate, 1998.

Nicholson, Helen J. *The Knights Templar: A New History*. Stroud, Gloucestershire, UK: History Press, 2004.

——. *The Knights Templar on Trial: The Trial of the Templars in the British Isles, 1308–1311*. Stroud, Gloucestershire, UK: History Press, 2009.

——, ed. *On the Margins of Crusading: The Military Orders, the Papacy and the Christian World*. Farnham, UK: Ashgate, 2011.

O'Callaghan, Joseph F. *Reconquest and Crusade in Medieval Spain*. Philadelphia: University of Pennsylvania Press, 2002.

Perry, Guy. *John of Brienne: King of Jerusalem, Emperor of Constantinople, c. 1175–1237*. Cambridge: Cambridge University Press, 2013.

Phillips, Jonathan. *Defenders of the Holy Land: Relations between the Latin East and the West, 1119–1187*. Oxford: Oxford University Press, 1996.

——. *The Second Crusade: Extending the Frontiers of Christendom*. New Haven, CT, and London: Yale University Press, 2007.

Phillips, Jonathan, and Martin Hoch, eds. *The Second Crusade: Scope and Consequences*. Manchester, UK: Manchester University Press, 2001.

Piquet, Jules. *Des Banquiers au Moyen Âge. Les Templiers; Étude de Leurs Opérations Financières*. Paris: Hachette, 1939.

Powell, James M. *Anatomy of a Crusade, 1213–1221*. Philadelphia: University of Pennsylvania Press, 1986.

Pryor, John H., ed. *Logistics of Warfare in the Age of the Crusades: Proceedings of a Workshop Held at the Centre for Medieval Studies, University of Sydney*. Aldershot, UK: Ashgate, 2006.

Read, Piers Paul. *The Templars*. London: Weidenfeld & Nicolson, 1999.

Reilly, Bernard F. *The Contest of Christian and Muslim Spain, 1031–1157*. Oxford: Blackwell, 1992.

Riley-Smith, Louise and Jonathan. *The Crusades: Idea and Reality, 1095–1274*. London: Edward Arnold, 1981.

Russell, Frederick H. *The Just War in the Middle Ages*. Cambridge: Cambridge University Press, 1975.

Sadeque, S. F. *Baybars I of Egypt*. Karachi: Oxford University Press, 1956.

Sargent-Baur, Barbara Nelson, ed. *Journeys Towards God: Pilgrimage and Crusade*. Kalamazoo, MI: Medieval Institute Publications, Western Michigan University, 1992.

Schein, Sylvia. *Fideles Crucis: The Papacy, the West, and the Recovery of the Holy Land, 1274–1314*. Oxford: Oxford University Press, 1991.

Schenk, Jochen. *Templar Families: Landowning Families and the Order of the Temple in France, c. 1120–1307*. Cambridge: Cambridge University Press, 2012.

Segal, J. B. *Edessa: "The Blessed City."* Oxford: Oxford University Press, 1970.

Sharon, M., ed. *Studies in Islamic History and Civilization in Honor of Professor David Ayalon.* Jerusalem: Cana, 1986.

Smail, R. C. *Crusading Warfare, 1097–1193.* Second edition. Cambridge: Cambridge University Press, 1995.

Smith, Katherine Allen. *War and the Making of Medieval Monastic Culture.* Woodbridge, Suffolk, UK: Boydell Press, 2011.

Stalls, Clay. *Possessing the Land: Aragón's Expansion into Islam's Ebro Frontier under Alfonso the Battler, 1104–1134.* Leiden: Brill, 1995.

Thorau, Peter, and P. M. Holt, trans. *The Lion of Egypt: Sultan Baybars I and the Near East in the Thirteenth Century.* London: Longman, 1992.

Tobin, Stephen. *The Cistercians: Monks and Monasteries of Europe.* London: Herbert Press, 1995.

Tolan, John V. *Saint Francis and the Sultan: The Curious History of a Christian-Muslim Encounter.* Oxford: Oxford University Press, 2009.

Tyerman, Christopher. *God's War: A New History of the Crusades.* London: Penguin, 2006.

Upton-Ward, Judith M., ed. *The Military Orders, Volume 4: On Land and by Sea.* Aldershot, UK: Ashgate, 2008.

Van Cleve, Thomas Curtis. *The Emperor Frederick II of Hohenstaufen, Immutator Mundi.* Oxford: Clarendon Press, 1972.

Woodacre, Elena. *Queens Regnant of Navarre: Succession, Politics and Partnership, 1274–1512.* New York: Palgrave Macmillan, 2013.

Articles

Amitai-Preiss, Reuven. "Mamluk Perceptions of the Mongol-Frankish Rapprochement." *Mediterranean History Review* 7 (1992).

Barber, Malcolm. "The Origins of the Order of the Temple." *Studia Monastica* 12 (1970).

———. "The Social Context of the Templars." *Transactions of the Royal Historical Society,* fifth series, 34 (1984).

Brown, Elizabeth A. R. "The Prince Is Father of the King: The Character and Childhood of Philip the Fair of France." *Medieval Studies* 49, no. 1 (1987).

Brundage, James A. "The Crusader's Wife Revisited." *Studia Gratiana* 14 (1967).

Cassidy-Welch, Megan. "'O Damietta!': War, Memory and Crusade in Thirteenth Century Egypt." *Journal of Medieval History* 40, no. 3 (2014).

Constable, Giles. "The Second Crusade as Seen by Contemporaries." *Traditio* 9 (1953).

Ferris, Eleanor. "The Financial Relations of the Knights Templars to the English Crown." *American Historical Review* 8 (1902).

Fletcher, R. A. "Reconquest and Crusade in Spain c. 1050–1150." *Transactions of the Royal Historical Society,* fifth series, 37 (1987).

Forey, Alan. "The Emergence of the Military Order in the Twelfth Century." *Journal of Ecclesiastical History* 36, no. 2 (1985).

———. "Letters of the Last Two Templar Masters." *Nottingham Medieval Studies* 45 (2001).

Forey, A. J. "The Failure of the Siege of Damascus in 1148." *Journal of Medieval History* 10, no. 1 (1984).

———. "Were the Templars Guilty, Even If They Were Not Heretics or Apostates?" *Viator* 42, no. 2 (2011).

Frale, Barbara. "The Chinon Chart: Papal Absolution to the Last Templar, Master Jacques de Molay." *Journal of Medieval History* 30, no. 2 (2004).

Franceschi, Francesco, Robert Bernabei, Peter Malfertheiner, and Giovannia Gasbarrini. "The Diet of Templar Knights: Their Secret to Longevity?" *Digestive and Liver Disease* 46, no. 7 (2014).

Gilmour-Bryson, Anne. "Sodomy and the Knights Templar." *Journal of the History of Sexuality* 7, no. 2 (1996).

Hamilton, Bernard. "Knowing the Enemy: Western Understanding of Islam at the Time of the Crusades." *Journal of the Royal Asiatic Society of Great Britain and Ireland* 7, no. 3 (1997).

———. "Our Lady of Saidnaiya: An Orthodox Shrine Revered by Muslims and Knights Templar at the Time of the Crusades." *Studies in Church History* 36 (2000).

Harari, Yuval. "The Military Role of the Frankish Turcopoles: A Reassessment." *Mediterranean Historical Review* 12 (1997).

Jackson, Peter. "The Crisis in the Holy Land in 1260." *English Historical Review* 95 (1980).

———. "The Crusades of 1239–41 and Their Aftermath." *Bulletin of the School of Oriental and African Studies, University of London* 50, no. 1 (1987).

Jacoby, Zehava. "The Tomb of Baldwin V, King of Jerusalem (1185–1186), and the Workshop of the Temple Area." *Gesta* 18, no. 2 (1979).

Joserand, Philippe. "The Templars in France: Between History, Heritage, and Memory." *Mirabilia: Electronic Journal of Antiquity and Middle Ages* 21 (2015).

Kedar, Benjamin Z. "On the Origins of the Earliest Laws of Frankish Jerusalem: The Canons of the Council of Nablus, 1120." *Speculum* 74 (1999).

Khamisy, Rabei G. "The Templar Estates in the Territory of Acre." *Ordines Militares* 18 (2013).

Lee, John S. "Landowners and Landscapes: The Knights Templar and Their Successors at Temple Hirst, Yorkshire." *Local Historian* 41 (2011).

Lotan, Shlomo. "The Battle of La Forbie and Its Aftermath—Reexamination of the Military Orders' Involvement in the Latin Kingdom of Jerusalem in the Mid-Thirteenth Century." *Ordines Militares* 12 (2012).

Lourie, Elena. "The Confraternity of Belchite, the Ribat, and the Templars." *Viator* 13 (1982).

———. "The Will of Alfonso I, 'El Batallador,' King of Aragón and Navarre: A Reassessment." *Speculum* 50, no. 3 (1975).

Mayer, Hans Eberhard. "The Concordat of Nablus." *Journal of Ecclesiastical History* 33, no. 4 (1982).

Mechoulan, Stéphane. "The Expulsion of the Jews from France in 1306: A Modern Fiscal Analysis." *Journal of European Economic History* 33, no. 3 (2006).

Meyvaert, Paul. "An Unknown Letter of Hulagu, Il-Khan of Persia, to King Louis IX of France." *Viator* 11 (1980).

Nicolle, David C. "The Reality of Mamluk Warfare: Weapons, Armour and Tactics." *Al-Masāq* 7 (1994).

O'Banion, Patrick J. "What Has Iberia to Do with Jerusalem? Crusade and the Spanish Route to the Holy Land in the Twelfth Century." *Journal of Medieval History* 34, no. 4 (2008).

Pringle, Denys. "The Templars in Acre c. 1150–1291." *Bulletin for the Council for British Research in the Levant* 2 (2007).

Prutz, Hans. "Ein Zeitgenössisches Gedicht über die Belagerung Accons." *Forschungen zur Deutschen Geschichte* 21 (1881).

Pryor, John H. "Two Excitationes for the Third Crusade: The Letters of Brother Thierry of the Temple." *Mediterranean Historical Review* 25 (2010).

Rother, Joachim. "Embracing Death, Celebrating Life: Reflections on the Concept of Martyrdom in the Order of the Knights Templar." *Ordines Militares* 19 (2014).

Sayous, Andre-E. "Les Mandats de Saint Louis Sur Son Trésor et le Mouvement International des Capitaux Pendant la Septième Croisade (1248–1254)." *Revue Historique* 167 (1931).

Sivan, Emmanuel. "La Genèse de la Contre-Croisade: Un Traité Damasquin du Début du XIIe Siècle." *Journal Asiatic* 254 (1966).

Slavin, Philip. "Landed Estates of the Knights Templar in England and Wales and Their Management in the Early Fourteenth Century." *Journal of Historical Geography* 42 (2013).

Smail, R. C. "Crusaders' Castles of the Twelfth Century." *Cambridge Historical Journal* 10 (1952).

Smith, Thomas W. "Between Two Kings: Pope Honorius III and the Seizure of the Kingdom of Jerusalem by Frederick II in 1225." *Journal of Medieval History* 41 (2015).

Sneddon, Jonathan. "Warrior Bishops in the Middle Ages." *Medieval Warfare* 3, no. 2 (2013).
Telfer, Alison. "Locating the First Knights Templar Church." *London Archaeologist* 10, no. 1 (2002).
Tsurtsumia, Mamuka. "Commemorations of Crusaders in Manuscripts of the Monastery of the Holy Cross in Jerusalem." *Journal of Medieval History* 38 (2012).
Warren, F. M. "The Battle of Fraga and Larchamp in Orderic Vitalis." *Modern Philology* 11 (1914).

Unpublished Theses

Crawford, Paul. "An Institution in Crisis: The Military Orders, 1291–1310." PhD diss., University of Wisconsin–Madison, 1998.
Peixoto, M. J. "Templar Communities in Medieval Champagne: Local Perspectives on a Global Organization." PhD diss., New York University, 2013.

INDEX